CLASSICS
OF THE AIR

An illustrated history of the development
of military planes from 1913-1935

Exeter Books

NEW YORK

Series Editor: Peter Allez-Fernandez
Book Editor: Len Cacutt

© Aerospace Publishing Ltd. 1986, 1988
© Pilot Press Ltd. 1986, 1988
© This edition Marshall Cavendish Ltd.
   1988

This edition published in the USA by
Exeter Books
Distributed by Bookthrift
Exeter is a trademark of Bookthrift
Marketing, Inc.
Bookthrift is a registered trademark of
Bookthrift Marketing, Inc.
New York, New York

ISBN 0–7917–0010–0

Typeset by J&L Composition Ltd, Filey,
North Yorkshire, England
Printed and bound in Spain

Contents

Contents

Introduction

This volume covers the period between 1913 and 1935, and all the aircraft it describes made their maiden flights between these two dates. World War 1 inevitably speeded up the development of a technology which was still in its infancy; the accent was always on the building of faster and more manoeuvrable aircraft, and the names of the fighter planes became just as well known as those of their pilots. But little attention tends to be paid to the fact that the nations involved in the war were also producing much larger aircraft during this period; one example described here is the Handley Page O/100, with a wingspan of more than 98 ft (30 m) making it a very large plane even by modern standards. In the years after the war the aircraft builders turned their sights towards civil trainers and light passenger aircraft. The de Havilland Moth took over the world market, and in passenger aircraft a new concept made a breakthrough. With its F.VII, Fokker developed the cantilever three-engined passenger craft, an idea which was soon being used by Ford in the USA. Later, the Junkers Ju 52 experienced worldwide success, but was not put solely to peaceful uses; the "Tante Ju" became the Luftwaffe's standard transport plane during World War 2. As the world situation worsened and war approached, military aircraft development was accelerated and in 1935 a number of prototypes first saw the light of day, versions of them being used right through the war. Two types, the Douglas DC-3 and the North American Harvard/Texan, which both flew for the first time in 1935, were still forming the backbone of many airforces and civil airlines even after the war was over. More than 50 years after its maiden flight, the Douglas DC-3 is still in active use in many countries today.

Peter Alles-Fernandez

Avro 504

Efficient product of Britain's great pioneering aircraft designer, Alliott Verdon Roe, the Avro 504 became the most widely-used British trainer during World War 1, and laid the foundations of formal flying training that were to persist for more than 30 years; it went on to become the sporting pilot's favourite mount during the 'barnstorming years' of the 1920s.

During the first decade of this century, when many major young talents were at work on the construction of aircraft, A. V. Roe was championing the idea of Britain having its own aircraft industry. In 1907 he built his first prototype, the Roe I biplane. But his first success in powered flight was not until 1909 when, on 13 July, twelve days before Louis Blériot's historic flight across the English Channel, he became the first British pilot successfully to fly an all-British powered aircraft, the Roe II triplane.

After considerable experimenting and the production of further triplanes and biplanes, Roe produced several examples of his two-seat E500 biplane, and in 1912 three such aircraft, fitted with dual controls, were ordered by the War Office, nine others being ordered by early 1913. This business made possible the formation of the private company of A. V. Roe and Co. Ltd.

The construction of a direct development, the Avro 504, was started in April 1913; this was completed within 12 weeks and started flying at Brooklands in July. On 20 September it was flown into fourth place in the Second Aerial Derby by Fred Raynham at a speed of 66.5 mph (107 km/h). The aeroplane was a well-proportioned biplane with two-bay, equal-span wings and wire-braced wooden box-girder fuselage. The engine originally fitted was an 80-hp (60-kW) Gnome rotary attached to a nose bearing mounting in a square cross-section cowling. A float version was also produced for sporting customers.

In the months immediately preceding the outbreak of World War 1 the War Office ordered 12 Avro 504s and the Admiralty one, and these were delivered between July and September 1914. However, although further orders quickly followed the declaration of war, Avro 504s did not feature in any numbers in RFC squadrons in France. It was an Avro of No. 5 Squadron that became the first British aircraft to be shot down when on 22 August the aircraft flown by Lieutenant V. Waterfall was brought down by infantry fire over Belgium. Avro 504s were also flown in a small number of audacious bombing raids, of which the most famous was the attack by RNAS aircraft on the Zeppelin sheds at Friedrichshafen, Lake Constance, on 21 November 1914, led by Squadron Commander E. F. Briggs. Aerial attacks were also made on Zeppelins in their own element by dropping 20-lb (9-kg) bombs on them from above.

The Avro 504A appeared early in 1915, retaining the 80-hp (60-kW) Gnome but with shorter and broader ailerons; some aircraft had the lower wing roots left uncovered so as to improve the downward field of vision. This was the main version produced during the years 1915–6. The Avro 504B, of which 240 were built by Avro, Parnall, Sunbeam and Regent Carriage for the Admiralty, reverted to the long ailerons and featured a large unbalanced rudder hinged to a prominent, low aspect ratio fin. The RNAS also insisted on wing spars of increased cross section, and the Avro 504B introduced a big ash tailskid, sprung with rubber cord and hinged to a pylon under the rear fuselage, a feature retained on all subsequent Avro 504s. Some Avro 504Bs served operationally at Dunkirk, at least two being fitted with a forward-firing gun with interrupter gear and an upward-firing Lewis gun. Later aircraft were powered by 80-hp (60-kW) Le Rhône engines.

This superb replica was built by Vivian Bellamy for an abandoned film and snapped up by Cole Palen for his Old Rhinebeck (New York State) airfield. It is a copy of E2939, an Avro 504K built by Morgan & Co. of Leighton Buzzard. The replica regularly shoots down von Richthofen's Fokker Dr.I with 'Le Prieur' rockets.

Avro 504

Specification

Avro 504K

Type: two-seat ab initio elementary trainer

Powerplant: one 110-hp (82-kW) Le Rhône rotary piston engine

Performance: maximum speed 95 mph (153 km/h) at sea level; climb to 3,500 ft (1065 m) in 5 minutes; service ceiling 16,000 ft (4875 m); range 250 miles (402 km)

Weights: empty 1,230 lb (558 kg); maximum take-off 1,829 lb (830 kg)

Dimensions: span 36 ft 0 in (10.97 m); length 29 ft 5 in (8.97 m); height 10 ft 5 in (3.17 m); wing area 330.0 sq ft (30.66 m²)

Armament: none

The Avro 504K shown here in pristine factory finish, E3785, was a wartime product of A. V. Roe's own Miles Platting works at Manchester. The small company logo was applied to almost all aircraft before delivery but was usually overpainted on arrival at the service aircraft parks. Although much is made of the Avro 504's suitability for the barnstorming 'work' it performed in the 1920s, it was unforgiving of slipshod maintenance, and many aircraft, purchased by shoestring companies run by enthusiastic ex-wartime pilots, came to grief as the result of inadequate servicing.

Avro 504 variants

Avro 504: prototype first flown in summer 1913; 80-hp (60-kW) Gnome, and later Gnome Monosoupape engine

Avro 504: first production, four commercial aircraft and 63 for RNAS and RFC, 80-hp (60-kW) Gnome or Le Rhône engines (Avro-built)

Avro 504A: production by Avro, Saunders, Humber, Biériot & Spad, Parnall and Eastbourne; total uncertain but seen under 540J, short ailerons; 80-hp (60-kW) Gnome or Le Rhône engines

Avro 504B: 240 built by Avro, Parnall, Sunbeam, and Regent in 1915–6, 80-hp (60-kW) Gnome or Le Rhône engines; RNAS version with long fin and long ailerons

Avro 504C: 80 built by Avro and Brush Electric, 80-hp (60-kW); Gnome engines, single-seaters for RNAS

Avro 504D: six built by Avro, as 504C but for RFC;

Avro 504E: 10 built by Avro; 100-hp (75-kW) Gnome Monosoupape engines; straight top longerons and long fin; served with RNAS

Avro 504F: one 504C (8603) with 75-hp (56-kW) Rolls-Royce Hawk engine

Avro 504G: unknown number of 504Bs modified as gunnery trainers for RNAS with two guns; 80-hp (60-kW) Gnome engines

Avro 504H: one 504C modified for catapult trials

Avro 504J: first major production variant built by Avro, Harland & Wolff, Sunbeam and Brush in 1917–18; introduced Gosport communication; 80-hp (60-kW) Le Rhône or 100-hp (75-kW) Gnome Monosoupape engine (unknown number built, but said to be about 1,050; total number of 504As and 504Js computed as 1,455)

Avro 504K: main production variant, total of 6,350 built by Avro, Sage, Henderson, Scottish, Hewlett & Blondeau, Grahame-White, Parnall, Harland & Wolff, Morgan, Savage, Humber, Eastbourne, Brush and Sunbeam (plus one built by RAF from spares); engines included 90-hp (67-kW) RAF 1A and Thulin; 100-hp (75-kW) Gnome Monosoupape, Curtiss K6 and Sunbeam Dyak; 110-hp (82-kW) Le Rhône, 130-hp (97-kW) Clerget; 150-hp (112-kW) Bentley B.R.1; 170-hp (127-kW) A.B.C. Wasp and 220-hp (164-kW) Hispano-Suiza; many sold to civilian customers, including 51 new-built; unknown number also privately built from spares; licence

production of 20 in Australia by Broadsmith and AAEC, 27 in Belgium by SABCA, two by CAL in Canada, 74 by Nakajima in Japan; others were presented or exported to Argentina, Australia, Belgium, Brazil, Canada, Chile, Denmark, Estonia, Finland, Guatemala, India, Ireland, Japan, Malaya, Mexico, Netherlands, Indies, New Zealand, Norway, Peru, Portugal, South Africa, Spain, Sweden, Switzerland, USA and Uruguay

Avro 504L: six aircraft (three-seat floatplanes), new built with 150-hp (112-kW) Bentley B.R.1 engines plus numerous conversions from 504K; imperial gifts of five conversions to Canada, two to Australia and two to New Zealand, some converted in Japan

Avro 504M: single conversion (G-EACX) of 504K as three-seat cabin aircraft by Avro (Hamble) for Avro Transport Co.; 100-hp (75-kW) Gnome Monosoupape

Avro 504N: principal peacetime production variant; engines included 100-hp (75-kW) Bristol Lucifer, 115-hp (86-kW) Lucifer IV; 150-hp (112-kW) Armstrong Siddeley Mongoose IIIA or Lynx; 180-hp (134-kW) Lynx IVC; 200-hp (149-kW) Wright Whirlwind; six prototypes and eight development aircraft, plus four interim aircraft for Armstrong Whitworth; 512 new-built plus 78 504K conversions for RAF; licence production in and export to: 17 to Belgium (plus 31 licence), four to Brazil (including 504Os), six to the Netherlands (including 504Os), six to Chile (including 504Os), one to Denmark (plus five licence), one to Japan, unknown number to South Africa, 20 to Thailand, one to Sweden

Avro 504P: unbuilt version of 504N with side-by-side seating

Avro 504Q: one three-seat aircraft (G-EBJD) with enclosed cabin for Oxford University Arctic Expedition; 160-hp (119-kW) Lynx engine

Avro 504R Gosport: six prototype and development aircraft, engines included 90-hp (67-kW) Avro Alpha; 100-hp (75-kW) Gnome Monosoupape; 150-hp (112-kW) Mongoose; 180-hp (134-kW) Lynx; 10 sold to Argentina (and 100 built under licence); about six to Estonia and an unknown number to Peru

U-1: copy of 504K mass-produced in USSR; NU-1 seaplane version

A Sunbeam-built Avro 504K, F2623, possibly belonging to the Central Flying School, Upavon, on a training flight over Salisbury Plain shortly after the end of the war. At the time of the Armistice the RAF held 2,999 504Js and Ks on charge, of which 2,267 were serving with flying schools.

Nostalgia abounds in this inter-war scene showing Avro 504Ks and their ground personnel awaiting an inspection at an RAF station. With huge quantities of war-surplus spares available at virtually no cost, the 504 was probably the most cost-effective military trainer of all time.

Early variants

Eighty Avro 504Cs were built by Avro and Brush Electrical Engineering: this model was a single-seat version produced for the RNAS with a big cylindrical fuel tank in place of the front cockpit to increase the aircraft's endurance to 8 hours 30 minutes. A gap in the top-wing centre section allowed a Lewis gun to fire upwards at an angle of 45°. Six examples of an equivalent RFC version, the Avro 504D, were ordered but doubt remains that they were ever delivered.

Ten Avro 504Es were produced for the RNAS with the 100-hp (75-kW) Gnome Monosoupape; the rear cockpit was moved aft to allow space for a fuel tank behind the front cockpit, and the resulting centre of gravity change was countered by reducing the wing stagger from 24 to 9 in (61 to 23 cm). These aircraft served at Chingford, Cranwell and Fairlop. Only one Avro 504F was produced, this being a converted Avro 504C with 75-hp (56-kW) Rolls-Royce Hawk six-cylinder inline engine, but for some reason nothing came of this version.

Some uncertainty surrounds the Avro 504G, said to have been an RFC gunnery trainer with 130-hp (97-kW) Clerget engine, and with a synchronized Vickers at the front and a Lewis gun in the rear; 10 such aircraft were produced, but the designation was also used to cover conversions of the Avro 504B for the RNAS with 80-hp (60-kW) Gnome and two guns. One Avro 504H was produced by converting an Avro 504C for catapult trials by Flight Commander R. E. Penny in 1917; the aircraft was specially strengthened and featured catapult pick-up points.

It may be said that the A to H versions of the Avro 504 were exploratory variants, undertaken before large-scale wartime production got under way of the widely used Avro 504J and Avro 504K. The Avro 504J, otherwise externally identical to the Avro 504A, was powered by a 100-hp (75-kW) Gnome Monosoupape in a characteristic lobed cowling; indeed many aircraft originally ordered as Avro 504As were completed as Avro 504Js, thus making it impossible to determine the exact production of each version; manufacture was undertaken by Avro, S.E. Saunders, Humber, Parnall, Sunbeam and Brush Electrical in 1916–8. The model was significant in introducing the 'Gosport' speaking tube which enabled the flying instructor to communicate with his pupil, thereby allowing the system of demonstration and explanation, a system that persisted in biplane training to the end of the Tiger Moth era in the Royal Air Force. The Avro 504J was also fully aerobatic, joining the School of Special Flying at Gosport and almost every other training establishment in the UK as well as many overseas. Some Avro Js were also fitted with surplus 80-hp (60-kW) Le Rhônes but without change of designation.

Best-remembered of all is the Avro 504K, which introduced a new type of universal engine mounting, designed by H. E. Broadsmith; consisting of two bearer plates which would accept any suitable engine, the mounting allowed the use of a smooth, open-fronted cowling, and the standardization of the airframe gave rise to a considerable increase in production. Forthwith Avro planned to produce 100 aircraft per week, plus spares; 20 further sets of parts were also despatched to Egypt for assembly at Aboukir. Fifty-two Avro 504Ks were purchased by the USA, and these were flown for advanced training by the American Expeditionary Forces in France in 1918, the survivors being shipped to the USA after

Avro 504K cutaway drawing key

1 Wooden leading edge and wing tip
2 Tubular steel trailing edge
3 Starboard upper aileron
4 Aileron control horn
5 Aileron interconnecting cables
6 Starboard upper wing panel
7 Inter-spar diagonal wire bracing
8 Starboard lower aileron
9 Outboard interplane struts
10 Diagonal bracing wires
11 Ventral aileron operating cables
12 Starboard wing tip skid
13 Wing panel fabric covering
14 Centre interplane struts
15 Two-bladed wooden propeller
16 Propellor hub fixing bolts
17 Landing skid front struts
18 Wooden landing skid
19 Skid bracing wires
20 Axle beam
21 Starboard mainwheel
22 Tyre inflation valve
23 Starboard shock absorber leg strut
24 110-hp Le Rhône nine-cylinder rotary engine

25 Engine mounting bulkhead
26 Aluminium engine cowling
27 Oil filler cap
28 Engine oil tank, 6½-Imp gal (29.5-litre) capacity
29 Diagonal engine bearer
30 Pilot's footboards
31 Sloping fuselage bulkhead
32 Carburettor air intake
33 Fuselage access panel
34 Main fuel tank, 20-Imp gal (91-litre) capacity
35 Fuel tank fixing straps
36 Fuel filler cap
37 Centre section struts
38 Wind driven fuel pressurizing pump
39 Windscreen panel
40 Fuel priming pump
41 Front pilot's seat
42 Ignition switch
43 Front throttle and mixture control levers
44 Rudder pedal bar
45 Control column
46 Cockpit coaming
47 Upper wing panel spar joints
48 Wing centre section
49 Fuel tank fixings
50 Fuel filler cap

One of 30 Avro 504Ks with Le Rhône engines ordered by Portugal from Vickers Ltd in November 1923 and reconditioned by Avro the following year. All were delivered by May 1924. Most were used by the Cintra flying school and four survived as late as 1934 with the Grupo de Esquadrilhas de Aviação 'Republica'.

Representing the enormously popular pastime of joy-riding between the wars, the Avro 504K G-EBIZ joined the Cornwall Aviation Company in 1924 and was not struck off the British Civil Register until August 1935. This company had been formed by Captain Percival Philips DFC and F. L. Hill, proprietor of a St Austell garage where their five Avro 504s were serviced.

51 Gravity fuel tank, 4-Imp gal (18-litre) capacity
52 Fuel contents sight glass
53 Trailing edge cut-out
54 Rear cockpit windscreen
55 Instrument panel
56 Rear throttle and mixture control levers

57 Boarding step
58 Rear pilot's seat
59 Cockpit section plywood decking
60 Fuselage top longeron
61 Plywood stiffening side members
62 Dorsal frame and stringer construction
63 Fuselage fabric covering
64 Elevator control cables
65 Starboard tailplane

66 Elevator control horn
67 Starboard elevator
68 Tubular steel rudder edge member
69 Rudder construction
70 Rudder control horn
71 Port elevator construction
72 Tailplane rib construction
73 Rudder hinge mounting
74 Tailplane attachment frame
75 Rubber block tailskid shock absorber

76 Tailplane tubular steel leading edge
77 Tailplane bracing strut
78 Castoring tailskid
79 Fuselage bottom longeron
80 Vertical spacers
81 Tailplane control cables
82 Fuselage ventral fabric lacing
83 Wing rear spar
84 Trailing edge ribs
85 Box section compression ribs
86 Front spar

87 Inter-spar diagonal wire bracing
88 Upper aileron interconnecting cables
89 Aileron control horn
90 Port upper aileron construction
91 Steel tube trailing edge
92 Aileron interconnecting cables
93 Port lower aileron
94 Aileron diagonal bracing ribs
95 Wooden leading edge and wing tip
96 Outboard interplane struts
97 Diagonal wire bracing
98 Lower wing panel rib construction
99 False centre spar
100 Centre interplane struts
101 Pitot tube
102 Boarding step
103 Fuselage fabric lacing panel
104 Wing spar root attachment joints
105 Wing footsteps
106 Skid rear bracing struts
107 Main undercarriage leg strut
108 Shock absorber fairing
109 Elastic cord shock absorber
110 Port mainwheel
111 Wheel hub fixing
112 Wheel disc fabric cover

Production of the Avro 504K continued long after the Armistice of 1918, this example being produced by the Henderson Scottish Aviation Factory of Aberdeen in 1919 or 1920.

The post-war Avro 504K joy-riding phenomenon was inaugurated by the Avro Company at Easter 1919 with three aircraft, including E4360 (later G-EABM), on Blackpool sands.

the war. Total wartime production of the Avro 504 exceeded that of any other British aircraft. The figure of 3,696 built by Avro and 4,644 by sub-contractors has frequently been quoted but the total of 8,340 appears to be an overstatement by about 236. By far the greater proportion was flown by training units (more than 4,800 in the United Kingdom and some 320 overseas).

Peacetime production

With so many war-time pilots being trained on the Avro 504 and such enormous stocks of the aircraft being declared surplus, it was not surprising that the type should survive well into the years of peace. There were, moreover, huge stocks (some estimates put them at almost 3,000) of un-delivered aircraft at storage parks and at the factories. Aircraft were sold at public auction at Hendon, until in 1920 Handley Page purchased all stocks and thereafter sold them through its subsidiary the Aircraft Disposal Co. at Croydon. New price of an Avro 504K, without engine, was £868, and a 130-hp Clerget cost £907; average price paid by civilian buyers in 1920 was around £650 for a Clerget-powered Avro 504K.

Among the multitude of popular flying events at which civil-registered Avro 504Ks appeared were the Aerial Derbies, the Wakes Weeks and Air Traffic Exhibitions, not to mention the countless displays mounted by the fast-growing numbers of local flying clubs up and down the country. Alan Cobham was among the newly demobilized service pilots

who started the famous 'barnstorming' tours with Avro 504Ks in the 1920s, and persisted until the 1930s. One of his pilots, Captain Percival Philips DFC, carried more than 91,000 passengers, almost all of them in one famous aeroplane, G-EBIZ, over a period of about 15 years.

The RAF continued to use the Avro 504K, aircraft of this type serving with Nos 1, 2, 3 and 5 FTS in the UK and with No. 4 FTS at Abu Sueir, and at East Retford, Throwley and Newmarket; others flew at the CFS at Upavon, and the Royal Air Force College, Cranwell, as well as the newly-created Auxiliary Air Force in the late 1920s. The Fleet Air Arm used Avro 504Ks at Leuchars and Netheravon.

Avro 504Ks enjoyed a brisk trade in the export market and some ex-Australian Flying Corps aircraft served with the RAAF until 1928. Others included 63 Imperial Gift Avro 504Ks to Canada and 20 to New Zealand. The largest overseas licence manufacturer of the Avro 504K was Nakajima of Japan. Far greater numbers were built without a licence in the USSR in 1922–8 as the U-1 and sea-plane NU-1, powered by the M-2 copy of the 100-hp (75-kW) Gnome.

The Avro 504L was a peacetime development employing two wooden pontoon-type floats and a 130-hp Clerget driving a four-blade propeller, The aircraft was not adopted by the RAF and new production was confined to six aircraft produced by Avro at Hamble, although numerous float conversions were carried out in the UK and overseas. The single Avro 504M (G-EACX) was a standard Avro 504K modified to feature enclosed accommodation for two passengers, and a similar version was put into licence

This Avro 504K was a parent company-built aircraft which served with the RFC/RAF's No. 8 Training Squadron in 1918. The end of the war brought about a rapid rundown of the RAF, which in turn resulted in large numbers of surplus Avro 504Ks being offered on the civil market at very low prices.

In February 1920, their success prompted the purchase of at least seven further Avro 504Ks (nos 15–21) by the Estonian air force in 1921, the first aircraft, shown here, being originally produced by the Grahame-White Aviation Company.

This Avro 504K was built in 1918 and has a 100-hp (75 kW) Avro Le Rhône nine-cylinder engine. It is now owned by the Shuttleworth Collection and occasionally still appears in flying displays. (*Photo: Air Portraits*)

The Avro 504R was not adopted by the RAF, but a small number was sold abroad to Argentina, Estonia and Peru. At least six went to the Estonian air force for service at Tallinn in November 1928, including the example depicted here, and some of them survived into the 1940s.

production in Japan as the Aiba Tsubami IV with 150-hp (112-kW) Gasden Jimpu engine.

The Avro 540N was the main production variant introduced after the end of World War 1. Prototypes and development aircraft were largely produced by converting Avro 504Ks, but six new-built aircraft appeared after 1924. The new version featured a wholly revised landing gear, comprising two main legs attached to the axle which in turn was hinged to two horizontal tubes by two rear Vee-struts behind and in line with the main legs. In this characteristic 'N-type' landing gear the central skid (for so long a feature of the Avro 504) was discarded. Production orders for the RAF, placed between 1927 and 1933, amounted to 512 aircraft, plus 78 conversions from Avro 504Ks, and these aircraft gave yeoman service with Nos 1, 2, 3, 4 and 5 FTS, No. 23 ERFTS, the RAF College, the Oxford and Cambridge University Air Squadrons, and Nos 500, 501, 502, 601, 602, 603, 604 and 607 Squadrons of the Auxiliary Air Force. In due course many of these Avro 504Ns were replaced by the Avro Tutor and Hawker Tomtit, and eventually found their way on to the commercial market. Among the modified versions of the Avro 504N was a single-float aircraft with Wright Whirlwind J-4 engine, produced by Canadian Vickers in 1926, and a light glider-tug version. Seven of the latter were produced in 1940 (as conversions) to equip a Special Duty Flight at Christchurch, towing Hotspur gliders 40 miles (66 km) out to sea to test radar reflection of wooden aircraft; other Avro

One of the many Avro 504 derivatives was the Avro 548, with Renault engine, for example, produced by Surrey Flying Services from ex-E3043 in 1921–2, was used in radio telegraphy work by Marconi Wireless Telegraph Co. in the early 1920s and sold to the Henderson School of Flying in 1926.

504N glider tugs were used during World War 2 at Ringway to develop towing techniques for the airborne forces.

The single Avro 504Q was a three-seat enclosed-cabin floatplane produced at Avro's Hamble works for the Oxford University Arctic Expedition; powered by a 160-hp (119-kW) Armstrong Siddeley Lynx and registered G-EBJD, this aeroplane sported a large dorsal fin and carried extra fuel tanks under the upper wing. During the course of an exciting voyage via Spitzbergen (on which G-EBJD was all but wrecked several times but repaired), it reached latitude 80° 15' on 8 August 1924, the farthest north yet reached by an aeroplane. G-EBJD was eventually abandoned to test the effect of Arctic exposure on wooden aircraft, but when examined in the 1930s it was found to have been partly devoured by polar bears!

The last version of the Avro 504 was the Gosport or Avro 504R. This was an attempt to produce a version which could emulate the performance of the RAF's Avro 504N, despite having a cheaper, lower-power engine than the Lynx. Various engines were tested, but most proved not to be powerful enough. Finally, the manufacturers came to the conclusion that a 150-hp (112-kW) Mongoose would give the best performance. Six test aircraft were built, and a few exported to Argentina, Estonia and Peru. The Fábrica Militar de Aviones, in Cordoba, Argentina, built 100 of these machines under licence. As far as is known, when SABCA in Belgium ordered ten Avro 504s in October 1937, it was the last time any of these aircraft were ordered.

Most celebrated RAF unit to fly the Avro 504N was the Central Flying School, Upavon, the aircraft shown here serving with the school from 1931 onwards. Just visible is the blind-flying hood for the student's cockpit, shown here folded down. When covering the rear cockpit the u/t pilot had to fly solely on instruments.

Handley Page O/100 and O/400

No other aircraft manufacturer achieved sufficient fame as to grace the pages of the Concise Oxford Dictionary with the definition 'Type of large aeroplane', and it was the impression created by Frederick Handley Page's O/100 and O/400 bombers of World War 1 which caused the name Handley Page to become a generic title for large aircraft

Two events shortly after World War 1 gave a definite boost to the development of these two great aircraft types. When the Royal Flying Corps and other Air Forces realised how useful aircraft could be for reconnaissance purposes they set off falteringly into the skies using BE2a biplanes, Blériot and Taube monoplanes and various other unsafe aircraft. But the Royal Navy, or at least a few keen young officers, notably the redoubtable Commander C. R. Samson, already had other ideas. Although Samson commanded the No. 1 Wing of the Royal Naval Air Service in France, in between flying missions he would wage war using a column of armoured vehicles. For him, war was synonymous with attack, and two weeks after World War 1 began he sent two of his tiny biplanes off to bomb Zeppelin hangars. Lieutenant Marix managed to blow up a hangar, and the Zeppelin it contained, with two 20-lb (9-kg) bombs, and shortly afterwards four Avro 504s attacked the Zeppelin factory on Lake Constance, causing considerable destruction.

Front-line service as RAF No. 214 Sqn (previously RNAS No. 14) ready their O/100s for another night raid into Germany from Coudekerke, which in early 1917 had been one of the first bases for naval Handleys. Note the wide but shallow fin flash, and long nacelles for the 266-hp (198-kW) Eagle IIs. The serial is probably on the extreme tail.

'A bloody paralyser to stop the Hun in his tracks' was the urgent signal sent by Commander Charles Rumney Samson in 1914 which led to the Handley Page O/100 and O/400 being developed. The O/400 had a 100-ft (30.48-m) wing span and exposed positions for gunners and pilots. Thankfully for the pilots and nose gunner, their positions ahead of the propellers spared them from most of the effects of turbulence, but nevertheless conditions were difficult. Note the wing folding joints immediately above the engine nacelles.

Handley Page O/400

Specification

Handley Page O/400 (HP-built)
Type: heavy bomber with crew three to five
Powerplant: two 360-hp (268-kW) Rolls-Royce Eagle VIII water-cooled Vee-12 piston engines
Performance: maximum speed (with full bomb load) 97.5 mph (157 km/h) at sea level; cruising speed at 10,000 ft (3048 m) 74 mph (119 km/h); time to reach 10,000 ft (3048 m) 40 min; endurance 8 hours
Weights: empty 8,502 lb (3857 kg); loaded 13,360 lb (6060 kg)
Dimensions: span 100 ft (30.48 m); length 62 ft 10¼ in (19.17 m); height 22 ft 0¾ in (6.72 m); wing area 1,648 sq ft (153.1 m²)
Armament: bombload varied but usually 16 of 112-lb (50.8-kg) size, with single 1,650-lb (748 kg) an alternative; defensive guns also varied but usually one or two 0.303-in (7.7-mm) Lewis guns on Scarff ring in nose, two single Lewis guns on side posts at mid-upper position, and single pin-mounted Lewis gun firing through lower rear trapdoor

Handley Page O/100 and O/400

Britain made a present of one of the first Handley Pages to the enemy. O/100, No. 1463, was landed by its RNAS crew on the first good field they saw after breaking cloud on their flight to France on 1 January 1917; it was 12 miles inside enemy territory, near Laon. Among the German evaluation pilots was Manfred von Richthofen.

Photographed at the Birmingham Carriage Company works in 1918, D5440 was part of initial 50-aircraft order constructed by this subcontractor. The finished aircraft were moved to the Aircraft Acceptance Park at Castle Bromwich from where they were delivered to their respective RAF squadrons.

Before 1914 was out Captain Murray Sueter at the Admiralty Air Department had asked Handley Page to build four production prototypes of a bomber of vast size to comply with Samson's signal to build 'a bloody paralyser of an aeroplane'. The fact that Handley Page had only built a few, rather unconventional, aircraft to this date deterred neither Sueter nor 'H.P.' himself, and 1915 saw work steadily progressing on the first of the aircraft, known as the O/100 — the Handley Page Type O with a 100-ft (30.48-m) span, at Cricklewood. As the parts emerged they were incorporated in the final assembly at Kingsbury, whence the completed aircraft was towed to Hendon. With the serial number 1455 this first machine arrived there on 10 December and took to the air on 17 December 1915 with Lieutenant Commander John Babington at the controls. Within a year of the Admiralty's decision this vast step forward in British bombing aircraft had emerged and flown.

The three subsequent prototypes had several different features, with an amidships gun position and extended nose, features later incorporated in the production aircraft, a batch of eight of which had already been ordered to follow the first four off the production lines. A RN Training Flight was established at Manston in the spring of 1916, receiving the second prototype and the first production machines (serial numbers were 1459 to 1466). An initial and potentially disastrous problem with tail flutter was soon cured with a new elevator.

Then the War Office looked with envy at the Royal Navy's new possession and ordered a batch of 12 for the Royal Flying Corps, to take their place after the next batch of 28 for the Royal Naval Air Service.

Two O/100s were delivered to the 3rd Wing at Luxeuil in

France in 1916, the first being taken by Babington, and plans were in hand to start operations in 1917. On New Year's Day, however, the third O/100 to set out for France was mistakenly delivered to the Germans when it landed behind the enemy lines. With spring weather the Handley Pages made their first sortie on the night of 16–17 March 1917 with a raid on a rail junction near Metz. The next month more aircraft went to France, this time to Coudekerke, where they began to form No. 7 Squadron, RNAS. These aircraft were from the second production batch (3115 to 3142), and soon after re-equipping No. 7 Squadron sent a detachment to Redcar in Yorkshire for anti-submarine patrolling. One of its aircraft was fitted with a 6-pounder (2.7-kg) Davis gun in the nose but this weapon was never used successfully in anger. In France three O/100s attacked five German destroyers with 14 65-lb (29.5-kg)

Pictured on a rare apron of concrete at Farnborough in early 1918, B8802 was the first of a batch of O/400s built by the Royal Aircraft Factory. The serials had originally been assigned to the first War Office (as distinct from RN) contract for Handley Pages, with RAF 3a engines.

F5417 was one of the standard Eagle VIII-powered O/400s assembled by National Aircraft Factory No. 1, at Waddon (Croydon). This was run by Cubitts to build bombers from parts fed in from hundreds of furniture and building firms in the London area. The markings are non-standard.

At the time the RAF was formed, the RFC's standard day bomber was the O/400, an aircraft from No. 207 Sqn at Ligescourt, France, in 1918 being shown here. This was the first British squadron used solely for long-range night bombing, and the first to operate Handley Page bombers.

G-EATN was one of the last O/400s built, as HP-built J2261 in 1918. It was then rebuilt as one of nine O/10 12-passenger airliners for Handley Page Air Transport, operating between Croydon and Paris in 1920. This particular O/10 was used for trials with the Aveline Stabilizer, an early two-axis automatic pilot.

bombs each and severely disabled one of them. A similar attack resulted in the loss of one of the bombers. Meanwhile one of the Manston aircraft (3124) flew out to Mudros in the Aegean in May 1917 for attacks on two German cruisers there. It succeeded in bombing the battle-cruiser *Goeben* and in carrying out some other raids before being forced to ditch in the Gulf of Xeros.

From O/100 to O/400

One of the problems at the time was the lack of Rolls-Royce Eagle engines for these giants, so 3117 became an engine test-bed at Farnborough, where no fewer than four different engine configurations were tried, including one with four Hispano-Suizas in tandem pairs. By September 1917, however, an aircraft powered by later Eagle engines and refined in many ways was flying at the Aeroplane & Armament Experimental Establishment at Martlesham Heath as the prototype O/400. This version had much increased fuel tankage, Eagle VIIIs and an increased bomb load. All sub-

sequent production was to this standard. No. 7 Squadron and its offshoot, No. 7A Squadron, were now keeping up a steady bombing offensive, having gone over to night bombing, and were joined by another RNAS unit, 'A' Squadron, later numbered No. 16 Squadron, which was based at Ochey from 17 October onwards.

The success of this giant aircraft resulted in quantity production orders for the RFC and RNAS and, when the Royal Air Force was formed on 1 April 1918, the naval units were renumbered Nos 207, 214 (ex-7A) and 216 Squadrons, RAF. These units were split, the first two supporting the army in the north, the latter being used for strategic bombing in the Nancy area. The RAF soon expanded these two groupings, adding No. 58 Squadron, now re-equipped with Handley Pages, to Nos 207 and 214 Squadrons in August and building up the strategic force with Nos 97, 100, 115 and 215 Squadrons, forming the 83rd Wing. This was part of the revolutionary Independent Force tasked with bombing industrial installations. This force, which was conceptually ahead of its time, showed to the rest of the world the possibilities of aerial bombardment inherent in an air force independent of the army and navy. Valuable lessons were learnt and digested by those involved in the force in the few short months of strategic bombing before the Armistice

In the impoverished post-war RAF the O/400 soldiered on in overseas theatres, and this example with No. 70 Sqn was photographed in 1921, at Heliopolis. The ladder strapped to the landing gear was often carried for crew exit at desert strips, and even a bicycle was an occasional adjunct.

D8350 was the last of a batch of O/400s assembled by Handley Page from British Caudron parts. She is pictured at Cricklewood (on which houses were now visible) after becoming a civil aircraft, *Vulture*; on 4 May 1919 Lt.Cdr Sholto Douglas took the first passengers from Cricklewood to Manchester.

This Handley Page O/100 was captured by the Germans on New Year's Day 1917; here it is shown still in its English markings shortly before its ill-fated landing on enemy territory to the obvious delight of German aviation experts.

of November 1918. Although the Independent Force flew several other types of bombers, there was no doubt in anybody's mind that the big Handley Pages set the pattern for the future. Despite the initial disbelief of the new Air Board in the effectiveness of night bombing the exploits of the Handley Page squadrons during 1918 gave them proof they could not ignore. Up to 40 of the big bombers would be airborne on good nights, ranging over German industrial areas, attacking factories, railway junctions and docks. Up until this time the biggest bombs normally carried were 112-lb (51-kg) weapons, but now the O/100s and O/400s were carrying 520- and 550-lb (236- and 250-kg) bombs, having a profound effect on the recipients. The farthest the squadrons reached was Mannheim, which was attacked on 25 August 1918 by two aircraft of No. 215 Squadron. The offensive was maintained right until the Armistice, and by then 1,650-lb (748-kg) bombs were being used. This all seems 'small beer' compared with the weapons of World War 2, but for those times it was formidable indeed.

Mention of 3124's exploit outside the Western Front has already been made. Two other O/400s set out for Egypt before the Armistice, one arriving in time to serve in the successful campaign through Palestine. This was C9681 which after arriving at Heliopolis, was attached to No. 1

The O/100 serial number 3124 belonged to the Royal Navy and was stationed in Manston, Kent. This bomber eventually made its name far from the Western Front, leading several attacks in the Aegean Sea, and in May 1917 by bombing the German battle-cruiser *Goeben*.

Handley Page O/400 cutaway drawing key

1 Twin 0.303-in (7.7-mm) Lewis guns
2 Rotatable Scarff ring
3 Gunner's cockpit (plywood construction)
4 Folding seat
5 Slat flooring
6 Entry hatch to gunner's cockpit
7 ASI pitot tube
8 Negative lens
9 Rudder pedals
10 Control wheel
11 Clear Pyralin windshield
12 Padded cockpit coaming
13 Pilot's seat
14 Observer's seat
15 Slat flooring
16 Light-bomb rack (manual)
17 Batteries
18 Trap-type forward entry door
19 Fabric lacing
20 Transparent panel
21 Plywood turtle-deck

34 Double flying cable braces
35 Spruce/plywood inner strut
36 Double flying cable braces
37 Single landing cable brace
38 Single stagger cables
39 Spruce/plywood outer strut
40 Double flying braces
41 Outer aileron control horn
42 Cabane braces (four point)
43 Steel cabane
44 Inner aileron control horn
45 Solid end ribs
46 Wing dihedral break-line
47 Gravity-feed fuel tanks in leading edge, two of 12-Imp gal (54.5-litre) capacity
48 Centre-section streamlined forward cabane strut
49 Centre-section streamlined aft cabane strut

58 Aft fuel tank, capacity 130 Imp gal (591 litres)
59 Solid rib at dihedral break-line
60 Upper gunner's seat
61 Transparent panels
62 Ammunition racks
63 Ventral gunner's hatch
64 Clear Pyralin panels
65 Gunner's slatted flooring
66 Plywood bulkheads
67 Single dorsal 0.303-in (7.7-mm) Lewis gun
68 Fabric lacing
69 Control cable pulleys
70 Fuselage frame
71 Multi-strand cable bracing
72 Elevator control cable
73 Interplane streamlined spruce strut
74 Starboard rudder
75 Fabric-covered upper tailplane
76 Elevator control horn
77 Fixed surface centre-section
78 Fabric-covered elevator
79 Port rudder spruce frame
80 Port lower elevator frame
81 Fabric-covered lower tailplane
82 Rudder hinge spar
83 Plywood tail covering
84 Rear navigation light

22 Aluminium fairing
23 Steel propeller hub
24 Four-blade walnut propeller
25 Four-blade walnut propeller
26 Radiator filler cap
27 Radiator
28 360 hp Rolls-Royce Eagle VIII engine
29 Exhaust manifold
30 Nacelle bracing strut/control spar
31 Oil tank, 15 Imp gal (68 litres) in each nacelle
32 Rigging lines
33 Streamlined steel struts

50 Forward cylindrical fuel tank (held by web straps), capacity 130 Imp gal (591 litre)
51 Filler cap
52 Cross member
53 Engine control pulley cluster
54 Centre-section main bomb-bay
55 Six volt wind-driven generator (port and starboard)
56 Perforated baffle plate
57 Air-driven fuel pumps

85 Interplane strut
86 Vertical stabilizer
87 Steel attachment point
88 Faired struts
89 Tailskid
90 Removable fabric panel
91 Lifting points (stations 10 and 12)
92 Port steel cabane
93 Rear upper mainplane spar
94 Forward upper mainplane spar
95 Plywood covering

Though Standard Aircraft, of Elizabeth, NJ, were under contract to supply parts for assembly in England, seven O/400s with Liberty engines were assembled in the USA. This was the first, given the name *Langley*. In 'Billy' Mitchell's trials to show that bombers could destroy warships, no. 62448 hit *Ostfriesland* and later dropped a 4,000-lb (1814-kg) bomb.

62447

Believed to have been taken at Langley Field, the heart of today's vast NASA research centre, this photograph shows the first of the seven Liberty-engined O/400s assembled in the USA for the US Army, from parts off the British production by Standard Aircraft. It made its first flight, as no. 62445, on 6 July 1918. Many O/400s were stored by the US Army Air Service.

96 Steel fitting
97 Solid drag strut
98 Wing structure
99 Port aileron structure
100 Port outer interplane struts (plywood-covered spruce)
101 Lower mainplane end rib
102 Wing structure
103 Leading-edge rib construction
104 Port inner interplane struts (plywood-covered spruce)
105 Hinge strut
106 Lower mainplane dihedral break-line
107 Steel tube engine nacelle support struts
108 Wing/fuselage attachment points
109 Wing root walkway
110 Fire extinguisher
111 Starboard undercarriage
112 Undercarriage forward strut
113 Port twinmain wheels
114 Faired rubber chord shock strut
115 Aft strut

Squadron, Australian Flying Corps. From Heliopolis it set out on 19 September to attack the Turkish HQ, a successful raid destroying the enemy's means of communications with its 7th and 8th Armies and hastening their demise. But its principal task in the Middle East was as a transport to take supplies and fuel to the advanced airstrip at Azrak, where Lawrence of Arabia centred his activities. The second machine, C9700, was too late for the war in Egypt but flew on east to Calcutta, pioneering what was eventually to become the air mail route. It ended its days in India, being wrecked at Lahore.

Post-war duties

As well as the bomber squadrons mentioned, the big Handley Pages also served as navigation trainers, at Andover and Stonehenge, and after the armistice these aircraft came to the fore. An imperial air mail service had already been considered a possibility, and with the war over O/400s from Andover began expanding their activities into longer-distance navigational exercises to prepare crews, experienced in navigation, for the long-awaited civil air transports. Long-distance navigation of a different kind took place when it was decided to move three of the Independent Force units to Egypt and to take them by air. It was an expensive expedition, for of the 51 aircraft of Nos 58, 214 and 216 Squadrons which set out from France 25 never made it. The survivors were used in Egypt into the early 1920s, flying operationally against troublesome Arab tribes amongst other tasks. The squadrons were regrouped into Nos 70 and 216 Squadrons, two units which formed the bomber-transport force in the Middle East until 1940.

The first genuine transport schedules on which this type flew were those run by No. 86 Wing RAF, which provided a link between London and Versailles during the peace treaty negotiations in 1919; the wing was based at Hendon. Nearby, at Handley Page's Cricklewood airfield, the company had acquired surplus aircraft and decked them out as 16-seat airliners. Here they flew familiarization flights for the joy-riding public and more serious routes to Paris, Brussels and Amsterdam (Handley Page Air Transport being one of the founder British air lines), sporting civil registration in place of roundels and serial numbers. Altogether about 25 served

in this way until 1924 and the advent of civil airliner derivatives of the O/400 put them out of service. Others of the breed found their way to South Africa and to China, where they formed the basis for an early air mail service and also, in one case, reverted to the military role.

As early as 1917 the Americans had been showing a great interest in the Handley Page. They were impressed with the considerable success it had experienced. A licence agreement was signed with the Standard Aircraft Corporation to manufacture the aircraft in the USA, but with Liberty 12 engines. A British aircraft (B9449) was sent to the United States to be used as a model, and complete sets of parts were shipped across the Atlantic. But only one-seventh of these ever reached the USA, and production took a long time to get off the ground. The Armistice brought the highly ambitious production schedule to a premature end. The US Army took only 13 of these aircraft, and a further 20 were put into storage. One of these was used for General 'Billy' Mitchell's experiments to persuade the US Navy that airborne bombers could be used to sink warships. At the beginning of the 1920s the Handley Page O/100 and O/400 bombers gradually disappeared from the scene, to be replaced by newer and more effective bombers and transport planes.

Handley Page O/100 and O/400 variants

O/100 no. 1455: first prototype, initially with 250-hp (186-kg) Rolls-Royce engines (later called Eagle) in armoured nacelles, with armoured and glazed nose for crew; later several times modified
O/100 nos. 1456/1458: prototypes with various detail improvements and 266-hp (198-kg) Eagle II engines
O/100 production, nos. 1459/1466 and 3115/3142: Eagle II engines, except (because of shortage of engines) 3117 flown with two RAF 3a and then four 200-hp (149-kW) Hispano Hs 8b engines; no. 3142 flown with two 300-hp (223-kW) Fiat A. 12 engines
O/100 production B9446/9451: powered by two 320-hp (238-kW) Sunbeam Cossack engines
O/400 prototype: in effect O/100 no. 3138 rebuilt with new fuel system with tanks in fuselage, air-driven pumps, and short nacelles for 275-hp (205-kW) Eagle II engines
O/400 production: by Handley Page. C3381/3480, C9636/9785 and F3748/3767, all with either 284-hp (212-

kW) Eagle IV, 360-hp (268-kW) Eagle VIII (Standard), 275-hp (205-kW) Sunbeam Maori or 350-hp (261-kW) Liberty 12; by RAF Farnborough, B8802/8813 and C3487/3498 (latter from HP-build parts) with Eagle VIII; by British Caudron Co. for erection at HP Cricklewood, D8301/8350; by Birmingham Carriage Co. D5401/5450, F301/320 and J2242/2291 (only 2242/2274 completed by Armistice) with Eagle VIII; by Metropolitan Wagon Co., D4561/4660 and J3542/3616 (none of last batch delivered); by Clayton & Shuttleworth, D9681/9730; by National Aircraft Factory No. 1 at Waddon, F5349/5448 (at least 70 delivered with Liberty 12, later re-engined with Eagle VIII)
O/400 US production: 1,500 ordered from Standard Aircraft for final assembly in England and 100 sets accepted in UK by Armistice, plus seven assembled at Langley Field with Liberty 12 engines as US Army Aviation Service Nos. 62445/62451, remainder cancelled
Total production: 46 O/100 plus 554 O/400 excluding US production

SPAD S.VII

When it appeared in 1916, the SPAD S.VII was a remarkable fighter: in comparison with its contemporaries, it was heavier and considerably faster; and while it lacked something of their agility, it also dispensed with their alarming tendency to break up in the air during prolonged manoeuvres. Successful in its own right, the S.VII also gave birth to the great S.XIII fighter.

During the critical months of 1917, French and Italian newspapers were also reporting on a great new brand of fliers: Charles Nungesser, Georges Guynemer and René Fonck in France, and Francesco Baracca in Italy.

Each gallant aviator was pictured with his unit or personal insignia in striking resemblance to medieval and renaissance knights with their colourful shields or pennants. World War 1 newspaper cuttings reveal Nungesser and his macabre skull and candles, Guynemer with the beautifully designed Stork badge of the Cigognes, and Baracca's finely outlined 91a Squadriglia 'Cavallino Rampante' (prancing horse). But there was scarce mention made of the aircraft which bore the insignia. Yet in most instances it was the same reliable design – the tough, highly stable little SPAD biplane which did so much to wrest aerial supremacy over the Western Front for precious months from the ever-threatening Albatros and Fokker single-seaters, presenting a threat to which the Germans did not react for several costly months.

The S.VII owed its conception to the successful development of a new aero engine. The Allied air arms had relied heavily during the first two years of war on Gnome, Le Rhône and Clerget rotary engines, which possessed limited development potential. It was hardly surprising, then, that the French and British air staffs showed great interest in the new water-cooled stationary engine developed by the famed Hispano-Suiza company under the direction of a talented Swiss designer, Marc Birkigt. The first examples of his new V-8 engine, the Hispano-Suiza 8Aa, delivering 150 hp (112 kW), were available early in 1916. The task of producing an airframe to be married to the new engine so as to achieve a world-beating single-seat fighter was allotted to the chief

engineer of SPAD (the Société Anonyme pour l'Aviation et ses Dérivés), a subsidiary of the famous Blériot company. This decision might have seemed foolhardy since the chief engineer was a certain Louis Béchereau, notorious for his Type A two-seaters, whose major design feature was the mounting of the engine and propeller in the fuselage, separating the observer-gunner in the nose from the pilot in the rear. French and Russian aircrew operating the A-2 production version had little good to say for it, since any nose-over on landing tended to kill the gunner.

Yet several features of the A-2 design, including the wing construction, were excellent and were retained by Béchereau for his new fighter. When the SPAD Type V prototype appeared in the spring of 1916, it was revealed as a neat and powerful tractor biplane. Flying initially in April 1916, it performed well in subsequent company and service trials. With a maximum level speed of over 130 mph (210 km/h), it promised a substantial performance improvement over the Nieuport sesquiplane scouts currently in Allied service. The French authorities were quick to order the new fighter into production, awarding the SPAD company a contract for 268 aircraft on 10 May 1916.

Strong and sure

Series aircraft incorporated a number of minor modifications, but the basic design of the prototype remained unchanged. The service designation S.VII was applied to the new fighter, although it was often described as the S.7 or Spa 7. The wings were of remarkably thin aerofoil section, a feature which became the hallmark of all derivatives of the basic

The detachable panel marked 'PHOTO' on this SPAD S.VII indicates that it was one of a limited number adapted to carry a camera for photographic reconnaissance work, a role in which the S.VII's speed and flight steadiness were important assets to survival and good photography. The technique of aerial photographic reconnaisance was new.

This SPAD S.VII is in the markings adopted by the air arm of the newly created state of Czechoslovakia in 1919. The concentric circles of the insignia were white (in the centre), blue and red. The roundels just visible on the rudder were replaced by a facsimile of the Czech national flag two years later. S.VII No. 3 was photographed at Cheb.

design. There were ailerons on the upper wing only. Although a single-bay biplane, with a pair of bracing struts on each side, the S.VII had the superficial appearance of a two-bay aircraft, since it had inboard intermediate articulated struts, which served as tie struts for the flying and bracing wires and thus gave added structural strength. As with the wings, the fuselage was of wooden construction: built up on four longerons, it had curved top and bottom decking and was fabric covered. The landing gear was of cross-axle Vee-type, with the axle articulated at the centre. Shock absorbers were of the then indispensable 'bungee' elastic cord.

Great care was taken to give the S.VII smooth contours. Attempts to fit a large propeller spinner were abandoned at an early stage, but the engine had curved metal cowlings formed round the circular shutter for the frontal engine radiator and extending back to a position just in front of the pilot's open cockpit. A single Vickers 0.303-in (7.7-mm) machine-gun was mounted on top of the engine cowling. Engine designer Marc Birkigt himself had developed the ingenious mechanical interrupter gear, which was driven off the rear of the starboard cam shaft.

The S.VII soon proved itself a nimble and rugged fighter, able to hold its own in dogfights. It had a respectable rate of climb and an ability to make sudden extended dives, which could be repeated without risk to the structure, features which gave it an ability to manoeuvre vertically in a way unequalled by any contemporary aircraft, Allied or German, in 1916. Above all the SPAD provided a stable gun platform.

The first SPAD S.VII to reach the front line was issued to Lieutenant Armand Pinsard of Escadrille N.26, and it was he who scored the first recorded victory by an S.VII on 23 August 1916. From then on the SPAD opened the road to glory and honour for a galaxy of French fliers whose names became household words. By the summer of 1917 the S.VII equipped more than 50 *escadrilles de chasse* (fighter squadrons) on the Western Front. This pre-eminence was achieved despite the failure of the grandiose production plans of the French high command, which relied on licence manufacture by a whole range of companies. That output was little more than half that anticipated was hardly surprising, since apart from a few experienced manufacturers, such as Blériot, the parent company of the SPAD firm, the bulk of contractors had negligible experience in building aircraft. Nevertheless, in the hands of veterans such as Georges Félix Madon, Marcel Noguès and Armand de Turenne, the S.VII continued to make its mark.

Ahead of the Germans

Efforts to improve the performance of the S.VII, always in danger of being overtaken by newer German types, were vigorously pursued. From April 1917 all S.VIIs leaving the

In this particular photograph of the SPAD the grill covering the lower part of the 180-hp (134-kW) Hispano-Suiza 8Ab engine has been removed, possibly as an aid to cooling. Engine cooling was a perpetual problem with SPADs, and this and other contemporary photographs reveal a wide diversity of louvring and even of radiator configuration.

The chosen successor of the SPAD S.VII was the S.XIII, first production examples of which entered French service in mid-1917. It featured many detailed refinements, was powered by a 200-hp (149-kW) Hispano-Suiza 8Ba or 220-hp (165-kW) Hispano-Suiza 8Bc engine, had a more powerful twin-Vickers 0.303-in (7.7-mm) machine-gun armament, and

featured an enlarged curved rudder. This S.XIII was the mount of Captain Edward Rickenbacker of the 94th Squadron, United States Air Service. 'Eddie' Rickenbacker was born on 8 October 1890. Commissioned in France in early 1918, Rickenbacker was assigned to the 94th Aero Squadron in March 1918. He found his first victim on 29 April, shooting down an Albatros D.Va. In just over six months, until the 11 November Armistice, Rickenbacker achieved the remarkable score of 26 enemy aircraft. Over 7,000 S.XIIIs were built and they continued in service in France, the United States and many other countries right through the 1920s.

SPAD S.VII

Specification

SPAD S.VII
Type: single-seat fighting scout
Powerplant: one 180-hp (134-KW) Hispano-Suiza 8Ab inline piston engine
Performance: maximum speed 132 mph (212 km/h) at sea level, and 124 mph (200 km/h) at 13,125 ft (4000 m); climb to 6,560 ft (2000 m) in 4 minutes 40 seconds; service ceiling 21,490 ft (6550 m); range 217 miles (350 km); endurance 1 hour 30 minutes

Weights: empty 1,102 lb (500 kg); maximum take-off 1,554 lb (705 kg)
Dimensions: span, upper 25 ft 8 in (7.82 m), lower 24 ft 10¼ in (7.57 m); length 19 ft 11¼ in (6.08 m); height 7 ft 2½ in (2.20 m); wing area 192.14 sq ft (17.85 m²)
Armament: one fixed forward-firing 0.303-in (7.7-mm) Vickers machine-gun with 500 rounds

factories had the new Hispano-Suiza 8Ab engine, developed from the original powerplant and offering 180 hp (134 kW). This kept the type ahead of the opposition, but other experiments, with a wing of revised aerofoil section, and with the temperamental 200-hp (149-kW) Hispano-Suiza 8B engine, were soon abandoned. With the personal encouragement of Georges Guynemer, Louis Béchereau designed the SPAD S.XII Ca.1, powered by a 200-hp (134-kW) Hispano-Suiza 8C engine and armed with the powerful 37-mm Hotchkiss gun, fitted between the cylinder blocks and firing through the hollow airscrew shaft. Guynemer received his S.XII in July 1917, promptly scoring four of his victories with it, but the type did not become popular, no more than 100 of the original order for 300 being completed.

The hopes of the French and their allies, however, were pinned on the SPAD S.XIII, natural successor to the S.VII. Retaining the good qualities of the S.VII, it had the more powerful 220-hp (165-kW) Hispano-Suiza 8Ba engine fitted with reduction gear, was armed with twin Vickers guns and had a number of other modifications, including increased rudder area, which rendered it a more manoeuvrable and formidable fighting machine. The prototype flew in April 1917, but production got under way only very slowly. Although eventually over 7,000 S.XIIIs were built, at the time of the last great German offensives in March 1918, only seven months before the war was to end, the S.VIIs in first-line service still exceeded the S.XIIIs. Thus the S.VII soldiered on past its prime, outclassed by the new Fokker D.VII in the fast-changing fortunes of war.

Precise figures for French production of the S.VII are not known, but at least 3,500 were completed. From French-built

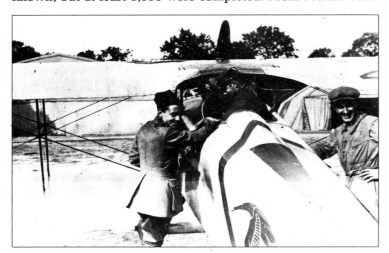

An aircraft of the famed French 'Cigognes', Groupe de Chasse 12, commanded by Capitaine Armand Brocard. In this view the flying stork insignia can be clearly seen on the fuselage side next to the coloured stripe. The French ace Georges Guynemer was also a member of this *Group de Chasse*.

SPAD S.VII variants

Type V: prototype of S.VII; one built, flew spring 1916; designated with letter V under SPAD company alphabetical system

SPAD S.VII (initial French production): powered by Hispano-Suiza 8Aa engine 150 hp (112 kW), estimated 500 built May 1916–March 1917

SPAD S.VII (Renault-powered): one-off 1916 experimental variant with 150-hp (122-kW) Renault 8G engine, back-up in event of difficulties with Hispano-Suiza engine

SPAD S.VII (main French production): powered by 180-hp (134-kW) Hispano-Suiza 8Ab engine, some 3,000 constructed by following French companies from March 1917: SPAD, Blériot, Janair, Kellner, de Marçay. Regy Frères and Sommer, wartime foreign sales to Italy (214) USA (189), UK (185 to RFC), Russia (43) and Belgium (15), post-war surplus French aircraft widely exported to countries that included Brazil, Czechoslovakia, Greece, Peru, Poland, Portugal, Romania, Thailand and Yugoslavia

SPAD S.VII (200-hp (149-kW) variants): only two S.VIIs have been identified as built with experimental 200-hp (149-kW) Hispano-Suiza 8B engine

SPAD S.VII (Russian production): 100 constructed by Duks Company. Moscow; specification identical with French aircraft, powered by imported engines

SPAD S.VII (British production): 100 built by British-based Blériot and SPAD company, serialled A8794 to A8893. 120 built by Mann, Egerton Company, serialled A9100 to A9161, B1351 to B1388 and B9911 to B9930; British-built SPADs mostly powered by British development of Hispano-Suiza, Wolseley W.4A Python engine. Python 1 of 150 hp (112 kW) succeeded by Python II of 180 hp (134 kW)

Total production was at least 3,500

42

This was the personal mount of the Commanding Officer of the XXIII Gruppo of the Italian Regia Aeronautica, stationed at Lonade Pozzolo in 1924. The pennant-type insignia enhanced the appearance of Italy's fighters and bombers after the creation of the independent air arm by the Mussolini regime in 1923. The shield included the insignia of the 74ª, 75ª, 76ª and 91ª *squadriglie* which made up the *gruppo*.

SPAD 7 cutaway drawing key

1 Steel wire trailing edge
2 Rudder construction
3 Rudder post
4 Sternpost
5 Rudder hinge control
6 Starboard elevator
7 Elevator construction
8 Elevator hinge control
9 Tailplane construction
10 Fin construction
11 Tailskid
12 Steel shoe
13 Elastic cord shock absorber
14 Port elevator
15 Port tailplane
16 Fin attachment
17 Fuselage fabric covering
18 Dorsal construction
19 Dorsal stringers
20 Top longeron
21 Tailplane control cables
22 Vertical spacers
23 Bottom longeron
24 Fuselage stringers
25 Diagonal wire bracing
26 Headrest fairing
27 Plywood decking
28 Headrest
29 Padded cockpit coaming
30 Fuel filler cap
31 Used cartridge belt storage drum

32 Exhaust pipe tail fairing
33 Control cable pulleys
34 Pilot's seat
35 Safety harness
36 Underfloor fuel tank
37 Starboard upper wing panel construction
38 Upper wing spars
39 Compression rib
40 Internal wire bracing
41 Aileron horn control
42 Starboard aileron
43 Leading edge carry-round
44 Leading edge stiffeners
45 Interplane strut
46 Aileron control rod
47 Aileron rod crank
48 Lower wing spars
49 Compression rib
50 Internal wire bracing
51 Leading edge rib construction

52 Flying wire bracing
53 Flying wire support strut
54 Spar root fixing
55 Fuselage wing root rib
56 Cockpit floor panel
57 Rudder pedal bar
58 Fuselage keel member
59 Control column
60 Instrument panel
61 Gun cocking lever
62 Engine throttle
63 Centre section strut
64 Windscreen
65 Padded trailing edge section
66 Service fuel tank
67 Steel wire trailing edge
68 Port aileron
69 Aileron horn
70 Port upper wing panel construction
71 Spar section joint
72 Interplane strut
73 Flying wires
74 Flying wire bracing strut
75 Lower wing panel fabric covering
76 Radiator header tank
77 Ammunition drum
78 Ammunition belt feed chute
79 Engine compartment bulkhead
80 0.303-in (7.7-mm) Vickers machine gun
81 Engine blister fairing
82 Radiator filler cap
83 Engine access panel
84 205 hp Hispano-Suiza 8Ab Vee-engine
85 Exhaust pipe
86 Engine bearer construction
87 Ventilation air intake panel
88 Nose cowlings
89 Radiator cowling ring
90 Water radiator
91 Radiator shutters
92 Propeller fixing bolts
93 Propeller hub
94 Two-bladed wooden propeller
95 Port mainwheel
96 Laminated wooden main undercarriage legs
97 Undercarriage leg top fixing
98 Undercarriage bracing wires
99 Fixed axle beam
100 Swing axle fixing
101 Elastic cord shock absorber
102 Wheel hub fixing
103 Fabric wheel disc fairing
104 Tyre inflation valve
105 Starboard mainwheel

29

A French-built S.VII bought by the British government and flown by the Royal Flying Corps during 1917 with the serial B1524. It belonged to No. 23 Sqn RFC flying from La Lovie aerodrome, France, summer 1917. Apart from the forward fuselage panelling, the entire finish was in natural doped fabric.

aircraft 185 were supplied to the Royal Flying Corps, 214 to the Aeronautica Militare Italiana, 43 to Russia, 15 to Belgian units and 189, mostly for training, to the US Air Service operating with the American Expeditionary Force in France.

In addition, at least 100 S.VIIs were licence-built by the Duks company in Moscow, and 220 in the UK. British-produced SPADs suffered many vicissitudes. Mann, Egerton & Co. of Norwich eventually built 120 examples, most of which revealed structural weakness and often varied considerably from specification. After several fatal crashes, acceptance was refused by the RFC until August 1917, by which time considerable strengthening had been undertaken. The British 'Bleriot and SPAD' company, based at Brooklands in Surrey, constructed the remaining 100 British SPAD S.VIIs.

SPAD S.VIIs began to reach Italy in March 1917, going first to the 77a Squadriglia and then to the 91a Squadriglia, whose commanding officer from May 1917 was Maggiore Francesco Baracca. In October 1917, when the Italian army and nation were reeling under the crisis created by the disastrous defeat at Caporetto, public morale was raised by news that 91a Squadriglia pilots had shot down 14 Austro-Hungarian aircraft within a few days. Baracca himself had destroyed two aircraft in a single skirmish on 21 October

1917. The Italian ace's affection for the S.VII was such that he retained his aircraft for some months in preference to the later S.XIII. He had 34 confirmed victories when he was shot down and killed on 19 June 1918, a high proportion of them achieved with the S.VII.

Although the S.VII was tested by the Royal Naval Air Service, an agreement was made whereby all Sopwith Tri-plane fighters went to the RNAS and all S.VIIs to the RFC, where they equipped Nos 19 and 23 Squadrons in France. Operational use was restricted to French-built aircraft, RFC pilots having a justified mistrust of British-built machines. The S.VII also flew in the Middle East with Nos 30, 63 and 72 Squadrons, RFC.

Several Russian SPADs survived the revolution to fly with the Red air arm during the Russian Civil War. Others operated with Polish units in the immediate post-revolution period. The American Expeditionary Force in France received its first S.VIIs in the summer of 1917, but they served mainly to train pilots for the S.XIII, supplied in large numbers to the USAS.

Post-war the S.VII remained in French service as an advanced trainer for nearly a decade. In 1924 eight Italian fighter *squadriglie* still had the S.VII on strength. Other countries to utilize the type included Greece, Portugal and Romania, together with the newly independent states of Czechoslovakia, Finland, Poland and Yugoslavia, as well as several countries in Latin America and the Far East.

Today the SPAD S.VII is remembered with affection and gratitude in its native country, where the *Vieux Charles* of Guynemer is preserved to remind pupil pilots at the Academy of the Armée de l'Air at Salon-de-Provence of the great traditions they have to uphold. Of the handful of remaining SPAD S.VIIs in Europe and North America, the most renowned is the aircraft flown by Baracca, now exhibited at Lugo di Romagna in a Museum dedicated to Italy's foremost World War 1 ace.

In the history of French flight, the SPAD fighter was inextricably linked to the famous Cigognes of the Aviation Militaire. Initially only one flight of aircraft (SPA.3) bore the coveted stork symbol, but as the number of S.VIIs gradually increased, the Cigognes were extended to the five flights of the Groupe de Chasse 12, commanded by Captain Armand Brocard. The French public soon took to these heroes of the air, pilots such as René Dorme of SPA.3 (23 Siège), Armand Pinsard (27 Siège) of SPA.26, and Bernard de Romanet of SPA.167 (18 kills), René Fonck (a record 75 kills), and the great Guynemer, who finally fell on 11 September 1917 after 54 victories, many of them in the S.VII. Their fame was due in no small measure to that small but remarkable fighter, the SPAD S.VII.

A number of S.VIIs have been beautifully restored and preserved by American private owners. Notable on this example is the star decoration on the landing gear wheels.

Sopwith Camel

Joining the Royal Flying Corps just too late to avert the 'Bloody April' slaughter of Allied aircraft in 1917 over the Western Front, the Sopwith Camel was a tricky aeroplane to fly but, once mastered, was the most successful and popular of the fighting scouts of what was popularly known as the 'Kaiser's War'.

Not a particularly easy aircraft to fly, the little Sopwith Pup wrought a considerable amount of damage on German fighters over the Western Front during the second half of 1916, even after the appearance on the scene of the Albatros D.I, with its twin machine guns. But it was soon apparent that the Albatros D.I and other German aircraft types were merely precursors of an aircraft technology that was rapidly gathering momentum. The chief designer for Sopwith, Herbert Smith, realised this at an early stage. In the late summer of 1916 he was busy designing a successor to the Pup. The first prototype, known as Sopwith F.1, was cleared to fly by the company on 22 December of the same year.

Although an obvious descendant of the Pup, the F.1 was a compact and purposeful-looking little aircraft with a deeper fuselage, accentuated by a humped fairing forward of the cockpit which covered the breeches of a pair of synchronized Vickers guns. Structurally the new aeroplane was conventional, the fuselage being a wire-braced wooden box girder with rounded top decking; immediately aft of the engine the structure was aluminium covered, then plywood covered as far as the rear of the cockpit, and fabric covered on the rear fuselage. Smith originally intended that both upper and lower wings should have equal dihedral, but Fred Sigrist, the chief engineer, favoured a flat upper wing to facilitate production by permitting construction as a single continuous unit. In compensation the dihedral of the lower

wing was arbitrarily doubled. Even when it was later decided to produce the top wing in three parts to assist maintenance and repair in the field, the top wing dihedral was not restored, and the Camel's 'tapered gap' remained one of its best-known characteristics.

The most important design feature was the concentration of propeller, engine, fuel tank, armament and pilot's cockpit within the front 7 ft (2.1 m) of the front fuselage; such a concentration of mass contributed to the extraordinary manoeuvrability of the new fighter, but also led to its tricky turning habits. On account of the considerable torque and its small inertia about the centre of gravity and marked gyroscopic movement, the Camel could be turned very tightly, but in a turn to the left the nose rose sharply, and to the right it dropped – demanding coarse use of rudder – without which the aircraft would rapidly spin without warning.

Company records suggest that three (or possibly four) F.1 prototypes were built at private expense (the F.1, F.1/1, F.1/2 and F.1/3, although the F.1/2 has never been authoritatively identified). The F.1/1 'Taper Wing Camel' featured tapered wings and single broad-chord interplane struts on each side; the F.1 was powered by a 110-hp (82-kW) Clerget 9Z rotary, and the F.1/3 by a 130-hp (97-kW) Clerget 9B; it has been suggested that the F.1/2 was identifiable by a cut-out panel in the top wing to increase pilot view.

First flown by Harry Hawker, probably at Brooklands early

Sopwith Camel

Specification

Sopwith F.1 Camel (Clerget)
Type: single-seat fighting scout
Powerplant: one 130-hp (97-kW) Clerget 9-cylinder air-cooled rotary piston engine
Performance: maximum speed 117 mph (188 km/h) at sea level;
climb to 10,000 ft (3050 m) in 10 minutes 35 seconds; service ceiling 19,000 ft
(5790 m); endurance 2 hours 30 minutes
Weights: empty 929 lb (421 kg); maximum take-off 1,453 lb
(659 kg)
Dimensions: span 28 ft 0 in (8.53 m); length 18 ft 9 in (5.72 m);
height 8 ft 6 in (2.60 m); wing area 231.0 sq ft (21.46 m²)
Armament: two 0.303-in (7.7-mm) Vickers machine-guns on nose and synchronized
to fire through the propeller, plus four 25-lb (11.35-kg) bombs carried on external racks
below the fuselage

A Sopwith-built 2F.1 Camel flown by the high-scoring Canadian pilot William Alexander with 'A' Flight, No. 10 (Naval) Sqn, RNAS, at Treizennes, a squadron that was to become No. 210 Sqn, RAF, on amalgamation of the RFC and RNAS on 1 April 1918.

An anonymous Gnome Monosoupape-powered F.1 Camel without nose Vickers guns fitted; this may indeed be the Boulton & Paul-built aircraft, B9278, which was later equipped with two downward-firing Lewis guns (not fitted here) and which became the Sopwith TF.1 trenchfighter.

in January 1917, the F.1 was quickly followed by the above prototypes plus two aircraft (N517 and N518) ordered by the Admiralty. The F.1/3 was tested at Martlesham Heath in March, and this was adopted as standard for production, although it returned in May with a 110-hp (82-kW) Le Rhône 9J and in July with a 130-hp (97-kW) Clerget.

Meanwhile the second Admiralty prototype was flown at Martlesham with the new AR.1 (Admiralty Rotary) of 150 hp (112 kW); designed by Lieutenant W. O. Bentley (later of motor car fame), this engine was the first production aero engine to employ aluminium as an air-cooled cylinder material and soon entered production as the BR.1, and was ready for the first production Camels for the Admiralty which started delivery from Sopwith on 7 May. They joined No. 4 Naval Squadron (commanded by Squadron Commander B. L. Huskisson) and were in action for the first time on 4 July when five attacked 16 Gothas north of Ostend, destroying at least one of the large German 'heavy' bombers. By the end of the month Nos 3, 4, 6, 8 and 9 Naval Squadrons had received Sopwith Camels.

The Camel was the private-venture stablemate to the S.E.5. It served with great distinction on the Western Front. Originally bought by the RNAS, it is seen here in service with a naval squadron which became No. 208 Sqn when the RAF was formed.

The first War Office contracts for Camels were given to Ruston Proctor & Co. at Lincoln for 250 aircraft on 22 May 1917 and to Portholme Aerodrome Ltd at Huntingdon for 50 aircraft on 2 June. The former contract specified the 130-hp (97-kW) Le Rhône 9J. A contract placed with Sopwith on 7 June specified the Clerget 9B as an alternative. Contract prices included £874 for the unequipped Camel airframe, and engine prices ranged from £907 for a 130-hp (97-kW) Clerget down to £643 for the 150-hp (112-kW) BR.1.

A Camel painted in the colours of Eskadra Kosciuszkowska, one of 20 such ex-RAF aircraft supplied to Poland which flew from Lwòw against the Russians in 1920; this aircraft is privately owned by an American, Ken Murray.

A Camel flown by the Belgian ace Jan Oleislagers (six victories) with Escadrille, Groupe de Chasse Belge, towards the end of the war; it was always said that this famous pilot destroyed many more German aircraft than his official tally shows, but he never formally claimed an aircraft shot down over German-held territory.

Fighting scout supreme

Between 4 July 1917 and 11 November 1918 the Sopwith Camel destroyed 1,294 enemy aircraft, more victories than achieved by any other type of aircraft in the war. Only the Fokker Dr.I triplane could match its manoeuvrability.

The first RFC unit to receive the F.1 was No. 70 Squadron at Boisdinghem in July 1917, in time to take part in the Battle of Ypres which opened on 31 July. It was followed quickly in France by No. 45 (also in July), and No. 43 with Clerget Camels; in October No. 28 Squadron took Camels from the UK to France. At the end of August three pilots of No. 44 Squadron, Major (later Group Captain) G. W. Murlis Green, Captain (later Air Vice-Marshal Sir Quentin) C. J. Q. Brand and Lieutenant C. C. Banks flew Camels at night against raiding Gothas proving that, though tricky, the little fighter could be flown in darkness.

In the great Battle of Cambrai in March 1918 the Camel squadrons played a conspicuous part, many being equipped with a rack for four 20-lb (9-kg) Cooper bombs. Nos 3 and 46 Squadrons were particularly prominent in their ground-attack work, such famous names as Bourlon Wood, Flesquières and Lateau featuring among their targets. In air combat individual Camel pilots were already becoming well-known. During the Cambrai battle Captain J. L. Trollope of No. 43 Squadron shot down six enemy aircraft in one day, 24 March, an RFC record. On 12 April, when the new Royal Air Force was but 12 days old, Captain H. W. Woollett, also of No. 43 Squadron, equalled the achievement.

On 21 April a Canadian pilot, Captain A. R. Brown of No. 209 Squadron (previously No. 9 Naval Squadron), flying a Bentley Camel, was credited with shooting down Rittmeister Manfred, Freiherr von Richthofen, the victor of 80 air combats and scourge of the Western Front. Indeed many of the RFC's and RAF's most illustrious pilots flew Camels, includ-

ing Lieutenant Colonel R. Collishaw, DSO, DSC, DFC (with 60 victories), Major D. R. MacLaren, DSO, MC, DFC (54 victories) and Major W. G. Barker VC, DSO, MC (53 victories).

The Camel itself had undergone some development. A total of 1,325 aircraft was completed during 1917 powered by Clerget, Le Rhône and Bentley rotaries (although the last were in a minority). However, with America now in the war not even the 3,450 Camels ordered by the end of that year appeared likely to meet the demand, and new contracts were placed with Boulton & Paul Ltd, British Caudron Co. Ltd, Clayton & Shuttleworth Ltd, Hooper & Co. Ltd, March, Jones & Cribb Ltd, Nieuport & General Aircraft Co. Ltd, Wm

Flown by Lieutenant J. A. Myers of the US Air Service, this F.1 Camel was one of a large batch built by March, Jones & Cribb Ltd, Leeds, and which flew with the 17th Aero Squadron on the Western Front in 1918. Its 'donor' – Thomas Carlyle – has his name at the rear.

A Boulton & Paul-built Camel, whose serial D8239 was incorrectly applied in the field and which served in Italy in January 1919; flown by Captain C. M. McEwen, the aircraft sported distinctive chequerboard markings that became increasingly popular after the end of hostilities.

Beardmore & Co. Ltd, Fairey Aviation Co. Ltd, and Pegler & Co. Ltd.

Numerous different rotary engines were flown in Camels, among them the 150-hp (112-kW) Gnome Monosoupape which featured an adjustable ignition switch which enabled the pilot to run the engine on one, three, five, seven or nine cylinders; a witness recalls seeing the Camel being flown near the ground on one cylinder only, when, accompanied by a blast of flame, the pilot cut in all nine cylinders. The name Camel, incidentally, was never used officially (the name being quite unofficially, but universally, adopted by

As part of a series of experiments to provide British airships with their own fighter defence, two F.1 Camels (N6622 and N6814) were modified for trials by No. 212 Sqn, RAF, with the airship R.23; N6814 is seen here, probably at Pulham, Norfolk. The first live release was made by Lieutenant R. E. Keys DFC.

Sopwith F.1 Camel cutaway drawing key

1 Two-blade wooden propeller
2 Propeller attachment plate
3 Attaching bolts
4 Engine cowling
5 130 hp Clerget nine-cylinder rotary engine
6 Engine mounting bulkhead
7 Engine bearing member
8 Gravity oil tank
9 Oil tank mounting
10 Fuselage cross member
11 Fuselage frame
12 Twin synchronized 0.303-in (7.7-mm) Vickers machine-guns
13 Ammunition tank
14 Ammunition feed chute
15 Cartridge ejector chute
16 Gun cocking lever
17 Gunsight
18 Hinged windscreen
19 Carburettor intake
20 Centre section front strut
21 Centre section bracing wires
22 Centre section rear strut
23 Wind driven fuel pressurizing pump
24 Hand operated fuel pressurizing pump
25 Front spar
26 Leading edge stiffeners
27 Spar connecting strut
28 Rear spar
29 Inner/outer wing spar joint
30 Wing ribs
31 Port aileron
32 Aileron operating horn
33 Diagonal cross bracing
34 Interplane strut
35 Strut bracing wires
36 Interplane bracing wires
37 Padded cockpit coaming
38 Pilot's basket-work seat
39 Seat mounting frame
40 Main fuel tank
41 Secondary fuel tank
42 Fuel filler cap
43 Control cables beneath seat
44 Fuselage top longeron
45 Fuselage bottom longeror
46 Vertical spacers
47 Cross members (frames)
48 Diagonal wire bracing
49 Dorsal frame
50 Dorsal stringers
51 Rudder cables
52 Elevator up cable
53 Elevator down cable
54 Port tailplane structure
55 Tailplane stay (upper)
56 Port elevator
57 Elevator operating horn
58 Elevator hinge
59 Fixed fin structure
60 Rudder
61 Rudder hinge
62 Rudder operating horn
63 Starboard elevator
64 Starboard tailplane structure
65 Tailskid
66 Tailskid pivot mounting
67 Elastic cord shock absorber
68 Starboard aileron (top)

the flying services), F.1 being the formal designation. This also covered a night-fighter version, introduced with Home Defence units, which featured a pair of Lewis guns on a double Foster mounting above the top-wing centre section, and the cockpit moved about 12 in (30 cm) aft to allow the pilot to operate the guns; navigation lights and flare brackets were also included.

Camels at sea

Two versions did, however, merit a change of designation, the TF.1 and the 2F.1. The former, a trench fighter with two down-firing Lewis guns and a third on the upper wing centre section did not enter production but paved the way for the Sopwith Salamander. The latter, the 2F.1 shipboard fighter, had slightly reduced wing span, jettisonable steel-tube landing gear and detachable rear fuselage (for ease of shipboard stowage). 2F.1s were flown from the aircraft carriers HMS *Furious* and *Pegasus*, as well as being catapulted from

platforms erected on the gun turrets and forecastles of many other warships. These Camels accompanied sweeps by the Harwich Force in the Heligoland Bight in 1918 and shot down a number of German seaplanes. Perhaps the most spectacular use of Camels at sea involved those that took off from towed lighters, a procedure pioneered by that extraordinary pilot Commander C. R. Samson; however, it was Lieutenant Stuart Culley who, flying from a lighter towed by the destroyer HMS *Redoubt*, shot down the last German airship, *L.53* (Kapitänleutnant Prölss), to fall during the war on 11 August near Terschelling. Other 2F.1 Camels were employed in trials to provide defence for the UK's own airships, the aircraft being suspended below the airship *R.23* flying from Pulham; Lieutenant R. E. Keys DFC of No. 212

69 Aileron interplane cable
70 Starboard aileron (bottom)
71 Aileron operating cable
72 Aft interplane strut
73 Forward interplane strut
74 Strut bracing wires
75 Rear spar
76 Spar connecting strut
77 Front spar
78 Wing ribs
79 Diagonal wire bracing
80 Leading edge stiffeners
81 Rear spar/fuselage attachment
82 Front spar/fuselage fitting
83 Undercarriage leg mounting
84 Undercarriage leg
85 Undercarriage bracing wires
86 Axle fairing
87 Starboard mainwheel
88 Pivoted half-axle
89 Elastic cord shock absorber
90 Port mainwheel
91 Tyre inflation valve

Sopwith Camel variants

F.1: prototypes; **F.1** with Clerget 9Z; **F.1/1** with tapered wings; **F.1/2** not positively identified; **F.1/3** with Clerget 9B, Le Rhône 9J and 130-hp (97-kW) Clerget
F.1: Admiralty prototypes (N517 and N518); AR.1 rotaries
F.1: production; 110- and 130-hp (82- and 97-kW) Clerget, 110-hp (82-kW) Le Rhône, 150-hp (112-kW) BR.1 and 100-hp (75-kW) Gnome Monosoupape rotaries; widely sub-contracted; a number also converted to two-seat trainers
TF.1: experimental trench fighter; one only (C57) built by Nieuport & General with three Lewis guns
2F.1: production shipboard fighter; majority with BR.1 rotaries; most with one Lewis and one Vickers gun, and some carried two 50-lb (22.7-kg) bombs; two (N6622 and N6814) used for airship trials with *R.23*

This Camel, N6616, was flown by Captain Claude Emery, who was seconded to the Estonian Aviation Company in 1919. The aircraft was obtained from HMS *Vindictive*, and served alongside other British aircraft such as the Avro 504K, D.H.9 and Short 184, which had been supplied by the British government.

Squadron made the first live release, but the rapid end to the war eclipsed his achievement and the trials were eventually ended in 1925.

In all, 48 squadrons of the RFC and RNAS (and RAF) flew Camels and, apart from those that served in the UK and France, Camels took part in the campaigns in Italy, the Aegean, Macedonia, Greece, Russia and Mesopotamia. At the time of the Armistice the RAF had on charge a total of 2,519 F.1s and 129 2F.1s, including 802 with the Expeditionary Force in France and 112 2F.1s with units of the Grand Fleet. Total Camel production was 5,490, comprising 1,325 produced in 1917 and 4,165 in 1918.

Flown by the famous Canadian pilot, 'Billy' Barker, originally with No. 28 Squadron, RAF, in France, who, took his Camel with him when posted to command No. 66 Squadron in Italy, and kept it with him when given command of a Bristol Fighter Squadron, No. 139. In all, while flying his faithful B6313, Barker destroyed 48 enemy aircraft before his epic fight in which he destroyed four German aircraft while flying a Snipe, and for which he was awarded the Victoria Cross. It is now generally believed that no other single aeroplane has ever matched the achievement of B6313.

Camels also served with several foreign air forces. About 36 were supplied to Belgium in 1918, remaining in service until 1922, and one of these has been preserved to this day. Six were delivered to Greece and were flown by pilots of the Royal Hellenic naval air service.

In June 1918 143 Clerget Camels were purchased for use by the American Expeditionary Force in France, and these served with the 17th, 27th, 37th and 41st Aero Squadrons. As a result of their unforgiving handling characteristics they were never very popular with the Americans and few were ever flown in combat; instead they were used as trainers to acclimatize pilots arriving at the front. A well-known American pilot declared 'I don't want to fly Camels and certainly not Clerget Camels ... those little popping firecrackers'.

At the end of the war most of the American Camels were left in France or the UK; six which had flown with the US Navy in France were shipped to the United States where they underwent shipboard trials, being flown from platforms erected on the warships USS *Texas* and *Arkansas*. A small number of Camels also went to Canada after the war,

and about 20 were supplied to Poland whose Eskadra Kosciuszkowska flew them from Lwòw against the Russians in 1920.

In 1918 Camels accompanied the Slavo-British Aviation Group to Russia, flying from Archangelsk, with 'B' Flight, No. 47 Squadron, RAF, at Beketovka in 1919 and No. 221 Squadron at Petrovsk until 1920. In 1919 a Sopwith 2F.1 Camel was operating from HMS *Vindictive* against the Bolsheviks in the Baltic.

For all its magnificent exploits the Camel would have completely disappeared from combat service with the RAF had the war continued to rage for three or four months longer – replaced by the Sopwith Snipe, an excellent fighter without the vicissitudes of what Captain Norman Macmillan described as 'a fierce little beast'.

A preserved Camel, displaying spurious markings. This view nevertheless emphasizes the compact concentration of engine, guns and cockpit in a very short length of fuselage nose, as well as the cut-out in the top wing to improve the pilot's field of vision.

British pilots scored more successes with the Sopwith Camel than with any other type of aircraft during World War 1. This Camel is an accurate replica. (*Photo: Air Portraits*)

Royal Aircraft Factory S.E.5

'It's a bloody awful machine!' With these words to General Trenchard, rising 'ace' Albert Ball, finally victor in 44 combats and prejudiced in favour of the rotary-engined Nieuports, dismissed the Royal Aircraft Factory's new S.E.5 fighter.

Left: The first prototype of the S.E.5 (A4561), which flew for the first time towards the end of 1916. It had no weapons and was powered by a 150 hp (111.9 kW) Hispano-Suiza engine with no reduction gears.

The S.E.5 was designed around the Hispano Suiza engine in 1915, with the aircraft itself being designed by H. P. Folland and J. Kenworthy. The unarmed prototype with its direct-drive propeller appeared in November of the following year, although the choice of a gearless engine obviously meant that the original plan to have a Lewis machine gun installed between the rows of cylinders would have to be abandoned.

Only seven days later a second prototype appeared. In all essentials this was identical to its predecessor, but an early test flight resulted in damage that was not put right until the end of the month. During repairs the opportunity had been taken to fit a new landing gear and the armament which was later to become standard, namely an offset Vickers gun on the fuselage and a Lewis gun on a Foster mounting above the upper wing centre-section alongside an external gravity tank.

The middle of the following month saw the maiden flight of a third prototype, which was very similar to the first except for details of the tanks and a somewhat different radiator occasioned by the geared 200-hp (149.1-kW) Hispano-Suiza. It also carried the centre-section and port upper wing of the first machine, and when these were replaced an enlarged cut-out was incorporated, as were a centre-section gravity tank, armament, and a windscreen with such large side panels that it in effect formed a hood

which severely obstructed the pilot's forward vision. Meanwhile the second prototype was lost when it broke up in the air, killing its pilot, so that ply webs were subsequently added to the compression struts and standardized strut fittings were introduced. The only other major modification took the form of less acutely raked wing tips to cure the claim by some pilots that the S.E.5 was 'almost uncontrollable' below 70 mph (112.7 km/h) if conditions were gusty.

First production S.E.5s equipped No. 56 Squadron, RFC, but to the dismay of the pilots these were fitted with even larger 'greenhouses' than before, so that their removal was ordered before the unit, which accounted for most of the machines built, was declared operational for service in France. Meanwhile a handful each went to Nos 24, 60 and 85 Squadrons.

Delayed in taking the new machines into action by the windscreen modifications, No. 56 carried out its first offensive patrol only late in April 1917, and Ball, together with other pilots, soon came to appreciate the strength and firepower of the type. However, a forgotten exponent of the S.E.5 with No. 56 Squadron was Lieutenant L. M. Barlow of B Flight, who finally brought down 18 of the enemy and won for himself three Military Crosses while flying these aircraft.

Typical of Barlow's actions was the special mission on the afternoon of 7 June when he shot up the sheds at Bisseghem which he identified by the adjacent mineral water factory. A few moments later a train was attacked twice from a height of only 20 ft (6.1 m), while another was left in a blanket of smoke and steam. The next targets were the troops in Wevelghem streets, as well as the railway station where a train was stopped. From an altitude of only 50 ft (15.2 m) Barlow then strafed Reckem aerodrome off the Menin road, a troublesome ground gunner being silenced, though not before he had succeeded in shooting away the port elevator of the S.E.5 while Barlow was flying below the level of the nearby roofs to make sure of his aim.

Meanwhile production of the fighter had got into its stride and models were no longer being delivered with the modified wing tips, although it is recorded that at least the first delivery of this fresh batch retained the large windscreen and boasted the external gravity tank of the prototypes. The total of all 150-hp (111.9-kW) S.E.5s built was probably fewer than 59, and it was soon replaced by the S.E.5a when there were available sufficient 200-hp (149.1-kW) Hispano-Suizas such as powered the third prototype S.E.5.

As might be expected, it was one of the prototype S.E.5s that later became the first version of what was to become known as the S.E.5a, a fact that was proven even by its external appearance. The historic machine in question was the third S.E.5 (A4563), but in a modified form as it appeared

A direct development of the third S.E.5 prototype (A4563) was the S.E.5a *(left and below),* which itself had been considerably modified by the time it first appeared in May 1917.

Royal Aircraft Factory S.E.5a

Specification
S.E.5a (Royal Aircraft Factory)

Type: single-seat fighting scout

Powerplant: one Hispano-derived V-8 water-cooled engine, usually a 200-hp (149-kW) Wolseley Viper

Performance: (Viper) maximum speed 138 mph (222 km/h) at sea level, falling to 123 mph (198 km/h) at 15,000 ft (4572 m); time to climb to 5,000 ft (1524 m) 4.9 minutes; endurance 2.5 hours

Weights: empty about 1,430 lb (649 kg); maximum loaded 1,940 lb (880 kg)

Dimensions: span 26 ft 7.5 in (8.12 m); length 20 ft 11 in (6.38 m); height 9 ft 6 in (2.90 m); wing area 244 sq ft (22.67 m²)

Armament: usually one 0.303-in (7.7-mm) Vickers machine-gun fixed in top of fuselage to left of centre, firing through propeller disc, with 400-round belt; plus one 0.303-in (7.7-mm) Lewis machine-gun on Foster mount, with four 97-round drum magazines; provision for four 25-lb (11.3-kg) Cooper bombs carried under fuselage

An RAF squadron that was to see outstanding success with the S.E.5a during World War 1 was No. 74. Receiving its first aircraft in March 1918, the squadron quickly moved to France where, on its first dogfight, five enemy aircraft were downed for no losses to the squadron. The majority of operations were of an offensive nature, often with

25-lb (11-kg) bombs for low-level attacks on retreating German forces, though by Armistice Day the squadron had a total of 140 aerial combat 'kills'. One of the unit's most deadly pilots was Major E. 'Mick' Mannock VC, who, despite having sight in only one eye, scored over 70 kills before his death. This is one of the aircraft he flew in achieving that figure.

Plans for mass production of the S.E.5a by the Curtiss company in America did not come to fruition, other than the assembly of 56 British-built airframes. In 1922–3 50 of these were rebuilt by the Eberhart Steel Company as advanced trainers.

This Royal Aircraft Factory S.E.5a replica was used, as were all modern rebuilds or copies, for sky writing before World War 2.

E5808 was one of a large batch of S.E.5as made by the Austin Motor Company at Birmingham, close to the Wolseley engine factory. It was assigned around the time of the Armistice to No. 56 Squadron, RAF, the original S.E.5 user in March 1917 (with large wrap-round windscreens). Note the long Aldis optical sight, an alternative to the ring-and-bead system.

at Martlesham Heath testing establishment in May 1917, its alterations including a head fairing behind the cockpit, gravity fuel and water tanks in the centre section, short-span wings and L-shaped exhausts. But more importantly, a 200-hp (149.1-kW) Hispano-Suiza engine had been retained, driving a four-blade propeller so that superior performance was assured.

Contracts for the new machine, designated S.E.5a, were placed as early as February 1917 with Martinsyde and Vickers, only a small number being manufactured by the Royal Aircraft Establishment itself, the resultant models differing little from the final form of the prototype. Some of these first variants were fitted with Wolseley-built engines despite the troubles associated with engines of the type from this source, and some of the first batch of new scouts again went to No. 56 Squadron, these even retaining the L-shaped exhausts of the prototype, although these were later replaced by a long horizontal type; any of this pattern which went to No. 56, however, were promptly cut down to mere extensions of the manifold.

As the year progressed, not only did the production tempo increase, but so too did the orders placed with other builders until the total expected was 3,600 by the end of the year, although only about 900 had been delivered at this time, a number which included S.E.5s which were still being manufactured.

Production problems

December found the S.E.5a in service with only five front-line squadrons, with a further one expecting re-equipment in the coming year. The reason for such a poor state of affairs lay in the fact that production of airframes had outstripped that of engines. In part this was due to the defective nature of the Wolseley products already mentioned, but added to this was the fact that those of French manufacture had in some instances shafts and gears manufactured poorly by the Brasier company, and although these were in some cases replaced by similar components of British make, demand eventually exceeded supply to the extent that faulty parts had knowingly to be passed and used. It was not until this

had been going on for some time that relief came in the form of a supply of engines which had been ordered on the advice of the Admiralty from other French companies.

A further precautionary measure was an order placed with the Wolseley company for Hispano engines of the earlier 150-hp (111.9-kW) type, but insufficient clarity of instruction resulted in the organization developing a 220-hp (164-kW) high-compression motor, and although this was eventually to prove a blessing in disguise (since this Viper power unit was to be specified for all 1918 contracts), the immediate result was a mere trickle of engines where a flood had been expected.

In combat the S.E.5a soon proved a formidable fighting machine, and its name was quickly to become associated with the foremost British pilots of the day, as well as those of

44

At least 20 ex-RAF S.E.5as were shipped to Poland as that newly-formed country's first fighters. Soon after their arrival, in 1920, they became hotly engaged in the war with the Russian Bolsheviks, mainly on the Ukrainian front. Photographs are known of a captured machine in Red Star markings.

the single Australian unit (No. 2 Squadron, AFC) and two from the United States (the 25th and 148th Aero Squadrons) which flew the type, not only on the Western Front, but in Macedonia (Nos 17, 47 and 150 Squadrons), Mesopotamia (No. 72 Squadron), Palestine (Nos 111 and 145 Squadrons), plus the units using the type on Home Defence (Nos 37, 50, 61 and 143 Squadrons of the RFC and RAF). These were the 'aces' of the war years, the top-scorers who seemed to live charmed lives, and they included not only Albert Ball who had become reconciled to the design he had been at first swift to condemn, but also those with comparatively modest claims of kills, such as Longton (12), Clayson (21), Shields (24) and Maxwell (27). However, at the opposite end of the list of famous S.E.5a pilots are the names of Mannock (with a total of 73 victims) and McCudden, who not only raised his

One of the first photographs ever taken of an S.E.5, this shows the prototype in its original form. Later it was fitted with a large windscreen, different exhausts for the Hispano-Suiza engine and other modifications. Sadly it was not given new wings, which broke in January 1917, killing Major Frank Goodden, who is seen in the cockpit.

total to 57 while flying the type but was also one of those who flew specially-modified machines, his B4891 having narrow-chord elevators when he took it over on 3 December 1917; factory workers responsible for this machine later recalled that they already knew to whom it was going, although the modification was by no means unique, B4890 also being on record as being thus modified.

Indeed, the S.E.5a was the subject of continuous change and refinement so that towards the end of 1917 a stronger landing gear became standard with substantially tapered forward legs, while other modifications included additional braces to the leading edge of the fin, which was itself revised; strengthened trailing edges; and improved oil tankage.

This was not all, for trials were conducted with a view to improving the armament: thus twin Lewis guns were experimentally fitted over the centre-section to augment the fixed Vickers gun below, and another triple-gun arrangement for Home Defence application included three Lewis guns on an Eeman fuselage mounting that carried the armament arranged to fire forwards and upwards at an angle of 45° through slots in the centre-section. Neither of these installations was adopted officially.

Modifications of a more academic nature were the fitting

The assembly lines at Wolseley Motors, where the radiators and other components were produced, and other parts were checked.

Royal Aircraft Factory S.E.5

Hundreds of S.E.5as were given to the fledgeling air forces in countries of the British Empire after the Armistice. One batch went to what was then the Union of South Africa, and No. 320 is pictured at the headquarters at Pretoria in early 1920. Finish was silver, and markings blue/white/orange.

of newly designed fins and rudders, underslung radiators and even a variable-pitch propeller, while there also existed the modifications necessary to produce two-seat S.E.5a aircraft, and although these did yeoman service for instructional purposes, the resultant flying qualities left much to be desired; meanwhile another series of test programmes was conducted to explore the question of stowage of both the Calthrop Guardian Angel and Mears parachutes.

Before the comparatively sudden termination of World War 1, plans were made for construction of the S.E.5a by the Curtiss company for use by the US Air Service. One thousand were ordered, and although 56 were assembled from British parts, only one (SC43153) was completed with a Wright-Martin (Hispano-Suiza derived) engine of 180 hp (134.2 kW), the designation of this variant being S.E.5E. More radical had been the changes in June 1917 resulting in the S.E.5b at Farnborough: this type emerged with unequal-span wings and a considerably cleaner nose with an underslung radiator, and although there were no plans to develop an operational version it is of interest to note that such was the improvement in performance that the single example

The S.E.5a registered as F904 is the only original machine still flying today (here with a Wolseley Viper engine).

survived the war by at least two years, being finally flown with standard wing panels. Total production of the S.E.5 and S.E.5a was 5,205.

With the end of the war, the S.E.5a vanished from military use fairly rapidly, although small numbers lingered on in Australia, Canada and South Africa, but as unwanted fighters became available to the civil market, they were quickly bought and pressed into use in some unexpected roles: included among these were experiments in fire prevention, while one went to Japan with the British Aviation Mission of 1921 and exerted some considerable influence on future single-seat design in that country.

Civil conversions

A number of S.E.5a aircraft came onto the civil register from May 1920, the first being G-EATE. Not all of the privately-owned machines were fitted with the original engines, G-EAZT for example having an RAF 1A motor, while G-EBCA had a Renault which offered a maximum speed of only 65 mph (104.6 km/h).

Royal Aircraft Factory S.E.5a cutaway drawing key

1 Laminated wooden propeller
2 Propeller attaching plate
3 Attaching bolts
4 Radiator

33 Ammunition drum
34 Gun elevating track
35 Firing cable
36 Fixed gun sight
37 Vickers 0.303-in (7.7-mm) machine-gun
38 Machine-gun mounting
39 Ammunition tank
40 Cartridge ejector chute
41 Plywood fuselage top decking
42 Forward fuselage upper longeron
43 Forward fuselage lower longeron
44 Vertical frame member
45 Priming pump
46 Rudder pedal bar
47 Instrument panel
48 Throttle control

78 Starboard lower aileron
79 Aileron horn
80 Operating cable
81 Front spar
82 Built-up centre spar
83 Rear spar
84 Diagonal bracing wires
85 Leading edge stiffeners
86 Wing ribs
87 Forward interplane strut
88 Aft interplane strut
89 Strut bracing wires
90 Spar root fitting
91 Undercarriage attachment
92 Steel tube undercarriage legs

93 Leg fairings
94 Hinged axle box
95 Elastic cord shock absorber
96 Axle fairing
97 Port mainwheel
98 Undercarriage bracing wires
99 Tyre inflation valve
100 Starboard mainwheel

The art of skywriting, pioneered by Major Jack Savage, utilized ex-military S.E.5as. This example served from 1928 to 1934 and shows the lengthened exhaust piping, within which the chemical formula reacted with the exhaust heat to produce the highly visible white smoke used in aerial writing.

5 Radiator shutter plates
6 Filler cap
7 Radiator mounting strut
8 Bottom fitting
9 200-hp (149-kW) Wolseley Viper V-8 engine
10 Engine mounting structure
11 Top cowling
12 Hinged bottom cowling
13 Oil tank
14 Oil filler cap
15 Engine cooling air duct
16 Main fuel tank
17 Fuel tank fixing
18 Centre section forward strut
19 Centre section aft strut
20 Front spar
21 Built-up centre spar
22 Rear spar
23 Wing ribs
24 Leading edge stiffeners
25 Diagonal wire bracing
26 Aileron connecting cable
27 Starboard upper aileron
28 Aileron horn
29 Auxiliary fuel tank
30 Radiator header tank
31 Lewis gun mounting
32 0.303-in (7.7-mm) calibre Lewis gun

49 Control column
50 Pilot's seat
51 Exhaust pipe
52 Tailplane incidence control
53 Access step
54 Headrest
55 Headrest fairing
56 Aft fuselage top longeron
57 Aft fuselage bottom longeron
58 Vertical spacers
59 Diagonal wire bracing
60 Dorsal structure
61 Rudder and elevator cables
62 Fin structure
63 Fin attachment
64 Rudder structure
65 Rudder hinge
66 Operating horn
67 Variable incidence tailplane
68 Tailplane actuator
69 Hinge point
70 Tailplane structure
71 Tailplane bracing wire
72 Elevator structure
73 Elevator horn
74 Ventral fin
75 Steerable tail-skid
76 Tail-skid shock absorber
77 Aileron interconnecting wire

Royal Aircraft Factory S.E.5 variants

S.E.5 prototypes: three built, A4561 unarmed and powered by a direct-drive 150-hp (111.9-kW) French-built Hispano-Suiza motor with a gravity tank in the leading edge of the upper, port wing; A4562 which was similar but later armed and fitted with an enlarged windshield and centre-section gravity tank mounted externally, and A4563 powered by a 200-hp (149.1-kW) geared Hispano-Suiza; armed, this last became in effect the prototype S.E.5a.

S.E.5 production: originally fitted with extra-large windshields, these were soon discarded as was the armoured seat of the prototypes; flown with or without headrest, span of later versions reduced by 1 ft 3.6 in (0.40 m) by reducing rake of wing-tips; 150-hp (111.9-kW) Hispano-Suiza engine.

S.E.5a prototype: modified A4563 fitted with four-blade propeller and having L-shaped exhausts.

S.E.5a production: powered by 200-hp (149.1-kW),

220-hp (164.1-kW) or 240-hp (179.0-kW) Hispano-Suiza, some of the early units of French manufacture, or (final standard) 200-hp (149.1-kW) Wolseley W.4a Viper, an underslung radiator being tried on one such; various trials conducted with different tail assemblies or a version armed with three upward-firing Lewis guns; also some flown with reduced dihedral and steel or wooden landing gears, narrow-chord ailerons etc; some modified as two-seaters, or as civil smoke-writers.

S.E.5b: only one (A8947) produced with 200-hp (149.1-kW) motor, underslung radiator and sesquiplane configuration at one time; original armament retained.

S.E.5E: designation for USA Curtiss-assembled variant with 180-hp (134.2-kW) Wright-Martin Hispano Suiza; only one (SC43153) completed, fuselage covered in ply.

S.E.6: uncompleted project to be fitted with 275-hp (205.1-kW) Rolls-Royce Falcon water-cooled motor

Royal Aircraft Factory S.E.5

The average cost of these machines offered for disposal was £700 each, and eight were procured for a unique race by the Royal Aero Club in 1921, the contest being a proposed speed trial between Oxford and Cambridge Universities on 16 July. Civil registrations on the fuselage apart, the six competing aircraft (one was held in reserve by each team) were to fly in their old military dope scheme relieved only by the appropriate shade of blue on the rear fuselage and tail assembly.

The race finally took place on one of the hottest afternoons of the summer and it was undoubtedly the choice by the Cambridge pilots to fly in the cooler conditions of the upper air that contributed to their taking the first three places and an accumulated prize of more than £400. All the competing aircraft were Viper-powered.

Perhaps better known than the privately owned or racing S.E.5a aircraft were the few that might be seen on a summer's day skywriting in white smoke trails the words of advertisements such as *Buick* or *Persil*. The S.E.5 aircraft used for this purpose were piloted by M. L. Bramson or Sidney St Barbe, or alternatively Major Jack Savage who invented the art of skywriting and was at the time the proprietor of the company formed for its exploitation.

The aircraft were in all essentials standard machines powered by 200-hp (149.1-kW) Wolseley Vipers but with a special modification to the exhaust pipes: these were lengthened down the fuselage to accommodate this. Into this the smoke-producing substance was introduced from a tank

D5995 was built by Vickers at Weybridge, and is depicted while serving with No. 143 Sqn, RFC, at Throwley on home defence duties. The Lewis gun on its Foster mounting can be seen clearly, in its upper position for firing. This looks as 'standard' an S.E.5a as one could find (there were hundreds of minor variations).

inside the fuselage, the flow being controlled by means of a cock inside the cockpit. The pilot had only to turn this cock to allow the entry of the chemical, the formula for which was always a closely kept secret, the heat of the pipes then transforming it into dense white smoke. Thus it was that astonished spectators lifted their eyes on 30 May 1922 to read the single word *Vim* against the backdrop of the sky, a word chosen for its simplicity.

Perhaps unintentionally, and possibly due in part to the Skywriter's Union, we still have a few examples of the S.E.5a around today. This is partly shown by the fact that all the museum models still extant in Britain today were used for skywriting at some stage in their lives. Perhaps the best example of these aircraft is in the Science Museum in London. With the exception of its headrest, former G-EBIB has been restored to its original military configuration.

Left: A replica S.E.5a built by trainees at the Royal Aircraft Establishment at Farnborough. *Below:* In this photo the additional Lewis machine-gun can be clearly seen on top of the wing.

Fokker Dr.I Triplane

Conceived as a counter to the Sopwith Triplane, the Fokker Dr.I was one of the most agile combat aircraft in history. Flown by such men as Manfred von Richthofen, the small number built shot down many times their own number of enemy aircraft on the Western Front. It was in one of these aircraft that von Richthofen, the legendary Red Baron, met his death.

Manfred von Richthofen and his scarlet Fokker Dr.I triplane have become a legend in their own right. This is despite the fact that Leutnant Werner Voss shot down many more aircraft from his Fokker triplane, and von Richthofen's kills were mostly achieved with other aircraft. What is more, the number of these aircraft flying in World War 1 was comparatively small, and it was only designed as an answer to, and built along the same lines as, the British Sopwith Triplane. But the renown of the Fokker Dr.I still eclipses that of any other aircraft which flew in this war.

Released by the Sopwith Experimental Department on 28 May 1916, the first Triplane was a very neat fighting scout with a fuselage and tail almost identical to those of the Sopwith Pup, perhaps the most agile and well-loved aircraft of its day. Sopwith designed the Triplane for several reasons. Its three wings were much narrower (smaller chord) than the biplane wings of the Pup, so that though span remained unchanged the wing area actually was reduced. The more powerful (130-hp/97-kW) instead of 80- or 100-hp/60- or 75-kW) engine made the Triplane significantly faster. The narrower wings gave the pilot a better view, especially as the middle wing was on the same level as his eyes. The narrow chord also meant that the centre of pressure (the point through which the resultant lift force acts) did not move so far from front to rear, or vice versa, as in a normal broad-winged machine during violent manoeuvres, and as this meant the fuselage could be short it enhanced manoeuvrability. Manoeuvrability was also assisted by keeping the span short, which with three wings was simple.

Frightening example

All the Triplanes went to the Royal Naval Air Service and, in no small measure because of the tremendous aggressiveness and skill of the pilots, soon struck a chill into the hearts of German flyers. The Triplanes really got into action during the Battle of Arras in April 1917. So great was their success that an official historian wrote: 'The sight of a Triplane

A replica of the Fokker Dr.I painted to represent von Richthofen's famous aircraft, though the face painted upon the engine cowling simulates that of the aircraft flown by Werner Voss.

The Fokker Dr.I serialled 152/17 (construction no. 1864) was one of a batch of 30 from early in the type's production run. Allocated to Jasta 11, this aircraft was on occasion flown by Manfred von Richthofen, and survived the war to go on display in a Berlin museum in an all-red scheme.

Fokker Dr.I

Specification

Type: single-seat fighting scout
Powerplant: one 110-hp (82-kW) Oberursel Ur.II nine-cylinder rotary piston engine
Peformance: maximum speed 115 mph (185 km/h) at sea level, and 103 mph (165 km/h) at 13,125 ft (4000 m); climb to 3,280 ft (1000 m) in 2 minutes 55 seconds; service ceiling 20,015 ft (6100 m); range 186 miles (300 km); endurance 1 hour 30 minutes
Weights: empty 894 lb (406 kg); maximum take-off 1,291 lb (586 kg)
Dimensions: span, upper 23 ft 7 in (7.19 m), centre 20 ft 5¼ in (6.23 m) and lower 18 ft 8½ in (5.70 m); length 18 ft 11 in (5.77 m); height 9 ft 8 in (2.95 m); wing area, including axle fairing 200.85 sq ft (18.66 m²)
Armament: two 7.92-mm (0.31-in) LMG 08/15 machine-guns with 500 rounds per gun

Fokker Dr.I

This all-black Dr.I had unusual white crosses on its fuselage and wings (it is believed other black German machines had white-outlined black crosses). It was the aircraft of Leutnant Josef Jacobs of Jasta 7, who finally gained 41 confirmed victories. This put him level with Hauptmann Bruno Loerzer in eighth place in Germany.

Perhaps the most famous fighter of all time, the triplane number 425/17 was the last mount of the 'Red Baron', Rittmeister Manfred, Freiherr von Richthofen, the top-scoring ace of World War 1 with 80 confirmed kills. He was shot down on 21 April 1918. Here the old cross can just be seen under the new one.

formation induced the enemy pilots to dive out of range.' The moment a Triplane crashed behind the German lines the wreckage was studied in the finest detail. Even the commander of the Imperial German Air Service, General von Höppner, publicly eulogized the British fighter. By the spring of 1917 almost every important aircraft company in the Central Powers – at least 14 – had a design team furiously trying to produce a triplane fighter. But it was the wily Dutchman, Anthony Fokker, who achieved success. So eager was he to beat his rivals that, as well as studying the Sopwith Triplanes at first hand, flying at the front, he completely illegally had the wreckage from the first crashed specimen sent to his own factory at Schwerin!

The latest fighter prototype at the Schwerin works at that time was the D.VI (a company designation unrelated to the later production D.VI), intended for the Luftfahrttruppe (air force) of Austro-Hungary. In June 1917 chief designer Reinold Platz quickly re-drew the drawings and the D.VI emerged round 1 July 1917 as the first triplane to fly in Germany. It was immediately tested by Lt Werner Voss, already a famed ace. Platz had already designed extremely advanced biplane fighters with completely cantilever wings, and he made the D.VI the same way, unbraced wings being easier on a short-span triplane. The two lower wings were attached to the top and bottom of the fuselage, and the only struts were long steel-tube inverted-Vee cabane struts carrying the top wing high above the fuselage. This wing was the only one with ailerons, whereas the Sopwith Triplane had had ailerons on all three wings, linked by light rods. Powered by a 110-hp (82-kW) Oberursel Ur.II rotary engine, the D.VI flew excellently, though before being sent to Hungary in August the upper wing, with its ailerons, was increased in span. To eliminate slight wing vibration, light wooden streamline I-type struts were added linking the wings near their tips. Armament was two synchronized 0.31-in (7.29-mm) LMG 08/15 guns.

52

Further developments

The D.VI, often incorrectly called the V 3, was succeeded by the first of the Fokkers to have a *Versuchs* (experimental) number, the V 4. Two V 4 triplanes, with balanced ailerons squared-off at the wingtips, were ordered on 11 July 1917. In August a number of V 7 triplanes were ordered with more powerful engines, such as the 160-hp (119-kW) Siemens-Halske Sh.III, 160-hp (119-kW) Ur.III, 145-hp (108-kW) Steyr-built Le Rhône and 170-hp (127-kW) Goebel Goe.III. These introduced modified wings with span increasing in equal steps from bottom to top. They retained the I-strut linking the wings, and all had horn balances on the ailerons and elevators, those on the ailerons projecting beyond the tips of the wings. No data survive, but because of their power the V fighter prototypes were probably more formidable than the eventual production fighter triplane.

Action at the Front

Lt Voss spent over 20 hours testing the two V 4 prototype triplanes in August 1917, and by the end of that month had them to his satisfaction. Both had by that time seen action at the front, and Fokker himself had also done a lot of active flying in them (previously he had had to don the uniform of a German officer and fly on active operational missions to test his synchronizing gear, despite the fact he was a Dutch civilian!).

Voss made the first operational flight in Fok.103/17 (Fokker No.103 for year 1917), the second V 4 prototype, on 30 August 1917. He claimed a victory on this mission. Two days later, on 1 September, von Richthofen flew the original V 4 (102/ 17) and scored his 60th victory. Flying with von Richthofen's *Jagdgeschwader* 1 (JG1) the two prototypes scored success after success. Voss monopolized the second Dr.I (103/17) scoring a remarkable 20 confirmed victories in it in 24 days before being killed in a classic fight on 23 September with no fewer than six S.E.5a fighters.

Structurally it was typical Fokker and Platz, with very strong mixed construction. The wings were almost wholly wood, with steel at the main joints and the attachments of bracing wires. Each wing had a single built-up box spar with main longerons of spindled (machined away for lightness on a router) hardwood, carrying built-up plywood ribs. Trailing edges were wire, resulting in the characteristic scalloped appearance when the fabric covering was doped and tightened.

Fokker Dr.I cutaway drawing key

1 Starboard upper wing tip
2 Wing panel fabric covering
3 Starboard upper interplane strut
4 Aileron cable run
5 Two-blade wooden propeller
6 Starboard centre wing
7 Lower interplane strut
8 Propeller hub fixing bolts
9 Ventilated engine cowling
10 Oberursel Ur.II (le Rhône) nine-cylinder rotary engine
11 Engine compartment fireproof bulkhead
12 Engine bearer struts
13 Reduction gearbox
14 Plywood side fairing panel
15 Carburettor
16 Rudder pedal bar
17 Pilot's footboards
18 Compass mounting
19 Control column
20 Control column-mounted secondary throttle control
21 Gun firing cables
22 Ammunition boxes
23 Fuel tank (20-Imp gal/91-litre capacity)
24 Wing spar box construction
25 Centre wing/fuselage attachments
26 Fuel filler cap
27 Twin 7.92-mm (0.31-in) LMG 08/15 machine guns
28 Ring-and-bead gunsight
29 Diagonal wire bracing
30 Centre section V-struts
31 Aileron cables
32 V-strut attachment
33 Plywood covered leading edge
34 Upper wing spar box
35 Wing ribs
36 Port upper interplane strut
37 Wing tip construction
38 Rib bracing tapes
39 Aileron horn balance
40 Welded steel tube aileron construction
41 Aileron control horn
42 Wire trailing edge
43 Port centre wing construction
44 Interplane strut attachment
45 Wing root cut-out, forward and downward visibility
46 Machine gun breeches
47 Padded cockpit coaming
48 Engine instruments
49 Engine throttle and fuel cock controls
50 Pilot's seat
51 Sliding seat adjustment
52 Welded steel-tube fuselage construction
53 Aft end of plywood side fairing panel
54 Plywood top decking
55 Port lower interplane strut
56 Fuselage top longeron
57 Horizontal spacers
58 Port lower wing tip
59 Wing tip skid
60 Tailplane centre section mounting
61 Welded steel tube tailplane construction
62 Rudder horn balance
63 Steel tube leading edge
64 Elevator horn balance
65 Steel tube elevator construction
66 Rudder fabric covering
67 Sternpost
68 Rudder control horn
69 Elevator control horn
70 Tailskid hinge mounting
71 Steel-shod tailskid
72 Elastic cord shock absorbers
73 Fuselage vertical spacers
74 Lifting handles
75 Fuselage fabric covering
76 Diagonal wire bracing (double wires)
77 Tailplane control cables
78 Fuselage bottom longeron
79 Control cable guides
80 Mounting step
81 Seat support frame
82 Dust proof fabric bulkhead
83 Pilot's floor
84 Control column mounting shaft
85 Lower wing centre section spar box
86 Undercarriage strut attachments
87 Main undercarriage V-struts
88 Port mainwheel
89 Wheel disc fabric covering
90 Wheel spokes
91 Pivoted half-axle
92 Axle fairing construction
93 Axle spar box
94 Elastic cord shock absorbers
95 Starboard mainwheel
96 Tyre valve access
97 Starboard lower wing tip skid

First of the Fokker triplanes, this neat prototype is commonly (but incorrectly) known as the V 3. Its true designation was D.VI, in an early-1917 series of D designations unrelated to the official series which included the famed D.VII. Powered by a 110-hp (82-kW) Ur.II rotary, it was flown by Leutnant Werner Voss in mid-1917.

One of the best surviving photographs of a genuine Dr.I. This aircraft provided the basis for the restored triplane N864DR which, after a busy flying career, was donated to the Australian War Memorial at Canberra. Numerous replicas of this famous fighter have been built in recent years, powered by non-rotary engines.

The small fuselage and tail were accurately welded in jigs from pre-shaped steel tubes, the fuselage then having light wooden fairings added prior to being covered in fabric. The traditional rubber-sprung main landing gears had an axle faired by a small wing, a feature of many Fokker fighters. Again a common feature of the day was the absence of a fin, the only vertical tail surface being the simple rounded rudder pivoted to the fuselage sternpost. The small riveted fuel tank was immediately behind the spinning engine, and beneath the guns; the usual armament, seldom altered in practice, comprised two LMG 08/15 (commonly called 'Spandau') machine-guns with belt magazines inside the fuselage behind the tank and the breeches immediately in front of the pilot inside the cockpit.

It added up to a simple, relatively cheap and fairly agile fighter, which with the standard 110-hp (82-kW) engine could climb faster than many more powerful aircraft and also turn inside them, a factor which in a dogfight was vital. But the speed was unimpressive by late 1917 standards and the range and endurance were exceptionally poor – only a skilled pilot could keep a Dr.I airborne longer than 80 minutes whereas 2 (if not 3) hours was easily within the grasp of all Allied fighter pilots.

Richthofen's Flying Circus

But for the brief period from October 1917 the 318 Fokker Dr.I triplanes, plus the two prototypes, were to carve out a niche in the hall of fame of military aviation. As with the Sopwith which inspired it, this was to some extent because of the brilliant flyers who went to war in it. No more famous flying unit has ever existed than von Richthofen's JG1, often called 'Richthofen's Flying Circus' because of the large number of fighters under one command, their carefully planned and organized combat techniques and, not least, their brilliant and often highly personal colour schemes. Of

course, the 318 production Dr.Is equipped not just the four Jagdstaffeln (fighter squadrons) of JG1 but several other Jagdgeschwäder, notably JG2 and JG3.

The successful service career of the Dr.I was briefly marred by a spate of crashes in the first two weeks of combat duty by production aircraft. The cause was eventually traced to shockingly bad workmanship at the Schwerin factory, and all Dr.Is were at once grounded until their wings had been stripped of fabric and inspected. In many cases properly made wing spars had to be produced, and the factory spent almost the whole of November 1917 urgently repairing or rebuilding the wings of Dr.Is. Thus it was not really until late November that the Dr.I became effective in numbers on the Western Front, and it is remarkable that such a relatively small number of a basically outdated design should have acquired so great a reputation.

This reputation is, of course, inextricably interwoven with the great Red Baron himself, Rittmeister Manfred, Freiherr von Richthofen, a German aristocrat who was the top-scoring ace of World War 1 and perhaps the most famous fighter pilot of all time. Though most of his victories had been gained on other types, such as the Albatros D.III, he favoured the Dr.I over faster biplanes and continued to fly one almost exclusively on combat missions in 1918. It was in one of two Dr.Is regularly flown by him that he met his death on 21 April 1918 – probably at the hands of Roy Brown, a Canadian captain with No. 209 Squadron, RAF (the RAF was then just 20 days old). The Freiherr (not actually a baron) died from a single bullet that went diagonally through his body, penetrating the heart.

The last Dr.I was delivered in May 1918, at a time when this type was rapidly being taken out of service in favour of the considerably superior Fokker D.VII. At no time were there more than 171 Dr.Is in active service – the maximum was reached in May 1918 – and by the middle of June this had fallen to 125. During the summer, most of them had been transferred back to Germany to defend their home territory. Other famous Dr.I pilots apart from Richthofen were Kurt Wolff, with 33 aircraft shot down, Voss with 48, Erich Löwenhardt with 53, and Ernst Udet with 62. Richthofen himself had 80 kills to his credit.

This Dr.I was on the strength of Jasta 18 in the final year of the war. After the Armistice it was acquired by France and preserved. The interplane strut linked the single spars of the three wings. Not all Dr.Is were fitted with the ash skid attached under the tips of the lowest wing to prevent damage.

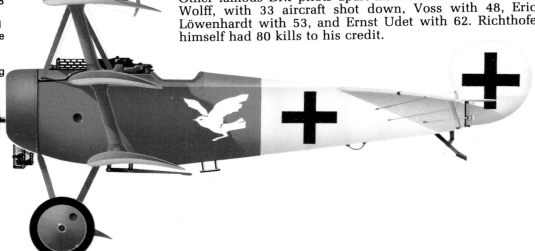

Vickers Vimy

Just too late to fight in World War 1, the Vimy bomber gained immortal fame when Alcock and Brown succeeded in flying the Atlantic nonstop for the first time. The Vimy gave long service with the Royal Air Force and made several outstanding long-range flights to distant destinations in the British Empire.

When one thinks that 'strategic' bombing began as early as 1915, especially on the Italian and Russian fronts, it is perhaps surprising that the British Air Board did not begin developing a heavy bomber until 1917, particularly since Britain had regularly been overflown by German aircraft. It is even more surprising that on 23 July of that year (only two months after a daylight attack on London by 30 Gotha G.IV bombers which left 162 people dead and 432 wounded), the Board cancelled its order for heavy bombers for the Royal Flying Corps. In the face of heated protests this decision was reversed, and in addition to a new order for more than 100 Handley Page O/400s, prototypes for new aircraft were ordered from Handley Page and Vickers.

Designed by Reginald Kirshaw Pierson, the Vickers F.B.27 project of which three prototypes were ordered, was in-

tended to feature two 200-hp (149-kW) RAF 4d air-cooled Vee-12 engines, but these were not ready in time and when first flown at Joyce Green by Captain Gordon Bell on 30 November 1917 the first aircraft (B9952) was powered by a pair of 200-hp (149-kW) Hispano-Suiza engines.

With a crew of three (pilot, nose gunner/bomb-aimer and mid-ships gunner) the Vimy (named after the famous battle-field of World War 1) was a three-bay biplane with upper and lower wings of equal span, the engines being strut-mounted between the wings, and had a twin-finned biplane tail unit and four-wheel landing gear with central nose-

Fine in-flight study of F9147, an Eagle-powered Vimy of No. 9 Sqn, one of a batch of 50 aircraft (F9146–F9295) produced by Vickers. No. 9 Sqn flew Vimys from Manston between April 1924 and June 1925.

Vickers Vimy variants

F.B.27: three prototypes (B9952–B9954) with Hispano-Suiza, Sunbeam Maori and Fiat A-12bis engines; first flight 30 November 1917
Vimy Mk I: 12 (F701–F712) built by Vickers, Crayford, 1918–9 with Fiat, BHP or Liberty engines specified; at least seven completed with Fiat A-12bis
Vimy Mk I: six (F2915–F2910) built by RAE, Farnborough; probably all with Fiat engines; F2915 with central fin and rudder for RAE trials
Vimy Mk I: 40 (F3146–F3185) built by Morgans, Leighton Buzzard with Rolls-Royce Eagle VIII; some reconditioned and re-engined in mid-1920s as trainers
Vimy Mk I: 50 (F8596–F8645) built by Vickers, Weybridge, all probably with Eagle VIIIs; F8625 became G-EAOL and flown to Spain; F8630 became G-EAOU for England–Australia flight by Smith brothers
Vimy Mk I: 50 (F9146–F9195) built by Vickers, Weybridge, all with Eagle VIIIs; 26 later reconditioned, 17 converted to dual-control trainers and four re-engined with Jupiter radials
F.B.27a Vimy Mk II: one prototype (F9569) with Rolls-Royce Eagle VIIIs
Vimy Mk III: 10 (H651–H660) built by RAE, Farnborough; Fiat engines specified but Eagles fitted; H651 used in automatic landing trials by RAE; redesignated Vimy Mk II
Vimy Mk IV: 25 (H5065–H5089) built by Westland, Yeovil, with Eagle engines: redesignated Vimy Mk II
Vimy Special: one prototype (H9963); believed used for torpedo trials in 1920; probably Vickers-built
Vimy Mk II: 10 (J7238–J7247) built by Vickers, Weybridge; these were first Vimys ordered post-war (in 1923), and at some time referred to as Vimy Mk IV
Vimy Mk II: 15 (J7440–J7454) built by Vickers, 1923–4, with Eagle VIII engines; some re-engined with Jupiter and Jaguar radials in 1926; J7451 with smoke-laying gear

Vimy Mk III: five (J7701–J7705) built by Vickers, 1924–5; most reconditioned and re-engined in 1927
Vimy Transatlantic: one aircraft, Vickers-built; no registration; flown by Alcock and Brown, April–June 1919, Eagle VIIIs, increased fuel
Vimy (Civil): one company-owned trials aircraft (G-EAAR allocated)
Vimy (Cape Flight): *Silver Queen*, one aircraft (G-UABA) flown by Van Ryneveld and Brand but crashed at Korosko, Upper Egypt, 11 February 1920; *Silver Queen II* was standard RAF aircraft
Type 66 Vimy Commercial: one prototype (K-107, later G-EAAV); used in flight attempt to Cape by Broome and Cockerell but crashed 27 February 1920
Vimy Commercial: Chinese aircraft; 40 built by Vickers between April 1920 and February 1921 and shipped out to fly Peking–Tsinan air post; not all flown
Vimy Commercial: two aircraft, namely G-EASI *City of London* flown by Instone and Imperial Airways, and F-ADER flown by Grands Express Aériens
Vimy Commercial: one aircraft with Lion engines; employed as Vernon prototype; sold to USSR in 1922
Vimy Ambulance: five aircraft (J6855, J6904, J6905, J7143 and J7144) with Lion engines; later converted to Vernons
Vernon Mk I: 20 aircraft (J6864–J6883) with Eagle VIII engines
Vernon Mk II: 25 aircraft (J6884–J6893, J6976–J6980 and J7133–J7142) with Lion engines
Vernon Mk III: 10 aircraft (J7539–J7548) with Lion III engines and extra wing tanks

F 318

The Vickers F.B.Mk 27 Vimy bomber arrived in RAF service just too late to see action in World War 1. It continued in production, however, and became the standard heavy bomber for the beginning of the 1920s. Several aircraft were sold for civilian use and were used for trail-blazing long-distance flights – across the Atlantic and from England to Australia being just two such feats. Those in RAF service were used mainly in the Middle East, with Nos 45, 58, 70 and 216 Sqns and No. 4 Flying Training School, whilst Nos 7 and 9 Sqns in the UK together with 'D' Flight of No. 100 Sqn also flew them until re-equipped with Virginias. The aircraft shown, F3184, served in Egypt with No. 70 Sqn.

Vickers Vimy

Specification

Vimy Mk IV (Vimy Mk II as redesignated in 1923)
Type: heavy bomber
Powerplant: two 360-hp (269-kW) Rolls-Royce Eagle VIII V-12 water-cooled engines
Performance: maximum speed 103 mph (166 km/h) at sea level; climb to 5,000 ft (1525 m) in 22 minutes; service ceiling 7,000 ft (2135 m); range 910 miles (1464 km) at 81 mph (130 km/h)
Weights: empty 7,101 lb (3221 kg); maximum take-off 12,500 lb (5670 kg)
Dimensions: span 68 ft 1 in (20.75 m); length 43 ft 6½ in (13.27 m); height 15 ft 7½ in (4.76 m); wing area 1,330 sq ft (123.56 m²)
Armament: two to four 0.303-in (7.7-mm) Lewis Mk III machine guns (with up to 12 97-round ammunition drums) in nose, dorsal and ventral positions, plus normal bombload of up to 2,476 lb (1123 kg)

Vickers Vimy

Purchased by the RAF for £6,300, Vickers Vimy ambulance J7143 displays the prominent Red Cross markings incorporated in the national insignia. Note the uncowled Napier Lion engines and deletion of the nosewheel.

mounted skid. The internal bombload comprised twelve 112-lb (51-kg) bombs stowed vertically in the centre fuselage; this was later increased to eight 250-lb (113-kg) and four 112-lb (51-kg) bombs, plus two 250-lb (113-kg) bombs under the fuselage and four 230-lb (104-kg) bombs under the wing centre sections. Indeed the Vimy astonished spectators at Martlesham Heath when it lifted a greater load than the O/400 on half the power. Fuel capacity was 92 Imp gal (418 litres) and armament four 0.303-in (7.7-mm) Lewis Mk III machine-guns with 12 97-round ammunition drums.

After trials at Martlesham Heath in 1918, during which the Hispano-Suiza engines gave persistent trouble as a result of over-heating, B9952 returned to Joyce Green to be re-engined with two 260-hp (194-kW) Salmson water-cooled radials; the wing dihedral was also increased from 1° to 2°. The second prototype was flown in February 1918 and featured plain elevators and ailerons in place of the first aircraft's horn-balanced surfaces; it was powered by 260-hp (194-kW) Sunbeam Maori engines driving four-blade propellers, each engine nacelle featuring its own instruments on the inboard side, where they were visible from the cockpit. This aircraft also introduced a ventral gun position.

The second Vimy (B9953) crashed in May following engine failure, and was followed in June by B9954 with 300-hp (224-kW) Fiat A-12bis engines in octagonal-section nacelles similar to those adopted in production aircraft. The rear upper gun mounting was a twin-Lewis Scarff ring, and the fuel capacity was increased to 226 Imp gal (1027 litres). This aircraft also crashed, at Martlesham on 11 September when the pilot stalled after take-off with a full load of bombs, which exploded. A fourth prototype, which appeared somewhat later, was powered by two 360-hp (269-kW) Rolls-Royce Eagle VIII V-12 engines.

Production was widely subcontracted by Vickers, but the end of the war brought cancellation of most orders. However, Vickers built 12 aircraft at Crayford and 132 at Weybridge (production continuing until about 1924); Morgan & Co, Leighton Buzzard, produced about 40 aircraft, and Westland Aircraft, Yeovil, a further 25. The Royal Aircraft Establishment at Farnborough also completed 10.

At the end of October 1918 the RAF had taken delivery of only three aircraft, of which one was on charge with the Independent (Bombing) Force, and none is known to have taken part in war operations. The Vimy only reached full service status in July 1919 when it replaced Handley Page O/400s with No. 58 (Bomber) Squadron at Heliopolis, Egypt, followed by No. 70 (Bomber) Squadron, also at Heliopolis, in February the following year.

Subsequent service with the RAF continued with deliveries to No. 45 (Bomber) Squadron at Almaza, Egypt, in November 1921; to 'D' Flight, No. 100 (Bomber) Squadron at Spitalgate, Lincolnshire, in March 1922; to No. 216 Squadron (a general bomber-transport unit) at Heliopolis in June 1922; to No. 7 (Bomber) Squadron at Bircham Newton in June 1923; to No.

9 (Bomber) Squadron at Upavon (and later Manston) in March 1924; and to No. 99 (Bomber) Squadron at Netheravon in April 1924. Also in April 1924 No. 58 Squadron, which had been renumbered No. 70 Squadron in February 1920 and had then given up its Vimys, was re-formed with Vimy Mk IVs at Worthy Down under the command of Wing Commander A. T. (later Marshal of the Royal Air Force Sir Arthur) Harris, perhaps the greatest advocate of strategic bombing in the history of the RAF. Finally, No. 502 (Ulster) Squadron, first of the Special Reserve Units to be incorporated in the new Auxiliary Air Force, received Vimys as initial equipment in June 1925 at Aldergrove in Northern Ireland.

Vickers Vimy cutaway drawing key

1. Aileron horn balance
2. Starboard upper aileron
3. Aileron control horn
4. Aileron balance cables
5. Compression ribs
6. Wing panel internal wire bracing
7. Fixed portion of trailing edge
8. Outer wing panel joint rib
9. Radiator header tank
10. Starboard lower aileron
11. Starboard interplane struts
12. Diagonal wire bracing
13. Aileron control cable runs
14. Wing panel fabric covering
15. Starboard four-bladed propeller
16. Radiator shutters
17. Engine nacelle support struts
18. Exhaust pipe
19. Starboard engine nacelle
20. Nacelle access panels
21. Fuel feed pipe and control cable duct
22. Engine instruments
23. Wing walkway
24. Cockpit propeller guard
25. Windscreen panels
26. Instrument panel
27. Scarff ring gun mounting
28. 0.303-in (7.7-mm) Lewis gun
29. Front gunner/bomb aimer's compartment
30. Nose compartment glazing
31. Drift sight
32. Spare ammunition containers
33. Compass
34. Gunner/bomb aimer's seat
35. Engine throttle and mixture control levers
36. Control column handwheel
37. Fuel system control panel
38. Flare stowage
39. Boarding steps
40. Pitot's footboards
41. Cockpit floor level
42. Pilot's seat
43. Front gunner/bomb aimer/observer's seat
44. Cockpit rear bulkhead
45. Elevator cable control lever
46. Forward main fuel tank capacity 86 Imp gal (391 litres)
47. Port propeller guard
48. Cockpit coaming
49. Pilot's head fairing
50. Aft main fuel tank, capacity 140 Imp gal (636 litres)
51. Dorsal decking
52. Fuel system header tank
53. Centre section inverted-V struts
54. Pitot tubes
55. Leading edge gravity feed fuel tank, capacity 15 Imp gal (68 litres)
56. Wing centre section rib construction
57. Port radiator header tank
58. Rear gunner's compartment
59. Spare ammunition containers
60. Scarff ring gun mounting
61. 0.303-in (7.7-mm) Lewis gun
62. Wing rear spar
63. Trailing edge ribs
64. Fuselage top longerons
65. Horizontal spacers
66. Tail control cables
67. Starboard fixed tailfin
68. Starboard rudder
69. Fabric covered tailplane
70. Elevator control horn
71. Upper elevator
72. Tailplane rib construction
73. Port rudder construction
74. Rudder control horn
75. Elevator interconnecting cables

Vickers Vimy

Bristol Jupiter IV-powered Vimy F9171, flown by No. 4 Flying Training School at Abu Sueir, Egypt, in the late 1920s. Conversion to these engines reflected the inability of the old water-cooled Eagle to achieve an acceptable standard of reliability, especially in Egypt.

Seventy-five Vickers F.B.Mk 27A Vimys (sometimes referred to as Mk IIs) were ordered from the Westland Aircraft Works at Yeovil but only 25 were completed, the second aircraft being depicted here. It was planned to use American Liberty engines in these but standard Rolls-Royce Eagle VIIIs were eventually fitted.

83 Fuselage diagonal wire bracing
84 Vertical spacers
85 Lower longeron
86 External control cable runs
94 Rib bracing stringers
95 Outer wing panel rib construction
96 Aileron control horns
97 Port upper aileron
98 Aileron horn balance
99 Wing tip rib
100 Outer interplane struts
101 Aileron interconnecting cables
102 Port lower aileron

103 Diagonal wire bracing
104 Port lower wing panel
105 Front spar
106 Leading edge rib construction
107 Inter-rib stiffeners
108 Inner interplane struts
109 Main undercarriage support struts
110 Twin mainwheels
111 Inspection panel
112 Engine maintenance walkways
113 Step
114 Engine nacelle support struts
115 Engine bearer
116 Oil tank
117 Oil filler cap
118 Exhaust pipe
119 Rolls-Royce Eagle 12-cylinder Vee engine
120 Cooling air louvres
121 Port radiator shutters
122 Propeller hub attachment plate
123 Port propeller
124 Wind driven fuel pump
125 230-lb (104-kg) HE bomb carried beneath fuselage longerons
126 Underwing bomb rack
127 Bomb release units
128 112-lb (51-kg) HE bombs, four per wing
129 Boarding step
130 Skid support struts
131 Front skid

76 Lower elevator
77 Tailplane tip skid
78 Port tailfin construction
79 Tailplane spar attachment
80 Tailskid
81 Elastic cord shock absorber
82 Tailplane centre section inverted-V struts
87 Fuselage fabric covering
88 Side window panels
89 Ventral gun cut-out
90 0.303-in (7.7-mm) Lewis gun
91 Ventral gunner's position
92 Rear fuselage floor panels
93 Outer wing panel double compression ribs

F8643

Production versions of the Vimy included the Vimy Mk II with 280-hp (209-kW) Sunbeam Maori engines, the Vimy Mk III with 310-hp (231-kW) Fiat A-12bis V-12 engines and the Vimy Mk IV with 360-hp (269-kW) Rolls-Royce Eagle VIIIs. Post-war trainers were fitted with 420-hp (313-kW) Bristol Jupiter IV radials, 450-hp (336-kW) Jupiter VIs or 420-hp (313-kW) Armstrong Siddeley Jaguar IV radials. Three ambulance aircraft were also produced for service with No. 216 Squadron in the Middle East.

RAF Vimys gave long and sterling service. The standard aircraft of No. 216 Squadron operated the air mail service between Cairo and Baghdad from 1923 until August 1926, reducing the service time from 16 days to two, while at home the Vimys of No. 7 Squadron constituted the RAF's entire home-based heavy bomber force from June 1923 until March 1924.

Three Vimys also served with the Night-Flying Flight at Biggin Hill from 1923 onwards for co-operation with searchlight and gun defences, and during the General Strike of 1926 they were employed to distribute the government's emergency news sheet, the *British Gazette*. The Jupiter- and Jaguar-powered versions were aircraft re-engined for use by flying training schools and as parachute trainers at Henlow. The Vimys with No. 502 Squadron remained in service until 1929, when they were replaced by Handley Page Hyderabads; those with FTS at home remained in service until 1931, and the last aircraft (H657) continued with No. 4 FTS at Abu Sueir, Egypt, until 1933 and its pilots averred that it still was as robust and reliable as ever.

Designation of Vimy versions was complicated indeed, despite attempts to rationalize it in 1923, and by 1925 semi-official designations had again proliferated, being further complicated by such appellations as the Vimy Reconditioned Mk I, Vimy Reconditioned Mk II, Vimy Reconditioned Mk III School, and Vimy Production School.

Vimys were found to be the best available aircraft for training purposes in the Middle East, and served for some years with No. 4 FTS at Abu Sueir, Egypt. Though shown here with Eagle engines, wear and tear in the hot dusty environment eventually caused most Vimys to be re-engined with air-cooled Jupiter or Jaguar engines.

A Westland-built Vimy H5089, serving with No.216 Sqn at Heliopolis, Egypt, in the early 1920s. Later re-registered HR5089, it underwent rebuilding at Abu Sueir for issue as a trainer to No. 4 FTS, probably with Jupiter radials.

Finally among the proposed versions there was the Liberty-powered Vimy, an aircraft re-engined with 400-hp (298-kW) Liberty 12 V-12 engines at the request in 1918 of the United States government in preparation for possible production in the USA (Liberty engines had also been specified for some RAF aircraft); however, when being prepared for flight at Joyce Green the aircraft caught fire and was destroyed, and the proposal was abandoned in 1919.

The great flights

Before World War 1 the *Daily Mail* had put up a prize of £10,000 to be awarded to the first airman to fly an aeroplane across the Atlantic nonstop, with anywhere in the British Isles as the destination achieved. Although some preparations had been made by various pilots (notably Fred Raynham) the war intervened, so that after the Armistice the prize remained unwon. Then in May 1919 the American Curtiss NC-4 was flown from New York to Plymouth (with intermediate landings at the Azores and Lisbon) by Lieutenant Commander A. C. Read of the US Navy. And at about the same time an attempt to make the flight nonstop failed when Harry Hawker and Lieutenant Commander K. F. Mackenzie-Grieve were forced down in a Sopwith biplane in mid-ocean (and were miraculously rescued).

Meanwhile in the UK Captain John Alcock DSC, RNAS and Lieutenant Arthur Whitten-Brown RFC had been testing a specially-prepared and company-owned Vimy; all its military equipment had been removed and extra fuel tankage installed, increasing its capacity to 865 Imp gal (3932 litres). Standard Eagle VIII engines were retained. After a few trial flights the Vimy was dismantled and shipped to Newfoundland where it was erected at Quidi Vidi airfield near St John's; this airfield was found to be unsuitable for take-off by the heavily-laden aircraft, which was moved to Lester's Field. At 16.13 (GMT) on 14 June 1919 Alcock and Brown took off, crossing out over the Newfoundland coast 15 minutes later. Most of the 1,890-mile (3042-km) flight was made during the hours of darkness, and at 08.40 on the following morning the Vimy landed in Derrygimla Bog, Clifden, Co. Galway in Ireland. The two naval officers were

A wry sense of humour was reflected by the name bestowed by the Australians Ross and Keith Smith, 'God 'elp all of us', on their Vimy G-EAOU for the first-ever England–Australia flight during November–December 1919.

given a tumultuous welcome in London, and received the *Daily Mail* prize of £10,000. The Vimy, which had nosed over in the ground on landing, was repaired and presented to the Science Museum, South Kensington.

Although overshadowed by this 'Blue Riband' achievement, the flight by the Australian brothers, Captain Ross Smith and Lieutenant Keith Smith, with Sergeants W. H. Shiers and J. M. Bennett (all of the Australian Air Force), from the UK to Australia must rank as one of the greatest of all feats in long-distance flying. Their aircraft, a Weybridge-built Vimy (F8630) was registered G-EAOU (and dubbed 'God 'elp all of us') and prepared for the flight which was undertaken in response to an offer by the Australian government of £A10,000 for the first flight by Australians from the UK to Australia within 30 days before the end of 1919. Pre-flight planning demanded the provision of fuel and stores at the various landing points.

Taking off from Hounslow, Middlesex, at 08.00 on 12 November, the Vimy eventually reached Darwin at 16.00 on 10 December, having successfully battled its way through tropical storms and undergone running repairs skilfully performed by the two flight mechanics en route. The 11,130-mile (17912-km) flight had been completed in just under 28 days, in 135 hours 55 minutes elapsed flying time, G-EAOU was presented to the Australian government by Vickers and was preserved in a special memorial hall at Adelaide airport.

Third of the great flights was that undertaken by Lieutenant Colonel Pierre Van Ryneveld and Major Christopher Quintin (later Air Vice-Marshal Sir Quintin) Brand from England to Cape Town, including a flight from Cairo to the Cape for a *Daily Mail* prize of £10,000. In a Vimy (G-UABA) named *Silver Queen*, Van Ryneveld and Brand left Brooklands on 4 February 1920 and landed safely at Heliopolis, setting off again after dark on 10 February; on the following day, when still 80 miles (130 km) short of Wadi Halfa, the aircraft was wrecked in a forced landing following engine over-heating.

A second Vimy was loaned by the RAF at Heliopolis (and named *Silver Queen II*), and this aircraft reached Bulawayo, Southern Rhodesia, before being badly damaged when it failed to get airborne in a 'hot-and-high' take-off. The two pilots eventually reached Cape Town in a borrowed de Havilland D.H.9, and were subsequently awarded £5,000 each by the South African government. In recognition of these three great pioneering flights, Alcock, Brown, the Smith brothers, Van Ryneveld and Brand all received knighthoods from HM King George V.

The Vimy Commercial and Vernon

Built in the Vickers factory at Bexleyheath, a considerably modified version of the Vimy made its first flight at Joyce Green on 13 April 1919 in the hands of Stan Cockerell. Originally known as the Monocoque, this crystallized as the Vimy Commercial with much enlarged fuselage of generous oval cross section capable of accommodating 10 passengers in padded-leather or wicker chairs. A rear freight hold of 300 cu ft (8.5 m^3) could accommodate 2,500 lb (1134 kg) of baggage. Originally registered K-107, and later G-EAAV, the prototype was followed by three production aircraft, of which one (with 450-hp/336-kW Napier Lions, and later 400-hp/298-kW Lorraine Dietrich engines) was purchased by the French airline, Grands Express Aériens. The Chinese government also ordered 40 Commercials to establish civil air travel in that country, but it seems that not all these aircraft were ever flown, some remaining in their crates. The other two British-registered aircraft G-EASI and G-EAUL, undertook some early route flying work with the pioneer airline S. Instone & Co. in Europe, the former being handed on to Imperial Airways and the latter shipped to China.

The last Vimy Commercial to be produced featured high-lift wings and Lion engines, and was effectively the prototype of a transport version being developed for the RAF; it was eventually sold to the USSR in September 1922, thereafter being loaned to the Russian airline Dobrolet in 1924.

The Atlantic Vimy of Alcock and Brown was specially built for the flight, featuring a long turtle-back fairing over the centre fuselage enclosing additional fuel tanks. It is pictured here at Brooklands during preliminary trials prior to shipment to Newfoundland.

Pictured in front of a Vimy (*not* their historic aircraft, G-EAOU) at Brooklands before the England–Australia flight are the famous Aussies, Captain Ross Smith, Lieutenant Keith Smith, Sergeant J. M. Bennett and Sergeant W. H. Shiers.

Airco D.H.4 and D.H.9

Geoffrey de Havilland always had a flair for producing aircraft that filled the bill for a specific requirement. In 1916, with World War 1 in progress, there was a need for an advanced bombing and reconnaissance aircraft, which would, in the event, make possible the RFC's entry into strategic bombing. The aircraft that more than met this need was the D.H.4.

The D.H.4 was a well-designed single-strut biplane made of spruce and ash covered with fabric, except for the front section of the fuselage which was panelled with plywood. The pilot sat beneath the centre of the wing, with the gunner behind him; between them was the 60-gal (273-litre) fuel tank. The engine was the only part that gave any problems while this aircraft was being introduced. The original prototype of the D.H.4 had a new BHP test engine, which gave just over 200 hp (149 kW) and was also used in the later versions. The D.H.4 showed such great promise that 50 were ordered. The prototype performed so well even in its first flight that large numbers were in use within a very short space of time. The second aircraft had a 250-hp (186-kW) Rolls Royce engine. The framework and the central wing struts had been modified slightly by this time, the pilot had been placed in a different position, and the gunner now had a swivelling machine gun. Other engines used in later production aircraft were the 200-hp (149-kW) RAF 3a, the Siddeley Puma with 230-hp (172-kW; a version of the BHP), the 260-hp (194-kW)

Another patrol mission for E844, a D.H.9A operated by No. 8 Sqn as part of its long association with the Middle East. Note the close proximity of pilot and observer, thus enabling effective communication – an improvement on the early D.H.4.

Fiat A-12 and the 250-hp (186-kW) Rolls-Royce, later the Eagle. Eventually, the 375-hp (280-kW) Eagle VIII engine was fitted, which required a higher undercarriage and a larger propeller.

The first aircraft to become operational went to France with No. 55 Squadron, RFC, which flew from Fienvilliers on 6 April 1917 to bomb Valenciennes. The aircraft was a great advance on previous bombers, having a higher ceiling, a maximum speed in excess of 100 mph (161 km/h) at 15,000 ft (4570 m) and, by flying in formation, the ability to provide a formidable fire power to tackle German fighters struggling at heights at which they were ill equipped to fight. So, at the beginning of its career, the D.H.4 was able to operate without fighter escort deep behind the enemy lines. The only disadvantage it had was the placing of the fuel tank between the pilot and gunner, making communication between the two almost impossible and ensuring that, when the aircraft was hit by enemy fire, both crew members were incinerated, giving the aircraft the soubriquet 'The Flaming Coffin'. Re-equipment went ahead, No. 57 Squadron receiving D.H.4s in May, No. 18 Squadron in June, and No. 25 Squadron in July, while new squadrons came to France already D.H.4-equipped.

The RNAS had also ordered the aircraft and this version was built by Westland at Yeovil, having the Eagle engine,

This is an Airco D.H.4 operated by No. 2 Sqn RNAS immediately prior to its redesignation as No. 202 Sqn RFC in 1918. Based at Bergues and Varssenaere during World War 1, the aircraft was used for bombing and reconnaissance missions over Belgium until the Armistice. The squadron also used the D.H.9 during the war, returning to the UK in March 1919.

Originally one of 100 D.H.4s produced under contract by Palladium Autocars, F5764 was converted to D.H.4A configuration to carry two passengers in the enclosed cabin. Up to five aircraft served with the RAF, and there were a further nine civil conversions.

two forward-firing Vickers guns in place of one, and a Scarff ring for the observer. The naval aircraft went first to No. 2 Squadron, at the same time as No. 55 Squadron received its D.H.4s, and then to Nos 5, 6 and 17 Squadrons. These were all based in the north of the Western Front and were used for a variety of tasks in addition to bombing, such as gunranging with ships, reconnaissance and photographic work. Most of their bombing targets were the naval installations at Ostend and Zeebrugge; it was also a first for the D.H.4 when No. 17 Squadron, by then renumbered No. 217 Squadron, RAF, sank a U-boat off the Belgian coast on 12 August 1918. The naval aircraft also flew with the coastal defence stations on North Sea patrols, and with Home Defence flights in the United Kingdom, having occasional brushes with Zeppelins; one D.H.4, flown by Major E. Cadbury, shot down the Zeppelin L70 on 5 August 1918, 40 miles (64 km) out over the North Sea when operating from the base at Great Yarmouth. To make the D.H.4 more suitable for such tasks a floatplane version was modified and tested at Felixstowe, but this variant was never put into production.

As well as forming part of the Independent Air Force when it was formed as the first strategic bombing organization in the world, the D.H.4 also served in small numbers in such overseas theatres as Italy and the Aegean.

The Americans showed much interest in the D.H.4 as they had nothing comparable, although they had a fine new engine, the Liberty 12, which was expected to develop 400 hp (298 kW). Accordingly, the Americans decided to build the D.H.4 under licence in America. The American flair for mass-production meant that by the end of 1918 some 4,587 American DH-4 aircraft (as the type was known locally) had been built, three times more than had been produced in

An Airco D.H.4A of the Belgian airline SNETA, which began operating its continental routes with the predecessor of this model, the Airco D.H.4. The picture was taken in 1921. Today's commercial passengers would hesitate before taking continental journeys in this aircraft.

the UK. In the United Kingdom the D.H.4 did not last long after the Armistice in RAF service, being superseded first by the D.H.9, but then overwhelmingly by the D.H.9A. Not a few were sent to Commonwealth countries to enable them to form their own air forces under what was known as the 'Imperial Gift Scheme'. Those which went to Canada performed a number of valuable roles, particularly in respect of the great forests where as single-seaters they flew fire patrols, and many were also used on early mail routes, remaining in service until 1928. D.H.4s were also sold after the war to Belgium, Persia and Spain from the United Kingdom. However, in the USA the DH-4 really took off after World War 1 because the government decreed that there would not be funds for new aircraft but that they would be available for rebuilding existing aircraft. As there were by then 4,846 DH-4s in existence in America, the possibilities were immense and, with the Americans' penchant for adaptation, no fewer than 60 different versions of the DH-4 were evolved, and even 10 years later many were still serving. The type flew with the US Army, US Navy and US Marine Corps, and was used as a bomber, trainer and transport. And for several years the DH-4 was the backbone of the airmail service flown by the US Postal Service in the United States. The type was still on the services' inventories in 1929, by which time many had entered civilian use.

Civilian versions of the D.H.4 appeared in the United Kingdom as well, for the production lines were still pumping out new aircraft at the time of the Armistice and an aircraft such as the D.H.4 had a basic airframe suitable for a variety of duties. The type entered into continental services in 1919 with Aircraft Transport and Travel until better aircraft were available, others went out to Australia and figured in the first air mail services of QANTAS, and one of their aircraft was still flying (on joy riding flights) in 1934. The first Belgian airline, SNETA, used four D.H.4s to open up its continental routes; but the D.H.4s did not last long in service with the Belgians.

One D.H.4 was highly modified, with the lower wing cut right down and the aircraft turned into a single-bay biplane

Without doubt the best Airco D.H.4s were those powered by the 375-hp (280-kW) Eagle VIII, but this engine was costly and in short supply (and, because of its bigger propeller, needed longer landing gears). Many other engines were therefore fitted, most of the earlier machines having the RAF.3a, a water-cooled V-12 of only 200 hp (149 kW) produced by the Royal Aircraft Factory. A7712 was one of the RAF-engined machines, built by Airco in summer 1917 and delivered to No. 18 Sqn RFC, which with No. 49 Sqn used the RAF-engined version exclusively from June 1917. The frontal radiator tapered slightly from top to bottom (the reverse of the BHP version) and had a single exhaust stack. At first the valuable D.H.4s were kept above 15,000 ft (4572 m), but during the crucial days of March 1918 No. 18 Sqn was ordered over the front at low level to harass the advancing enemy troops.

Airco D.H.4 and D.H.9

Specification

Airco D.H.4 (Eagle VIII)

Type: two-seat bomber

Powerplant: one 375-hp (280-kW) Rolls-Royce Eagle VIII water-cooled V-12 piston engine

Performance: maximum speed 143 mph (230 km/h) at sea level; cruising speed about 108 mph (174 km/h); time to reach 15,000 ft (4572 m) 16.5 minutes; service ceiling 22,000 ft (6700 m); endurance (maximum) 6 hours 45 minutes

Weights: empty 2,387 lb (1083 kg); loaded (clean) 3,472 lb (1575 kg) (two 230 lb [104.3 kg] bombs) 3,932 lb (1784 kg)

Dimensions: span 42 ft 4.625 in (12.92 m); length (Eagle) 30 ft 8 in (9.347 m); height (Eagle VIII) 11 ft 0 in (3.353 m); wing area 434 sq ft (40.32 m²)

Armament: one 0.303-in (7.7-mm) Vickers machine-gun firing ahead; single or twin Lewis of same calibre mounted on observer's Scarff ring; racks under lower wing for two bombs of 230 lb (104.3 kg), four of 112 lb (50.8 kg), depth charges or other stores

Airco D.H.4 and D.H.9

The lack of suitable American aircraft for use in World War 1 led to the United States producing the D.H.4 as the 'Liberty Plane', with 4,846 being built by three companies. This DH-4B served with the 168th Aero Squadron as part of the American Expeditionary Force in France, one of 13 squadrons equipped with the type. But there were severe problems with the aircraft, most notably the landing characteristics and the lethal positioning of the fuel tank between pilot and observer.

with outboard bracing struts to become the D.H.4R racer with a new Napier Lion engine, with which it set up a British closed-circuit speed record of 129.3 mph (208.08 km/h) in the Aerial Derby on 21 June 1919. It subsequently flew at 150 mph (241 km/h). This and other civil D.H.4s were one-off conversions by their new owners, mainly differing in the rearrangements made to the rear (observer's) position by the fitting of different seating arrangements. However, there was in existence in 1919 an official civil conversion of the D.H.4, known as the D.H.4A. It arose from the fact that D.H.4s were being used by No. 86 (Communications) Wing of the RAF on its cross-Channel passenger services around the time of the Armistice, providing transport for civil servants, military attachés, MPs and ministers flitting to and fro. One of the cabinet ministers, Bonar Law, requested that a modified version should be built to accommodate its passengers in a cabin. In the event this became a major variant because, by the time the windowed cabin had been built of plywood, the centre of gravity had moved considerably aft and therefore the upper mainplane had to be rerigged aft so that the biplane became unstaggered. The resulting aeroplane became known as the D.H.4A and at least eight aircraft were modified to this configuration. They went into service with No. 2 (Communications) Squadron of the wing flying the route between Kenley and Buc, and continued regular services until September 1919, when the wing was disbanded for lack of the traffic to sustain it.

The remaining aircraft were sold to Handley Page Ltd, which immediately prepared them for use on its impending routes. At the same time four brand new D.H.4s were converted to D.H.4A standard and sold to Aircraft Transport and Travel, and one such made its niche in British aviation history by flying the first British commercial cross-Channel service with one passenger and freight consisting of news-

papers, grouse, Devonshire cream and leather! AT&T carried on with services until the end of 1920, when the company went into liquidation. In the meantime, Handley Page Air Transport had started regular services using D.H.4s and D.H.4As from Cricklewood to Paris and Schiphol (Amsterdam), and two more D.H.4As were used by SNETA. A further D.H.4A served with Instone Air Line out of Croydon on the Paris route, transferring to the Central Aircraft Company in 1922 and winning the King's Cup in that year, the first in which the race was run. A further D.H.4A went to Argentina.

The D.H.4 had become one of the greats of World War 1, pioneering true strategic bombing, and also being the mainstay of budding aviation in the USA. But aircraft development does not stand still, and even as the D.H.4 was beginning to win its spurs over the Western Front a successor was starting flight trials at Hendon. As mentioned above, the original D.H.4 prototype had used a prototype BHP engine which showed much promise. As time went by this engine was developed into the Galloway Adriatic, which powered the prototype of a new aircraft with basically the same wings and tail of the D.H.4 but a new fuselage, placing the pilot and observer back to back. In the meantime, the Siddeley-Deasey Car Company had modified the BHP engine for mass production, improving it for service use and calling it the Puma. Forecasts estimated that this new engine would produce 300 hp (224 kW), but it had extended teething troubles and was derated to 230 hp (172 kW). In the meantime the new aircraft had been ordered in quantity. Aircraft came pouring off the production lines, but the commander of the RFC in France, hearing about the D.H.9 (for this was the designation of the new aircraft) and its poor performance, tried to stop its entry into squadron service as it was clearly inferior to the D.H.4 it was intended to replace. Alternative engines were tried, and

Having served in World War 1, this D.H.9 was transferred to the South African Air Force and fitted with a 200-hp (149-kW) Wolseley Viper, a change which for some inexplicable reason led to the aircraft being named the Mantis.

Prior to development of the three-passenger D.H.9C, the D.H.9B offered places for two people, one fore and one aft of the pilot. Twenty were built for civil use in the UK, this machine having passed later to the Dutch civil register for use with KLM.

some production aircraft entered service with the Fiat A-12, but with production wheels so squarely set in motion, there was no turning back and the D.H.9 entered service with the RFC and RNAS. The first units to fly them in France were Nos 6 and 11 Squadrons, RNAS, and again the type was used mainly for attacks on naval installations on the Belgian coast. The first RFC units were Nos 98 and 99 Squadrons, followed by Nos 103, 104, 107 and 108, No. 98 moving to France on 3 April 1918, two days after the Royal Air Force had been formed.

Not only was the performance of the D.H.9 poorer than that of the D.H.4, the main disadvantage being its low ceiling of 13,000 ft (3960 m), but the Puma engine was chronically unreliable. Early raids by the squadrons resulted in between one third and one half of the aircraft taking part being lost on each raid, a totally unacceptable figure. It is significant that the Netherlands army was able to operate a squadron of nine D.H.9s, all aircraft of the RAF that had force landed in the Netherlands and been interned!

What the boffins in the UK could not do, the mechanics on the squadrons in France attempted to do, namely make 'home brewed' modifications to improve the reliability of the D.H.9, and it says much for their brilliant improvisation that their squadrons stayed in business and managed to achieve some successes; for, in its favour, the aircraft was a pilot's aeroplane (like most of de Havilland's) and could manoeuvre well in a dogfight and, with the revised seating arrangements, the pilot and observer were well placed to cope with enemy fire. In fact, one observer of No. 49 Squadron managed to shoot down four enemy fighters in one sortie.

The D.H.9 was also used in overseas theatres, chiefly the Mediterranean, and here it made some outstanding long-range reconnaissance flights; whether the hot, dry climate made the Puma more reliable is not recorded.

The D.H.9 squadrons fought on through 1918, and the type was even used in the UK for anti-Zeppelin and coastal defence work, and after the Armistice was used initially on the cross-Channel mail services. This was short-lived, for by July 1919 the RAF had thankfully rid itself of the D.H.9 for its replacement. The aircraft was not finished yet, however, and various airframes continued on the research and development scene, chiefly as engine test-beds for a variety

Captain Gerald Gattergood won the 'Aerial Derby' at Hendon in the Airco D.H.4R, registration K141, with a 450 hp (336 kw) Napier Lion engine. His average speed was 128 mph (206.88 km/h), racing over a private course.

of new and alternative powerplants. A few were used for deck landing trials when the new HMS *Eagle* appeared in 1921, and the most significant piece of development that any of the D.H.9s accomplished was by H9140. This aircraft was bought by Handley Page, which used it as a test-bed for the company's new aerodynamic theory of leading-edge slats. The theory ran that these slats, being auxiliary aerofoils fitted on the front of each upper wing, would provide a smooth airflow over the upper surface even when the wing would normally stall, and thus enable the aircraft to fly under full control at a slower speed. Handley Page designated the aircraft the H.P.17 and flew it in demonstrations against a standard D.H.9, demonstrating the tremendous advantages of a slatted wing.

Surplus stock operators

Although the RAF disposed of D.H.9s as quickly as possible, this was not the case elsewhere. Many emergent air forces were forming after the 'war to end all wars', and there were literally hundreds of D.H.9s in the hands of the Aircraft Disposal Company. Thus impecunious small nations could construct a sizable bomber/reconnaissance force at a price

Airco D.H.4 and D.H.9 variants

D.H.4: two prototypes and 1,449 production aircraft, the latter built by the Aircraft Manufacturing Company (Airco). F.W. Berwick & Co. Ltd, Glendower Aircraft Co. Ltd, Palladium Autocars Ltd, Vulcan Motor & Engineering Co., Waring & Gillow Ltd and Westland Aircraft Works; an additional 15 aircraft to this pattern were built for the Belgian army air arm by SABCA in Belgium; of this total 21 found their way onto the civil register after World War 1 (three in the UK, four in Belgium, two in Australia and 12 in Canada); engines used in the D.H.4 were the 200-hp (149-kW) RAF 3A, the 230-hp (172-kW) BHP, the 230-hp (172-kW) Siddeley Puma, the 250-hp (186-kW) Rolls-Royce Mk III, the 250-hp (186-kW) Rolls-Royce Mk IV, the 260-hp (194-kW) Fiat and the 275-hp (205-kW) Rolls-Royce Eagle VI; there were also 15 experimental installations

D.H.4A: designation of Liberty-engined aircraft modified to carry two passengers in a small enclosed cabin aft of the open pilot's cockpit; it is believed that five such machines were operated by the RAF, while civil conversions amounted to two Belgian and seven British aircraft

D.H.4R: designation of one special racing aircraft with the 450-hp (336-kW) Napier Lion engine and clipped lower wings

DH-4: designation applied to US-built aircraft; orders amounted to 12,348 aircraft, but of these only 4,846 were built (less than 200 being delivered to units in France before the Armistice); this baseline American model was powered by the 420-hp (313-kW) Liberty engine, though other versions of the Liberty engine were used in the various developed models listed below; manufacturers were the Dayton-Wright Airplane Co. (3,106 aircraft), the Fisher Body Corporation (1,600 aircraft) and the Standard Aircraft Corporation (140 aircraft)

DH-4Amb-1: ambulance model with the ability to carry one litter

DH-4Amb-2: ambulance model with the ability to carry two litters

DH-4Ard: dual-control cross-country model with additional fuel capacity

DH-4B: much-modified development with the pilot and main fuel tank exchanged and with the fuselage covered in ply

DH-4B-1: improved version of the DH-4B with additional tankage

DH-4B-2: revised model with 'crashworthy' fuel system

DH-4B-3: version with considerably increased fuel capacity

DH-4B-4: airways version with standard fuel tankage

DH-4B-5: US equivalent to the D.H.4A three-seater with small cabin

DH-4BD: DH-4B equipped for crop-dusting

DH-4BG: DH-4B equipped for the laying of chemical smoke screens

DH-4BK: night-flying version of the DH-4B

DH-4BM: messenger version with rear-fuselage compartment

DH-4BM-1: dual-control transport version of the DH-4BM with additional fuel capacity

DH-4BM-2: increased-tankage version of the DH-4BM-1

XDH-4BP: experimental photographic aircraft with cameras in front cockpit

DH-4BP-1: photographic aircraft

XDH-4BP-2: experimental photographic aircraft with additional tankage and the wings of the USD-9

DH-4BP-3: improved version of the DH-4BP-1

XDH-4BS: experimental version of the DH-4B with a supercharged engine

DH-4BT: dual-control trainer version of the DH-4B

DH-4BW: test-bed aircraft for the 300-hp (224-kW) Wright-Hispano 'H' engine

DH-4C: test-bed aircraft for the 350-hp (261-kW) Packard 1A-1237 engine

XDH-4L: aerodynamically improved cross-country racer with large fuel capacity

DH-4M: much improved development with steel-tube fuselage; 59 built by Boeing

DH-4M-1: improved version of the DH-4M; 97 built by Boeing, as well as another 30 used by the US Marine Corps with the designation O2B-1

DH-4M-1K: DH-4M-1 equipped as a target tug

DH-4M-1T: dual-control trainer version of the DH-4M-1, of which 22 were produced by conversion from standard airframes

DH-4M-2: version of the DH-4M-1 with increased fuel capacity; 135 built by the Atlantic Aircraft Corporation

DH-4M-2A: airways version of the DH-4M-2

DH-4M-2K: target tug version of the DH-4M-2

DH-4M-2P: photographic version of the DH-4M-2

DH-4M-2S: supercharged version of the DH-4M-2 with reduced fuel capacity

DH-4M-2T: dual-control trainer version of the DH-4M-2

Twin DH-4: designation of a twin-engine version developed by LWF (Lowe, Willard and Fowler) in 1919 as an airmail aircraft; span was increased to 52 ft 6 in (16.00 m) and maximum take-off weight to 5,490 lb (2490 kg), power being provided by two 200-hp (149-kW) Hall-Scott L-6 inlines for a maximum speed of 105 mph (169 km/h); twin vertical tails were added, and production amounted to 20 Post Office and 10 US Army aircraft

XCO-7: single Boeing-built corps observation development with the wings developed for the Loening COA-1 amphibian

XCO-7A: single Boeing-built development of the XCO-7 with DH-4M-1 fuselage and Loening tapered wings, larger tailplane and split oleopneumatic landing gear

XCO-7B: single Boeing-built development of the XCO-7 with an inverted Liberty engine

XCO-8: single conversion of a DH-4M-2 with Loening wings

D.H.9: recast version of the D.H.4 with the pilot and observer/gunner located closer together for enhanced tactical capability; production amounted to one prototype (converted from a D.H.4) and 3,204 production aircraft, the latter being built by the Aircraft Manufacturing Co., Alliance Aeroplane Co. Ltd, F. W. Berwick & Co. Ltd, Crossley Motors Ltd, Cubitt Ltd, Mann, Egerton & Co. Ltd, NAF 1, NAF 2, Short Bros, Vulcan Motor & Engineering Co., Waring & Gillow Ltd, G. & J. Weir Ltd, Westland Aircraft Works and Whitehead Aircraft Co. Ltd; other examples were built in Belgium by SABCA (30 aircraft) and in Spain by Hispano-Suiza (perhaps 500 aircraft); de Havilland also exported aircraft to the Netherlands, and among the many handed on to other air forces were

machines redesignated **Mantis, M'pala I** and **M'pala II** by the South African Air Force when re-engined with the 200-hp (149-kW) Wolseley Viper, 450-hp (336-kW) Bristol Jupiter VI and 480-hp (358-kW) Bristol Jupiter VIII respectively; seven trial engine installations were made in British D.H.9s, but the standard powerplants were the 230-hp (172-kW) Siddeley Puma, the 250-hp (186-kW) Fiat A-12, the 430-hp (321-kW) Napier Lion and the 435-hp (324-kW) Liberty 12A; many D.H.9s later passed on to the civil registers of several countries, 34 in the UK, nine in Australia, five in New Zealand, six in Belgium, four in India and four in Denmark

D.H.9A: much-improved version of the D.H.9 designed round the Liberty engine, though the first two of three prototypes had the 375-hp (280-kW) Rolls-Royce Eagle VIII; production amounted to 2,300 aircraft built by the Aircraft Manufacturing Co., Mann, Egerton & Co. Ltd, Whitehead Aircraft Co. Ltd, Vulcan Motor & Engineering Co., Westland Aircraft Works, F. W. Berwick & Co. Ltd, Handley Page Ltd, Gloucester Aircraft, Parnall Aircraft Co. and de Havilland Aircraft Co. Ltd; civil conversions amounted to 13 British and 11 Canadian aircraft

D.H.9AJ: single prototype with 465-hp (347-kW) Bristol Jupiter VI radial and divided landing gear

D.H.9B: designation of 20 aircraft converted for the British civil register as three seaters with two passenger seats (one forward and one aft of the pilot)

D.H.9C: designation of aircraft modified to carry three passengers (one forward and two aft of the pilot); these civil conversions appeared in the UK (13 aircraft), Australia (three aircraft) and Spain (three aircraft)

D.H.9J: designation of modernized aircraft produced by conversion in the late 1920s with 385-hp (287-kW) Armstrong Siddeley Jaguar III radials, Handley Page leading-edge slats and a number of control and structural improvements; the designation was also used for the South African M'pala development; 14 such civil conversions were carried out in the UK

D.H.9R: single racing aircraft with sesquiplane wing and 465-hp (347-kW) M Napier Lion II engine

USD-9A: US version of the D.H.9, of which only 13 (nine by the engineering Division at McCook Field and four by Dayton-Wright) of a planned 4,000 were completed

Airco D.H.4 and D.H.9

Service in the Middle East saw the use of aluminium dope on the main airframe, this No. 45 Sqn D.H.9A also sporting the red rim of 'A' Flight and the winged camel badge signifying the squadron's long association with the Middle East. This aircraft was based at Heliopolis in 1928 for patrol duties in Egypt and Palestine. Note the auxiliary radiator under the nose for desert use.

they could afford. If the aircraft were not the best for fighting, they were certainly good value for training budding airmen in the arts of aerial warfare, so business was brisk. Belgium took 18 to form its day bomber force, and Poland had a squadron's worth, 12 aircraft. Afghanistan, Greece, Eire, Latvia and the Netherlands all took aircraft, and the Netherlands, having returned those interned, then purchased 46 for service at home and in the East Indies and began assembling its own. An amazing fact about the Dutch aircraft is that they were re-engined in 1934 with Wright Whirlwinds and some were still in service in 1937, a tribute to the correctness of the basic airframe. Peru, Romania, Spain and Switzerland all took D.H.9s into their complements, and the aircraft figured in the Imperial Gift to Commonwealth nations. Biggest recipient of the D.H.9 was South Africa, which acquired 48 that served in the Union for a long time, many being re-engined with Bristol Jupiters and named M'palas. They were in action in 1922 during the Boudelzvartz rebellion, and one aircraft made the first Pretoria to Cape Town flight, taking 9 hours 25 minutes in March 1924. So the D.H.9 was greater in its latter days than it had ever been in RAF service. But its fame paled when compared with that of its replacement.

Both the D.H.4 and the D.H.9 had been hampered in production because of the lack of sufficient suitable engines. To remedy this overall shortage, and when convinced that a winner could be found across the Atlantic, large orders were placed for the American Liberty 12 which produced 400 hp (298 kW). This engine was lined up for a D.H.9 replacement as quickly as possible. Unfortunately, the de Havilland design team was up to its ears in producing the organization's first production twin-engine bomber, the D.H.10, so the responsibility for developing this new single-engine day bomber was given to Yeovil-based Westland Aircraft, which had produced D.H.4s and D.H.9s for the RFC and RNAS. This was an opportunity to take the good qualities of both

earlier types, marry them to the excellent Liberty engine and produce what by any standards would be an outstanding aeroplane. And this Westland achieved by strengthening the fuselage for the heavier engine and by increasing the span and chord of the mainplanes.

The first two prototypes, in order to speed things along, were fitted with scarce Rolls-Royce Eagle VIII engines in order to work out the type aerodynamically, then the production aircraft had the Packard Liberty. The aircraft could carry up to 660 lb (299 kg) of bombs on external racks, and the observer's cockpit had provision for twin Lewis guns, otherwise the configuration was as before. By June 1918, enough production aircraft had been delivered to form one squadron. This was No. 110, which began receiving its aircraft at Kenley in that month; all its aircraft had been subscribed by the Nizam of Hyderabad and were suitably decorated, the squadron henceforth being known as the Hyderabad Squadron. It went to France on the last day of August 1918 and flew its first bombing raid on Boulay aerodrome two weeks later. This was followed by raids deeper into Germany, and losses mounted as a result not of any fault in the aircraft but of the fact that the crews were generally 'green'. The squadron fought on until the Armistice, having by then dropped 10½ tons of bombs. One other squadron, No. 99, received some 'Nineacks' (as the

One of de Havilland's 'own' D.H.9s was the D.H.9J, the most notable difference from previous models being the adoption of a 385-hp (287-kW) Armstrong Siddeley Jaguar III radial engine. Other modifications, made in the 1920s, included Handley Page leading-edge slats. Fourteen D.H.9Js were produced.

type became known in the service) in time to use them in action, and the comparison between the performance of the D.H.9A and that of the D.H.9 was very apparent as the squadron was also operating the older type at the same time.

The type also went into service with the Americans on the Western Front, principally with the Marine Corps Northern Bombing Groups which began operations in October, just before the Armistice called a halt to all bombing. By then Nos 18 and 105 Squadrons, RAF, had also received the type. As other squadrons disbanded, the D.H.9A units soldiered on with the Army of Occupation in Germany, providing a useful component to run scheduled mail services on the continent, but within a year of the Armistice this task was over and by January 1920 only No. 99 Squadron was left with the D.H.9A in service.

The aircraft, however, continued in production in the UK for it was seen to be suitable for the post-war Royal Air Force. This was soon proved to be so for already the service had become operational once more, with fighting on India's border with Afghanistan. Reinforcements were sent out to India, one such being the only D.H.9A squadron, No. 99. Flying from Mianwali, it was immediately thrown into the arid operations involved in taming the tribes up amongst the mountains. The first lesson learnt was that the Nineack's performance in the heat of India was but a fraction of its temperate abilities. Even with extra radiators, its ceiling, on a good day, was only some 13,500 ft (4115 m), so it had perforce to wind its way through the mountain passes. On 1 April 1920, No. 99 was renumbered No. 27 Squadron, sporting the flying elephant badge on its fins. Although the

De Havilland D.H.9A cutaway drawing key

38 Streamlined flying wires
39 Trailing edge cut-out
40 Front spar
41 Wing rib construction
42 Compression ribs
43 Wing internal wire bracing
44 Leading edge ribs
45 Port navigation light
46 Rounded wing tip
47 Port upper aileron
48 Aileron control horns
49 Aileron cable
50 Rear spar
51 Trailing edge ribs
52 Rear strut
53 Windscreen
54 Instrument panel
55 Machine-gun ammunition boxes
56 Pilot's control column
57 Engine throttle controls
58 Rudder pedal bar
59 Tailplane trim wheel
60 Pilot's seat
61 Cockpit coaming
62 Observer's control column
63 Observer's seat

77 Fin construction
78 Rudder horn balance
79 Rudder control horn
80 Sternpost
81 Rudder construction
82 Tail navigation light
83 Port tailplane
84 Port elevator
85 Elevator control horns
86 Tailplane incidence control screw jack
87 Ventral fairing
88 Tailplane trim cables
89 Steel tailskid shoe
90 Tailskid
91 Elastic cord shock absorber
92 Fuselage diagonal wire bracing
93 Bottom longeron
94 Port wing tip skid
95 Rear fuselage bulkheads
96 Bottom longeron joint
97 Elevator control hinge
98 Deep section front fuselage bottom longeron
99 Spare wheel mounting
100 Bottom wing spar attachments

1 Two-bladed fixed pitch wooden propeller
2 Starter attachment dog
3 Propeller hub fixing bolts
4 Radiator shutters
5 Filler cap
6 Cooling intake
7 Radiator
8 Radiator mounting
9 Drain cock
10 Starboard wing tip skid
11 Aircraft picketing cable
12 400-hp (298-kW) Liberty 12-cylinder Vee engine
13 Exhaust pipe
14 Engine cowling louvres

15 Starboard upper wing leading edge
16 Wing panel fabric covering
17 Starboard interplane struts
18 Front fuselage frame construction
19 Ash engine bearer
20 Tropical radiator
21 Water pipe
22 Engine bay fireproof bulkhead
23 Oil tank
24 Oil filler cap
25 Centre section front struts
26 Diagonal wire bracing
27 Fuel vent

28 Gravity fuel tank, capacity 8 Imp gal (36 litres)
29 Wind driven fuel pumps
30 Fuel filler cap
31 Main fuel tank mounting
32 Starboard main fuel tank, capacity 50 Imp gal (227 litres)
33 Port main fuel tank, capacity 50 Imp gal (227 litres)
34 Vickers 0.303-in (7.7-mm) machine-gun
35 Pilot's gunsight
36 Centre section rear struts
37 Inboard interplane struts

64 Scarff elevating gear
65 Gun elevating gear
66 Observer's Lewis gun
67 Outboard interplane struts
68 Reconnaissance camera mounting
69 Fuselage upper longeron
70 Plywood rear decking
71 Port lower wing leading edge
72 Diagonal wire bracing
73 Squadron Leader's pennant
74 Aileron connecting cable
75 Rudder cables
76 Tailplane bracing wire

101 Undercarriage rear strut
102 Fuselage bomb racks
103 Two 112-lb (51-kg) bombs
104 Port mainwheel
105 Wheel spokes
106 Tyre valve access
107 Split axle beam
108 Wheel disc fabric cover
109 Elastic cord shock absorber
110 Starboard mainwheel
111 Undercarriage front struts
112 Undercarriage wire bracing
113 Starboard wing bomb racks
114 Four 20-lb (9.1-kg) bombs

Airco D.H.4 and D.H.9

While many war surplus aircraft found their way to lesser military powers, 19 D.H.9s were converted as civilian passenger aircraft carrying four people, including the pilot. Thirteen such aircraft were operated in the UK (with three going to Australia and three to Spain) with this example, operated by Northern Air Lines, being the last D.H.9C in service in 1932 at Barton.

Third Afghan War was supposed to have ended in May 1920, in fact the squadron was almost continuously in action during the 1920s, being supplemented by No. 60 on D.H.9As in 1923 when the latter shed its temperamental D.H.10s. It fell to these two squadrons to pioneer the peacetime use of the RAF in India and, apart from the intermittent operations, they flew several long-distance flights across the sub-continent. In 1925, the RAF was allowed to conduct a whole 'war' by itself, and managed to contain one such tribal war with only two casualties, largely as a result of the effectiveness of the D.H.9A squadrons. In 1928, the two squadrons were involved in the emergency flights to evacuate Kabul, escorting the Vickers Victorias of No. 70 Squadron to accomplish this feat. The Nineacks actually stayed in service in India until 1930 when Westland Wapitis, a new aircraft, but fitted with surplus D.H.9A wings, took their place.

The D.H.9A was not confined to India. It had been chosen to be the standard day bomber for the reconstituted Royal Air Force in the UK and, as and when Trenchard could form new squadrons, so the D.H.9A moved in. No. 207 Squadron re-formed at Bircham Newton on 1 February 1920 and No. 39 two months later. In the autumn of 1922 the former went to Turkey for a year because of the crisis there, returning after a fruitless year. These two squadrons maintained the light bomber force of the RAF through the 1920s, their D.H.9As being replaced by Wapitis during 1928. But they were augmented in the day bomber role during the 1920s by the formation of the Auxiliary Air Force, and six of these squadrons received D.H.9As as their initial equipment, starting with 602 (City of Glasgow) Squadron in September 1925. It was on this safe and doughty aircraft that this volunteer force cut its teeth and laid the foundations for the formidable air force it became in time for World War 2. By 1930 the Nineack had left the AAF and was virtually out of service in the UK. It had also served at Martlesham Heath where it became a ready tool of the experimental squadrons, and had spent a brief period in the early 1920s with No. 3 Squadron on coastal reconnaissance duties.

In September 1922 Captain F. L. Barnard won the first King's Cup race in this Airco D.H.4A (G-EAMU) at an average speed of 122.3 mph (196.8 km/h).

Success in the Middle East

It is probably in the Middle East, however, that the D.H.9A flew its most significant role. In 1921 it was agreed in Cairo that the Royal Air Force alone would accept responsibility for control of the area – a bold step indeed. The new Iraq Command had four squadrons, all equipped with the D.H.9A: Nos 8, 30, 55 and 84. These units had already been in action in 1919–20 when the first Arab revolt took place, although not all of them were fully equipped with the D.H.9A at the time. Now these squadrons began a system of air policing whereby, with regular flights over key areas, any inter-tribal enterprises were discouraged. If raids by tribesmen began, their villages were notified by messages dropped that bombing raids would take place at a specified time a few days later. This gave the factions the opportunity to evacuate personnel and thus preserve life while at the same time hampering the tribes by removing their possessions. It was a very effective method which had great success. Despite this, sporadic outbreaks of fighting continued during the 1920s.

The method was transferred to Palestine in the mid-1920s when trouble flared there, and a newly equipped No. 14 Squadron used its Nineacks to good effect in the fighting against Ibn Saud. Two more Middle East squadrons received the D.H.9A, No. 47 at Helwan in 1920 (remaining as a base squadron in Egypt with detachments in the Sudan) and No. 45 Squadron at Heliopolis in 1927 (converting from Vickers Vernon bomber transports).

In 1927, No. 8 Squadron transferred to Aden and started its unique control of the Protectorate, converting to Fairey IIIFs shortly after this and the Westland Wapiti began to replace the D.H.9A overseas in the late 1920s, and by 1930 the last D.H.9As were leaving the Middle East. Now there were but few of the breed left, most of them in England with training units (a two-seater trainer version had been produced and used in the flying training schools) and with experimental establishments such as Farnborough. It had been a wonderful mainstay for the decade after World War 1, had been the instrument with which the RAF's revolutionary policing methods had been worked out and honed in the Empire, and had seen the Auxiliary Air Force established at home.

The type had gone into service with Commonwealth air forces in small numbers, and a few had appeared in civil guise though to nothing like the same extent as the D.H.4. The D.H.9A racer version, the D.H.9R, had appeared in 1919 but was not as punchy as the D.H.4R. Despite this it established a closed-circuit record at 149.43 mph (240.48 km/h) in November 1919. A large number were used in research and development flying, carrying on Handley Page's slot trials, trying out a plethora of different engine types and being used to test new propellers, landing gear legs and many other ancillary devices. Even when the Nineack itself was finished, its many surplus wings flew on in the Westland Wapiti into the early years of World War 2.

All these aircraft, from the D.H.4 to the D.H.9A, were amongst the most important aircraft of World War 1 and the ten years afterwards. The specifications they fulfilled with their abilities, flexibility and adaptability were being imitated as late as the 1930s by other aircraft builders.

Fokker F.VII:
the Dutch master

After World War 1 the best-selling airliners did not come from the Allies but from defeated Germany's Junkers and 'Flying Dutchman' Anthony Fokker, whose German factory had produced the enemy's top fighters. Fokker's series of high-wing monoplane transports also supported a major industry in the USA.

Germany's military defeat in 1918 was followed by the collapse of the political system. Sailors from the navy mutinied in Wilhelmshaven, and then in Kiel. The mutiny spread to the hinterland of these cities and rebellion was in the air in many large towns. In Bavaria the Wittelsbachers had fallen and on 9 November the November Revolution, as it was called, reached its high point: Kaiser Wilhelm II was forced to abdicate. On the same day Philipp Scheidemann declared the German Republic against the will of Friedrich Ebert, and shortly afterwards Karl Liebknecht proclaimed a Free Socialist Republic. During this time of political confusion Anthony Fokker managed to escape from his aircraft factory in Schwerin, which was being guarded by revolutionaries. The guards are believed to have been shot because they failed to recognise Fokker. Fokker transferred large sums of money to his Dutch homeland, and only two years later he completed an audacious project. The Allies had strictly forbidden Germany to build large aircraft during the postwar period. But in 1920 Fokker still had large stocks of aircraft parts left over from wartime production, and using six freight trains, each with sixty wagons, he smuggled these components past the eyes of the Allies from his old factory in Schwerin to Amsterdam, where by now he had built a new factory.

However, back in early 1919 Fokker and chief designer Reinhold Platz had decided they had better start designing passenger aircraft. The first result was the F.I. There was no argument about the structure. The fuselage was to be made of steel tubes, accurately cut and, where necessary, curved, and welded together in a precision jig, with fabric covering. This was how they had made their fighters. Platz had pioneered unbraced wooden wings whose plywood covering was an early form of stressed skin. By making the wing deep it could be light yet strong enough to need no external bracing. The wing of the F.I. was almost a direct scale-up of that of the D.VIII fighter. This was to be mounted in the parasol position above the fuselage, the latter having an impressive row of open cockpits for the pilot and six passengers, the latter in three side-by-side pairs. But before this prototype (the V 44) had got very far, Fokker and Platz took a decision that probably made the difference between failure and success. They decided to redesign the fuselage to accommodate the passengers in comfort, internally.

The result was the V 45 prototype, or F.II, first flown by Fokker's trusty chief pilot and school head, Bernard de

This single-engine version of the Fokker F-VIIA was flown by Swissair in the early 1930s and has now become a museum piece.

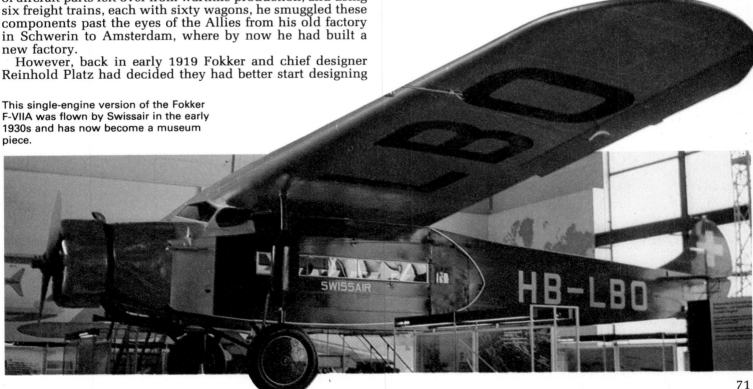

Fokker F.VII

Specification

Fokker F.VII-3m

Type: 8/10 seat medium range passenger transport monoplane

Powerplant: three 215-hp (160-kW) Armstrong Siddeley Lynx air-cooled radial piston engines fitted with two-blade wooden fixed-pitch propellers*

Performance: maximum speed at sea level 115 mph (185 km/h); cruising speed 93 mph (149 km/h); range with standard tanks at cruising speed 477 miles (768 km); service ceiling 10,170 ft (3100 m); landing approach speed 62 mph (100 km/h)

Weights: empty weight 6,393 lb (2900 kg); maximum take-off 11,023 lb (5000 kg)

Dimensions: span 71 ft 2½ in (21.71 m); length 47 ft 7 in (14.50 m); height 12 ft 9 in (3.88 m); wing area 727.66 sq ft (67.6 m²)

Accommodation: two crew in side-by-side seating in forward enclosed cockpit and eight passengers in two rows of four seats either side of a central aisle in main cabin

* Note: Fokker F.VIIs were fitted with a variety of engines, and the performance of different aircraft varied slightly from that shown above

This is the F.VII-3m commissioned by Mr R. Wanamaker for a special New York to Paris flight in 1927. Under the command of Commander Richard E. Byrd, this was intended to explore the possibilities of transatlantic commercial services. The aircraft was fitted with the long-span Fokker wing, long-range tanks and Wright J-5 Whirlwind engines together with an extended cockpit and an unusual forward-sloping windscreen. Named *America*, the Fokker finally departed with its four-man crew on 29 June 1927, but was forced to ditch in the English Channel near Le Havre when appalling weather conditions over Paris enveloped Le Bourget and the aircraft ran out of fuel after over 40 hours in the air.

Fokker F.VII variants

F.VII: original enlarged transport, 360-hp (268.5-kW) Rolls-Royce Eagle, six passengers
F.VIIA: improved model with eight passengers, smaller wing, aerodynamically cleaned-up and fitted with various engines in 450-hp (335.6-kW) class
F.VIIA-3m: tri-motor version of F.VIIA with same wing of 63 ft 3.8 in (19.3 m) span and 630 sq ft (58.5 m²) area, typically three engines in 200-hp (149.1-kW) class such as Wright Whirlwind or Armstrong Siddeley Lynx
F.VIIB-3m: enlarged aircraft with wing of 71 ft 2.7 in (21.71 m) span and 727 or 728 sq ft (67.5 or 67.6 m²) area and cleared to much greater weights, with various engines of 200–350-hp (149.1–261.0-kW)
F.9: US Atlantic Aviation derivative of F.VIIB-3m, usually with wing of 74 ft 2.2 in (22.61 m) span and 718 sq ft (66.7 m²)
C-2: US Army version of F.9, followed by **C-2A** series
TA-1 (later **RA-1**): US Navy version of C-2 for US Marine Corps
TA-2 (later **RA-2**): US Navy equivalent of C-2A
TA-3 (later **RA-3**): final US Navy model with 300-hp (223.7-kW) R-975 (J-6) Whirlwinds
F.10: enlarged 12-passenger Atlantic Aircraft version with 79 ft 2 in (24.13 m) span and 854 sq ft (79.34 m²) wing and 425-hp (316.9-kW) Wasp engines

F.10A: Atlantic **Super Trimotor** with enlarged 14-seat cabin
C-5: US Army version of F.10A but with 300-hp (223.7-kW) Wright R-975 engines
XC-7: US Army C-2A re-engined with 330-hp (246.1-kW) R-975s
C-7A: production development of XC-7 with larger wing, new tail and F.10A fuselage
RA-4: single F.10A for US Navy
XLB-2: single bomber derived for US Army from C-7 but with two 410-hp (305.7-kW) Wasps
F.VIII: next Dutch airline model, 893 sq ft (83 m²) wing and two Jupiters
F.IX: Dutch airliner with 1,109 sq ft (103 m²) wing and three Jupiters (also Czech **Avia F.IX**, **F.39** and **F.IXD** bomber)
F.XII: Dutch airliner with 893 sq ft (83 m²) wing and three Wasps
F.XVIII: Dutch airliner with 904 sq ft (84 m²) wing and three Wasps
F.XX: redesigned Dutch airliner with 1,033 sq ft (96 m²) wing, three 640-hp (477.2-kW) Cyclones and retractable landing gear, last Fokker trimotor

M. Badtocke

Fokker F.VII

Sir Charles Kingsford Smith's famous F.VII-3m – the *Southern Cross* – arrived at Brisbane's Eagle Farm Airport on 9 June 1928 following a 7,390-mile (11890-km) flight across the Pacific from Oakland, California. The American registration (1985) was changed to VH-USU.

The Italian airline Avioline-Italiane received a batch of three F.VIIa-3ms, including I-BBED (c/n 5059). This was sold by them in 1933 to Societá Aérea Mediterranea and then, in company with the other ALI aircraft, it was taken on charge by the Ala Littoria company and is believed to have been scrapped in 1939.

Waal, in October 1919. The wing, originally intended for the V 44, was simply bolted direct to the top of the enlarged fuselage. The cabin was furnished for four passengers, and a fifth could sit in the open front cockpit under the leading edge alongside the pilot. Powered by a 185-hp (138-kW) BMW IIIa 6-cylinder inline water-cooled engine, the F.II was slow but to the passenger vastly better than the crudely converted military machines produced by British and French companies. One odd feature was the absence of a fin, the weathercock stability being provided by the long flat-sided rear fuselage to which was hinged the diminutive rudder. There was nothing lacking, however, from the tailplane, elevators and ailerons, all controls being fully balanced and the ailerons projecting distinctively beyond the wingtips.

De Waal secretly flew the V 45 prototype to the Netherlands on 20 March 1920. Subsequently the type entered service with several airlines, some being built by Fokker and others

The first prototype of the single-engined Fokker F.VII is seen here making its maiden flight on 11 April 1924. The vertical tail shown in this photograph was later changed for a redesigned version with greater area and a rounded rudder profile. This aircraft was subsequently given the registration H-NACC.

under licence by Grulich, the latter having 250- or 320-hp (186.4- or 238.6-kW) BMW engines and usually some wing bracing struts and an enclosed cockpit. They firmly established Fokker as a builder of practical passenger airliners. Despite their wooden wings and fabric-covered fuselages, they proved to be robust and long-lived, and they rather

Of typical Fokker design, with a plywood-covered two-spar wooden wing and fabric-covered welded steel tube fuselage, the four production F.VIIs had accommodation for eight passengers and two crew members.

F.VIIB-3m PH-AFS was used initially by KLM, who named it *Specht* (woodpecker). It was sold in August 1936 to Crilly Airways, but did not see any further airline service because it was then passed on to the Spanish Nationalist forces, who took it on charge at Burgos and used it in the fight against the Republican army.

Sabena was a prominent F.VIIB-3m user, and flew aircraft built under licence by the Belgian manufacturing company SABCA. This particular example, OO-AGH, was delivered on 20 September 1932 and flew on European routes until May 1940, when it was taken over by the invading German forces at Haren Airport near Brussels.

The first three-engined Fokker F.VII (c/n 4900) was flown in the 1925 Ford Reliability Tour and was subsequently sold to Edsel Ford. Carrying the name *Josephine Ford*, it made an historic flight from Spitzbergen to the North Pole on 9 May 1926 under the command of Lieutenant-Commander Richard E. Byrd and piloted by Floyd Bennett.

surprisingly remained in scheduled service with several operators (including even Deutsche Lufthansa) well into the 1930s, one still flying in 1940.

Naturally Fokker developed the F.II, moving via the bigger F.III to the F.IV of 1921. The former, powered by a BMW, Eagle, Puma or Jupiter, was a best-seller and by far the most important airliner in northern Europe, including the Soviet Union, in 1922–5. The F.IV was much bigger but was still only single-engined, with a 420-hp (313.2-kW) Liberty. Two were sold to the US Army, which called them T-2s. One gained immediate fame on 2–3 May 1922 by flying nonstop across the USA, from New York to San Diego. This triggered off major sales to the US Army and US Navy, which in turn

led to an outcry among US manufacturers. Fokker overcame this by setting up a US subsidiary, Atlantic Aircraft Corporation, at Teterborough, New Jersey. Subsequently, Atlantic Fokkers tended to depart from the parent product in design details and engines, until from 1925 Atlantic's manager, R. B. C. Noorduyn (later a famed builder of his own well-liked and efficient Norseman), developed Fokker transports quite independently.

In early 1923 Fokker and Ing. Walther Rethel (later famed at Arado) began designing the F.VII, a straightforward machine with a 360-hp (268.5-kW) Rolls-Royce Eagle and six passenger seats. It had a wing of 772-sq ft (71.72-m²) area, compared with 421 sq ft (39.11 m²) for the F.III and 958 sq ft (89.00 m²) for the F.IV. It worked well enough, but the way to improve it was obvious. With a newer and more powerful engine and smaller wing it would be possible to carry more yet fly faster, and thus reduce the operating costs. Only five F.VIIs were built, but the improved F.VIIA was another smash hit.

First flown in early 1925, the Fokker was given a wing reduced in area to only 630 sq ft (58.53 m²), with the ailerons at last accommodated within the outline of the wing. The usual engine was a 450-hp (335.6-kW) Bristol or Gnome-Rhône Jupiter, but one early example had the 400-hp (298.3-kW) Packard A-1500 (improved Liberty). Carrying eight passengers and two crew, the F.VIIA was what a modern observer might call 'a real airliner'. Minor improvements were the fitting of a larger rudder with a fixed fin, and a neater landing gear with vertical shock struts (sprung by multiple elastic cords inside a fairing) pinned under the front wing spar.

The F.VIIB-3m c/n 5028 was delivered for use on the 1928 Antarctic expedition planned by Lieutenant-Commander Richard E. Byrd. In the event, a Ford Trimotor was used instead and the Fokker, named *Friendship*, was fitted with twin floats and, with the great Amelia Earhart as passenger and Wilmer Stultz piloting, made a record transatlantic flight from Trepassey Bay to Burry Port.

The US Army received eight C-2A aircraft, which differed from the normal F.VIIB-3m in having a larger, 10-seat fuselage, a modified cockpit and three 220-hp (164-kW) Wright J-5 engines. This example, named *Question Mark* and a US Army crew of Spaatz, Eaker, Quesada and Halvorsen, was used to establish an inflight-refuelling endurance record of 150 hours during January 1929.

Famous Fokker flights

2–3 May 1923: Lieutenants Macready and Kelly fly nonstop from New York to San Diego in a Fokker T-2 of the US Air Service, the flight time being 26 hours 50 minutes

24 November 1924: Van der Hoop starts the first airline flight from Amsterdam to Batavia in the Netherlands East Indies in a Fokker F.VII of KLM

27 July 1925: M. Grase sets an endurance record of 3 hours 30 minutes 30 seconds with a payload of 3,307 lb (1500 kg) in a Fokker F.VIIA

September 1925: Anthony Fokker wins the Ford Reliability Trial in the Fokker F.VII-3m

9 May 1926: Floyd Bennett flies the Byrd expedition's Fokker F.VII-3m from Spitzbergen over the North Pole

28–29 June 1927: Lieutenants Hegenberger and Maitland of the US Army fly the Fokker C-2 *Bird of Paradise* from Oakland, Cal., to Wheeler Field, Hawaii, in 25 hours 15 min

29 June–1 July 1927: The F.VIIB-3m prototype is flown by Bernt Balchen and Byrd from Roosevelt Field, USA, to Ver-sur-Mer, France, in 43 hours 21 minutes in fog

15–23 July 1927: An F.VIIA of KLM flown by Geysendorffer and Scholte makes the first revenue flight from Amsterdam to Batavia

31 May 1928: Charles Kingsford Smith and his crew in an F.VIIB-3m make the first aerial crossing of the Pacific Ocean from Oakland, California, to Sydney in Australia (via Honolulu, Suva and Brisbane) in 88 hours for the 7,800-mile (12555-km) trip

10 June 1928: Flown by Barnard and Alliott, an F.VIIA sets off for a round trip from the UK to India; the outward leg was delayed by the need for an engine change, but the return leg was accomplished in 4½ days

17–18 June 1928: Amelia Earhart piloted by Wilmer Stultz becomes the first woman to cross the Atlantic Ocean by air, flying from Trepassey Bay to Burry Port in the F.VII-3m *Friendship*

10–11 September 1928: Kingsford Smith makes the first aerial crossing of the Tasman Sea from Australia to New Zealand in an F.VIIB-3m; he makes the return flight in the same year

January 1929: The Fokker C-2A *Question Mark* is flown by a US Army crew (Spaatz, Eaker, Quesada and Halvorsen) for an inflight-refuelled record flight of 150 hours 40 min 15 sec

10 July 1929: Kingsford Smith and his crew arrive at Croydon from Australia in their F.VIIB-3m in 12 days 18 hours

24–26 June 1930: Kingsford Smith and his crew fly from Portmarnock to Harbour Grace and New York in their F.VIIB-3m

KLM specification

In the summer of 1924 the Dutch airline KLM, by then almost entirely Fokker-equipped, issued a specification for an airliner to carry 10 passengers and be able to fly with one engine stopped. It suggested the use of three Siddeley Puma engines. However, Fokker was intensely interested in the tri-motor Junkers G.23 when this flew in November 1924. Most significant of all, in his autobiography he wrote 'When Byrd sought to buy the first tri-motored Fokker he was unknown to me. That plane had been constructed on the basis of my cabled instructions to put three Wright motors on an F.VII'. It is therefore odd that Fokker later claimed that he built the F.VIIA-3m tri-motor purely in order to compete in the Ford Reliability Trial in the USA, which began in September 1925. Be that as it may, Fokker had his eye initially on the US market, and in any case was always intensely interested in publicity. So the first F.VIIA-3m was given American engines, 200-hp (149.1-kW) Wright J-4 Whirlwinds, and fitted for the American trial. Fokker wanted the outboard engines on the leading edges, but for reasons of balance and thrust-line axis designer Platz put them in separate nacelles on the vertical main legs, braced to fuselage and wings. This machine was completed with rather crude exhaust stacks wrapped round right in front of the air-cooled cylinders and discharging under the nose and above the wings. In typical

Fokker F.VIIB-3m cutaway drawing key

1 Starboard wing tip tie-down shackle
2 Starboard navigation light
3 Aileron cables
4 Aileron control horn
5 Starboard aileron
6 Plywood wing skinning
7 Fixed trailing edge construction
8 Rear spar
9 Wing ribs
10 Front spar
11 Leading edge nose ribs
12 Starboard engine nacelle mounting struts
13 Engine instruments
14 Control cable duct to engine nacelle
15 Cooling air louvres
16 Starboard main undercarriage leg
17 Starboard engine
18 Three-blade propeller
19 Exhaust collector ring
20 Wright J-6 Whirlwind nine-cylinder radial engine
21 Engine accessories
22 Engine mounting struts
23 Fireproof bulkhead
24 Oil cooler
25 Centre engine oil tank
26 Oil tank filler cap
27 Cockpit floor level
28 Nose baggage compartment
29 Landing/taxiing lamp
30 Wind driven generator
31 Undercarriage strut mounting
32 Mail locker
33 Rudder pedal bar
34 Elevator control linkages
35 Instrument panel
36 Windscreen panels
37 Co-pilot's seat
38 Control column handwheel
39 Pilot's seat
40 Radio
41 Cockpit bulkhead
42 Wing spar/fuselage attachment
43 Fuel selector cocks
44 Aileron cable runs
45 Wing lifting lugs
46 Fuel tank filler cap
47 Fuel tanks
48 Fuel vent pipes
49 Starboard cabin window panel
50 Passenger seats
51 Rear spar/fuselage attachment
52 Overhead luggage racks
53 Cabin rear bulkhead
54 Cabin doorway
55 Toilet compartment
56 Water tank
57 Starboard baggage door

Fokker F.VIIs were pressed into service with both sides in the Spanish Civil War. This example was one of three F.VIIB-3ms originally delivered to Lineas Aereas Postales Espanolas (LAPE) in November 1933 and used by the Republicans. Makeshift external bomb racks were fitted on spars secured to the window frames.

The Avro Ten G-AASP was delivered as *Achilles* to Imperial Airways at its Cairo station during April 1931, and flew pipeline patrols on contract to the Iraq Petroleum Transport Co. It later returned to the UK, where Imperial Airlines found charter work for it. It was eventually withdrawn from use and scrapped in 1939.

Fokker fashion the aircraft was painted with the name in gigantic capitals along the wings and fuselage. It first flew on 4 September 1925, required little alteration, and was dismantled and shipped to the USA.

The machine's appearance was sensational, and it performed almost faultlessly throughout the trial. It proved it could (just) fly with one outer engine stopped, and Henry and Edsel Ford took a keen personal interest. The Fokker won the trial easily, and Edsel Ford bought the aircraft for Commander Richard E. Byrd's scientific expedition over the North Pole. Named *Josephine Ford*, and now with refined rear exhaust collector rings and fitted with skis, it was flown by Byrd and Floyd Bennett over the Pole on 9 May 1926. The same aircraft is now in the Ford Museum in Dearborn. Ford later produced his own tri-motor, with Junkers-type all-metal structure with corrugated skin.

From the start, demand for the F.VIIA-3m was almost more than Fokker's Dutch and US plants could handle. Later he did a deal with industrialists in Wheeling, West Virginia, who thought aircraft might replace part of their declining steel industry; soon Wheeling was building a 10-seat tri-motor every five days. Licences were purchased by Belgium, Italy, Poland and the UK, the British licensee being A. V. Roe, which produced several derived designs which included a nice-looking twin, the Avro 642. This was a much

more graceful design than Fokker's own derived twin, the F.VIII. The latter was a hefty 15-passenger machine, of which two were made by Manfred Weiss in Hungary.

Until 1934 Fokker's mainstream airliner developments were tri-motors. In 1926 two Dutch-built F.VIIs were ordered for Sir Hubert Wilkins' Arctic expedition. One was a Liberty-F.VIIA, but the other was a tri-motor of a new and enlarged type which gradually became the standard model, the F.VIIB-3m. This had a bigger wing of 727 or 729 sq ft (67.54 or 67.72 m²), but not as big as that on the original F.VII, which was designed at Fokker's Dutch factory for the American Fokker F.9 (see variants list). Thus the second machine was a unique in-between, for it retained the 200-hp

58 Entry door
59 Rear baggage compartment
60 Steel tube upper longerons
61 Fuselage stringers
62 Control cable runs
63 Horizontal spacers
64 Starboard tailplane
65 Elevator horn balance
66 Starboard elevator
67 Fin construction
68 Rudder horn balance
69 Sternpost
70 Fabric covered rudder construction
71 Tailplane bracing wire
72 Elevator control horn
73 Fabric covered port elevator construction
74 Elevator horn balance
75 Tailplane construction
76 Rudder control horn
77 Tailplane bracing strut
78 Fuselage fabric covering
79 Tailplane trim adjustment
80 Tailskid
81 Elastic cord shock absorber
82 Vertical spacers
83 Diagonal wire bracing
84 Steel tube bottom longeron
85 Welded fuselage construction
86 Rear spar girder construction
87 Step
88 Spar plywood facing
89 Trailing edge ribs
90 Port aileron construction
91 Aileron control horn
92 Wing tip tie-down shackle
93 Wing tip stringer construction
94 Port navigation light
95 Leading edge construction
96 Pitot tube
97 Aileron cables
98 Plywood ribs
99 Front spar girder construction
100 Passenger cabin floor level
101 Engine nacelle rear struts
102 Nacelle attachment joints
103 Port engine instruments
104 Oil tank
105 Exhaust pipe
106 Oil cooler
107 Welded steel tube nacelle construction
108 Port Wright J-6 engine
109 Exhaust collector ring
110 Cooling air intake louvres
111 Main undercarriage leg strut
112 Elastic cord shock absorber
113 Mudguard
114 Undercarriage lower V-struts
115 Port mainwheel
116 Hydraulic brake
117 Tyre valve access
118 Wheel disc cover/tyre facing

The Polish government ordered a bomber version of the F.VIIB-3m, which was built by the Plage & Laskiewicz factory at Lublin. This aircraft served with No. 2 Sqn of the Dywizjon Bombowy (bomber group) and was equipped with an open mid-upper turret and bomb racks under the fuselage. The engines were J-5 Whirlwinds.

(149.1-kW) Whirlwind and fuselage of the F.VIIA. After expedition flying in Alaska this special long-range Fokker was overhauled by Boeing and sold to an Australian, Squadron Leader Charles Kingsford Smith. Re-engined with 237-hp (176.7-kW) J-5 Whirlwinds and boldly painted with the name *Southern Cross*, the Fokker took off from Oakland, California, on 31 May 1928. This was the start of a career that was to make the Fokker the most famous aircraft between the world wars, surpassing even Lindbergh's Ryan. Some of its flights figure in a separate listing of famous Fokker flights. Today it is on display at Eagle Farm, Brisbane.

The 'big-wing' tri-motor had great potential, especially with greater power, and the F.VIIB-3m was formally marketed from 1928, usually with the J-6 series Whirlwind of 300–330 hp (223.7–246.1-kW). The first production example was another 'special' built in late 1927 as the *America* for the Byrd transatlantic flight. Later renamed *Friendship* (a prophetic name for Fokker) it participated in many further epic flights. Several of the enlarged tri-motors were F.VIIA rebuilds, one of the most famed starting life as H-NADP, powered by a Jupiter. This carried a wealthy American on the first KLM passenger flight to the Dutch East Indies (see list of flights). In 1928 it was rebuilt as an F.VIIB-3m with Gnome-Rhône (Bristol) Titans, and was again hired by Black for a trip to Cape Town. It was later fitted with Whirlwinds and almost commuted between Croydon, Cape Town and the Far East, amazing for 1929–30.

Licence-building

The F.VIIB-3m was the world's premier airliner of the 1927–33 period. Fokker and Atlantic built 147, and basically similar machines (with many makes of engine) were built under licence in Belgium, Czechoslovakia, France, Italy, Poland and the UK. Nine of the licensed sub-types were military, four being bombers. Probably the most important tri-motor Fokker bombers, however, were the Avia F.IXs. The Czech Avia company had built 21 F.VIIB-3m aircraft, one a bomber, and it followed with 12 F.IX bombers based on the Fokker F.IX, a much more powerful machine with 500-hp (372.9-kW) Walter-built Jupiters and able to take off at a weight of 19,842 lb (9000 kg). An ex-KLM F.IX later found its way to the Spanish Republicans where it too became a bomber.

Fokker's American team ended in a blaze of glory with 10 giant F.32s, the designation indicating the number of seats. Powered by four push/pull 575-hp (428.8-kW) Pratt & Whitney Hornets, they were generally judged too big for the market. But back in Amsterdam the traditional Fokker tri-motors just kept on being improved. In 1930 the important F.XII made its appearance, with an 893-sq ft (82.96-m²) wing and 425-hp (316.9-kW) Pratt & Whitney C-series Wasp engines. Normally seating 16 passengers, the F.IX was the KLM main liner and also served with Sweden's ABA and Denmark's DDL, two actually being built in Denmark. This model in turn led to the further-enlarged F.XVIII of 1932. These proved to be the ultimate production Fokker tri-motors. KLM's incredibly experienced crews did marvels with what were becoming outdated machines. F.XVIII PH-AIP *Pelikaan* took 1933 Christmas mail to Batavia in 73 hours 34 minutes flight time, and PH-AIS *Snip* took 1934 Christmas mail to Curaçao in under 56 hours.

In 1932 Fokker gradually realised the advantages of an all-metal fuselage. But he obstinately stuck to traditional methods. The result was the F.XX of 1933, which kept in step with technical progress with 640-hp (477-kW) Cyclone engines and retractable undercarriage. For the first time a conscious effort was being made to reduce resistance, and the new twelve-seater could reach a speed of 190 mph (305 km/h). but now it had to prove itself against the Boeing 247 and the Douglas DC-1. KLM reluctantly decided in 1933 to negotiate with Douglas. But Fokker did not give up that easily. His last two transport planes were the great F.XXXVI, which flew in June 1934, and a year later the somewhat smaller F.XXII. This time the numbering of the type was based on the American method used for the F.32, where the number represented the maximum number of passengers. Both machines were traditional high-wing aircraft made of steel tubing, fabric and wood. But they had four wing-mounted engines. The '36' had a 750-hp (559-kW) Cyclone engine, and the '22' Wasp one of 500 hp (373 kW). Four machines were fitted with these, but only two were left by the beginning of World War 2. These were kept by the RAF, which used them in Scotland together with the only F.XXXVI ever to be built.

Hugh Wells piloted this Fokker F-VII in Pan American's first official flight from Miami to Havana.

Breguet 19

Almost certainly produced in larger numbers than any other military aircraft between the world wars, the inelegant Breguet 19 established numerous world records and served with great distinction for almost a quarter of a century.

The design for the Breguet 19, which was intended to capitalise on the success of the Breguet 14, the well-known World War 1 bomber, was taken charge of by M. Vuillerme in the design offices in Vélizy-Villacoublay. The prototype Bre.19 A.2 No. 01 was displayed in the VIIe Salon d'Aéronautique from 12 to 27 November 1921 in the Grand Palais in Paris. The structure of this large two-seater was made entirely of duralumin. The front half of the fuselage had a duralumin skin, while the rear half was tensioned using lacquered fabric. The huge upper wing was also tensioned with fabric and consisted of two pre-fabricated spars and ribs made of duralumin. It sat on two tandem wing struts above the fuselage and was joined to the much smaller bottom wing above a single Y-shaped wing strut. The prototype had a single Breguet-Bugatti 16-cylinder V-engine giving 450-hp (336-kW) and driving a four-bladed propeller. In fact, two Bugatti eight-cylinder engines were used in series. As the first ground test revealed vibration and cooling problems, the 16-cylinder engine which Robert Thiery used for the maiden flight in March 1922 in Villacoublay was replaced by a Renault 12Kb 12-cylinder V-engine with direct drive.

Already assembly of 11 pre-production aircraft had started

The 'Fuel Can', as it was nicknamed, flew around the world as the *'Nungesser-Coli'* in 1927–8. This journey of 35,420 miles (57000 km) also involved the first-ever crossing of the South Atlantic.

at Vélizy-Villacoublay, it being intended to offer the Bre.19 in two versions, the A.2 (Armée-biplace) two-seat reconnaissance aircraft and the B.2 (Bombardement-biplace) two-seat bomber, with a number of alternative engines; these preliminary aircraft featured the Renault 12Kb, 480-hp (358-kW) Renault 12Kd, 370-hp (276-kW) Lorraine-Dietrich 12D, 450 hp (336-kW) Lorraine-Dietrich 12Eb, and a Hispano-Suiza 12. The pre-production aircraft also differed from the prototype in having a 2-ft (0.6-m) longer fuselage.

Following trials with the Service Technique de l'Aéronautique in August 1922, which fully justified the manufacturers' earlier confidence, plans were authorized for an initial batch of 112 aircraft.

Production and proliferation

Roughly half the first production batch was powered by the Renault 12Kd, these aircraft being delivered for service with France's Aviation Militaire; however, well aware that a huge market was opening up internationally as nation after nation sought to establish or re-establish military air services and the post-war pacifism evaporated, Breguet offered the type with the many other powerplant options. First to inspect the Bre.19 was General Uzelac, commanding Yugoslavia's army aviation (already using the Bre.14), and in 1923 a pre-production Bre.19 was delivered for evaluation in that country. Meanwhile Thiery had flown Bre.19 No. 01 at an

Unquestionably the most illustrious Breguet 19 was the record-breaking Super-Bidon, the *Point d'Interrogation*, whose manufacture was sponsored by François Coty, the perfume magnate. After Dieudonné Costes and Maurice Bellonte had failed to fly the Atlantic in July 1929, a direct-drive Hispano-Suiza 12Lb engine was fitted and in this form the aircraft established a new world record of 4,912 miles (7905 km) when the same crew flew from Le Bourget to Tsitsihkar in Manchuria on 27–29 September 1929. It was again re-engined, this time with a 650-hp (485-kW) Hispano-Suiza 12Nb engine, and made the first direct aeroplane flight from Paris to New York. Thereafter it embarked on a 'Voyage of Friendship' in the USA, its landing points being recorded on the rear fuselage chevron as shown in this illustration. Other remarkable achievements are also recorded between the chevrons.

Breguet 19

Specification

Breguet Bre.19 A.2
Type: two-seat day bomber
Powerplant: one 513-hp (383-kW) Renault 12Kd water-cooled 12-cylinder Vee engine
Performance: maximum speed 146 mph (235 km/h) at sea level; climb to 16,405 ft (5000 m) in 29 minutes 50 seconds; absolute ceiling 22,640 ft (6900 m); maximum range 746 miles (1200 km)
Weights: empty 3,796 lb (1722 kg); normal loaded 5,174 lb (2347 kg); maximum take-off 6,856 lb (3110 kg)
Dimensions: span 48 ft 7¾ in (14.83 m); length 31 ft 2½ in (9.51 m); height 12 ft 1¼ in (3.69 m); wing area 538.2 sq ft (50.00 m²)
Armament: one forward-firing synchronized Vickers 0.303-in (7.7-mm) machine-gun with 500 rounds, two Lewis 0.303-in (7.7-mm) guns on Scarff TO-7 ring mounting on rear cockpit and one ventral Lewis 0.303-in (7.7-mm) gun with 1,552 rounds, plus a maximum internal bombload of 882 lb (400 kg) and 882 lb (400 kg) on external racks

Breguet 19

Versatility was a characteristic of the Bre.19 design, with two main versions being produced in France: the A.2 (Armée-biplace) reconnaissance aircraft, and the B.2 (bombardement-biplace) bomber, coupled with a great range of equipment provisions, and powerplants ranging from 350 hp (261 kW) to 650 hp (485 kW). Illustrated is a French Aviation Militaire Bre.19 A.2.

international military aircraft contest in Spain in February 1923, eclipsing all other contenders; subsequently Spain negotiated licence rights to manufacture the Bre.19.

Distributed among the first 112 production series were aircraft powered by the Lorraine-Dietrich 12Db and 12Eb, 500-hp (373-kW) Salmson 183Ma and 420-hp (313-kW) Gnome-Rhône 9Ac engines. By the time production deliveries started from Villacoublay in 1924 foreign interest in the aircraft was such that Breguet negotiated sub-contracted production with Avions Henri et Maurice Farman at Billancourt, and the Société d'Emboutissage et de Constructions Mécaniques at Colombes (SECM-Amiot). By mid-1928 no fewer than 1,936 Bre.19s had been built in France, of which more than 1,100 were exported.

Deliveries of the Bre.19 A.2 for the Aviation Militaire started in October 1924 to the 32e, 33e, 34e and 35e Regiments d'Aviation, and in June 1926 the 11e Regiment d'Aviation de Bombardement de Jour (RABJ, or day bomber regiment) took delivery of its first Bre.19 B.2s, followed by the 11e RABJ. In all, by mid-1927 46 Escadrilles de Reconnaissance, d'Observation and de Bombardement were flying the Bre.19 A.2 and B.2.

Meanwhile Breguet was hard pressed to keep pace with demand abroad. Yugoslavia had ordered 100 Bre.19 A.2s and B.2s, the former powered by the Lorraine-Dietrich 12Db and the latter by 12Eb engines; one of these aircraft, flown by Captain Radović and Lieutenant Rubčić, established a speed record between Paris and Belgrade in 8 hours 25 minutes on its delivery flight. The Yugoslav army's 2nd Regiment at Rajlovac near Sarajevo was the first to introduce the Bre.19.

In 1926 Romania ordered 50 Bre.19 A.2s and B.2s with which to start modernizing her air force, the first of a total of 108 Bre.19s (supplemented by about 12 Bre.19.7s, of which more later). In the Far East, following the purchase of four Bre.19s in 1924 by the Central Chinese government in Peking, 70 Lorraine-Dietrich 12Db-powered Bre.19s were bought for the Manchurian air arm under Marshal Chang Tso-lin, and some of these fought against the Japanese in the Manchurian campaign of 1931–2.

A measure of the high esteem in which the Breguet 19 was held at this time may be gained by the decision by Poland to create a powerful air force largely composed of Bre.19s. Following a visit by a purchasing mission from Poland,

One of the first long-distance flights (*grands raids*) by the Bre.19 was that flown by Lieutenants Pelletier d'Oisy and Bésin in the Lorraine-Dietrich 12Db-powered Bre.19 no.3. They flew from Paris to Shanghai in May 1924; the aircraft is seen here during its stop at Hinaidi.

General Wlodzimierz Zagórski authorized the first of a number of orders for Bre.19 A.2s and B.2s at the end of June 1925, and less than a month later Zagórski led a mixed formation of Bre.19s and Potez 25s from France to Poland – the first of 250 Bre.19s delivered to the Polish Lotnictwo Wojskowe between then and 1930 (including 20 examples of a special long-range version). It was a Polish Bre.19 A.2, flown by Colonel Ludomil Rayski and Sergeant Leonard Kubiak, which flew 4,660 miles (7500 km) round the entire Mediterranean between 16 and 22 September 1925. A Bre.19 was flown from Warsaw to Tokyo, a distance of 14,290 miles (23000 km) by Captain Boleslav Orlinski; on the return flight the aircraft ran into a severe storm and lost a large area of fabric from its port lower wing but, after the crew had landed in a field and torn away an equivalent area of fabric from the wing on the other side, continued safely on its way.

Polish Bre.19s served with the 2nd, 3rd, 5th and 6th Regiments of the Lotnictwo Wojskowe, but by the end of 1936 they had been relegated to training duties; 20 were sold to the Nationalists early in the Spanish Civil War. Just before the fateful events of September 1939 a small number of Polish Bre.19s took part in exercises to test the control of Warsaw's anti-aircraft defences, but were grounded immediately afterwards and took no part in the operations to fight Germany's invasion.

Greece and Turkey also purchased Bre.19s in the mid-

Yugoslav Kraljevo-built Bre.19 A.2 no. 1330 with 420-hp (313-kW) Gnome-Rhône 9AB radial of the fourth production batch, shown in the markings of the Yugoslav air force in about 1935. The engine, the French version of the Bristol Jupiter, was licence-built at a factory at Rakovica.

Operated by the 51ᵉ Escadre (2ᵉ Escadrille) of France's Aviation Militaire, this Bre.19 A.2 (Armée-biplace) was powered by a Lorraine-Dietrich 12Db 12-cylinder Vee-type engine.

Britain was among the foreign nations to acquire single examples of the Bre.19 for evaluation, this B.2 with a Renault 12Kd engine being registered J7507 and flown by pilots of the Royal Aircraft Establishment during 1925.

1920s. The former took delivery of 30 Bre.19 A.2s and B.2s (bought by popular subscription), powered by 500-hp (363-kW) Hispano-Suiza 12Hb engines, for the 1st Air Regiment newly formed at Tatoi and the 3rd Air Regiment at Salonika-Mikra; and the latter received 20 Lorraine-Dietrich 12Eb-powered Bre.19 B.2s for the 1st Air Regiment.

A number of orders were placed for Bre.19s by South American countries, a sequence initiated by Argentina with an order for 25 Lorraine-Dietrich 12Eb-powered Bre.19 A.2s and B.2s, the first of which were delivered in 1926. In 1930 a dozen of these aircraft, flying from El Palomar, played an active part in the revolution which erupted that year. In 1928 12 Bre.19 A.2s and B.2s constituted the initial combat element of Venezuela's newly-formed Military Aviation Service, and at the same time Brazil bought five Renault 12Kb-powered Bre.19s. Fifteen Bre.19 B.2s purchased by Bolivia in 1928 took part in the war with Paraguay in the following year.

Breguets under licence

As mentioned above, Robert Thiery's demonstration of the Bre.19's superiority at the Cuatro Vientos military aircraft contest in February 1923 led to Spain's decision to acquire licence manufacturing rights, but these could not be implemented until completion of the Construcciones Aeronáuticas SA (CASA) factory south of Madrid in 1924. Three pattern aircraft were delivered, together with components for 26 other aircraft for assembly by CASA; except for one, which was powered by a 500-hp (373-kW) Hispano-Suiza 12b, all were fitted with Lorraine-Dietrich 12Ebs. Simultaneously the latter engine entered licence production in Spain by Elizalde SA as the A-4. Before licence-built Bre.19s could be completed, the campaign in Spanish Morocco forced the Spanish government to import 16 Breguet-built aircraft, and these took part in military operations with the Aeronáutica Militar Espanola in July 1925. In due course the first licence-built order for 77 Bre.19s (50 with imported HS 12Hb and 27 with indigenous A-4 engines) was completed, and was followed by a contract for 80 aircraft in 1929 and one for 20

in 1931, all these aircraft having Hispano-Suiza 12b A-4.

Production of the Bre.19 in Spain ended in 1935, but in the following year the Spanish Civil War broke out, by which time about 135 Bre.19s were serving with the Aviación Militar. Owing to the disposition of the air force (a number of Bre.19s were, for example, serving in North Africa), Bre.19s fought with both Republican and Nationalist forces, but with the arrival of modern aircraft on the scene all were withdrawn from combat status by May 1937. Losses from all causes were said to have been 10 by the Nationalists and 28 by the Republicans. As already mentioned, 20 Bre.19s were also acquired by the Nationalists from Poland.

At about the time that Spain first decided on licence production of the Bre.19, Belgium ordered six Bre.19 B.2s in 1924 as pattern and evaluation aircraft. Evaluation of various alternative engines led to the choice of the Hispano-Suiza 12Ha but in the event, when production was undertaken by Société Anonyme Belge de Constructions Aéronautiques (SABCA) at Haren, aircraft were produced with both this engine and the Lorraine-Dietrich 12Eb. Belgian-built Bre.19s joined the Aéronautique Militaire in 1927, eventually equipping the 1ère Régiment d'Aeronautique and the 2ème Groupe de Bombardement until replaced by the Fairey Fox in the 1930s. Belgian production amounted to 146 Bre.19s.

A number of nations contemplated licence production, and purchased pattern and evaluation aircraft. Japan, where production by Nakajima was suggested, acquired two Bre.19 A.2s for assembly in that country, one being completed as a landplane, the other as a floatplane; licence production was not undertaken, however. Italy purchased one Bre.19 A.2 and one Bre.19 B.2 in 1924, and Persia took two Bre.19 A.2s. The UK obtained an early Bre.19 B.2 in 1925 (with Renault engine), and this was evaluated by the RAE at Farnborough as J7507.

Yugoslavia proved to be the largest foreign customer for the Breguet 19 and, following delivery of the 100 Bre.19 A.2s and Bre.19 B.2s in 1925–6 (already mentioned), a contract was signed on 14 October 1927 for the import and licence construction of a minimum of 425 aircraft. The first order covered 50 completed aircraft delivered by rail from France;

The second Bidon-type Bre.19 GR, powered by a Hispano-Suiza 12Lb, was flown by Commandants Girier and Weiss on 25 May 1929 to establish a world speed record of 116.88 mph (188.1 km/h) over a distance of 3,107 miles (5000 km).

Breguet 19

CASA-built Bre.19s served on both sides during the Spanish Civil War. This Elizalde A-4-powered aircraft was flown by a Nationalist observers' school in about 1938 after the type had been relegated to second-line duties.

After the famous *'Point d'Interrogation'* only one other Super-Bidon was produced; this was the CASA-built Bre.19 *'Cuatro Vientos'*, which was flown by Barberián and Collar the 4,722 miles (7600 km) from Seville to Camaguey, Cuba, on 10–11 June 1933, but which disappeared on a subsequent flight to Mexico.

an order, signed in December 1928, stipulated 35 completed aircraft delivered by rail, 25 aircraft in parts to be assembled at Kraljevo and 15 to include some Yugoslav-made components; the next order for 75 aircraft and the fourth for 100 aircraft were to be completed by Yugoslav manufacture, the last aircraft being delivered in 1932. The aircraft in the second and third batches were powered by Hispano-Suiza 12Hb or 12Lb engines, but those in the last order had Yugoslav-built Gnome-Rhône Jupiter 9Abs. The fifth batch of Yugoslav Bre.19s comprised 125 Bre.19.7s, a new version whose development is now described.

Some of the spectacular long-distance flights undertaken by modified Bre.19s have already been mentioned, and France's own Aviation Militaire had already flown a number of *grand raids* (long-distance flights), including one by Lieutenants Pelletier d'Oisy and Bésin from Paris to Shanghai in May 1924; on 3–4 February 1925 Capitaines Lemaitre and Arrachart established a new world distance record with a flight of 1,967 miles (3166 km) from Etampes to Villa Cisneros in the Spanish Sahara.

Breguet 'fuel cans'

As a result of international interest in these long distance flights, three standard Bre.19s were taken from the production line in 1926 and extensively modified to accommodate 641 Imp gal (2915 litres) of fuel, compared with 97 Imp gal (440 litres) in the standard Bre.19 B.2, and to feature an enlarged upper wing. These three aircraft embarked on a series of extraordinary flights, the first, flown by Capitaine Girier and Lieutenant Dordilly from Villacoublay to Omsk on 14–15 July 1926, raised the record to 2,930 miles (4715.9 km); another, flown by Breguet's chief test pilot Dieudonné Costes together with Capitaine Rignot, increased the record to 3,353 miles (5396 km) on a flight from Le Bourget to Djask on 28–29 October 1926. These achievements were crowned

---

Breguet Bre.19 variants

Bre.19 A.2.01: prototype, originally with Breguet-Bugatti 16-cylinder engine but changed to Renault 12Kb for first flight in March 1922
Bre.19 A.2 and B.2.02 to 012: pre-production, nos 03, 04 and 05 with Renault 12Kb, no. 02 with Lorraine-Dietrich 12D, nos 06, 07, 08, 010 and 012 with Renault 12Kd, no. 09 with Hispano-Suiza 12, and no. 011 with LD 12EB
Bre.19 A.2 and B.2: production by Breguet, Farman and SECM; powered by LD 12Db, LD 12Eb, LD 12Ed, Renault 12Kb, Kd, Ke and Kf, Salmson 18CMa, Gnome-Rhône 9Ac and Farman 12We; 100 to Yugoslavia, 108 to Romania, 4 to China (Central government), 70 to Manchuria, 30 to Greece, 45 to Spain, 20 to Turkey, 250 to Poland, 25 to Argentina, 12 to Venezuela, 15 to Bolivia, five to Brazil, two to Japan (one completed as floatplane), two to Italy, two to Persia and two to UK; remainder (excluding experimental conversions, see below) to Service Aviation
Bre.19 A.2 and B.2: foreign licence production; assembly and production of 300 aircraft at State factory, Kraljevo, Yugoslavia, with Lorraine 12Eb, HS 12Hb or 12Lb engines; 177 by CASA, Spain, with LD 12Eb (and licence A-4) engines; 146 by SABCA of Belgium
Bre.19 Grand Raid: increased fuel capacity in French Bre.19 A.2 (converted)
Bre.19 Bidon type: Bre.19 nos 1685, 1686 and 1687

rebuilt with 641-Imp gal (2915-litre) fuel capacity; no. 1685 (later became *Nungesser-Coli*) powered in turn by HS 12Ha and HS 12Lb; nos 1686 and 1687 powered by Renault 12Kb; also one Belgian aircraft similar to no. 1685, one Greek aircraft with HS 12Hb (named *Hellas*), and two built by CASA in Spain, nos 71 and 72 (the latter named *Jesús del Gran Poder*)
Bre.19 Super Bidon: fuel capacity 1,137 Imp gal (5170 litres); one aircraft built in France (*Point d'Interrogation*) and one by CASA in Spain (*Cuatro Vientos*)
Bre.19.1132: twin-float conversion of Bre.19 no. 1132 in 1926
Bre.19ter: prototype; long-range service derivative of Bidon type; became F-AIXP; HS 12Lb engine
BRE.19.7: 10 rebuilt aircraft similar to Bre.19ter, five to Yugoslavia and five to Romania; 125 newly built in Yugoslavia; HS 12Nb engines
Bre.19.8: prototype; Yugoslav-built aircraft fitted by Breguet with GR 14Kbrs Mistral Major radial, re-engined with GR 14Kdrs; various propellers and cowlings
Bre.19.8: production; 48 Yugoslav-built Bre.19.7s completed with Wright Cyclone GR-1820-F56 radials
Bre.19.9: single Yugoslav prototype (converted Bre.19.7) with 860-hp (642-kW) Hispano-Suiza 12Ybrs
Bre.19.10: single Yugoslav prototype (converted Bre.19.7) with 720-hp (537-kW) Lorraine 12Hfrs Petrel

Breguet Bre.19 B.2 Type 1926 cutaway drawing key

1 Two-bladed fixed-pitch wooden propeller
2 Spinner
3 Propeller boss
4 Exhaust manifold (to starboard)
5 Carburettor intake
6 Port carburettors
7 Radiator
8 Engine support lower bearer
9 Water pump
10 Engine main support member
11 Upper engine bearer
12 Port magneto
13 Forward fuselage frame
14 Renault 12Kd 12-cylinder 60° Vee water-cooled engine

19 Synchronized 7.7-mm Vickers machine gun (offset to starboard)
20 Oil tank (11 Imp gal/50 litre capacity)
21 Forward fuel tank (70 Imp gal/320 litre capacity) to starboard (obscured by port tank/bomb magazine)
22 Optional 88 Imp gal (400 litre) long-range tank (replacing Type D magazine for 32 22-lb (10-kg) or eight 110-lb (50-kg) vertically-disposed bombs)
23 Diagonal bracing wires
24 Lower mainplane bracing wire

30 Leading-edge stiffeners
31 Diagonal bracing wires
32 Aileron control conduit
33 Wing ribs
34 Mainplane forward spar
35 Interplane strut upper attachments
36 Mainplane rear spar
37 Wing fabric
38 Aileron outer hinge
39 Aileron control hinge
40 Port aileron
41 Aileron inner hinge

51 Control linkage
52 Pilot's seat
53 Seat support frame
54 STIAé bomb sight (external starboard)
55 Handhold
56 F120 vertical camera installation
57 Underwing bomb release switches (starboard side)
58 Fuselage Type D (forward) and Type F (rear) bomb release switches (portside)

73 Fin navigational light
74 Rudder upper hinge
75 Rudder frame
76 Port tailplane upper bracing
77 Port elevator
78 Elevator torque tube
79 Port tailplane lower bracing
80 Rudder post and hinge
81 Tailskid
82 Tailskid attachment
83 Fuselage fabric
84 Aft-firing 7.7-mm Lewis machine gun

42 Aileron ribs (Note: ribs between ailerons are continuous from leading to trailing edge)
43 Interplane strut fairing
44 Windscreen frame
45 Instrument panel
46 Cockpit coaming
47 Control column (Note: dual control standard on both A2 and B2 models)
48 Starboard aft (jettisonable) fuel tank of 26 Imp gal (120 litre) capacity
49 Lower mainplane/undercarriage bracing attachment
50 Underwing bomb rack attachments

59 TO-7 Scarff-type gun mount
60 Twin 7.7-mm Lewis machine guns
61 Fuselage decking
62 Port lower mainplane tip
63 Type R-7 radio installation
64 Lewis cartridge drum stowage racks (16 × 97-round drums)
65 Radio support tray
66 Fuselage frames
67 Rudder controls
68 Elevator controls
69 Fuselage frame diagonal bracing
70 Fin forward attachment
71 Fin structure
72 Electrical lead

85 Signal flares stowage
86 Lewis cartridge drum stowage
87 TO-7 gun mount support/fuselage frame
88 Aerial winch
89 Aerial duct
90 Oscillator/variometer
91 Gaumont photographic plate magazine
92 Port underwing GPU rack (one 441-lb/200-kg bomb each)
93 Fuselage Type F bomb magazine (12 × 22-lb/10-kg bombs)
94 Lower mainplane/undercarriage bracing
95 Mainwheel leg fairing
96 Bomb bay panel
97 Mainwheel leg fairing
98 Lift wire attachments
99 Cross-axle fairing
100 Port mainwheel

15 Camshaft drive
16 Upper mainplane/fuselage support frame
17 Fuselage/wing centre section support strut fairing
18 Centre section forward support strut

25 Wing centre section/fuselage aft support frame
26 Aft fuselage/wing centre section support sturt fairing
27 Wing centreline joint
28 Aileron control linkage
29 Interspar bracing tubes

Breguet 19

Not surprisingly the Axis powers were glad to throw any available aircraft into the fight against the numerous partisans who were active in Yugoslavia during the war. This Wright Cyclone-powered Kraljevo-built Bre.19.8 served with the Croatian air force in about 1943.

when Dieudonné Costes and Lieutenant de Vaisseau le Brix made their famous 35,420-mile (57000-km) round-the-world flight in 350 flying hours in *Nungesser-Coli* (inevitably dubbed the *Bidon*, or Fuel Can) between 10 October 1927 and 14 April 1928; the flight also included the first flight across the South Atlantic.

Further Bidons [and Super-Bidons with 1,137 Imp gal (5170 litres of fuel)] appeared; the most famous was *Point d'Interrogation* (Question Mark), sponsored by the perfume company Coty; flown by Dieudonné Costes and Maurice Bellonte and powered by an Hispano-Suiza 12Lb, this aircraft was flown from Le Bourget to Tsitsihkar in Manchuria between 27 and 29 September 1929, a new world distance record of 4,912 miles (7905 km). The aircraft had a theoretical range of 5,405 miles (8700 km) and the margin was to allow for unforecast headwinds.

Night fighters

Bidon-type Bre.19s (termed Bre.19.7s) were acquired by Belgium (where the nickname originated), Turkey, Romania and Greece (as well as Yugoslavia, already mentioned) while in France the standard Bre.19 was being introduced as a night-fighter, equipping the 21e, 22e, 23e and 24e Escadrilles de Chasse de Nuit between 1931 and 1935. Peak inventory of Bre.19s reached 702 in July 1931, including 34 deployed in North Africa. Thereafter the total declined, until the last examples (the night-fighter models) were phased out of

Bre.19.7 was the name given to an aerodynamically improved version with an Hispano-Suiza 12Nb engine. These engines were produced in Kraljevo, Yugoslavia. The aircraft illustrated here was used in Turkey.

operational front-line service during the spring of 1935.

Production by the parent company ended in 1932, but Breguet re-engined a Yugoslav-built Bre.19.7 with a 690-hp (515-kW) Gnome-Rhône 14Kbrs Mistral Major, this aircraft being redesignated the Bre.19.8; it was evaluated but discarded by the Yugoslav *opitna grupa* (test squadron) and attention switched to the Wright Cyclone GR-820-F56, of which an installation was undertaken at Kraljevo, retaining the Bre.19.8 designation. (An experimental version, the Bre.19.10 with 720-hp/537-kW Lorraine 12Hfrs Petrel, was also produced in prototype form.) In all, 55 Cyclone-powered Bre.19.8s were built at Kraljevo between December 1936 and November 1937. As late as 1936 Bre.19s equipped all six of Yugoslavia's air regiments.

Breugets fly for Croatia

In the period from 1938 to 1940 most of the Yugoslavian Bre.19 bombers were used only for training purposes, 103 reconnaissance aircraft with Jupiter engines being taken out of service in 1939. But when Germany attacked Yugoslavia on 6 April 1941, more than a hundred Bre.19s were still in use in 14 Army Co-operation Squadrons. Apart from an attack on a bridge over the river Vardar, however, most of these machines stayed on the ground and were destroyed where they lay. Thirty of them fell into the hands of the German forces, and six were taken over by the Italians to equip the new Croatian Air Force. This unit was stationed in Mostar, Sarajevo and Zagreb to be used in attacks on partisans. One Br.19 pilot defected to the partisans with his aircraft, and another was used by Major Arkadije Popov in October 1943 to cross the Adriatic and join the Allies, who were fighting in Italy. The Yugoslavian liberation army discovered the last two Bre.19s in April 1945 at Sarajevo Airfield, but even these two were scrapped a year later.

This Kraljevo-built Bre.19.7, F-ALPN, was modified at Vélizy-Villacoublay by installation of a Gnome-Rhône Mistral Major but, although it established a number of records, neither it nor the engine found favour with the Yugoslavs.

Dornier Flying-boats

In April 1983 Dornier flew the Do 24TT, a big turboprop amphibian derived from the pre-war Do 24. No company is better fitted to test the market for marine aircraft than this famous German firm, with a heritage of all-metal flying-boats no other company can match.

Professor Dr Claude Dornier was probably the best builder of flying boats anywhere in the world in the years before 1930, as well as being one of the great exponents of the modern all-metal aircraft. His very first design, the RS I in 1915, was not only made almost entirely of steel and aluminium alloys, but was also the largest aircraft in existence, with a wingspan of 142 ft 8 in (43.5 m). This was the first in the RS series (RS stood for *Riesenflugzeug See*, or Extra Large Seaplane) which was used after the war ended in 1918.

As well as the RS series Dornier's company, Zeppelin-Werke Lindau GmbH, had almost completed the prototype of a smaller but still very capable flying-boat, the Gs I. Powered by two 270-hp (201-kW) Maybach Mb.IV water-cooled engines arranged in tandem at the centre of a rectangular monoplane wing, the Gs I had a slim and very efficient hull, stabilizing sponsons of the kind favoured by Dornier, and a twin-finned biplane tail. The four-seat enclosed cockpit in the bows gave an appearance like the head of a serpent, but as a tough transport flying-boat it had no equal when it flew on 31 July 1919. It was later flown from Lindau to the Netherlands, but the fact remained that the machine contravened the rules imposed by the Allies and the Allied Control Commission had it sunk off Kiel on 25 April 1920.

Dornier went ahead with small aircraft, such as the Delfin, Libelle and Komet, but he never gave up his work on big and powerful flying-boats. His wartime design for the Gs II, rather larger than the Gs I with 1,033.4 sq ft (96 m²) of wing instead of 861.1 sq ft (80 m²), and a laden weight raised from 9,513 lb (4315 kg) to 12,566 lb (5700 kg) appeared to be just what the infant airlines and air forces needed. Under the noses of the hated Control Commission, Dornier set up an Italian subsidiary, Societá di Costruzioni Meccaniche di Pisa, at Marina di Pisa. He carried on designing at Lindau, the works there being renamed Dornier Metallbauen GmbH in 1922, and licensed the big Gs II machines to the Italian subsidiary, even buying two 300-hp (224-kW) Hispano-Suiza engines from Paris for the prototype of the improved Gs II. Dornier redesignated it as the Type J, and named it Wal (whale). The prototype flew on 6 November 1922.

Dornier was correct in his assessment of the market. The Wal was ideally suited to both commercial and military operations for the next 15 years, having very satisfactory performance and payload, a robust all-metal structure and

This Wal was one of the later examples of the 17,637-lb (8000-kg) gross weight civil family, in this case with BMW VI engines. These later variants had the same 1,033-sq ft (96-m²) wing area, but rounded tips and span increased from 74 ft (22.5 m) to 76 ft (23.2 m). D-2069 *Monsun* (monsoon) served with Deutsche Lufthansa. Note the giant D/F loop aerial.

Dornier Superwal

Specification

Dornier Superwal (four engines)
Type: transport flying-boat
Powerplant: (this example) four 460/485-hp (343/362-kW) Napier Lion VIII W-12 water-cooled piston engines
Performance: maximum speed 130 mph (210 km/h); cruising speed (typical) 100 mph (161 km/h); normal operating ceiling 6,500 ft (2000 m); range with maximum payload 620 miles (1000 km)
Weights: empty 21,781 lb (9880 kg); maximum loaded 30,865 lb (14000 kg)
Dimensions: span 93 ft 10 in (28.6 m); length 80 ft 8.5 in (24.6 m); height 19 ft 8.2 in (6 m); wing area 1,475 sq ft (137 m²)
Accommodation: normal operating crew of four and up to 19 passengers; maximum payload 8,375 lb (3800 kg)

Dornier built three of the twin-engined Superwals, with 650-hp (485-kW) Condor engines, followed by 16 of the four-engined version. The first of the four-engined machines was this example, one of seven (together with all three twin-Condor Superwals) delivered to the German airline Deutsche Lufthansa. D-1337 was the only one powered by 485-hp (362-kW) Napier Lion engines, the other Lufthansa machines having the 525-hp (391-kW) Siemens-built Bristol Jupiter air-cooled radial. The radiators for the Lions can be seen mounted athwartships above the push-pull nacelles, and the side-by-side cockpit offset to port was enclosed in this version.

Dornier Flying-boats

This regular Military Wal was one of a substantial number operated by the Spanish navy. Many earlier Spanish Wals had been built by CMASA, but the example shown was a Dornier-built Do J IId, with BMW VI engines. It is shown during the Civil War while serving with I-G 70 Grupo at Puerto de Pollensa, in Majorca.

The Luftwaffe Do 18D reached the peak of its brief career in 1939–40, when the type equipped four *Staffeln* (squadrons) of the *Küstenfliegergruppen* (coastal groups). This example served at Kamp, on the Pomeranian coast, with 2/KüFlGr 906. By 1941 the Do 18Ds were being converted as Do 18H crew trainers, the more powerful Do 18Gs then becoming Do 18Ns.

The 22,046-lb (10000-kg) gross weight Wal was the last and largest version, dating from 1933. Span was increased to 89 ft 2.9 in (27.2 m) and wing area to 1,206 sq ft (112 m²). This example was one of those that made 328 scheduled crossings of the South Atlantic, operating from the ships *Westfalen* and *Schwabenland*. Note the length of the hydraulic catapult.

of the hull from which bombs and other stores could be hung, and there were various schemes for defensive guns.

Of course, with the benefit of hindsight the Wal can be criticized. Tandem engines are inefficient, can lead to cooling problems and can cause severe stresses in the rear propeller. The Wal's very broad wingtips were aerodynamically poor, and the high induced drag inevitably reduced the attainable range. The large 'park bench' balancing surfaces attached to the ailerons were a scheme outmoded by 1930, and the open cockpit of most Wals would have been disliked by the softer pilots of later times. But in overall terms no other marine aircraft came near it. Altogether at least 300 and possibly more than 320 Wals were built, including between 157 and 177 in Italy (156 by SCMP and its successor CMASA of 1929, a Fiat subsidiary), at least 56 by Dornier at Friedrichshafen from 1932, 40 by CASA in Spain, about 40 by Aviolanda in the Netherlands and three by

excellent reliability. Airline Wals set new standards in interior appointments, and with glass portholes resembled staterooms in luxury yachts. The many military versions were fitted with four small stub wings along the upper part

One of the three Wals built under licence by Kawasaki. Dornier Wals were also built under licence in Italy, Spain and Holland with the result that the variations of this model were in many ways very different from one another.

Kawasaki in Japan. It is doubtful if any aircraft has left the original factory in so many different variations. There were four major and nine minor variations in span, six quite different designs of nose and cockpit, eight different designs of tail, at least 17 different basic types of engine, and a host of gross weights from 8,818 lb (4000 kg) to more than 22,046 lb (10000 kg).

Though some early customers continued to specify the Hispano, many of the pre-1925 Wals were powered by the 360-hp (268-kW) Rolls-Royce Eagle IX, and this rather outdated V-12 was fitted to a Wal that set 20 world records for speed/height/range with payloads up to 4,409 lb (2000 kg) on 4, 9, 10 and 11 February 1925. Other Wals, with three different types of engine, made crossings of the North and South Atlantic, flew from Europe to near the North Pole and to various places in the Far East, and also flew round the world. Airline Wals often had an enclosed cockpit (always from 1931) and began as six- to nine-seaters, with space for loose cargo. In 1931 Dornier began production of the '8-tonne Wal' first flown the previous year with 690-hp (515-kW) BMW VI engines and a 1,033.4-sq ft (96-m²) wing. This became the standard model, though again with many variations, and it led to the 8.5-tonner in 1933, and the corresponding Militär-Wal 33 which was produced for the Luftwaffe as the Do 15. In the same year appeared the biggest version, the 10-tonne Wal, with 1,205.6 sq ft (112 m²) of wing, which was operated by Deutsche Lufthansa from the

The original Do X 12-engined monster is seen here after its refit with Curtiss Conqueror water-cooled engines. It is shown after its long trip to the Americas in brief service with Lufthansa. It then went to the DVL research organization before becoming the biggest exhibit in the Berlin air museum, where it was destroyed by bombs.

depot ships *Westfalen* and *Schwabenland* and made 328 crossings of the South Atlantic in regular mail service. Among export customers were Argentina, Chile, Colombia, Italy, Japan, the Netherlands, Portugal, the Soviet Union, Spain, the UK and Yugoslavia.

Different enough to have a different name, Superwal, the Type R enlarged version first flew on 30 September 1926. This was constructed at another Dornier factory, at Manzell on the Swiss shore of the Bodensee (Lake Constance). The prototype of this much bigger boat had two Rolls-Royce Condors of 650 hp (485 kW) each, and another had two 800-hp (597-kW) Packard A-2500s, but most other Superwals had two push/pull pairs, the most common engines being the Siemens-built Bristol Jupiter, Pratt & Whitney Hornet, and, for the CASA-built military Superwals, the 500-hp (373-kW) Hispano-Suiza.

Model X monster

Just as the RS I had been the biggest aeroplane of its day, so did Dornier's liking for size manifest itself in an extreme

D-AEAV was one of a small batch of Fokker-built Do 24T-1 flying-boats completed as unarmed civil aeromedical transports operated by the *Reichsluftdienst* (air service). They operated mainly within and around Germany in 1941–4, carrying seven stretchers or a larger number of sitting patients or war casualties.

This Do 24T-2 was one of the later (1943) production series from the Dutch assembly line, the main external difference being the tall HDL 151 dorsal turret fitted with a Mauser MG 151/20 cannon instead of the French HS 404 cannon of the Do 24T-1. This boat served with 7 *Seenotstaffel* SBK XI in the Aegean Sea, chiefly on rescue duties.

form in 1926 when work began at Manzell on the Model X. This monster flyingboat was the ultimate scaled-up Wal, with no fewer than six push/pull pairs of engines, still the largest number ever used to propel a single aircraft. The Do X first flew in the hands of Richard Wagner on 12 (often reported as 25) July 1929, powered by Siemens Jupiters. Planned as a long-range passenger machine with 66 to 72 seats, it took off on 31 October 1929 with 10 crew, 150 passengers and nine stowaways, a total not exceeded for 20 years. On 4 August 1930 the Do X emerged after a rebuild with water-cooled Curtiss Conqueror engines with plain struts instead of auxiliary wings between the nacelles, the US engines giving extra power (640 instead of 525 hp/477 instead of 391 kW) and avoiding customs problems on a visit to the USA in 1930–1. The Italian air force used two of these monsters with 580-hp (433-kW) Fiat A 22R engines.

On 26 September 1939 a Blackburn Skua flown by Lieutenant B. S. McEwan scrambled from HMS *Ark Royal* and shot down a shadowing Do 18D, the first aircraft shot down by British forces in World War 2. The Do 18 was the natural successor to the Wal, designed in early 1934 to meet both a requirement for an updated Militär-Wal and a more modern South Atlantic boat for Lufthansa. The prototype Do 18a flew on 15 March 1935, powered by tandem 540-hp (403-kW) Junkers Jumo 5 diesel engines giving great range and endurance. Similar to the 8-tonne Wal in size and weight, the Do 18 was naturally much improved aerodynamically, with a tapered wing with rounded tips and 'double wing' flaps and ailerons, a central wing pylon incorporating the cooling radiators, and a well-streamlined hull of graceful form. Small numbers of several versions were produced for civil applications, and in summer 1936 deliveries began from the Weser company of the military Do 18D series, most of which had 600-hp (447-kW) Jumo 205C diesels and were used for armed reconnaissance with coastal units. Delay in development of the Blohm und Voss Bv 138 led to continued

D-ABYM *Aeolus* was the Do 18 V3 (third prototype). Powered by tandem 600-hp (447-kW) Jumo 205C diesel engines, all three were later designated as Do 18E transports and used from 1936 on Lufthansa's routes on the North, and later South, Atlantic. Just before joining the airline, on 10–11 July 1936, *Aeolus* made a 30-hour 21-minute test flight over the Baltic.

Dornier Do 24T cutaway drawing key

1 Bow navigation light
2 Towing/mooring ring
3 Fore hull structure
4 Retractable mast
5 Ammunition magazine racks
6 Spent cartridge chute
7 Bow compartment (see equipment stowage)
8 Turret mechanism
9 Bow 7.92-mm MG 15 machine-gun
10 Bow turret
11 Removable turret dome
12 Nose decking
13 Nose mooring lug
14 Mooring rope stowage
15 Bulkhead
16 Crawlway
17 Rudder pedal assembly
18 Bulkhead door frame
19 Instrument panel shroud
20 Co-pilot's control column
21 Compass
22 Windscreen panels
23 Cockpit roof glazing
24 Sliding entry panels
25 Hatch runners
26 Flight deck windows
27 Navigator's station
28 Co-pilot seat
29 Pilot's seat
30 Seat adjustment lever
31 Side-mounted control column
32 Floors support frame
33 Radio-operator's position
34 'Vee' bottom hull structure
35 Fuselage/sponson fairing
36 Access panels
37 Sponson nose ribs
38 Sponson main fuel cells (four, approx 77 Imp gal/350 litre capacity each)
39 Sponson abbreviated fuel cell (36.6 Imp gal/180 litre capacity)
40 Port sponson mooring lug
41 Rib reinforcement
42 Sponson main spar/fuselage frame
43 Sponson/forward wing strut lower attachment
44 Fuel collector tank (46 Imp gal/210 litres)
45 Access panels
46 Fuselage hull step
47 Sponson rear spar/fuselage frame
48 Sponson/aft wing strut lower attachment
49 Mooring lug
50 Non-slip sponson walkway
51 Forward midships bay (two-stretcher accommodation; 28 oxygen bottles stowed along centre-line walkway)
52 Forward bay hinged entry hatch
53 Sponson/forward wing strut
54 Fuselage main frame bulkhead

Dornier Wal variants

Gs I: wartime flying-boat design, first flown in 1919 and sunk by Allied authorities.
Wal: initial military version of 1922 built by Marina di Pisa and licensees; Rolls-Royce Eagle, Hispano, Lorraine, Napier, Bristol, Packard, Liberty, Wright, BMW, Junkers, Piaggio and other makes of engine; 1,033.4-sq ft (96-m²) wing, gross weight 5.7 tonnes
Wal Type J: initial commercial model from early 1923, generally as for military with enclosed cockpit
8.0-to Wal: strengthened and more powerful 1931 model, usually with 690-hp (515-kW) BMW VI engines, still 1,033.4 sq ft (96 m²) but span increased from 73 ft 9.8 in to 76 ft 1.4 in (22.5 to 23.2 m); passenger seating increased from nine to 14
8.5-to Wal: further uprated version generally as 8.0-to but cleared to 18,739 lb (8500 kg) in 1933

10-to Wal: further enlarged 1933 model with span of 89 ft 2.9 in (27.2 m), 1,205.6-sq ft (112-m²) wing area, usually 690-hp (515-kW) BMW VI engines
Do-15: Luftwaffe designation for uprated military version of 1933; 18,739-lb (8500-kg) weight, 1,033.4-sq ft (96-m²) wing, usually BMW VI engines in German service
Superwal/2m: various twin-engine Type R Superwals usually with two 650-hp (485-kW) Condor or 800-hp (597-kW) Packard engines, 93 ft 10 in (28.6 m) span, 1,539.3-sq ft (143-m²) wing, 19 passenger seats, gross weight 10.5 tonnes
Superwal/4m: four-engine Superwal series, with 480-hp (358 kW) Jupiter VI, 525-hp (391-kW) Siemens Jupiter, 550-hp (410-kW) Hornet or 460-hp (343-kW) Napier Lion; same span but wing reduced to 1,474.7 sq ft (137 m²) area and gross weight increased to 14 tonnes

Dornier Flying-boats

A49-4 was the fourth of five of the oldest Do 24K-1s flown from the Dutch East Indies to Australia on 19 February 1942. Many later escapees reached Broome, Northern Territory, a fortnight later, only to be destroyed there by Japanese fighters. A49-4 served with RAAF No. 41 Sqn on transport duties to the New Guinea theatre.

production of the Do 18 into World War 2 the total of all versions being in the region of 160 including 75 Do 18Ds. The main wartime version was the Do 18G and the unarmed Do 18H crew trainer, both powered by the 880-hp (656-kW) Jumo 205D. By 1941 most surviving Do 18s of all types were converted as Do 18N air/sea rescue aircraft.

The last aircraft that can be said to have descended from the Wal was the Do 24, a considerably larger boat that at last abandoned tandem engines, though it adhered to the use of sponsons for stability on the water. It had its origins in the requirement of the MLD, the Dutch naval air force, for a successor to its mainstay, the trusty Wal. In 1934 the MLD

55 Medical attendant: station
56 Fuselage/wing strut attachment fairing
57 Port engine nacelle intake
58 Fuselage porthole
59 Starboard crew entry door
60 Bulkhead
61 Radio equipment installation
62 Roof external strakes
63 Three-blade VDM metal propellers
64 Spinners
65 Starboard sponson
66 Roof (starboard) entry hatch
67 Centre engine nacelle intake
68 Engine exhausts
69 Engine upper air intakes
70 1,000-hp (746-kW) Bramo 323R-2 radial engine
71 Cowling ring
72 Hinged engine inspection/ maintenance panels

73 Cooling louvre
74 Oil tank cover
75 Servicing handgrip
76 Engine bearers
77 Firewall/bulkhead
78 Centre engine oil tank
79 Centre nacelle frames
80 Centre nacelle pick-up/ hoist bar
81 Starboard wing fuel tank
82 Starboard engine nacelle fairing
83 Starboard aerial mast
84 Wing front spar
85 Aerial
86 Wing ribs
87 Wing metal skinning
88 Starboard navigation light
89 Starboard formation/ identification light
90 Starboard aileron

91 Aileron hinge fairings
92 Wing rear spar
93 Aileron control runs
94 Aileron trim tab
95 Wing centre/outer-section join
96 Aileron inboard profile
97 Centre-section underwing flap
98 Flap actuating hinges
99 Antenna
100 D/F loop
101 Rear spar structure
102 Wing rib/flap cut-out
103 Flap control runs
104 Port engine nacelle fairing
105 Port wing fuel tank
106 Port aerial mast

113 Sponson/forward wing strut upper attachment
114 Twin landing lights
115 Sponson/wing strut diagonal bracing
116 Fuselage/wing aft inverted 'Vee' struts (housing fuel lines from sponsons)

133 Wing rear spar
134 Port navigation light
135 Port formation/ identification light
136 Port aileron
137 Hull aft step

160 Tailplane rear spar/tailfin attachment
161 Starboard tailfin structure
162 Aerial attachment
163 Rudder balance
164 Rudder frame
165 Rudder upper trim tab
166 Starboard rudder post
167 Rudder lower trim tab
168 Trim tab actuating linkage
169 Starboard elevator tab
170 Port rudder balance
171 Starboard elevator structure
172 Elevator control linkage

107 Oil tank cover
108 Front spar
109 Hinged leading-edge (inspection/servicing access)
110 Fuselage/wing centre-line diagonal brace strut
111 Fuselage/wing forward inverted 'Vee' struts (housing control runs)
112 Wing centre/outer section front spar join

117 Wing centre/outer section join rib
118 Sponson/aft wing strut upper attachment
119 Midships dorsal decking
120 Sponson/aft wing strut
121 Fuselage air ventilation plant
122 Fuselage main frame bulkhead
123 Centre-line walkway
124 Aft bay hinged entry hatch
125 Aft midships bay (four × stretcher accommodation)
126 Hull 'Vee' bottom structure
127 Galley/hot plate (port)
128 Blanket/survival clothing cupboard (starboard)
129 Fuselage midships mooring lug
130 Aileron hinge fairings
131 Bulkhead door
132 Aileron underwing mass balances

138 'Vee' bottom sternpost frame
139 Reinforced fuselage frame
140 Turret support
141 Compressed air bottles
142 Turret ring
143 Dorsal turret
144 20-mm MG 151 cannon
145 Toilet
146 Peat bag (toilet sanitary refill)
147 Porthole
148 Master compass
149 Aft fuselage centre-line catwalk
150 Tail surface control rod linkage
151 Fuselage aft frames
152 Fuselage skinning
153 Ventral stringers
154 Control rods
155 Fuselage/tailplane fairing
156 Tailplane front spar
157 Elevator control rod
158 Elevator hinges
159 Tailplane ribs

173 Rudder linkage
174 Port aerial attachment
175 Tailplane inboard end rib structure
176 Tailplane front spar/ fuselage frame attachment
177 Fuselage aft main frame
178 Control linkage
179 Stern mooring rope stowage
180 Tailplane brace struts
181 Port tailfin
182 Tailplane/fin attachment
183 Port elevator hinge
184 Rear turret ammunition stowage
185 Port rudder post
186 Rear turret
187 Turret ring
188 Tail gunner's armour plating
189 Port rudder
190 Rudder lower trim tab hinge fairing
191 Port rudder lower trim tab
192 Tail navigation light
193 Tail mooring ring
194 7.92-mm MG 15 stern machine-gun

Dornier Flying-boats

The last military flying-boats in service in Europe, the Spanish Ejercito del Aire's Do 24T-2s survived on coastal patrol and rescue duties from Puerto de Pollensa until 1970, serving with the 58th Escuadrilla de Salvamento. Their superb rough-water seaworthiness has never been equalled by any other aircraft of any size.

refined its ideas and opened talks with Dornier, soon deciding that the Do 18 was not quite big enough. The MLD wanted not only long range and more than two engines but also the ability to operate safely at great distances from land and, if necessary, alight on quite rough seas. During 1935 Dornier went ahead with the design of the three-engine Do 24 purely for the MLD, charging the Dutch government a fee for the design process as well as selling a licence to Aviolanda, which had finished building Wals in 1931. Four prototypes were put in hand, the Do 24 V3 being the first to fly and being powered, like the Do 24 V4, with the engine specified by the customer for commonality with its Martin 139WH-1 bombers, the Wright Cyclone F52. Dornier fitted the first two prototypes with the heavier and less powerful Jumo 205 diesel for possible use by the Luftwaffe, but not much was done with them before the war.

Successful trials

A wholly modern stressed-skin boat, the Do 24 hung its shapely hull under the rectangular centre section on two pairs of inverted-V struts, with a fifth diagonal strut to react to the pull of the engines (in contrast to the big streamlined pylon of the Do 18). The tail had twin fins on the ends of the wide-span tailplane, and there was provision for a gun turret in the bow, amidships and at the extreme tail. The MLD also specified wing bomb racks for up to 12 stores of 220 lb (100 kg) each, and a heavy load of mission equipment. Flight trials, including operations from very heavy seas, showed that the Do 24 possessed exceptional strength and good performance. In autumn 1937 the MLD signed for 60, to be licence-built in the Netherlands, but in the event Dornier built 12 (including the Do 24 V3 and V4 prototypes), with the designation Do 24K-1, using the 875-hp (652-kW) F52 engine, while Aviolanda, De Schelde and other Dutch companies undertook to build the other 48, designated Do 24K-2, powered by the 1,000-hp (746-kW) Cyclone G102.

Continuing the story of the Do 24 into the 1980s, this ex-Do 24T-2 has acquired a new wing and triple turboprop powerplants while retaining the original hull and tail units. Currently undergoing flight testing and research into composite materials and corrosion problems, a commercial future for the Do 24TT remains to be realized.

This Do 24MS minesweeper was one of a small number (possibly only two) converted for the task from regular Luftwaffe Do 24T-1 rescue/reconnaissance machines. An auxiliary motor/generator set in the hull fed the heavy current pulses through the duralumin ring conductor; the magnetic field exploded mines below the aircraft.

All the Do 24K-1s had been delivered by the outbreak of war, but when Germany invaded the Netherlands on 10 May 1940 only 25 of the Do 24K-2s had been despatched. Three were captured intact, and when these were tested at Travemünde the Luftwaffe discovered they were superb boats, and Dutch production was quickly restarted. Under the control of the Weser company the Do 24K-2s were modified without bomb gear but with MG15 nose and tail guns and captured Hispano 20-mm cannon in the amidships turret, as well as large hatches and comprehensive internal furnishings for the air/sea rescue mission. Designated Do 24N-1, the production boats entered Luftwaffe service from August 1941, 11 being delivered by November when the stock of engines was exhausted. Production then continued with the Do 24T-1 with the 1,000-hp (746-kW) BMW Bramo Fafnir 323, a total of 170 in all being supplied. Such was the demand for this fine boat that a second source was organized at the former Potez-CAMS factory at Sartrouville, France, where 48 additional Do 24s were built.

From early 1943 most were of the Do 24T-2 sub-type with extra radio and sometimes radar, as well as an MG 151 replacing the Hispano cannon amidships. Very similar boats designated Do 24T-3 were prepared for Spain, 12 being flown to the Spanish seaplane base at Puerto Pollensa, Majorca, in 1944.

Every Do 24 was heavily involved in the events of the war. The MLD boats in the Dutch East Indies had almost all been destroyed by the end of March 1942. Towards the end of the war, the Luftwaffe's losses of flying boats were very high, but the Spanish Do 24T-3s were still in use long after the war. As late as 1972, holidaymakers in Majorca were able to see a number of Do 24T-3s. The last of these was flown to the Dornier factory in Friedrichshafen to be preserved for posterity. A number of squadrons of the French Aéronavale were using about 40 Do 24T-2s between them, and one machine which a Luftwaffe flight engineer flew to Sweden in 1945 was used by the Flygvapen as a Tp 24 for a total of seven years.

Curtiss Hawk Biplanes

Dependence upon licence production of British aircraft at the end of World War 1 deprived the USA of design experience with which to maintain a flow of indigenous designs during the post-war period. Instead, a host of small companies scrambled for attention; the best-known results were the Curtiss Hawk fighters, manufactured by a company run by a famous American. Glenn Curtiss, a noted flier in his own right, produced the Curtiss Hawk over a period of 10 years, though fewer than 250 were built.

One of the USA's most famous pioneers of flight, Glenn Curtiss, was also one of the country's first aircraft manufacturers. He mass-produced planes based on wholly American designs, although later on the Curtiss JN ('Jenny') trainer was built mainly from designs by B. Douglas Thomas, who was working for Sopwith in England at the time. Towards the end of World War 1, trainers were the only planes designed in America and mass-produced for the US Army.

However, one of the best-known foreign combat aircraft, selected by the Bolling Commission for US production, was the Royal Aircraft Factory S.E.5a, and although the planned mass production of this excellent fighter by Curtiss never materialized the company gained important experience in the field when ordered to modify and assemble 57 British-manufactured examples. In the meantime the company also embarked on a series of racing aircraft in which military pilots were to compete in the prestigious Pulitzer contest of 1922, and the two Curtiss R-6s (68563 and 68564) were flown into first and second place by Lieutenants Russell Maughan and Lester J. Maitland; shortly after the race Brigadier General Billy Mitchell raised the world speed record over 0.62 mile (1 km) to 222.97 mph (358.84 km/h) while flying one of the racers.

The success of the R-6 encouraged the Curtiss company to enter the field of interceptor fighters (known in those days as pursuit aircraft), and before the end of 1922 a prototype was under construction at private expense. However, whereas the R-6 biplanes had employed single-bay wings (and demonstrated inadequate strength when one aircraft shed its wings at the start of the 1924 Pulitzer race), the new fighter reverted to two-bay configuration, being officially adopted by the Air Service as the XPW-8 (experimental, pursuit, water-cooled-8). In due course Curtiss won a contract for 25 PW-8 production aircraft, and these served with the 17th Pursuit Squadron between 1924 and 1926. When one of the three XPW-8s was modified (at the request of what had become the US Army Air Corps on 4 June 1920) to feature completely redesigned wings of tapered planform and Clark Y aerofoil section (similar to that on the contemporary Boeing PW-9), the resulting aircraft, the XPW-8B, became in effect the prototype of a new design family, the P-1 Hawk (under a simplified designation system omitting reference to

A few of the nine P-6As with the Prestone cooling system were fitted with three-blade propellers, this aircraft carrying the markings of an Air Base Squadron, probably in about 1930. Top speed of this version was 179 mph (288 km/h) at sea level.

The XP-6 was in fact a P-2, 25-423, experimentally powered by a 600-hp (447-kW) V-1570 Conqueror engine; the famous 'Snowy Owl' insignia suggests previous service with the 17th Pursuit Squadron, 1st Pursuit Group.

Curtiss P-6 Hawk

Specification

Curtiss P-6E Hawk

Type: single-seat pursuit aircraft

Powerplant: one 600-hp (448-kW) Curtiss V-1570-23 12-cylinder Vee liquid-cooled piston engine

Performance: maximum speed 197 mph (317 km/h) at sea level; initial climb rate 2,400 ft (732 m) per minute; service ceiling 24,700 ft (7530 m); range 570 miles (917 km)

Weights: empty 2,699 lb (1224 kg); maximum take-off 3,392 lb (1539 kg)

Dimensions: span 31 ft 6 in (9.60 m); length 23 ft 2 in (7.06 m); height 8 ft 10 in (2.69 m); wing area 252.0 sq ft (23.41 m²)

Armament: two 0.3-in (7.62-mm) machine-guns with 600 rounds per gun on sides of nose

Curtiss Hawk variants

XPW-8B: serialled 23-1203, this was the third of three prototypes with single-bay wings; became P-1 Hawk prototype; Curtiss D-12 engine

P-1 Hawk: 10 aircraft (25–410 to 25-419); Curtiss V-1150-1 engines

P-1A Hawk: 25 aircraft (26-276 to 26-300); Curtiss V-1150-1 engines; fuselage lengthened by 3 in (7.62 cm); one aircraft (26-296) became **XAT-4** and one more (26-295) became **XP-6A** racer

P-1B Hawk: 25 aircraft (27-063) to 27-087); Curtiss V-1150-3 engines with modified radiators

P-1C Hawk: 33 aircraft (29-227 to 29-259); Curtiss V-1150-5 engines; wheelbrakes fitted

XP-1C: one P-1C (29-238) with Heinrich radiator and Prestone cooling

AT-4: 35 aircraft (27-088 to 27-097, and 27-213 to 27-237); trainers with Wright V-720 engines; re-engined with Curtiss V-1150-3s and designated **P-1D Hawk**

AT-5: five aircraft (27-238 to 27-242); trainers with Wright R-790-1 radial engines; re-engined with Curtiss V-1150-3s and designated **P-1E Hawk**

AT-5A: 31 aircraft (28-042 to 28-072); trainers with Wright R-790-1 radials; re-engined with Curtiss V-1150-3s and designated **P-1F Hawk**

P-2 Hawk: five aircraft (25-420 to 25-424); first aircraft (25-420) with experimental turbocharger; fourth (25-423) became **XP-6** with V-1570-1 engine; remaining three became standard **P-1A** fighter

XP-3A: conversion of last P-1A (26-300) with Pratt & Whitney R-1340-9 radial

P-3A Hawk: five aircraft (28-189 to 28-193); Pratt & Whitney R-1340-3 radials; one aircraft (28-189) became a second XP-3A

P-5 Hawk: five aircraft (27-327 to 27-331); turbocharged V-1150-3 engines; the first aircraft (27-327) was termed **XP-5**

XP-6: conversion of P-2 (25-423) with V-1570 engine for racing

XP-6A: conversion of P-1A (26-295) with high compression V-1570 for racing

P-6 (YP-6) Hawk: 18 aircraft (29-260 to 29-273, and 29-363 to 29-366); test batch with V-1570 engines; first

nine aircraft with water cooling and remainder with Prestone cooling; nine aircraft later converted to P-6D

P-6A: eight P-6s (29-260 to 29-267) converted to V-1570-23 with Prestone cooling

XP-6A: (2nd aircraft); conversion of one production P-6A (29-263) for trials

XP-6B 'Hoyt Special': long-range conversion of the last P-1C (29-259) with V-1570 engine

XP-6D: conversion of first P-6A (29-260) with turbocharged V-1570C

P-6D Hawk: conversion of nine P-6s and three P-6As with turbocharged V-1570 engines

XP-6E: conversion of third P-11 (29-374) with single-leg landing gear

P-6E Hawk: 46 aircraft (32-233 to 32-277); Curtiss V-1570-23 engines, final aircraft (32-277) became XP-23

XP-6F: conversion of XP-6E (29-374) with V-1570F engine and enclosed cockpit

XP-6G: conversion of one P-6E (32-254) with unsupercharged V-1570F engine; reverted to P-6E

XP-6H: conversion of first P-6E (32-233) to mount six machine-guns

P-11: three aircraft intended for Curtiss H-1640 engine, but two completed as P-6 (29-367 and 29-268), and one as YP-20 (29-374) with Wright Cyclone engine

XP-17: conversion of first P-1 (25-410) with V-1470 engine

YP-20: conversion of third P-11 (29-374) with Wright Cyclone engine

XP-21: conversion of XP-3A (26-300) and first P-3A (28-189) with R-985 Wasp Junior engine; 26-300 became **XP-21A**, and 28-189 became a P-1F

XP-22: conversion of third P-6A (29-262) with modified nose, tail surfaces and three-blade propeller

Y1P-22: original designation of 46 production aircraft that became P-6E

XP-23: conversion of the last P-6E (32-277) with monocoque fuselage; became **YP-23**

Export Hawk: eight aircraft for Netherlands East Indies air force, and eight for Cuba (with Pratt & Whitney R-1340 radials); one aircraft purchased by Mitsubishi, Japan

One of the two classic Army biplane pursuit aircraft designs of the 1920s and 1930s, the long-lived Hawk series was epitomized by the last of the production versions, the P-6E. Its basic shape had evolved through a long line of Hawk biplanes, originating with Army and Navy racers that Curtiss built between 1921 and 1925. The developed P-6E form was elegant, with tapered wings and a fuselage that faired into the 600-hp (448-kW) Curtiss Conqueror liquid-cooled engine. The initial order was for 46 of the E models, and most were delivered to the 17th and 94th Pursuit Squadrons during 1932. The single-leg landing gear and the belly radiator position were the major differences between the P-6E and earlier Hawks, with their more conventional landing gear and nose radiators. This particular aircraft is painted in the characteristic black and white markings and Army Air Corps insignia of the 17th Pursuit Squadron of the 1st Pursuit Group, while based at Selfridge Field, Michigan. This scheme, named after the Arctic snow owl painted on the fuselage band, was a short-lived one; but it is the best-remembered one, as well as the most elaborate, of all Hawk markings.

engine type and manufacturer) but only ten were assembled.

Adoption of the smaller, tapered wing on the XPW-8B, combined with growing familiarity with the causes and effects of wing flutter, allowed reversion to the single-bay layout, and the 10 production Curtiss P-1s, ordered on 7 March 1925, differed from the prototype only in inclusion of an extra strut in the centre-section bracing and a slightly modified rudder shape. These aircraft served with the 27th and 94th Pursuit Squadrons, 1st Pursuit Group, at Selfridge Field, Michigan, commanded by Major Thomas G. Lanphier. Power was provided by the 435-hp (325-kW) Curtiss D-12 12-cylinder water-cooled Vee engine which, under a new designation system denoting cubic capacity, became the V-1150-1. The first P-1 underwent tests at McCook Field starting on 17 August 1925.

The P-1 contract covered production of five additional

Service P-6Ds differed from the prototype XP-6D in having three-blade propellers. Fitted with turbo-superchargers, nine P-6Ds and some P-6As were converted to P-6D standard, the aircraft shown being flown by the 8th Pursuit Group in 1932.

aircraft designated P-2 and powered by the 505-hp (377-kW) Curtiss V-1400, also water-cooled. The first of these P-2s was flown in December 1925, and was later fitted with an experimental turbocharger which increased the service ceiling from 22,980 ft (7005 m) of the standard P-1 to 32,790 ft (9995 m)

Meanwhile the P-1 itself had undergone minor improvement that resulted in a contract for 25 P-1As being placed in September 1925; this version featured a fuselage lengthened by 3 in (7.62 cm), changed cowling lines and a D-12C engine, and had improved bomb release gear (all pursuit fighters were still required to feature a light bomb-carrying ability). Only 23 P-1As were completed as such, one aircraft emerging as the XAT-4 trainer with Wright-Hispano E engine, and

the other became the XP-6A racer (with XPW-8A wings).

The next production version, the P-1B with V-1150-3 engine and improved radiator, was ordered in August 1926, 23 examples serving alongside earlier Hawks and starting delivery only two months later. With larger landing wheels and some equipment changes, the normal loaded weight increased to 2,932 lb (1330 kg), and the maximum speed was reduced from the 163 mph (262 km/h) of the P-1 to 159.6 mph (257 km/h).

Largest order for the Curtiss pursuit fighters to date was for 33 P-1Cs, their delivery being completed in April 1929. The V-1150-3 was retained and once more, on account of increased weight (wheel brakes were fitted), the speed dropped, this time to 154 mph (248 km/h). One aircraft, modified with an experimental Heinrich radiator and Prestone cooling system, was termed the XP-1C. No further P-1s were produced but, following successful trials with the XAT-4 in October 1926, 35 production AT-4s with Wright V-720 engines and five AT-5s with Wright R-790 engines were ordered; the former were later re-engined with the standard Curtiss V-1150-3 and reverted to the pursuit category as P-1Ds; when similarly re-engined the five AT-5s became P1Es. These aircraft served with the 43rd School Squadron at Kelly Field; this unit became the 43rd Pursuit Squadron in 1935.

Trainers into fighters

A further conversion involved 31 Curtiss AT-5A trainers which had been ordered by the US Army on 30 July 1927 with R-790 engines; their poor performance (maximum speed only 122 mph/196 km/h) caused them to be re-engined with D-12s in 1929, their designation changing to P-1F; one other P-1F was created by reconverting an XP-21 (see below).

The designation P-2, as mentioned above, covered the last five aircraft ordered on the first P-1 contract, powered by Curtiss V-1400 engines. In the event this engine proved disappointing and three aircraft were converted to P-1As; only one aircraft (25-240) remained XP-2, and the last P-2 became the XP-6.

The P-3 was the first radial-engine Hawk pursuit fighter. The XP-3A designation was applied to the last P-1A, which was completed with a 410-hp (306-kW) Pratt & Whitney R-1340-9, this radial engine being flown both uncowled and with a variety of deep-chord NACA cowls. Later, when re-engined with the 300-hp (224-kW) Pratt & Whitney R-985-1 Wasp Junior, the aircraft was redesignated the XP-21. Five production P-3As with R-1340-3 radials were ordered in 1928 and four of these were delivered the following year to the 94th Pursuit Squadron, then commanded by the famous US Army Air Corps pilot, Major (later Major General) Ralph Royce. The other P-3A (28-189) was retained for further engine cowling trials and became the second XP-3A. Later it also became an XP-21 with R-985-1 Wasp Junior before being converted to a P-1F. Maximum speed of the standard P-3A

One of 23 P-1Bs ordered by the US Army Air Corps in August 1926, this aircraft served with the 27th Pursuit Squadron, 1st Pursuit Group, commanded by the famous Major Ralph Royce at Selfridge Field (now Air National Guard Base), Michigan, in 1929–30.

with narrow-chord cowling was 153 mph (246 km/h) at sea level; however in June 1930 one of the P-3As was flown with an SR-1340-C cowling, spinner and side fairings, refinements which resulted in a top speed of 193 mph (311 km/h).

Strangely, the US Army Air Corps decided to discontinue the radial engine 'Hawk' (despite favouring the radial-powered Boeing P-12), and the next Curtiss variant was the P-5, of which only five were ordered and delivered to the 94th Pursuit Squadron in 1928. Produced to allow service evaluation of the turbocharged Curtiss D-12F engine, this Hawk possessed a sea-level maximum speed of only 144 mph (232 km/h), but at 25,000 ft (7620 m), well above the ceiling of unsupercharged P-1s, the top speed was 166 mph (267 km/h). By the time the P-5s were delivered, however, the new Curtiss V-1570 Conqueror was ready for production. No further development was undertaken on the D-12.

Enter the P-6 Hawk

After almost four years of development the definitive Curtiss P-6 Hawk was considered ready for production. Once again aircraft prepared for racing played an important part in the development. For the 1927 National Air Races to be held at Spokane, Washington, the US Army ordered two Curtiss racers, the fourth P-2 (25-423) with the new 600-hp V-1570 Conqueror as the XP-6, and a P-1A (26-295) with a high-compression V-1570 in a different cowling as the XP-6A (this also employed wing radiators). The XP-6A won the unlimited race at a speed of 201 mph (324 km/h), and second place went to the XP-6 at a speed of 189 mph (304 km/h). The XP-6A was destroyed shortly before the 1928 air races, however.

The use of the Conqueror engine in the two racers served

Best known of all P-6 squadrons was probably the 17th Pursuit Squadron, 1st Pursuit Group, one of whose aircraft is seen here with ski undercarriage. The rear fuselage band was black with white borders and a 'Snowy Owl' superimposed on it.

Third of the three P-11s, 29-374, was completed with a Wright R-1820 Cyclone radial engine as the XP-20; it was then given the engine and landing gear of the XP-22 and became the prototype XP-6E, later being re-designated the XP-6F.

Identified by the Prestone cooling system label and turbo-supercharged engine, the P-6D was handicapped by considerable powerplant weight, and only 35 examples were produced.

Standard P-6E of the 94th Pursuit Squadron, 1st Pursuit Group, in about 1933 when commanded by Lieutenant-Colonel (later Major General) Frank M. Andrews at Selfridge Field, Michigan. Though only 46 P-6Es were produced, they represented the zenith of the 'Army Hawk' biplane family.

not only to demonstrate its suitability in the Hawk but also its reliability, and on 3 October 1928 18 P-6s (sometimes referred to as YP-6s) were ordered for service evaluation; they were delivered to the 27th Pursuit Squadron in 1929. To speed delivery, the first nine aircraft were completed with V-1570-17 engines with water cooling, the remainder having the intended V-1570-23s with Prestone (ethylene glycol) cooling which permitted smaller radiators. Two additional P-6s were produced by completing two of the three P-11s (see below) on order with water-cooled V-1570-17s.

Eight of the water-cooled P-6s were subsequently re-engined with Prestone-cooled V-1570-23s their designation being changed to P-6A; some of these flew with three-blade variable-pitch propellers. One of the aircraft (29-263) was assigned to radiator trials under the designation XP-6A no. 2, and the designation XP-6B covered a special conversion of the last P-1C (29-259) with Conqueror engine, and popularly known as the Hawk Hoyt Special; intended for a long-distance flight from New York to Alaska by Captain (later Brigadier General) Ross G. Hoyt, the Hawk crashed short of its destination and, after repairs, was assigned to experimental work.

The designation P-6D referred to turbocharged aircraft. The XP-6D covered the first P-6A (29-260) fitted experimentally with a supercharged V-1570C, performance figures including a sea-level maximum speed of 172 mph (277 km/h) and a speed of 197 mph (317 km/h) at 15,000 ft (4570 m). No new production followed, but nine P-6s and three P-6As were fitted with turbochargers and redesignated P-6D; they were issued to the US Army Air Corps in April 1932.

Best known of all Hawks was the P-6E variant. The prototype XP-6E had begun life as the third XP-11 (29-374), was completed as the YP-20 (see below) and then fitted with

Last of the P-6Es, 32-278, was held at the factory and completed with aluminium monocoque fuselage, turbo-supercharged and geared G1V-1570-C engine, and designated the XP-23; after removal of the supercharger and fitting a two-blade propeller, as shown here, the aircraft was re-designated YP-23.

Curtiss P-6E Hawk cutaway drawing key

1 Starter dog
2 Propeller hub
3 Three-blade Hamilton Standard metal propeller
4 Oil cooler chin intake
5 Nose cowling front panel line
6 Gear housing
7 Front curved panel
8 Carburettor air intake
9 Intake trunk
10 Curtiss V-1570-C Conqueror engine
11 Exhaust stubs (2 per cylinder)
12 Stainless steel trough surround
13 Gun trough
14 Machine-gun muzzle
15 Cowling access panel line
16 Diagonal brace
17 Struts
18 Main engine support bearer
19 Filter
20 Lower panel lines
21 Oil cooler assembly
22 Telescopic access/ servicing step
23 Radiator attachment mounts
24 Prestone radiator
25 Radiator fairing
26 Intake
27 Starboard mainwheel spat

28 Starboard undercarriage strut
29 Axle
30 Starboard low-pressure mainwheel tyre
31 Anchor point
32 Inboard access panel (brake servicing)
33 Port mainwheel spat
34 Flathead screw panel line
35 Port axle assembly
36 Port low-pressure mainwheel tyre
37 Hub assembly forging
38 Angled undercarriage strut
39 Removable spat half-section
40 Undercarriage leg fairing
41 Strut/fairing attachment
42 Strut support forged frame member
43 Strut pivot
44 Hinged cover plate
45 Front wires fuselage attachment
46 Engine accessories
47 Fuselage forward frame
48 Port ammunition magazine (600 rounds per gun)
49 Deflector panel
50 Cartridge chute
51 Gun support strut
52 Ammunition feed fairing
53 Oleo shock strut/rebound spring
54 Upper pivot point
55 Cabane forward attachment
56 Oil access point
57 Bulkhead panel
58 Starboard wires
59 Aluminium leading-edge panels

60 Upper wing centre-section
61 Cabane struts
62 Cabane wires
63 Cabane upper wing attachment points
64 Reinforced strut
65 Starboard lower wing plan
66 Front spar
67 Interplane 'N'-struts
68 Upper wing ribs
69 Internal bracing wires
70 Interplane strut upper attachment points
71 Reinforced rib
72 Outer rib assemblies
73 Starboard navigation light
74 Aerial mast
75 Aileron/rear spar join
76 Welded steel aileron (fabric-covered)
77 Aileron hinge link
78 Metal plate
79 Aileron interplane actuating link
80 Aileron profile
81 Rear spar
82 Trailing-edge rib assembly
83 Centre-section cut-out
84 Handhold
85 Telescopic gunsight
86 Gunsight supports
87 Hinged fuel access panel
88 Filler neck
89 Fuselage main fuel tank (50 US gals/189 litres)
90 Engine controls
91 Port 0.30-in (7.62-mm) Browning machine-gun
92 Lower longeron
93 Fuel tank bearer
94 Lower wing front spar attachment
95 Wingroot walkway

96 Diagonal strut frame
97 Lower wing rear spar attachment
98 Aileron control linkage
99 Hanging rudder pedal assembly
100 Control column
101 Fuselage frame
102 Cabane rear attachment
103 Instrument centre panel
104 Main instrument panel
105 Windscreen
106 Control grip
107 Side switch panel
108 Engine control quadrant
109 Throttle lever
110 Upper wing trailing-edge
111 Padded forward coaming
112 Cockpit cut-out
113 Headrest/turnover frame
114 Bad-weather cover (snap-on rubber tarpaulin)
115 Oxygen access panel (starboard)
116 Pilot's seat
117 Seat support frame
118 Inspection 'Vee' panel
119 Cockpit floor
120 Fuselage diagonal side frames

121 Oxygen cylinder (starboard)
122 Metal door flap
123 Parachute flare stowage (port)
124 Baggage compartment hinged side door
125 Hasp and lock
126 Baggage compartment hinged upper panel
127 Snap fasteners
128 Fuselage top frames
129 All-metal dorsal decking
130 Diagonal brace wires
131 Elevator control cables
132 Rudder control cables
133 Fuselage structure
134 Pulleys
135 Cross-member
136 Dorsal cross-section transition (round/point)
137 Tailplane front beam attachment
138 Bearer frame
139 Tailfin front beam attachment
140 Tailfin leading-edge
141 Starboard tailplane
142 Aerials
143 Tailfin structure
144 Tailplane brace wires
145 Rudder balance
146 Aerial post
147 Tail navigation light recess
148 Rudder upper hinge
149 Rudder frame
150 Spacers
151 Rudder post
152 Elevator control horns

153 Tailfin rear beam attachment
154 Elevator control cable
155 Rudder control horns
156 Port elevator frame
157 Brace wire attachment
158 Port (adjustable) tailplane
159 Tailplane front beam
160 Tail dolly lug

161 Swivel/steerable tailwheel
162 Axle fork
163 Metal grommet collar
164 Fuselage strut
165 Tailwheel shock-strut leg
166 Leather grommets (elevator control cables)
167 Tailwheel leg upper attachment
168 Access 'Vee' panel
169 Diagonal brace wires
170 Lower longeron
171 Ventral skinning
172 Port aileron
173 Aerial mast
174 Lower wingroot cut-out
175 Ventral tank aft fairing
176 Rear spar
177 Interplane 'N'-struts
178 Upper wing leading-edge
179 Drop tank filler cap
180 Drop tank (41.6 Imp gal/ 189 litres)
181 Vent
182 Lower wing aluminium leading-edge panels
183 Nose ribs
184 Wire turnbuckle clamp
185 'N'-strut lower attachments
186 Port navigation light
187 Reinforced rib
188 Aileron actuating linkage
189 Lower wing trailing-edge
190 Rear spar
191 Outer rib assemblies
192 Front spar
193 Wingtip structure
194 Handling point

the engine and landing gear of the XP-22 and designated XP-6E. It later became the XP-6F.

Forty-six production aircraft (32-233 to 32-278) were ordered under the initial designation Y1P-22, subsequently changed to P-6E to simplify administration. Their most prominent distinguishing feature was the single-strut cantilever landing gear with wheel 'pants' (streamlined fairings which covered the upper halves of the wheels). The radiator was moved back from the 'chin' location to a position just forward of the main landing gear units, while the balance area of the rudder was decreased by the top rib of the fin. The two-gun nose armament was revised by moving the guns from the top of the nose cowling to the sides of the fuselage. Other airframe refinements (including a tailwheel in place of a skid) raised the sea-level speed to 197 mph (317 km/h).

P-6Es served with the 1st Pursuit Group (17th, 27th and 94th Squadrons) at Selfridge Field, California, under Lieutenant Colonel Frank M. Andrews, and with the 8th Pursuit Group (33rd, 35th and 36th Squadrons) at Langley Field, Virginia, under Major Byron Q. Jones.

A formation of P-6E Hawks, the most important version of the Hawk series, here shown in the distinctive markings of the 17th Pursuit Squadron, 1st Pursuit Group, at Selfridge Field.

Experimental developments

Several other experimental variations of the P-6E were produced, including the XP-6F – the fastest of all Hawks. This was the XP-6E with turbocharged V-1570-55 Conqueror and an enclosed cockpit; gross weight increased to 3,842 lb (1743 kg) and this limited the sea-level speed to 194 mph (312 km/h), but at 18,000 ft (5510 m) the maximum speed increased to 225 mph (362 km/h). However, the impossibility of controlling the engine cooling at greater altitudes with the possibility of disastrous failure caused tests on this aircraft to be ended on 1 August 1933.

The designation XP-6G covered a P-6E (32-254) with the supercharger removed; the 'X' was dropped when the aircraft was delivered to the 8th Pursuit Group, but it later reverted to a standard P-6E. The XP-6H had also started out as a P-6E (32-233) but was returned to the manufacturers to have four additional machine-guns fitted (two in the upper and two in the lower wings, all free-firing outside the propeller arc). Carrying a total of 3,300 rounds of 0.3-in (7.62-mm) ammunition, the six-gun XP-6H was not considered a feasible combat aeroplane by the US Army Air Corps and the project was dropped.

Export Hawks included eight P-6s for the Netherlands East

Indies and a small number for Cuba with Pratt & Whitney R-1340 radials, produced around 1930. One Hawk was purchased by Mitsubishi in Japan where the technical inspector was one Jiro Horikoshi, later the chief designer of the famous Zero-Sen naval fighter.

Unsatisfactory Chieftain

Finally, there was a host of designations tentatively applied to new projects, and many of these reverted to standard after completion of trials. Three P-11s were ordered to a standard comparable with the P-6 but powered by the new Curtiss H-1640 Chieftain engine; this powerplant proved unsatisfactory and the first two P-11s were completed as P-6s, while the third became the YP-20, which was powered by a Wright Cyclone engine.

The XP versions appear

The designation XP-17 was applied to the first P-1 (25-410) when experimentally fitted with the Curtiss V-1470, a 480-hp (358-kW) 12-cylinder inverted-Vee engine. The YP-20 was so designated when the third P-11 was fitted with a 575-hp (429-kW) Wright R-1820 Cyclone radial; after being modified with the cantilever landing gear of the XP-22, the aircraft became the XP-6E, and later still the XP-6F. The XP-22 itself was the third P-6A (29-262), with all the modifications (including the revised single-strut landing gear) subsequently adopted on the P-6E. It later reverted to a standard P-6A. As already mentioned, the Y1P-22s became P-6Es.

YP-23 was the designation given to the final P-6E (32-378), which was retained by the manufacturer and featured an entirely new monocoque aluminium fuselage, new tail surfaces and a supercharged and geared Curtiss G1V-1570-C engine; top speed of this version was 220 mph (354 km/h) at 15,000 ft (4570 m).

The delivery of the Curtiss P-6E and Boeing P-12 during 1932 and 1933 marked the end of the procurement of biplanes for pursuit fighter purposes by the US Army Air Corps.

It was becoming very evident to US and other military aircraft designers that the era of the pursuit biplane was rapidly coming to an end. Already brilliant minds overseas were dreaming of monoplane fighters capable of high speeds. Sydney Camm, for one, had the embryo Hurricane on his drawingboard.

A view under the engine cowl of an XP-6A Hawk. With its V-1570 Conqueror engine this machine won the 1927 National Air Races at a speed of 201.3 mph (324 km/h).

de Havilland Moths

A product of the 1920s, the classic Moths represented a successful venture to enable the public to enjoy the sport of flying, and sowed the seeds of private aircraft ownership that were to blossom throughout the inter-war years.

The de Havilland Moth was much more than simply a series of light aircraft. With this plane, de Havilland proved their theory that the British middle classes loved recreational flying and represented a previously untapped market. For the same reasons, in 1923 the Daily Mail sponsored a competition for light aircraft – we would call them ultra-lights today – at Lympne. There was a demand for the production of an aircraft that a small flying club or even the man in the street could afford and would be correspondingly easy to fly. A number of interesting small aircraft were entered for the competition, but de Havilland realised that a machine with a capacity of less than 1.1 litre was too under-powered for an inexperienced pilot and would be dangerous.

Accordingly the works at Stag Lane set about producing a scaled-down version of the D.H.51 three-seater, the new aircraft being a two-seat single-bay biplane, tough enough to withstand the rigours of instructional work and not so cramped as to be uncomfortable during cross-country flying. Powered by a four-cylinder 60-hp (45-kW) engine specially designed by Major F.B. Halford and named the A.D.C. Cirrus I, the new D.H.60 was a model of robust simplicity, its fuselage being in effect a plywood box built round spruce longerons and stiffened by vertical and horizontal members screwed to the plywood.

Named Moth in recognition of Geoffrey de Havilland's renown as a lepidopterist, the first D.H.60 (G-EBKT) was flown at Stag Lane by 'DH' himself on 22 February 1925. On that day was set a pattern for private flying that was to be emulated the world over until World War 2. Efforts to canvass support from government sources were successful when Sir Sefton Brancker, Director of Civil Aviation, announced the founding of five Air Ministry-subsidized Moth-equipped flying clubs, the Lancashire Aero Club, the London Aeroplane Club, the Newcastle Aero Club, the Midland Aero Club and the Yorkshire Aeroplane Club. By the end of 1925 20 Cirrus Moths had been completed, of which 16 had been delivered to the clubs and two to private owners. 1926 brought forth 35 more Moths, of which 14 were exported, nine of them to Australia; Major Halford produced an 85-hp (63-kW) Cirrus II engine which was fitted in a Moth to be piloted by Geoffrey de Havilland in the King's Cup Race, but a broken oil pipe let through Hubert Broad into first place in a Cirrus I Moth. Another famous British sporting pilot, Neville Stack, flew the second Moth proto-type (G-EBKU), powered by the first production Cirrus II, from Croydon to India where it attracted much interest as it embarked on six months joyriding in the sub-continent.

G-ATBL was a D.H.60G Gipsy Moth which was exported to Switzerland. It returned to England where it continued to fly, and is seen here at the Shuttleworth Trust at Old Warden, a perfect setting for the aircraft that established light aeroplane flying as a purely enjoyable pastime.

de Havilland D.H.82A Tiger Moth

Specification

D.H.82A Tiger Moth Mk II
Type: two-seat ab initio trainer biplane
Powerplant: one 130-hp (97-kW) de Havilland Gipsy Major 1 four-cylinder air-cooled inverted inline piston engine
Performance: maximum speed 104 mph (167 km/h) at sea level; initial climb rate 635 ft (194 m) per minute; service ceiling 13,600 ft (4145 m); range 300 miles (483 km)
Weights: empty 1,115 lb (506 kg); maximum take-off 1,825 lb (828 kg)
Dimensions: span 29 ft 4 in (8.94 m); length 23 ft 11 in (7.29 m); height 8 ft 9½ in (2.68 m); wing area 239 sq ft (22.20 m²)
Armament: none

A de Havilland D.H.82A Tiger Moth of the University of London Air Squadron based at RAF Fairoaks in 1950. The University Air Squadrons received Tiger Moths to replace Avro Tutors in 1939, retaining them until they received de Havilland Chipmunks in the early 1950s. The RUL code prefix on this aircraft signifies Reserve Command, University of London Air Squadron, and it carries standard post-war yellow training bands on its fuselage and wings. This aircraft is fitted with a blind flying hood for instrument flying training; in use this would unfold on a metal framework to cover the rear cockpit.

Moth variants

D.H.60 Moth (Cirrus I): 1925–26 model; two prototypes (G-EBKT and G-EBKU); eight pre-production; 31 production aircraft
D.H.60 Moth (Cirrus II): 1926–27 model; 32 built
D.H.60 Genet Moth: six aircraft (J8816–J8821) for Air Ministry; Genet engines
D.H.60X Moth (Cirrus III): 1928 model; 338 built by de Havilland at Stag Lane
D.H.60G Gipsy Moth: introduced 1928; 595 built by de Havilland at Stag Lane; 40 aircraft built by Morane-Saulnier in France; 18 built by Moth Aircraft Corp, in USA; 32 built by Larkin Aircraft Supply, Melbourne, for Australian government
D.H.60M Moth (Metal Moth): introduced 1928; four pre-production aircraft; 536 built by de Havilland at Stag Lane; 40 built by DH Canada; 161 built by Moth Aircraft Corp, in USA; 10 built by Norwegian Army Aircraft Factory in 1931
D.H.60GIII Moth: Gipsy III in wooden Moth; introduced in 1932; 47 built by de Havilland at Stag Lane
D.H.60GIII Moth Major: Gipsy Major III or IIIA; introduced in 1934; one prototype (G-ACNP) and 96 production aircraft
D.H.60T Moth Trainer: Gipsy II; military trainer; introduced 1931; two prototypes (G-ABKS and G-ABKU) and initial production of 47 aircraft
D.H.61 Giant Moth: six/eight-passenger cabin biplane; Jupiter VI or XI, Jaguar VIC or Pratt & Whitney Hornet engines; introduced in 1928
D.H.71 Tiger Moth: two experimental monoplanes G-EBQU (Gipsy) and G-EBRV (Cirrus II) produced in 1927
D.H.75 Hawk Moth: first high-wing Moth; one D.H.75 prototype (de Havilland Ghost engine), five **D.H.75A** (Lynx, Whirlwind or Cheetah engine), and one **D.H.75B** (Whirlwind)
D.H.80A Puss Moth: high-wing cabin monoplane; Gipsy III, Gipsy Major or Gipsy (high compression) engines; introduced 1930; one **D.H.80** prototype (G-AAHZ) and 259 production aircraft built at Stag Lane; 25 built by DH Canada
D.H.81 Swallow Moth: two-seat low-wing monoplane, only one built
D.H.82T Tiger Moth: eight similar to D.H.60T but with Gipsy III; service trials led to D.H.82 and D.H.82A
D.H.82 Tiger Moth: 114 initial military training biplanes built by de Havilland at Stag Lane
D.H.82A Tiger Moth: in RAF, **Tiger Moth MkII**; basic ab initio trainer; total of about 7,290 produced between 1934 and 1945; 795 built by de Havilland at Hatfield, 3,216 by Morris at Cowley, remainder by DH Canada, DH Australia, DH New Zealand, and in Portugal (91), Norway (37) and Sweden (23); Gipsy III and Gipsy Major (various versions); total includes 786 **D.H.82C** with Menasco Pirate D4 engine built by DH Canada (200 sold to USA as **PT-24** in 1942); at least 17 converted to **Thruxton Jackaroo** (four-seat cabin conversion), 1957–9
D.H.82B Queen Bee: radio-controlled gunnery target; RAF 380, Royal Navy 420
D.H.83 Fox Moth: four-passenger cabin biplane; introduced in 1932; Gipsy Major or Gipsy Major IC
D.H.85A Leopard Moth: three seat high-wing cabin monoplane; introduced in 1933; Gipsy Major (**D.H.85**) and Gipsy Six R (**D.H.85A**); one prototype (G-ACHD) and 131 production aircraft
D.H.87 Hornet Moth: two-seat cabin biplane; introduced in 1934; Gipsy Major I; prototype D.H.87 (G-ACTA), **D.H.87A** with elliptical wings and tips
D.H.87B with squared wings and tips; 163 made
D.H.94 Moth Minor: two-seat low-wing monoplane; introduced in 1937

The prototype D.H.60 Moth G-EBKT, which was first flown by Captain Geoffrey de Havilland on Sunday 22 February 1925 at Stag Lane. It differed from subsequent production aircraft in having an unbalanced rudder and exhaust pipe on the starboard side. Moving the pipe to the port side allowed access to an aft baggage locker.

The so-called 1927-model Moths, of which 150 were produced, were all powered by the Cirrus II, and one of these (G-EBPP) was shipped to Australia where Major Hereward de Havilland set up an agency in Melbourne to assemble imported Moths. Numerous outstanding lightplane flights were made by enthusiastic private owners, typical being Lady Bailey's altitude record for light aircraft of 17,283 ft (5268 m) on 5 July of that year, and Lieutenant R. R. Bentley's two extraordinary return flights between the UK and Cape Town totalling 51,652 miles (83125 km) in G-EBSO. Six aircraft, powered by 75-hp (56-kW) Armstrong Siddeley Genet radials, were bought by the Air Ministry for use at the Central Flying School.

1928 introduced the 90-hp (67-kW) Cirrus III engine and a split-axle landing gear which, on account of the new cross-braces between the landing gear, resulted in this model being termed the D.H.60X Moth. By the end of the year 403 Moths of all types had been produced and production was running at 16 per week; moreover, licences to build Moths had been negotiated with the Finnish Government Aircraft Factory and Veljekset Karhumäki O/Y (also of Finland) and the General Aircraft Co. of Sydney, Australia.

Meanwhile stocks of war-surplus Renault engine components, employed in the Cirrus engines, had been exhausted and in 1926 'DH' asked Major Halford to design a new replacement engine; the first example of this, the legendary Gipsy, was completed in July 1927 and within 16 weeks a production shop at Stag Lane was built. After trials in an early Moth (G-EBOH), the new engine gained its certificate and appeared in the production D.H.60G Gipsy Moth. One of

The Thruxton Jackaroo was a post-war four-seat cabin conversion of the Tiger Moth undertaken by Jackaroo Aircraft Ltd, starting in 1957, G-AOIR (shown here), being the fourth produced that year. Most were powered by the 145-hp (108-kW) Gipsy Major 1C in place of the more usual 130-hp (97-kW) Gipsy Major I of the Tiger.

these, flown by W. L. Hope, won the 1928 King's Cup Race at 105 mph (169 km/h). Records tumbled, and many memorable flights followed; 'DH' himself in his own Gipsy Moth (G-AAAA) established a new lightplane height record at 19,980 ft (6090 m) on 25 July 1928, and Hubert Broad remained aloft for 24 hours (using extra fuel tanks in the fuselage); DH's son Geoffrey flew a Gipsy Moth for 600 hours in nine months during 1929; covering 51,000 miles (82075 km) with only routine inspections; when tested afterwards

de Havilland D.H.82A Tiger Moth cutaway drawing key

1 Starboard navigation light
2 Automatic leading edge slat, open
3 Slat hinges
4 Starboard upper and wing panel
5 Wing fabric covering
6 Starboard interplane struts
7 Pitot static tubes
8 Starboard lower wing panel
9 Diagonal wire bracing
10 Leading-edge stiffening ribs
11 Lattice rib construction
12 Fuel tank, capacity 22.8 Imp gal (104 litres)
13 Fuel contents gauge
14 Filler cap
15 Main spar attachment joint
16 Centre section 'N' struts
17 Cowling step
18 Detachable engine cowlings
19 de Havilland Gipsy Major four-cylinder inline engine
20 Fixed nose cowling
21 de Havilland two-bladed fixed-pitch wooden propeller
22 Spinner
23 Splined propeller shaft
24 Cooling air intake
25 Internal air duct
26 Engine mounting points
27 Engine bearer struts
28 Accessory equipment
29 Sloping engine bay bulkhead
30 Oil filler cap
31 Forward rudder pedals
32 Oil tank, capacity 2.5 Imp gal (11.4 litres)
33 Control column
34 Instrument venturi
35 Front pilot's (instructor's) seat
36 Tailplane trim control lever
37 Rear rudder pedals
38 Seat safety harness
39 Engine throttle lever
40 Instructor's instrument panel
41 Slat locking lever
42 Rear view mirror
43 Fuel tank sump and gravity feed pipe
44 Centre section root rib
45 Rear spar attachment joint
46 Cockpit side hatches
47 Cockpit bulkhead
48 Windscreen panel
49 Ignition switches
50 Student pilot's instrument panel
51 Throttle lever
52 Fire extinguisher bottle
53 Rear pilot's (student or solo flight) seat
54 Gosport speaking tube
55 Padded facia panel
56 Outline of blind flying hood closed position
57 Seat harness attachment
58 Blind flying hood, folded down
59 Starboard side locker door
60 Stowage locker
61 First aid kit
62 Plywood covered turtle decking
63 Anti-spin strakes
64 Control cable runs
65 Starboard tailplane
66 Starboard fabric covered elevator
67 Tailfin construction
68 Rudder horn balance

the cost of replacement parts was only just over £7! (The cost of a Gipsy Moth, ex-works, was a mere £475.)

The introduction of the inverted Gipsy III in 1931 led to the D.H.60GIII Moth, whose prototype (G-ABUI) first flew in March 1932. This was followed by orders from all over the world. The third production aircraft was fitted with a special high-compression Gipsy IIIA which developed 133 hp (99 kW); flown by Hubert Broad, it finished fifth in the 1932 King's Cup Race at 131.34 mph (211.5 km/h). One long-distance flight by a D.H.60GIII is worthy of mention, that by the Portuguese pilot Carlos Bleck, who flew from Lisbon to Goa (Portuguese India), averaging 105 mph (169 km/h) over the 6,000 miles (9655 km) in February 1934. From the 58th airframe onwards the designation was changed to Moth Major to mark a change to the standard 130-hp (97-kW) Gipsy Major, although externally the aircraft was indistinguishable from the earlier type (the cooling fins of the Major's cylinders tapered inwards towards the crankcase, while those of the Gipsy III did not). Among British sporting owners of Moth Majors was the Duchess of Bedford; at the age of 72 the old lady took off for a solo flight in the G-ACUR over the North Sea on 23 March 1937, but was never seen again.

Last of the classic D.H.60s, and a link between them and the famous Tiger Moth ab initio trainer, was the D.H.60T Moth Trainer of which 63, including two prototypes, were produced, prompted by an order for 10 aircraft for the

Swedish air force in 1931. Light training armament (such as camera gun, light reconnaissance camera and practice bombs, etc) were specified, and subsequent batches were supplied to the Egyptian air force, the Brazilian air arms, and Iraq.

Also in 1927 were produced in great secrecy two small monoplanes, designated D.H.71 and intended for high-speed lightplane research. Given the name Tiger Moth (in no way to be confused with the later D.H.82), G-EBQU and G-EBRV were each powered initially by 85-hp (63-kW) A.D.C. Cirrus II engines, but the former was soon re-engined with Major Halford's new 135-hp (101-kW) Gipsy engine. Both were entered for the 1927 King's Cup Race, but one was scratched and the other withdrew from the race having averaged 166 mph (267 km/h). Shortly afterwards, with wings reduced in span from 22 ft 6 in (6.86 m) to 19 ft 0 in (5.79 m), the first aircraft was flown by Broad to establish a world Light-plane Class III speed record over a 62.1-mile (100 km)

69 Fabric covered rudder construction
70 Tail navigation light
71 Rudder operating lever
72 Sternpost
73 Elevator operating lever
74 Elevator construction
75 Tailplane rib construction, fabric covered

76 Sprung tailskid, linked to rudder
77 Tailplane bracing strut
78 Fuselage lower longeron
79 Elevator cables
80 Fuselage fabric covering
81 Primary fuselage structure, square-section tube
82 Rudder cables

83 Port upper wing panel rear spar
84 Inter-spar bracing strut
85 Front spar
86 Wing internal wire bracing
87 Fixed trailing-edge construction
88 Wing tip construction
89 Port navigation light

90 Port automatic leading-edge slat, closed
91 Interplane struts
92 Early type air pressure airspeed indicator
93 Diagonal wire bracing
94 Aileron pulley and operating lever
95 Port aileron construction
96 Rear spar
97 Wing tip construction
98 Main spar

99 Interplane strut attachment joint
100 Leading-edge stiffening ribs
101 Inter-spar bracing strut
102 Lattice rib construction
103 Wing walkway
104 Main undercarriage shock
105 Port mainwheel
106 Pivoted axle strut
107 Drag strut
108 Starboard mainwheel

The light aeroplane that made the greatest impact on sporting aviation throughout the world in the 1920s was the D.H.60 Gipsy Moth, and it was flown in almost every country that supported flying facilities. Shown here with Australian registration, the Gipsy Moth was used by flying clubs at Adelaide, Brisbane, Longreach, Melbourne, Perth and Sydney.

The classic Tiger Moth was licence-built in Canada, New Zealand, Australia, Portugal, Norway and Sweden. The example depicted here was one of 20 D.H.82As produced by AB Svenska Järnvagsverkstaderna, Lindingö, as the Sk 11A for the Flygvapen.

closed circuit at 186.47 mph (300 km/h) on 24 August 1927.

Much closer to the true Moth tradition was the D.H.75 Hawk Moth, a four-seat cabin high-wing monoplane for which a new engine had been developed by Major Halford by inclining two Cirrus Is to mate on a common crankshaft as a V-8. The new engine, the Ghost, provided power of only 198-hp (148 kW), and after the prototype Hawk Moth had flown on 7 December 1928 the first two D.H.75A production aircraft were powered by 240-hp (179-kW) Armstrong Siddeley Lynx geared radials. Only five other aircraft were believed to have been built, of which one, designated D.H.75B, was fitted with a 300-hp (224-kW) Wright Whirlwind R-975 radial.

The next Moth, the D.H.80 Puss Moth, was also a high-wing cabin monoplane, this time a 'club three-seater' with the pilot seated forward of a two-place bench seat. This attractive little aeroplane remained in production for three years from mid-1930 until a total of 350 had been built, of which roughly half were exported. A spate of early accidents (in one of which the famous sporting pilot Bert Hinkler was killed on 7 January 1933) was diagnosed as the result of wing failure following control flutter, cured by mass-balanced ailerons and strengthened wing struts. Jim and Amy Mollison (the latter was Amy Johnson before her marriage) were the outstanding Puss Moth pilots; the former in G-ABXY *The Heart's Content* made the first solo east–west crossing of the North Atlantic on 18–19 August 1932; he also became the first to fly from England to South America, the first to make a solo east–west crossing of the South Atlantic and the first to make crossings of both North and South Atlantic.

Next in line, however, the D.H.82, was to eclipse even the magnificent D.H.60. The D.H.60T Moth Trainer had been in use by the RAF for some years when Air Ministry Specification 15/31 was issued calling for an improved version. Eight pre-production aircraft, using D.H.60 fuselages, were produced, but with the top wing centre-section moved forward and the outer sections swept back 19 in (48.26 cm) at the tips, thereby avoiding large changes in the centre of gravity position; this change in effect created the basis of the famous D.H.82 Tiger Moth. The first 35 production aircraft to Specification T.23/31 for the RAF were designated Tiger Moth Mk Is and entered service with the CFS and FTS, followed by two float-equipped aircraft to Specification T.6/33, but large-scale production started at Stag Lane early in 1934 with the issue of T.26/33, only to be switched to de

Havilland's new factory at Hatfield later in that year. Known in the RAF as the Tiger Moth Mk II, the new version departed from the Moth's traditional use of fabric and stringers behind the cockpits in favour of plywood decking, as well as provision for a blind-flying hood over the rear cockpit. Further contracts as well as Specification T.7/35 were received in 1935, so that pre-war production amounted to 1,150 at Hatfield, 227 by the de Havilland factory at Toronto, one by de Havilland at Wellington, New Zealand, and three by the DH Technical School. The vast majority had entered RAF service, but many had also gone to foreign owners and air forces as well as British flying clubs. On the outbreak of war most of the civil aircraft in the UK were impressed, the civilian schools providing the aircraft for the service's Elementary Flying Training Schools. In 1941 production of the de Havilland Mosquito at Hatfield forced the company to move Tiger Moth production to Morris Motors at Cowley, Oxford, where a total of 3,216 examples was produced before manufacture ended on 15 August 1945. Many of these Tiger Moths were shipped overseas where they provided the ab initio flying equipment of the schools that constituted the great Empire and Commonwealth Air Training Plan. Indeed, there were precious few wartime RAF pilots whose first experience of flight was not in the cockpit of a 'Tiger'.

After the war surplus Tiger Moths flooded into the civil market, while others continued to serve in the RAF for a number of years until replaced by the Percival Prentice and de Havilland Chipmunk.

Exuding nostalgia for RAF pilots of a former generation, this photo shows a de Havilland-built Tiger Moth being flown solo in 1941. So sensitive was the little trainer that it was possible to induce yaw simply by putting one's hand out into the slipstream as if to signal one's intention to turn!

Ford Tri-Motor

Popularly called the Tin Goose (and also, like the same company's Model T car, the Tin Lizzie), the Ford Tri-Motors combined the capable high-wing trimotor configuration of Fokker with the tough, all-metal construction of Junkers. This alone was enough for success in the tough airline world of the 1920s, but who could predict that these machines would make snap rolls and loops, fight fires, and still fly in the 1980s?

At the beginning of 1925 the Automobile King, Henry Ford, announced a reliability trial for transport planes. The race would begin at his company's headquarters in Dearborn, Michigan, and pass through most of the United States. Henry Ford had decided to extend his manufacturing to that of civil aircraft, and he sponsored this competition to find out who made the best transport planes. The Dutchman, Anthony Fokker, rapidly converted his remaining F.VII to run on three Wright engines and flew the first F.VII/3m to the USA in July 1925. He proved to be virtually unrivalled, and won the Ford Tour without any real problems. Henry's son, Edsel Ford, bought the Fokker for Byrd's North Pole expedition. He also persuaded his father that the three-engine high-wing aircraft was the best plane for his requirements. But Fokker was not interested in signing a licence contract with Ford to produce this model.

The Fokker was made of steel tube, wood and fabric, and after taking a lot of advice Henry Ford became convinced the future lay with what were at the time called 'all-metal ships'. Instead of just copying the Fokker, which is what Fokker himself insisted, incorrectly, was what happened, Ford decided to build an all-metal tri-motor high-wing transport of his own. In August 1925 he bought the Stout Metal

Airplane Company, whose founder, William Bushnell 'Bill' Stout, had pioneered the internally braced metal monoplane in the USA. From 1922 Stout had built reliable and aerodynamically clean transports, with Liberty, Wright and other engines, with an outer skin entirely of Alclad (described later).

Ford purchased several of these single-engine transports, and like many other companies jumped on the mail bandwagon made possible by the Kelly Act of 1925, which enabled private companies to bid for air mail routes. On 15 February 1926 Ford's Stout Air Services began flying the Detroit–Cleveland and Detroit–Chicago routes. But Ford could see that the future called for a bigger multi-engine aircraft, and he told Stout to build him a tri-motor. Stout had the ball at his feet, but he rushed through his Model 3-AT as if timing mattered more than the result. It will probably never be known precisely what happened, but

Tri-motors nos 69, 74 and 75 were all of the Model 5-AT-CS type with twin floats for water-based operation. It is shown as built, with two engines fitted with ring cowls and registered as a US civil aircraft (NC414H). Later it is believed to have served, with at least one other Model 5-AT-CS, with the Chilean air force.

Ford Tri-Motor

Specification

Ford Model 5-AT-B

Type: passenger transport

Powerplant: three 420-hp (313-kW) Pratt & Whitney Wasp C-series nine-cylinder radial piston engines

Performance: maximum speed 161 mph (259 km/h); cruising speed 123 mph (198 km/h); normal range 440 miles (708 km)

Weights: empty (typical, as built) 7,600 lb (3447 kg); maximum 12,650 lb (5738 kg)

Dimensions: span 77 ft 10 in (23.72 m); length 50 ft 3 in (15.3 m); height (tail down) 12 ft 0 in (3.66 m); wing area 835 sq ft (77.57 m^2).

Accommodation: flight crew of two side-by-side plus normal seating for up to 15 passengers, or (later) 13 plus steward, or 3,350 lb (1520 kg) cargo

Ford Model 5-AT-39 has had a long and very active life, passing through many minor changes and different paint schemes. She is depicted as she was when four years old in 1933, flying for American. After leaving American she toiled for operators in many Latin American countries as well as Alaska and Mexico before being completely refurbished in 1962 by Aircraft Hydro-Forming (a US company which made a prolonged attempt in the past 20 years to re-establish production of an improved Tri-Motor, the Stout Bushmaster 2000). A year later she was bought by American (long since Airlines instead of Airways) and repainted with her old number for publicity flying.

Ford Tri-Motor

The fourth Tri-Motor built was the lone XJR-1 ordered by the US Navy in March 1927. A Model 4-AT, it was tested at Anacostia in 1928 and put into service as a cargo and personnel transport before being damaged beyond repair in April 1930. It was the precursor of eight additional Tri-Motors in navy/marines service.

what seems beyond dispute is that the Model 3-AT was a crude and unimpressive lash-up. It may have flown only once before it was destroyed in a fire on the ground, which also destroyed the factory at Ford Airport, on 17 January 1926. Ford and Stout had a violent argument which ended in Stout being fired.

In February 1926 Ford decided to proceed with an improved aircraft, the Model 4-AT, whose design was based on that of the Model 3-AT but differed in almost all details and especially in the engine installations, cockpit, landing gear and fuselage. The small engineering team was headed by Harold Hicks and Tom Towle, but it is difficult today to determine whether they or Stout should receive the main credit for this classic and long-lived aircraft.

The first of the sucessful Ford tri-motors was flown for the first time on 11 June 1926. Most surviving pictures, and all surviving Fords, are of the larger Model 5-AT variety, but the Model 4-AT was as important as its successor and will now be described.

Though some of the high-wing transports of the day, including the Fokkers, had their wing mounted above the fuselage, the Ford wing was recessed so that the three spars significantly reduced headroom in the cabin. Each spar was

The Model 4-At-3, the third Tri-Motor to be built, typified the early production machines with enclosed cockpit, revised cabin windows and many other changes, but still with wire wheels with mudguards. It operated on the Ford Freight Line from late 1926 with 200-hp (149-kW) Whirlwind J4 engines. Gross weight was 9,200 lb (4173 kg).

This unique Ford was Model 6-AT-1, basically a Model 5-AT-C fitted with low-powered Wright Whirlwind J6 engines, sold as a sea/ski-plane to the Royal Canadian Air Force in 1929. It is pictured with only the last two letters of its civil registration G-CYWZ. Its main duty was forest patrol and dusting, followed by radio research.

After the false start with the Model 3-AT the Stout Metal Airplane division built the first true ancestor of the Tri-Motors in the Model 4-AT-1, flown on 11 June 1926. The assistant chief engineer was a young man of Scottish ancestry named James S. McDonnell, a recent graduate from MIT, whose later aircraft went faster.

a Warren-braced truss assembled mainly by riveting, and the ribs were likewise built up from rolled strip and sections. The wing was a generation earlier in form than the superb multi-spar stressed-skin wings of John R. Northrop, one of which was the basis of the Douglas DC series in the early 1930s. The Northrop (Douglas) wings proved to have hardly any fatigue problem, but Fords have suffered a certain amount of cracking after flying over 5,000 hours, a figure seldom even approached in commercial service between the world wars.

Rugged structure

Like that of Douglas, the Ford wing was made in three parts, the rectangular centre section being integral with the fuselage. The latter was a capacious box, though unlike that of the Fokkers it had a rounded top which may have reduced drag. The three engines, which in the Model 4-AT were 200-hp (149-kW) Wright J-4 Whirlwinds driving two-blade metal propellers, were uncowled and in most Fords not even provided with cooling airflow baffles or fairings. In the Model 3-AT the nose engine had been mounted low to balance the thrust lines of the two wing-mounted engines, but in the Model 4-AT the centre engine was mounted exactly on the nose and the other pair brought down so that all thrust lines were at the same level, the wing engines now

US Army Air Corps aircraft 31-401 was the first of three Tri-Motor Model 5-AT-Ds with the Army designation C-4A. It was the 91st Tri-Motor, delivered in 1931. Like most army Fords it had Townend rings round its R-1340 Wasps and spats over the mainwheels. The Army bought 13 Fords, seven being less-powerful C-3As.

being carried on the front of separate strut-mounted nacelles well below the wing. The wing engines had short stub exhausts or, from 1927, an exhaust manifold leading to a short pipe on the outboard side of the nacelle. The nose engine, however, sent its gas through a pipe running (in most versions) half way back to the tail, surrounded by a muff open at the front so that, in cold weather, heated fresh air could be admitted to the cabin.

Unlike those of many later metal stressed-skin aircraft, the movable control surfaces, as well as the fixed tail, were metal-skinned. The extreme nose and the top and bottom of the fuselage were often skinned with smooth metal sheet, but almost all other surfaces were of Junkers-style corrugated sheet. Such sheet could be made in thin gauges yet resist local impacts or buckling loads, and it was retained in Junkers aircraft up to the last Ju 52/3m in mid-1944. In fact, it was only after World War 2 that careful measurements revealed that the drag penalty of corrugated skin was con-

This Ford 5-AT passenger/mail plane of National Airlines had specially built mail compartments in its wings; here they have been opened for loading.

siderable, the air hardly ever flowing in the direction of the corrugations! The one good thing about the skin of the Fords was that, from the first Model 4-AT, the material used was Alclad, duralumin coated with non-corrosive pure aluminium. For good measure the assembled structure was then given a sprayed coating of varnish. This explains the outstanding longevity of these aircraft.

All the Fords had an oval entrance door on the right side, used for passengers, cargo and also by the two pilots. In the Model 4-AT the latter had the usual open cockpit, a feature of which was a sharply angled Vee windshield which had glass panes that were not vertical but sloped outwards from bottom to top, to give a better view for landing. Panels in the windshield could be slid open in really bad weather. The Model 4-AT had four passenger seats on each side of a central aisle, and was available with a lavatory at the rear. Light personal baggage could be placed in a typical suspended mesh rack along each side of the cabin above the windows, level with the bottoms of the wing spars. In a few Model 4-ATs further baggage and mail was stowed in drop-down lockers between the spars at the inner end of each outer wing panel, though this was really a feature of later models. Other features by no means common in 1926 were wheel brakes, which enabled a tailwheel to be used instead of a skid, and an electrical system with the battery charged by a generator in the nose engine. This system served navigation lights and, in most aircraft, leading-edge landing lamps and two-way radio. On the other hand, the Fords adhered to the old practice of running the tail control cables along the outside of the fuselage from large rocker arms on the sides of the nose.

One of the first customers was Stout himself, who had formed Stout Air Services to fly schedules from Detroit to Chicago and other cities in the Great Lakes region. But the first and largest customer was a Los Angeles car dealer, Jack Maddux. He first had to be satisfied with the Ford's ability to operate over the mountains of California and neighbouring states, and of its reliability; then he eventually bought 16 of different versions for Maddux Air Lines.

Subsequent Fords had an enclosed cockpit with sliding side windows, and various other refinements, and almost all were more powerful. As listed in the separate Variants section, there were almost as many sub-types as there were aircraft built, partly because there were numerous rebuilds and conversions. The initial Model 4-AT-A eight-seater entered service with Ford's own air service on 2 August 1926. Ford Airport at Dearborn had by this time become the first in the world with paved runways and full electric lighting, and later Ford not only made many other improvements to the buildings but also set up one of the world's first training schools for commercial flight crews.

One of the almost priceless survivors, Ford Model 5-AT-39 served with American Airlines in 1933–5. Then followed many years of trucking all over the Americas from Chile to Alaska. In 1962 the still highly airworthy ship was bought by American, completely refurbished and used for publicity and promotional purposes.

Though the Model 4-AT had been the biggest all-metal aircraft then built in the USA, and possibly in the world, it was rightly judged too small and the Model 4-AT-B of 1927 had a span increased from 68 ft 10 in (20.97 m) to 73 ft 11 in (22.53 m), matching the greater power of 220-hp (164-kW) J-6 Whirlwind engines. Though the fuselage was almost the

Most famous of all Tri-Motors, the Model 4-AT-15 was donated by Henry and Edsel Ford for the Antarctic expedition of Commander Richard E. Byrd. Pilot Bernt Balchen found it needed more range, so the span was increased to 74 ft (22.55 m), tankage was augmented and a powerful Cyclone was put on the nose. It overflew the South Pole.

Ford Tri-Motor variants

Model 3-AT: original Stout tri-motor prototype, destroyed 17 January 1926
Model 4-AT: first Ford tri-motor; three J-4 Whirlwind radials and eight passengers
Model 4-AT-A: initial production model, similar to Model 4-AT; 14 built
Model 4-AT-B: increased span and J-5 Whirlwind radials; accommodation for two pilots and 12 passengers; 35 built
Model 4-AT-C: similar to the Model 4-AT-B but with 400-hp (298-kW) Wasp radial; 1 built
Model 4-AT-D: used wing similar to that of the Model 5-AT; total production was three, one having J-4 Whirlwind radial, another with two J-5 Whirlwind radials and one 300-hp (298-kW) J-6-9 Whirlwind radials; and the last with three J-6-9 Whirlwind radials
Model 4-AT-E: detail changes and three 300-hp (298-kW) J-6 Whirlwind radials; 24 built
Model 4-AT-F: one aircraft similar to the Model 4-AT-E and built in 1931
Model 5-AT-A: enlarged variant with three 420-hp (313-kW) Wasp radials; 3 built
Model 5-AT-B: new 15-seater of 1929 with three 420-hp (313-kW) Wasp C-1 or Wasp SC-1 radials; 42 built
Model 5-AT-C: improved 17-seat version; 48 built
Model 5-AT-D: increased-weight version with three 450-hp (336-kW) Wasp SC radials; 24 built
Model 6-AT-A: similar to the Model 5-AT-C but with J-6 Whirlwind radials; 3 built
Model 7-AT-A: rebuild of 6-AT-A with a nose-mounted 420-hp (313-kW) Wasp radial
Model 8-AT: single Model 5-AT-C converted as a freighter without wing-mounted engines
Model 9-AT: conversion of Model 4-AT-B with 300-hp (224-kW) Wasp Junior radials; 1 converted

Model 11-AT: one Model 4-AT-E rebuilt with 225-hp (168-kW) Packard DR-980 diesels
Model 13-A: conversion of one Model 5-AT-D with two J-6 Whirlwind radials and one 575-hp (429-kW) Cyclone radial
Model 14-A: one much larger aircraft of 1932 with two 715-hp (533-kW) and one 1,100-hp (820-kW) Hispano-Suiza engines; this 40-seater was completed but not flown
C-3: US Army no. 28-348; based on Model 4-AT-B
C-3A: US Army nos 29-220/226, seven aircraft with 235-hp (175-kW) R-790-3 Whirlwind radials
C-4: US Army no. 29-219; basically a Model 4-AT-B for military service
C-4A: US Army nos 31-401/404, four aircraft based on the Model 5-AT-D with 450-hp (336-kW) R-1340-11 radials
C-9: redesignation of all seven C-3As after the installation of 300-hp (224-kW) R-975-1 radials
XJR-1: US Navy no. A7526, based on Model 4-AT
JR-2: US Navy nos A8273/8274, two aircraft based on the Model 4-AT-E for the US Marine Corps
JR-3: US Navy nos A8457 and A8598/8599, three aircraft based on the Model 5-AT-C
RR-2: redesignation of JR-2
RR-3: redesignation of JR-3
RR-4: additional Model 5-AT-C with US Navy no. A8840
RR-5: US Navy nos 9205/9206, two aircraft based on the Model 5-AT-D, one of them delivered to the US Marine Corps
XB-906-1: single prototype (NX9652) for a bomber version with internal racks and two gunner's positions; crashed on 19 September 1931 killing Ford's chief test pilot, Leroy Manning

Possibly Model 5-AT-11, this Tri-Motor in the 5-AT series was one of four supplied in 1930 to Cia Mexicana de Aviacion, an affiliate of Pan American. All had uncowled Wasp engines, but after World War 2 various powerplants appeared on Ford Tri-Motors throughout Latin America, including cowled Wasp Juniors from BT-13s.

same as before, the seating limit went up to 12. There followed various sub-types of Model 4-AT, differing chiefly in engine arrangement. Almost all the Fords were originally built with spatted main wheels, and their modern image did much to promote sales.

When the Ford was a new and very modern aircraft, most had Wright engines in the 200/220-hp (149/164-kW) bracket, but production of this Model 4-AT family came to an end (except for the single Model 4-AT-F) in 1929. By this time the much more powerful, and further enlarged, Model 5-AT family was selling even better than its predecessors, and output of Model 5-ATs reached a remarkable four per week in 1929, before the Wall Street crash.

A8840 was the US Navy RR-4, basically a Model 5-AT-C with the enlarged wing and three 450-hp (335-kW) Wasp engines with Townend ring cowls. The Tri-Motor in the US Naval Aviation Museum at NAS Pensacola is painted and presented as this aircraft, but its true identity is not certain.

Ford Tri-motor 5-AT-D cutaway drawing key

1. Starboard tailplane
2. Starboard elevator
3. Rudder
4. Tail navigation light
5. Rudder horn balance
6. Tailplane bracing wire
7. Tailfin
8. Corrugated tailplane skins
9. Elevator hinge strut
10. Tailplane bracing strut
11. Tailwheel shock absorber
12. Tailwheel
13. Tailplane incidence screw jack
14. Fin attachment
15. Rear fuselage construction
16. Port elevator
17. Port tailplane
18. Incidence control shaft
19. Fuselage top decking
20. Corrugated fuselage skins
21. Tail control cable pulleys
22. Flare dispenser
23. Wash basin
24. Step
25. Cabin door
26. Toilet compartment
27. Fire extinguisher
28. Rear cabin seating
29. Cabin roof luggage racks
30. Cabin windows
31. Fuselage strut bracing construction
32. Bottom longeron
33. Starboard mainwheel
34. Shock absorber leg strut
35. Starboard Pratt & Whitney Wasp radial engine
36. Two bladed propeller
37. NACA cowling ring
38. Engine cooling air shutters
39. Engine mounting framework
40. Oil tank
41. Exhaust pipe
42. Engine cowling fairing
43. Engine pylon struts
44. Centre wing panel
45. Wing corrugated skins
46. Spar attachment joints
47. Drop-down mail and baggage lockers
48. Outer wing panel spars
49. Wing spar strut bracing
50. Aileron hinge control
51. Starboard aileron
52. Wing rib bracing
53. Wing tip construction
54. Starboard navigation light
55. Reinforced leading edge
56. Aileron cable pulley
57. Landing and taxi lamp
58. Corrugated leading edge skin
59. Outer wing panel attachment rib
60. Fuel tanks
61. Cabin roof fairing
62. Fuselage main frame
63. Passenger seats
64. Starboard undercarriage swing axle
65. Cabin floor
66. Cabin heater duct fairing
67. Centre engine exhaust pipe
68. Air vents
69. Battery
70. External control cables
71. Co-pilot's seat
72. Cockpit side windows
73. Instrument panel
74. Control column hand-wheel
75. Cockpit roof windows
76. Sliding windscreen panel
77. Windscreen frame
78. Centre engine fairing air louvres
79. Oil tank
80. Centre engine mounting framework
81. Rudder pedals
82. Exhaust collector ring
83. Centre Pratt & Whitney Wasp engine
84. NACA cowling ring
85. Two-bladed propeller
86. Port Pratt & Whitney Wasp engine
87. NACA cowling ring
88. Engine pylon fairing
89. Port landing and taxi lamp
90. Reinforced leading edge
91. Instrument pitot head
92. Port wing tip
93. Port navigation light
94. Outer wing panel construction
95. Aileron hinge control
96. Port aileron
97. Port mainwheel
98. Mudguard fairing
99. Shock absorber leg fairing
100. Swing axle struts

Ford Tri-Motor

On 9 May 1926 Lieutenant Commander Richard E. Byrd, USN, noted polar explorer, had reached and flown over the North Pole in a prototype tri-motor Fokker F.VIIA/3m piloted by Floyd Bennett. However, the trip was not without its problems for the Fokker, called *Josephine Ford*, developed oil-leaks in the engines, so it was Byrd's intention to use another aircraft to overfly the South Pole, his next ambition. The plane he chose was a Ford Tri-Motor Model 4-AT-15, called *Floyd Bennett*, Byrd's pilot having died of pneumonia.

But this venture proved more hazardous than the Arctic flight, for the South Pole had no occupied base within a radius of 1,000 miles (1600km) and the Tri-Motor was not up to the job, being unable to carry four men, all the necessary equipment and fuel for the return leg. A base, some 440 miles (708km) south of Little America, was established in the Bay of Whales and it was intended to use it for the return trip. A Scandinavian, Bernt Balchin, was named pilot.

The Tri-Motor rose into the air on 28 November 1929 and the plane became the first to fly over the Pole, but not without its moments. Sufficient height became a problem at one stage and food had to be jettisoned but at last Byrd became the first man to fly over both Poles.

More engines, more sales

Thanks to the use of the Pratt & Whitney Wasp engine, the Model 5-AT was a much more capable aircraft. First flown in mid-1928, the Model 5-AT had a further enlarged wing, the fuselage deepened to give more headroom under the wing, Townend-ring cowled wing engines (often a cowled nose engine also), and a structure strengthened for operation at greater weights. No fewer than 117 were built in 1929–31, many of them having float or ski landing gear. Many were built with the wing baggage/mail lockers, and others were thus equipped as a modification. The cabin could be equipped to seat up to 17, with eight seats on the right and nine on the left even with a rear lavatory.

Some of the versions of this aircraft were built for military purposes. The first companies to buy the 198 civil aircraft built were American, British Columbia, CLASSA (Spain), Colonial, Colonial Western, CMA (Mexico), Curtiss Flying Service, Eastern, Ford, Jefferson, Maddux, Mamer, Mohawk, NAT (National), Northwest, NYRBA (New York, Rio and

US Army Air Corps X (NX) 9652 was the one-off XB-906-1 bomber, built at the firm's expense and using what was mainly a Model 5-AT-D airframe (but with a redesigned vertical tail). There were guns above and below at the rear and a bombardier's station under the cockpit. This aircraft disintegrated fatally in a dive in 1931.

Buenos Aires), Pacific, Pan American, Pan American Grace, Pennsylvania, Pitcairn, Queen City (Ohio), Rapid, Robertson, SCADTA (Colombia), SAFE (Southwest Air Fast Express), Spokane, Stout, TAT (Transcontinental Air Transport) and Universal Flyers. After 1930 many Fords appeared on the secondhand market and were soon snapped up. Standard Oil was the first industrial company to buy Ford aircraft (the first one they bought was new), and Royal Typewriters wrote on the fuselage of the plane they bought: 'Capacity 210 portable typewriters'. Several aircraft were exported to England, where the airport at Ford in Sussex bought them for their name and became a maintenance base for the many triple-engined machines which people were optimistically hoping to sell in Europe.

In 1934 W.S. Shackleton, of Piccadilly, London, sent four aircraft from Piccadilly to New Guinea, where they and various Junkers were used to service mining operations. One machine belonging to the Guinness family was given a set of roundels and became no. X5000 of No. 271 Squadron of the RAF. Many flew with the US Forces, the RAAF, the RCAF, the Colombian Air Force and the Republicans in the Spanish Civil War. The many Fords sold to Latin American countries remained in service longest. The Honduran company TACA had a particularly large number: at one point it owned thirty. The plane with the most unusual history was the Model 5-AT-11 (the eleventh Model 5-AT), whose first owners were Pan American and TACA. The latter sold it in August 1945 for $4,500 to the Mexican company TATSA, which flew the aircraft between Mazatlan and a tiny airstrip at the bottom of a canyon to service a mine at Tayoltita. As this was the only aircraft TATSA used for this purpose, it transported over 65,000 passengers and 6,700 tonnes of freight without a hitch and clocked up 5,376 hours of flight. In 1966 Island Airlines in Port Clinton, Ohio, bought the aircraft, by which time it had flown 23,000 hours. By the mid-1980s the old Ford Tri-Motor was still being used.

Built as NX8499, the lone Ford Model 8-AT was a single-engined machine completed as a freighter but used from 1929 until 1933 to test the Wright Cyclone (seen here), Pratt & Whitney Hornet, Hispano-Suiza 12 and Bliss-built Bristol Jupiter. From 1933 it had a fully cowled Cyclone and served as shown with Pacific Alaska Airways.

N414H may have been the last Tri-Motor on the US active register. Owned by Scenic Airways Inc., of Las Vegas, Nevada, it is still in existence and has been used for local pleasure flying (for example, as far as the Grand Canyon). One Scenic 5-AT caught out its pilot — unused to taildragger landing gears — and ground-looped.

Bristol Bulldog

If tenacity is an attribute of the bulldog, it was certainly evident in the manner by which the outmoded Bulldog clung to service with the Royal Air Force. By no stretch of the imagination an outstanding design of fighter aircraft, even in its day it nevertheless constituted the RAF's fighter backbone during the early 1930s.

In 1924 the British Air Staff issued specifications for an interceptor; the main criterion was good climbing performance rather than the range that would be needed for longer patrol flights. If possible the machine was to have a Rolls-Royce Falcon X engine, which later became famous as the Kestrel, even though this engine was too heavy, because it was still common to cast the cylinders individually. Frank Barnwell and Roy Fedden advocated the use of a radial engine. Specification F.17/24 was then replaced by specification F.9/26, which involved either a V-engine or a radial engine. Barnwell recommended the Bristol type 102A to fulfil this specification, and for the requirements of a fighter wanted by the Navy, N.21/26, a type 102B for float planes. As none of the Rolls-Royce V-12 engines being developed in 1926 was suitable for use in an interceptor, specification F.9/26 was partially replaced by F.20/27, for which Fedden recommended a Bristol Mercury III radial engine with gears.

In due course Bristol started work on a Mercury-powered prototype, the Type 107 Bullpup (J9051), which was scheduled for competitive evaluation with designs from Hawker, Gloster, Vickers and Westland. However, as a result of the limited availability of the geared Mercury engine, Barnwell produced a private-venture design, the Type 105 Bulldog

with a Bristol Jupiter VII radial, and, as this presented no installation problems, the Bulldog prototype was first flown by Cyril Uwins on 17 May 1927 while the Bullpup still awaited its Mercury.

The Bulldog's structure employed high-tensile steel strip using flat gusset plates in place of bolted joints, the wings and fuselage being fabric-covered. The lower wing was of much reduced span and chord, and of Clark YH section, while the big upper wing, of Bristol IA section, carried the fuel in two centre-section gravity tanks. Characteristically, armament remained the time-honoured pair of forward-firing Vickers guns on the sides of the nose, firing between the engine cylinders and synchronized to avoid the propeller.

Although regarded as an outsider in the F.9/26 evaluation at Martlesham Heath, the Bulldog quickly disposed of all opposition but the Hawker Hawfinch, with which it entered the final stage. A second Bulldog (designated a Mk II and serialled J9480) was ordered in November 1927 for extended

Prototype Bulldog, referred to as the Mk I, at Filton in May 1927, with Cyril Uwins in the cockpit. Seen here in its original form with small rudder, this aircraft was subsequently fitted with enlarged rudder and wings for high altitude trials at Farnborough.

Bristol Bulldog

Specification

Bulldog Mk IIA

Type: single-seat interceptor

Powerplant: one 440-hp (328-kW) Bristol Jupiter VIIF air-cooled radial piston engine

Performance: maximum speed 178 mph (286 km/h) at 10,000 ft (3050 m); climb to 20,000 ft (6095 m) in 14 minutes 30 seconds; service ceiling 27,000 ft (8230 m); normal range 310 miles (499 km)

Weights: empty 2,222 lb (1008 kg); maximum take-off 3,660 lb (1660 kg)

Dimensions: span 33 ft 11 in (10.34 m); length 25 ft 2 in (7.67 m); height 9 ft 10 in (3.00 m); wing area 306.5 sq ft (28.47 m²)

Armament: two forward-firing synchronized 0.303-in (7.7-mm) Vickers machine-guns on the sides of the nose, plus occasional provision for four 20-lb (9-kg) bombs

A Bristol Bulldog Mk IIA of No. 32 (Fighter) Sqn, RAF. These aircraft first arrived on the squadron in September 1930 when it was based at Kenley, commanded by Squadron Leader B. E. (later Air Marshal Sir Brian, CB, DSO, MC, AFC) Baker. Two years later it moved to Biggin Hill, retaining its Bulldogs until replaced by Gloster Gauntlets in July 1936. The blue squadron flash was crossed by white diagonals, although the number of such diagonals does not appear to have been consistent throughout the squadron.

Bristol Bulldog

competition with the Hawfinch in 1928, and was finally judged the winner, largely on account of its steel construction.

Meanwhile the Bulldog Mk I prototype underwent extensive modification (for an attempt on the world climb and altitude records) by the installation of a high aspect ratio wing and supercharged Jupiter VII radial.

The prototype Bulldog Mk II was flown by Uwins on 21 January 1928 and after achieving success in competition against the Hawfinch was purchased by the Air Ministry for £4,800. A production batch of 26 aircraft was laid down, comprising 25 (J9567–J9591) for the RAF and one company demonstrator (G-AAHH). The first RAF Bulldog Mk IIs were allocated to Nos 3 and 17 (Fighter) Squadrons at Upavon, replacing Hawker Woodcocks. One of the first batch was diverted to the company agents in Japan, but this aircraft was replaced by an additional aircraft as J9591, and this became a test-bed for the geared Mercury IV.

The next batch of 23 RAF aircraft (K1079–K1101), delivered in 1930, completed the establishment of No. 17 Squadron as well as equipping No. 54 (Fighter) Squadron at Hornchurch.

Already the Bulldog was proving popular among RAF pilots, its manoeuvrability setting it well ahead of its predecessors, the Gloster Grebe and Gloster Gamecock, and it was this partisan esteem (not to mention the relatively low cost of the long-established Jupiter engine) that prompted considerable follow-up orders. It was thus during the depressed years of 1930–3, when defence appropriations were strictly limited, that the unimaginative Bulldog gained preference on account of its low cost. However the competitive Kestrel V-12 engine had emerged from Rolls-Royce, first in the Hawker Hart bomber and then in the Hawker Fury fighter, both aircraft possessing a superior performance to that of the Bulldog.

The first improved Bulldog for the RAF was the Bulldog Mk IIA with Jupiter VIIF engine, revised wing spars and local strengthening to allow increased all-up weight, and was the subject of an RAF order for 92 aircraft placed in May 1930, yet the new variant's speed performance remained unaltered at 178 mph (286 km/h) at 10,000 ft (3050 m). In 1931 an additional 100 Bulldog Mk IIAs were ordered, and by the end of that year 10 of the 13 home-based RAF fighter squadrons were equipped with Bulldogs (Nos 3, 17, 19, 23, 29, 32, 41, 54, 56 and 111); the others were equipped or equipping with the Hawker Fury Mk I, while one flight of No. 23 Squadron was flying the Hart Fighter, or Demon.

As early as 1933 Bulldogs started phasing out of service, No. 23 Squadron completing a changeover to Demons in April. In 1935 Nos 19 and 29 followed with Gloster Gauntlets and Demons, and in June 1937 (only six months before the Hawker Hurricane appeared in service) No. 3 Squadron at Kenley became the last to discard its Bulldogs; No. 3 had been the only RAF fighter unit to fly Bulldogs in the Middle East, taking its aircraft to Khartoum in October during the crisis in Abyssinia. Of the 441 Bulldogs produced at Filton,

Although No. 17 Sqn, RAF, received its first new Bulldog Mk IIs in October 1928, its full complement of aircraft was achieved by taking over some of No. 3 Sqn's aircraft, also based at Upavon. In this photograph the nearest aircraft retains No. 3 Sqn's green flash and others have yet to be fully painted in No. 17's famous zig-zag flashes.

Later to be distinguished as the first squadron to fly Gauntlets, and later Spitfires, No. 19 (Fighter) Sqn received Bulldog Mk IIAs in September 1931; this ex-No 17 Sqn aircraft carried the familiar blue and white checks on the tail and wing surfaces denoting the aircraft flown by Squadron Leader (later Air Vice-Marshal) J. R. Cassidy.

Ex-Latvian Bulldog Mk II (one of five supplied to that country late in 1929) shown in markings carried during the Spanish Civil War when, in 1936–7, it was flown from Lmiaco by foreign volunteer pilots supporting the Basque forces.

Sweden purchased a total of 11 Bulldogs, including three Mk IIs and eight Mk IIAs. One of the latter is here depicted in the markings of F 1 (Västerås Flygkär), as carried in 1935; it was later presented to Finland where it served as a trainer until 1940.

Bristol, a single example survived in flying condition in the UK until the 1960s, but this was destroyed in an accident during a display at Farnborough following what appears to have been pilot error during low-level aerobatics.

The Bulldog two-seater

At the end of 1931 one of the production batch of 100 Bulldog Mk IIAs for the RAF was retained by the manufacturer for conversion to a two-seater, and this dual-control trainer, K2188 (known as the Bulldog TM, or training machine) was evaluated by the Central Flying School during 1932. A production order for 17 aircraft followed, these aircraft being distributed between the CFS and Coastal Area at Leuchars, as well as to six of the RAF's fighter squadrons; later aircraft served at the Royal Air Force College, Cranwell.

A total of 59 Bulldog TMs was eventually built, some of these remaining in service with flying training schools until 1939; they were also the only Bulldogs to serve on a permanent basis with the RAF in the Middle East, some examples equipping No. 4 FTS at Abu Sueir in Egypt.

As already mentioned, the final Bulldog Mk II of the first production batch was retained for test-bed work by Bristol with a geared Mercury IV engine. Thereafter numerous installations were undertaken, including an aircraft marked R-1 which flew with a Mercury III driving a four-blade

The demonstration Bulldog G-ABBB (R-II) with Bristol Aquila I sleeve-valve radial in 1935. This was the aircraft that, restored post-war with a Jupiter VIIFP engine, was made airworthy with the spurious registration K2227 and presented to the Shuttleworth Trust before being destroyed in a flying accident at Farnborough.

Characterized by the mounting of Madsen guns lower on the fuselage sides, the four Type 105D Danish Bulldogs equipped No. 1 Sqn, Danish Army Aviation Troops in 1931; three, the Type Mk IIa, were still in service as fighter trainers at the time of the German invasion of Denmark in April 1940.

propeller, followed by installation of a Gnome-Rhône Jupiter VI; in the latter guise, while practising for a foreign demonstration tour, the aircraft crashed when T. W. Campbell baled out rather than risk landing after damaging the rudder bar in a flick roll. A replacement demonstrator was produced with a Gnome-Rhône 9Asb, and after a number of demonstrations this Jupiter was replaced by a Bristol Aquila sleeve-valve radial; it was this aircraft, with a re-built Jupiter, that became the sole British survivor after World War 2.

In an early attempt to improve the Bulldog, Bristol produced the private-venture Bulldog Mk IIIA in 1931 with a Mercury IVA (later Mercury IVS2), and this was flown in competition with the Gloster SS.19B to decide a Bulldog replacement in the RAF. Pursuing much the same course as Gloster in the progressive development of a single prototype, Bristol did considerable work on the Bulldog Mk IIIA, but in the end the SS.19B emerged the winner and entered service as the Gauntlet. Bristol then produced the Bulldog Mk IVA with four guns in 1934 for competition under Specification F.7/30 requirements, with a Mercury VIS2 radial, but once again the Bulldog's 224 mph (360 km/h) speed was no match for the SS.37's 250 mph (402 km/h), and the latter entered service with the RAF as the Gladiator.

Bulldog two-seaters were also employed as engine test-beds for the Armstrong Sideley Cheetah and Alvis Leonides radials, and the Napier Rapier air-cooled inline.

Foreign Bulldogs

From the earliest days of the Bulldog's RAF service the aircraft attracted considerable interest overseas, nurtured by a constant programme of demonstrations by company pilots throughout Europe, the Bulldog's relatively low cost once more proving a considerable attraction. Apart from the aircraft diverted to Japan from the first production batch and mentioned above, the first true overseas order was for five Gnome-Rhône Jupiter VI-powered aircraft with twin Oerlikon machine-guns which followed that first batch in 1929 and were shipped to Latvia.

The next Bulldog on the production line was delivered to the United States where it underwent tests at Anacostia as a dive-bomber; this aircraft was destroyed after an aileron failed in a dive and the pilot, Lieutenant Cuddihy, was killed. With local strengthening incorporated, a replacement Bulldog Mk II was delivered in 1930 for US Navy tests.

Third of the second batch of Bulldogs, a Mk IIA, sold to Sweden and delivered in May 1931, shown at Filton shortly before delivery to Malmslätt. All the Swedish aircraft were from time to time flown with ski undercarriages.

Bristol Bulldog variants

Bristol Type 105 (F.9/26): prototypes as private venture; Bristol Jupiter VII radial; no serial
Bulldog Mk I: company display aircraft; completed but not flown; no serial
Bulldog HA: conversion of private-venture prototype for high-altitude record attempt; supercharged Jupiter VII and high aspect ratio wings
F.9/26 Bulldog Mk II: prototype for RAF evaluation; J9480
Bulldog Mk II: production for RAF in 1928–29; 49 aircraft (J9567–J9591) and K1079–K1101; Jupiter VII
Bulldog Mk II: one aircraft shipped to Japan for evaluation; Nakajima Jupiter as test-bed with Mercury IVA in various cowlings
Bulldog Mk II: three aircraft (1202–1203) for evaluation in Sweden
Bulldog Mk II: European display aircraft; shipped to Chile for evaluation but returned to UK
Bulldog Mk II: European display aircraft, G-ABBB, with Gnome-Rhône 9Asb, later Bristol Aquila; restored post-war, but crashed and destroyed
Bulldog Mk II: 12 aircraft for Estonia in 1930; Gnome-Rhône Jupiter VI engines
Bulldog Mk IIA: production for RAF in 1930–1; 254 aircraft (K1603–K1694, K2135–K2234, K2476–K2495, K2859–K2872, K2946–K2963 and K3504–K3513); Jupiter VIIF; strengthened for increased all-up weight
Bulldog Mk IIA: four aircraft for Denmark in 1931; Jupiter VIFH engines and Madsen guns
Bulldog Mk IIA: eight aircraft (5211–5218) for Sweden in 1931; Jupiter VIIF; three aircraft (5214–5216) presented to Finland in 1939
Bulldog Mk IIA: one aircraft (K4189) to Spec. 11/31 with stainless-steel structure
Bristol Type 124 Bulldog TM: two-seat trainer prototype; conversion of one standard RAF

Bulldog Mk II: 12 aircraft for Latvia, 10 with Gnome-Rhône Jupiter VI and two with Gnome-Rhône 9Asb; Oerlikon guns; delivered in 1929–30
Bulldog Mk II: two aircraft for evaluation by US Navy; delivered 1929–30
Bulldog Mk II: two aircraft to Royal Siamese air force, January 1930; Jupiter VII
Bulldog Mk II: eight aircraft (A12-1 to A12-8) for Royal Australian Air Force, January 1930; Jupiter VIF
Bulldog Mk II: one test-bed, marked R-1, for Mercury III radial; later Gnome-Rhône Jupiter VI; became G-ABAC
Bulldog Mk II: conversion of J9591 (as G-AATR) Bulldog Mk IIA (K2188)
Bulldog Mk IIIA: two prototypes, marked R-5 and G-ABZW; former with Mercury IVA and Mercury IVS2; later converted to Bulldog Mk V
Bulldog Mk IV: prototype converted from Mk III with four guns; evaluation as K4292
Bulldog Mk IVA: prototype (new aircraft), G-ACJN; flown with Mercury IVS2, Perseus IA and Mercury VIS2 with Hamilton three-blade propeller
Bulldog Mk IVA: 17 aircraft for Finland; Mercury VIS2; often flown with ski landing gear
Bulldog TM: to Specification T.12/32; production two-seat trainers for RAF; 59 aircraft (K3170–K3186, K3923–K3953 and K4566–K4576); Jupiter VIF; delivered 1932–4
Bulldog test-beds: conversions of aircraft included above; Alvis Leonides and Napier Rapier in Bulldog TM (K3183), and Armstrong Siddeley Cheetah IX in Bulldog TM prototype (K2188)
JSSF: Japanese-built Bulldog derivatives; two aircraft; Nakajima Jupiter VII
Bullpup: one prototype (J9051) to F.20/27; flown in turn with Mercury IIA, Short-stroke Mercury, Jupiter VIIF and Aquila I

Bristol Bulldog Mk IIA cutaway drawing key

1 Starter dog
2 Spinner
3 Two-blade wooden propeller
4 Starboard navigation light
5 Starboard aerial mast
6 Forward-facing fuel vent pipe
7 Starboard fuel tank capacity 35 Imp gal (159 litres)
8 Bristol Jupiter VIIF or VIIF-P engine
9 Cowling ring
10 Engine mounting plate
11 Cylinder head fairings
12 Cross-bracing
13 Gun synchronizing generator (port and starboard)
14 Supercharger
15 Firewall
16 Centre-section support struts
17 Wing centre-section
18 Bracing wire
19 Starboard fuel pipe
20 Oil tank, capacity 7.5 Imp gal (34.1 litres)
21 Forward fuselage framework

22 Gun trough
23 Oleo leg attachment
24 Rudder pedals
25 Accumulator (lighting system)
26 Air bottle (high-pressure cylinder)
27 Elevator link tube
28 Aileron rockshaft
29 Ammunition box, capacity 600 rounds (one each gun)
30 Control column
31 Empty case chute
32 Port Vickers 0.303-in (7.7-mm) Mk II or Mk IIIN gun
33 Gun cooling louvres
34 Instrument panel
35 Ring sight (combined with Aldis tube front mounting)

36 Bead sight
37 Windscreen
38 Padded coaming
39 Cockpit
40 Fibre acorns
41 Pilot's adjustable seat
42 Tailplane adjusting wheel
43 Chain and sprocket
44 Handhold step
45 Elevator cable arm
46 ASI cable on strut leading edge
47 Fuselage lacing
48 Wireless compartment and crate
49 ASI horn
50 Aerial mast
51 Interplane bracing
52 Port fuel pipe

53 Fuel lead fairing
54 Port fuel tank, capacity 35 Imp gal (159 litres)
55 Front interplane strut
56 Upper mainplane leading edge ribbing
57 Front spar
58 Port navigation light
59 Wing rib
60 Spar strip steel sections
61 Upper mainplane tip
62 Aileron balance
63 Aileron construction
64 Rear spar
65 Aileron cable
66 Rear interplane strut
67 Interplane bracing
68 Aerials

69 Strut cross-bracing
70 Fuselage tubular framework
71 Rudder/tailplane controls
72 Elevator controls
73 Handholds with lifting-bars behind
74 Tailskid spring
75 Rear fuselage lacing
76 Fuselage decking
77 Fin solid section
78 Fin frame structure
79 Upper rudder hinge
80 Aerial anchor point
81 Rudder frame
82 Rear navigation light
83 Rudder post
84 Centre rudder hinge

85 Port tailplane
86 Lower rudder hinge
87 Support pad with trolley-fitting track rail
88 Stern frame construction
89 Tailskid
90 Lower mainplane tip
91 Port lower mainplane
92 Tie-down lug
93 Light bomb racks
94 Air-driven generator mounting cradle
95 Centre-section lower frames
96 Oil cooler
97 Exhaust pipes
98 V-strut undercarriage
99 Cross-bracing wires
100 Fixed-length radius rod
101 700 × 100 Palmer Cord Aero Tyre
102 Tyre valve
103 Wheel spokes
104 Axle strut
105 Wheel cover

In addition to the three Bulldog Mk IIAs presented to her by Sweden in 1939, Finland had purchased from Britain 17 Mk IVA aircraft early in 1935. Powered by Mercury radials, and some operating on skis, the Bulldogs were flown in combat in the Winter War, gaining several victories. The aircraft shown served with TLeLv 35 early in 1942.

The same Bulldog seen on page 121 (bottom left) and showing the incorrect registration K-2227 and the Jupiter VIIFP motor. Here it is part of the famed Shuttleworth Collection before crashing to destruction at Farnborough in the 1960s.

In January 1930 two Bulldog Mk IIs were delivered to the Royal Siamese air force, and in the same month eight similar aircraft, with Jupiter VIF engines, were shipped out for service with the Royal Australian Air Force. Later in that year, following a demonstration in Sweden by the Bulldog G-AAHH, three Bulldog Mk IIs were shipped to that country in August for competitive evaluation with the indigenous Jaktfalk, the trials confirming the Bristol aircraft's superiority in the air. Simultaneously seven further Bulldogs (five with Gnome-Rhône Jupiter VI and two with Gnome-Rhône 9Asb engines) were shipped to Latvia. Also in August 1930 a dozen Gnome-Rhône Jupiter VI-powered Bulldogs were sold to Estonia.

Germany captures the Bulldog

The appearance of the RAF's first strengthened Bulldog Mk IIAs was accompanied by an order in 1931 for four similar aircraft (but with unsupercharged high-compression Jupiter VIFH engines, Viet gas starters and Madsen machine-guns) for the Royal Danish flying corps; these were flown by the Danish No. 1 Squadron, and three were still being used as trainers when Germany invaded the country in April 1940. At one time negotiations were in hand to build the Bulldog under licence at the Danish Naval Dockyard following evaluation of one of the Bristol-built machines by the Danish naval air service, but these plans did not come to fruition.

The four Danish Bulldogs were shipped from Filton in March 1931, and two months later eight further Bulldog Mk IIAs were flown out from the Bristol factory by Swedish service pilots to Malmslätt, where they gave long service, often operating with ski landing gear. The last three survivors of this romantic but sadly dated aeroplane were presented to Finland in December 1939 for service against the invading Soviet forces during the Winter War then raging.

Indeed it was Finland, fifth of the Baltic nations to equip with the Bulldog, that flew the old biplane into combat. The Bulldog Mk IVA attracted the Finns' attention in 1933, and in December of that year the manufacturers received an order for 17 Mercury-powered fighters. The situation was complicated by the fact that Finland lay within the Gnome-Rhône engine franchise area agreed with Bristol, and French production of the British engine was regarded by the parent company as disappointing. In due course the Bristol directors waived the licence franchise and went ahead with delivery of the aircraft with Bristol-built Mercury VIS2 radials in January 1935. Most of the 17 aircraft were still serving with the Finnish fighter squadron LLv 26 at the beginning of the Winter War of 1939–40, about five Russian aircraft being said to have been shot down by their pilots before the Bulldogs (including those presented by Sweden) were replaced by the Gladiator at the end of January 1940. A single aircraft survived both the Winter War and Continuation War, and survives to this day in superbly restored condition in Finland.

The Finnish Bulldogs were the last to be built at Filton. However, following evaluation of the original aircraft sent out to Japan in 1929, powered by a licence-built Nakajima Jupiter, the Japanese government sponsored an indigenous adaptation of the Bulldog under Bristol design supervision in Japan. Although differing in several respects (namely the fuel tank installation, landing gear and tail unit) two Nakajima Jupiter-powered prototypes (the first with cylinder helmets and the second with narrow-chord Townend ring and wheel spats) were flown. No Bulldog production was undertaken, although several subsequent Japanese aircraft incorporated Bulldog features without attribution.

It is true that in the early 1930s the RAF was very dependent on the Bulldog, but bombers were very important during this period and people were trying to spend less money on interceptors. It did not seem to matter very much that most of the fighters being used differed very little from those of World War 1.

Hawker Fury and Nimrod

Graced with superbly clean and simple lines, Sydney Camm's beautiful Hawker Fury biplane was the first RAF fighter to enter service with a top speed of over 200 mph (320 km/h). In the early 1930s the select body of Fury pilots came to be regarded as the fortunate élite in 'the best flying club in the world'.

The successful debut of the Rolls-Royce F.XI V-12 engine (which differed from the earlier Falcon in its cylinder blocks cast from a single piece of metal, giving a much better performance/weight ratio), meant that Hawker's chief designer, Sydney Camm, was able to break with the old tradition of using a radial engine for interceptors. Camm was striving for ever-improving speeds from his fighters, and had a particularly good working relationship with Rolls-Royce. As a result, he was able to take two fundamental paths in the building of the new F.XI engine: one led to the light Hart bombers, and the other to the Hornet, Fury and Nimrod fighters.

The basis of this fighter design lay in the experimental Hoopoe naval single-seater, produced as a private venture in 1927 and conforming to the general requirements of naval Specification N.21/26. Originally powered by a Bristol Mercury radial and with two-bay wings, the Hoopoe progressed to single-bay wings and finished up with a 560-hp (418-kW) Armstrong Siddeley Panther III which gave a fairly creditable top speed of 196 mph (315 km/h).

Early in 1928 the Hoopoe's design was tailored to accommodate a Rolls-Royce F.XI, it being found possible to enclose the engine totally in an exceptionally finely contoured nose with the associated radiator bath located between the landing gear legs. This design exceeded by a handsome margin the requirements of Air Ministry Specification F.20/27, and a prototype, named the Hornet, went on display at the 1929 Olympia Show where its appearance caused a sensation, the more so when, re-engined with a supercharged F.XIS, it returned a top speed of 205 mph (330 km/h) during flight trials by Flight Lieutenant P. W. S. Bulman a few weeks later.

Owing to 'shortsighted, superfluous and stultifying' demands expressed in F.20/27, the specification was officially withdrawn and a new set of requirements was drawn up around the Hornet, Camm himself frequently being consulted.

K8249 was a Fury Mk II built by General Aircraft. It differed from the Hawker-built aircraft by having a tailwheel and no spats. Eighty-nine were built in this batch and this example flew with No. 1 Sqn based at Tangmere, sporting the squadron's two red bars and winged '1' on the fin.

Hawker Fury

Specification

Hawker Fury Mk I
Type: single-seat interceptor fighter
Powerplant: one 525-hp (392-kW) Rolls-Royce Kestrel IIS vee 12-cylinder supercharged water-cooled piston engine
Performance: maximum speed 207 mph (333 km/h) at 14,000 ft (4270 m); climb to 10,000 ft (3050 m) 4 minutes 30 seconds; service ceiling 28,000 ft (8535 m); range 305 miles (491 km)
Weights: empty 2,623 lb (1190 kg); maximum take-off 3,490 lb (1583 kg)
Dimensions: span 30 ft 0 in (9.14 m); length 26 ft 8 in (8.13 m); height 10 ft 2 in (3.10 m); wing area 252.0 sq ft (23.41 m²)
Armament: two fixed forward-firing 0.303-in (7.7-mm) Vickers Mk III machine-guns on nose with 600 rounds per gun

During the mid-1930s, the Fury was a front-line fighter for the RAF. One squadron, No. 25(F), was based at Hawkinge, and two, Nos 1(F) and 43(F) at Tangmere. The latter is represented here in the shape of K3731, the aircraft of the red flight leader, denoted by the red coloured fin. Known as the 'Fighting Cocks', No. 43 flew Furies from May 1931 to November 1938, and often participated in the annual Hendon Air Pageant.

Hawker Fury and Nimrod

Three Hawker Furies were supplied to the Portuguese Arma de Aéronautica in 1935. Several European countries would have bought more Furies, but its cost and the slow delivery of the Kestrel engine halted several exports, while aircraft such as the Bristol Bulldog flourished.

Specification 13/30 was issued, the Hornet itself was purchased by the Air Ministry with the serial J9682, and a preliminary order for three development aircraft placed with the H.G. Hawker Engineering Company. Already the Rolls-Royce F.XI had been named the Kestrel and, despite some disappointment by the manufacturers as well as within the Air Ministry itself, the name Hornet was changed to Fury.

It was always Camm's intention that the Fury and Hart families should come to be regarded as the Bentleys and Rolls-Royces of the RAF, representing the peak of engineering expertise, yet in themselves they did little to advance technology save in an extraordinary attention to design detail. The Fury perpetuated Fred Sigrist's dumbbell-section wing spars, the wings themselves being of unswept parallel-chord configuration; the fuselage was a steel and aluminium structure with aluminium panels enclosing the nose as far aft as the cockpit, and with fabric covering on rear fuselage, wings and tail. The gun armament (twin synchronized Vickers guns) remained the same as had been introduced in RFC scouts more than a dozen years earlier. Ailerons were fitted to the top wing only, yet these were adequate to bestow extremely sensitive control and a brisk rate of roll.

As the Hornet prototype was taken abroad on a demonstration tour by Bulman, the Air Staff decided to equip a single RAF squadron with Furies (a decision possibly difficult to justify having regard to the prevailing economic depression, the fact that the Bristol Bulldog was only then just entering service as the RAF's standard interceptor and that the Fury was undeniably expensive at a unit price of

£4,800, itself reflecting the new Kestrel's unamortized costs). As jigging and tooling for the new fighter got under way at Kingston-upon-Thames, an order for six Furies was received from Yugoslavia, one of them to be powered by the Hispano-Suiza 12Nb engine and the others by standard Kestrel IIS engines.

First deliveries

The three development Furies and 18 production aircraft were all flown early in 1931, 16 of them being delivered to No. 43 (Fighter) Squadron, commanded by Squadron Leader L. H. (later Air Marshal Sir Leonard) Slatter at Tangmere. The Yugoslav Furies followed on immediately after, the Hispano-powered aircraft being found to be unsatisfactory and therefore modified to standard form.

Such was the enthusiasm with which the Fury was received by Slatter's pilots that an immediate follow-on order for 48 RAF aircraft was placed, and these joined No. 25 (Fighter) Squadron, commanded by Squadron Leader Walter Bryant at Hawkinge during the winter of 1931–2, and No. 1 (Fighter) Squadron, commanded by Squadron Leader Charles Spackman at Tangmere. At once intense rivalry sprang up among these three premier fighter squadrons, particularly to win the RAF's coveted air gunnery challenge trophy (eventually won outright by No. 25 Squadron with its Furies).

Despite the type's speed superiority over the Bulldog, efforts to argue support for standardization of the Fury nevertheless failed, largely on account of the faster amortization of Bulldog costs and limited availability of Kestrel engines (already slated for the large orders being placed for the growing family of Hawker Hart variants). Thus only 48 further Fury Mk Is were ordered for the RAF, spread over the

Developed from the Mercury-powered Hoopoe and the Hornet, there were three prototype Furies. The first flew initially on 25 March 1931. Production aircraft were little different from K1926 pictured here and were soon in service with No. 43 Sqn, which was receiving aircraft, armed with Vickers Mk III machine guns, as early as May 1931.

128

Devoid of any markings except for the 'Fighting Cocks' symbol on the tail, this aircraft is a Fury Mk II of No. 43 Sqn at Tangmere, sporting the dark green/dark earth camouflage adopted about the time of the Munich Conference in 1938.

Three Furies were delivered to Spain powered by 700-hp (522-kW) Hispano-Suiza 12Xbrs engines, and featuring a single strut undercarriage in common with contemporary types such as the Gloster Gladiator. These aircraft originally flew in aluminium colour schemes with red panels on the fuselage.

period 1932–5, the majority of these being replacements issued to the three squadrons already mentioned. That is not to suggest that the accident rate on the Fury was inordinately high, a total of 12 flying accidents being recorded on the three units in five years; however, there were other losses: on 7 August 1933 a No. 504 Squadron Horsley crashed at Hawkinge, falling on the hangar housing the Furies of No. 25 Squadron and destroying six in the fire that followed.

While the RAF Fury squadrons provided superb displays, including the memorable tied-together formation aerobatics at Hendon and elsewehere, foreign air forces were taking a lively interest in the fighter, although once more its high cost and the limited delivery rate of the Kestrel kept individual orders small. Norway ordered a single evaluation example with a Panther radial, and this was flown on a ski landing gear for a short time; the 14-cylinder engine proved too heavy, however, and this version was not considered a

success. Largest overseas customer was Persia, for whose air force 16 aircraft were produced with Pratt & Whitney Hornet radials. Most of these were delivered in 1933, and were followed the next year by an order for six further aircraft with Bristol Mercury VISP radials, the Hornet engine having given persistent trouble; some of the earlier aircraft were returned to Kingston to have the British engine substituted, a small number of Mercury Furies surviving in 1941 when they were encountered by the RAF during the Raschid Ali revolt.

Further exports

Other foreign customers included Portugal (with three aircraft delivered in 1935), and Spain, which also received three aircraft; the latter were powered by 700-hp (522-kW) Hispano-Suiza 12Xbrs engines and featured Gloster Gladiator-type single-leg cantilever landing gear legs, and were flown in action during the Spanish Civil War. Yugoslavia returned one of its original Furies to Kingston to have a 720-hp (537-kW) Lorraine Petrel Hfrs engine fitted; although this example returned a top speed of 229 mph (369 km/h) on test, the Yugoslavs opted to order 10 Kestrel XVI-powered aircraft (so as to share a common powerplant with that nation's Hawker Hinds) which featured the single-leg landing gear, low-drag radiator and four-gun armament. With a top speed of 242 mph (389 km/h) these Yugoslav aircraft were the fastest of all export Furies.

Hawker was undoubtedly fortunate to gain the relatively small Fury Mk I orders it did, bearing in mind that it had been pre-empted by the Bulldog and that the 1930 depression and the pervading mood for disarmament could be held as adequate excuse to ignore the aircraft altogether. Issue of Specification F.7/30, however, showed that the Air Staff at least was looking beyond the scope of the 'Ten-Year Rule', which claimed that 10-year warning of a European conflict would be available, and which was abandoned within a year in any case. It was this covert attitude, shared among those with a favoured ear in Whitehall, that spurred Camm and the Hawker management to persist with privately-funded development of the Fury, with a descendant in mind for possible tender to the F.7/30 specification itself.

This is an exact replica of the aicraft flown by Squadron Leader L. H. Slatter of No. 43 Squadron, itself one of the first examples of the Hawker Fury delivered in 1931.

Several aircraft for export had radial engines which necessitated an enlarged fin. This example was one of the six Mercury-engined Furies supplied to Persia. Earlier, 16 Pratt & Whitney Hornet-engined aircraft had been delivered. These saw much service and were used as late at 1941.

First step was to produce an almost standard, company-owned trial installation aircraft, known as the Intermediate Fury and registered G-ABSE. On this aircraft, first flown by P. E. G. Sayer on 13 April 1932, were tested such innovations as wheel spats, Goshawk supercharger (and eventually the Goshawk engine itself) and steam-condenser evaporative cooling. The next logical step was to produce a company-funded aircraft on which high performance flight trials could be conducted without the complication of service equipment. This was the High-Speed Fury, first flown on 3 May 1933 and variously used for the exploration of low-drag tapered wings, low-drag V-type interplane struts, evaporating cooling and Goshawk engine (by then mandatory in the F.7/30 specification). When eventually it underwent service-style evaluation with the 730-hp (545-kW) Goshawk B 43 engine with semi-retractable radiator and two guns fitted, the High-Speed Fury (sometimes known in this form as the Fury Mk II) returned a top speed of 277 mph (446 km/h) at 12,500 ft (3810 m), possibly the highest speed recorded by a fully-armed British biplane. It is also worth mentioning that, although not strictly a member of the Fury family, Camm's P.V.3 contender for the F.7/30 contest was a direct development of the High-Speed Fury; compromised by the unsuitable steam-cooled Goshawk, and weighed down by the ungainly condensers, mandatory four-gun armament, night-flying equipment, wheel spats and full fuel load, the P.V.3. could manage no more than 224 mph (360 km/h), at 14,000 ft (4265 m). It is hardly surprising, therefore, that the Gloster Gladiator, which was faster by some 25 mph (40 km/h) earned the winner's verdict. Incidentally the High-Speed Fury was also flown by Rolls-Royce in 1935 with the 1,000-hp (746-kW) P.V.12 Merlin prototype engine although, as a result of considerable ballasting to restore the centre of gravity position, there were no measured top speed trials.

Fury Mk II and Nimrod

That was not, however, the end of the Fury saga. Half-way through the High-Speed Fury development the aircraft (K3586) was evaluated at Martlesham Heath with a Kestrel VI and wheel spats, returning a top speed of 228 mph (367 km/h). When formally tendered to the existing Specification F.14/32, this version was accepted as the basis of an interim RAF fighter needed to serve during the Hawker Hurricane's development period. With an additional fuel tank to compensate for higher consumption this version, the Fury Mk II, entered service with No. 25 Squadron in November 1936, followed within a year by Nos 41, 73 and 87 Squadrons.

With a speed of only 223 mph (359 km/h), and already outclassed by the Gladiator (not to mention the Hurricane and Spitfire) the Fury was virtually at the end of its front-line service by the time of the Munich Crisis of September 1938. Nevertheless, production of the Fury Mk II totalled 98.

It has often been suggested that in much the same manner that the Hart underwent 'navalization' to become the Osprey, so the Fury joined the Fleet Air Arm as the Nimrod. This is entirely incorrect, and the two fighters were no more than distant cousins rather than brothers, albeit generically descended from the Hoopoe, which was, as already explained, itself a naval fighter.

Encouraged by the initial success of the Hornet as well as continuing enquiries from Denmark, Sweden and Norway

Hawker Fury Mk I cutaway drawing key

1 Starter dog
2 Spinner
3 Watts two-bladed wooden propeller
4 Propeller attachment bolts
5 Spinner backplate
6 Propeller reduction gear
7 Engine cowling
8 Cowling fairing
9 525 hp Rolls-Royce Kestrel II.S engine
10 Cowling attachments
11 Exhaust stubs
12 Front engine mounting
13 Rear engine mounting
14 Engine support framework
15 Supercharger
16 Water system header tank
17 Water system filler cap
18 Coolant pipe
19 Supercharger air intake
20 Engine compartment bulkhead
21 Centre section 'N' struts
22 Wing centre section structure
23 Handgrips
24 Outer wing spar attachment
25 Plywood-covered leading edges
26 Pitot/static tubes
27 Tubular steel front spar
28 Tubular steel rear spar
29 Spar bracing strut
30 Diagonal bracing wires
31 Port aileron
32 Aileron crank
33 Aileron cable
34 Gravity fuel tank, 27 Imp gal (123 litres)
35 Filler cap
36 Main fuel tank, 23 Imp gal (105 litres)
37 Tank mountings
38 Filler cap
39 Oil tank
40 Fuselage tubular framework
41 Upper longeron
42 Lower longeron
43 Riveted framework joints
44 Vickers 0.303-in (7.7-mm) machine guns
45 Gun muzzle trough in fuel tank
46 Cartridge case and link ejector chute
47 Ammunition tank, 600 rounds each gun
48 Gunsight
49 Pilot's windscreen

Hawker Nimrod variants

Hawker Norn: one private-venture naval prototype, later purchased by Air Ministry and renamed Nimrod; Rolls-Royce F.XIMS
Hawker Nimrod: two prototypes (S1577 and S1578) to Specification 16/30; Kestrel IIs
Hawker Nimrod Mk I: 10 production aircraft (S1579–S1588) to Specification 16/30; Kestrel IIS; interchangeable wheel/float landing gear
Hawker Nimrod Mk I: production of 43 aircraft (S1614–S1637) and K2823–K2841) in 1932–3 to amended Specification 16/30 with minor modifications
Hawker Nimrod Mk II: production of 27 aircraft (K2909–K2914), K2925, K2926, K3654–K3662 and K4620–

K4629) in 1933–5 to Specification 11/33 with strengthened rear fuselage; Kestrel V introduced in some aircraft; sweptback top wing K2909–K2911 of stainless-steel construction
Hawker Danish Nimrod: two pattern aircraft with Kestrel IIIS engines; supplied in 1934, followed by licence production in Denmark
Hawker Japanese Nimrod: one aircraft with Kestrel IIIS engine, supplied in 1934
Hawker Portuguese Nimrod: one aircraft supplied in 1934, first with Kestrel IIS but later changed to Kestrel V

The Fury Mk II went into service with No. 25 Sqn in November 1936 with the more powerful Kestrel VI. The first (Hawker) production batch were distinguished from their predecessors by having spats. This aircraft served with No. 25 Sqn flying from Hawkinge.

Hawker Fury variants

Hawker Hornet: one private-venture prototype (J9682) to amended Specification F.20/27; F.XIA engine (later F.XIS); first flight in March 1929
Hawker Fury Mk I: three development aircraft (K1926–K1928) with Kestrel IIS engine
Hawker Fury Mk I: production in 1931 to Specification 13/30; 18 aircraft (K1929–K1946) with Kestrel IIS; one aircraft (K1935) became Fury Mk II prototype; Vickers Mk I guns
Hawker Fury Mk I: production in 1932–3 to amended specification 13/30 with minor modifications; 63 aircraft (K2035–K2082, K2874–K2883 and K2889–K2903) with Kestrel IIS; Vickers Mk III guns
Hawker Yugoslav Fury (1st Series): six aircraft delivered in 1932; Kestrel IIS (one aircraft temporarily with Hispano-Suiza 12Nb engine)
Hawker Norwegian Fury: one aircraft delivered in November 1932; Armstrong Siddeley Panther IIIA radial; also flown with ski landing gear
Hawker Persian Fury (1st Series): 16 aircraft delivered in latter half of 1933 with Pratt & Whitney Hornet S2B1G radials and three-blade Hamilton Hydromatic propellers
Hawker Persian Fury (2nd Series): six aircraft delivered in 1935 with Bristol Mercury VIS2 radials (plus

some converted from 1st Series)
Hawker Portuguese Fury: three aircraft (50–52) delivered June 1934 with Kestrel IIS
Hawker Yugoslav Fury (2nd Series): 10 aircraft delivered 1936-7 with Kestrel XVI, low-drag radiator, cantilever landing gear and four-gun armament
Hawker Spanish Fury: three aircraft (4-1 to 4-3) delivered June 1936 with Hispano-Suiza 12Xbrs, cantilever landing gear and two-gun armament
Hawker Intermediate Fury: one company-sponsored trials aircraft (G-ABSE) flown with Kestrel IIS, IVS (with Goshawk supercharger), VI and VI Special, and Goshawk III engines; also on occasion with wheel spats, cantilever landing gear and electro-magnetic bomb gear
Hawker High-Speed Fury Mk I and Mk II: one company-sponsored trials aircraft (K3586) flown with Kestrel IIS, IIIS, IVS, Kestrel (Special), Goshawk III, B41 and B43, and Rolls-Royce P.V.12 (Merlin prototype) engines; various wing configurations also flown
Hawker Fury Mk ii: production in 1936 to Specification 6/35 by Hawker; 23 aircraft with Kestrel VI
Hawker Fury Mk II: production in 1936–7 to Specification 19/35 by General Aircraft Ltd; 75 aircraft (K8232–K8306); four aircraft to Habbaniyah in 1938, some others to South Africa in about 1939

50 Padded cockpit coaming
51 Throttle and mixture control levers
52 Control column
53 Instrument panel
54 Tailplane incidence control handwheel
55 Safety harness
56 Harness release cable
57 Pilot's seat
58 Seat adjusting lever
59 Priming handpump
60 Footboards
61 Rudder pedal bar
62 Oxygen bottle
63 Battery accumulator
64 Cockpit plywood back bulkhead
65 Rear fuselage top decking
66 Safety harness attachment
67 Dorsal frames
68 Wooden stringers
69 Rear fuselage structure

70 Tailplane control cables
71 Fin attachment
72 Fin structure
73 Fabric covering
74 Aerial post
75 Rudder structure
76 Sternpost
77 Rudder hinge
78 Tailplane bracing wire
79 Tailplane incidence control jack
80 Tailplane front mounting
81 Starboard elevator
82 Elevator operating arm
83 Fixed bracing strut
84 Access panel
85 Tailskid
86 Tailskid shock absorber
87 Aircraft trestling point
88 Fuselage bottom longeron
89 Access to rear fuselage structure
90 Lower wing rear spar attachment

91 Front spar attachment
92 Undercarriage strut mounting
93 Lower wing structure
94 Interplane struts
95 Wooden ribs
96 Plywood covered leading edge
97 Double tubular section spars
98 Water system radiator
99 Radiator attachment
100 Main undercarriage leg
101 Oleo strut
102 Rubber pad shock absorber
103 Leg fairing
104 Axle fairing
105 Starboard mainwheel
106 Tyre inflation valve access
107 Port mainwheel
108 Brake plate
109 Undercarriage bracing wires

Although not the same basic aeroplane, the Nimrod was the naval equivalent of the Fury. Nearly 100 Nimrods were produced by Hawker under licence, and several were still serving with the Danes when the Germans invaded in 1940. This example was a Nimrod Mk II.

about a possible naval development, Camm set about adapting the Kestrel-Hoopoe concept to the requirements of naval fighter Specification N.21/26, issued to bring about a replacement for the ageing Fairey Flycatcher. By the time this had been updated in Specification 16/30 Hawker had almost completed two prototypes at company expense. At first known unofficially as the Norn (a Scandinavian Fate), these aircraft were purchased by the Air Ministry, one for flight evaluation and the other for flotation trials. Renamed Nimrod, the new naval fighters certainly resembled the Fury but differed in a number of important respects. High energy-absorption, long-travel landing gear oleos, slightly enlarged fin, and metal fuselage panels extending slightly farther aft were the main external distinguishing features; internally there were such features as flotation boxes in the top wing and rear fuselage, some use of stainless steel components in wing attachments and engine bearers, and provision for interchangeable float or wheel landing gear. Much less perceptible was the relocation of the cockpit 3 in (7.6 cm) farther forward to give improved field of vision over the lower-wing leading edge.

After initial evaluation at Martlesham, the first Nimrod (S1577) was embarked early in 1931 in HMS *Eagle* to attend the British Empire Trade Exhibition at Buenos Aires, being flown in the El Palomar air display by Flying Officer C. P. Barker. On return, it completed its evaluation successfully and was joined by a second aircraft (S1578) for floatplane trials at Felixstowe. A production order for 34 aircraft was placed, and these aircraft first entered service in June 1932 with No. 408 Flight, commanded by Lieutenant Commander (later Vice-Admiral Sir Edward) E. M. C. Abel-Smith RN, aboard HMS *Glorious*, and soon after with Nos 402 and 409 Flights, in each case replacing Flycatchers. A final batch of 19 Nimrod Mk 1s included the addition of arrester hook and catapult spools, and of a headrest fairing found necessary during catapulting. Some of these modifications were retrospectively introduced to the earlier aircraft.

Production of the Nimrod continued slowly until well into 1935 with the Nimrod Mk II version, of which 27 were completed; originally intended to be a Kestrel V-powered version with swept-back top wing, strengthened rear fuselage and increased use of stainless steel in its structure, most aircraft were in fact completed with no more than the strengthening to distinguish them from Nimrod Mk Is, the Kestrel V being substituted later; only three aircraft are known to have widely employed stainless steel.

In 1933 Fleet Air Arm units underwent a change of designation, the old flights being renumbered in the 800s; Nimrods served with two flights on each of Nos 800 and 801 Squadrons (HMS *Courageous*) and No. 802 Squadron (HMS *Furious*), the third flight being equipped with Hawker Ospreys. Almost all had disappeared from service (replaced by Gloster Sea Gladiators and Blackburn Skuas) by the outbreak of World War 2. A total of four Nimrods was exported, two to Denmark as pattern aircraft for proposed licence production, one to Japan and one to Portugal.

Once it had been fitted out for ship-supported use, the Nimrod with its wheeled undercarriage and a Kestrel IIS engine was able to reach a maximum speed of only 196.4 mph (316 km/h) at a height of 11,800 ft (3600 m). But from all reports the plane handled quite well.

After having been rebuilt by Hispano-Suiza, this Fury, originally supplied to the Spanish air force, was captured by the Nationalist forces and flown by them. It features the Hispano-Suiza engine (note paired middle exhaust ports in the cowling) and single strut undercarriage.

Several ex-RAF Furies were handed over to the South African Air Force after their front-line days were over. This aircraft flew with No. 3 Sqn, SAAF, in 1942.

de Havilland Dragon and Rapide

Producing more than twice as many transport aircraft as any other British manufacturer, the de Havilland Aircraft Company carved its niche in aviation history. The Dragon family of biplane transports formed a high proportion of the company's output; with their reliable pedigree and overall performance attracting both civil and military customers, the three major designs logged over 30 years of operations, with some aircraft still flying today.

In the late 20s and early 30s, de Havilland was establishing itself a superb reputation with its series of light aircraft based on the D.H.60 Moth. The company had built the eight-passenger D.H.61 Giant Moth and the D.H.66 Hercules for

Aer Lingus flew its first passengers from Dublin to Bristol in a D.H.84 Dragon. To mark the company's 50th anniversary in 1986, a beautifully restored Dragon retraced this journey. At the speed it flew, and the height, a road map would have been enough for navigation.

Owned and operated by the Prince of Wales in the 1930s, this immaculate D.H.84 Dragon 1 wore a red, blue and silver colour scheme. Powered by two 130-hp (97-kW) Gipsy Major engines with a 30-Imp gal (136-litre) fuel tank in each nacelle, this two-bay strut and wire-braced biplane had seating for between six and 10 passengers.

use by Imperial Airways and elsewhere in the British Empire, while the needs of smaller users were covered by the D.H.83 Fox Moth.

One of the main Fox Moth operators was Hillman's Airways. It had been founded by Edward Hillman, who moved into aviation as a natural extension of his motor coach business. This colourful character was responsible for pressing de Havilland to design a larger 10-seat twin-engine aircraft to meet the expanding demand for his airline's services. Hillman's Airways was accordingly the first operator of de Havilland's new light airliner, the D.H.84 Dragon. The Dragon was actually rather smaller than Hillman's initial specification and provided accommodation for a pilot and six passengers in a slab-sided fuselage built of spruce and plywood. The biplane wings were built with outer panels which folded backwards just outboard of the engines and the shape of the wings themselves was somewhat complex. Two 130-hp (97-kW) de Havilland Gipsy Major 1 engines were mounted on the lower wings with the main landing gear legs directly mounted to the engine firewall bulkheads and, in some cases, the wheels were enclosed with streamlined spats to give some drag improvement. A swept-back fin and rudder assembly was used, perpetuating the de Havilland 'trademark' which had become familiar on the sport biplanes, and the pilot was housed in an extensively glazed cockpit in the extreme nose of the aircraft.

The prototype Dragon (E-9, c/n 6000) made its first flight at Stag Lane on 24 November 1932. The period of flight testing was incredibly short compared with present-day experience and the prototype was soon resprayed with the registration G-ACAN and delivered to Mr Hillman during December 1932. Four production Dragons followed in quick succession and were an immediate success. Hillman's Airways offered very low fares (by the device of keeping overheads down and paying the pilots and the bus drivers the same wage rates) and this soon resulted in two further Dragons being ordered and the existing machines being converted to eight-passenger configuration by eliminating the rear baggage compartment.

Many other small airlines started to order the Dragon for passenger services and carrying mail and for ambulance operations in Scotland and other isolated areas. Another bus company, the Scottish Motor Traction Co. Ltd, had established an integrated system of coach and air services and used the Dragon for this purpose and the type entered service with Highland Airways and Aberdeen Airways,

de Havilland D.H.84 Dragon cutaway drawing key

1 Starboard upper wing panel
2 Inter-spar bracing struts
3 Starboard upper aileron
4 Wing internal wire bracing
5 Outboard interplane struts
6 Diagonal wire bracing
7 Starboard lower aileron
8 Wing panel fabric covering
9 Outer wing panel joint rib
10 Folding segment of trailing edge
11 Rear spar hinge fixing
12 Inboard wing panel rib construction
13 Leading edge rib construction
14 Inboard interplane struts
15 Pitot tubes
16 Cockpit roof glazing
17 Starboard propeller
18 Windscreen panels
19 Instrument panel
20 Moulded plywood nose section
21 Rudder pedals
22 Compass
23 Tailplane rim control handwheel
24 Control column
25 Engine throttle and mixture control levers

26 Venturi tube
27 Seat support box
28 Safety harness
29 Pilot's seat
30 Direct vision opening side window panel
31 Fire extinguisher
32 Cockpit bulkhead
33 Main cabin flooring
34 Fuselage side panel framework

35 Diagonal frame member
36 Cabin window panels
37 Passenger seats (six)
38 Cabin roof framing
39 Ventilating air duct
40 Cabin wall trim panels
41 Leading-edge ventilating air scoop
42 Wing spar centre-section carry-through

The prototype D.H.84 Dragon made its first flight with the test registration E-9 but was re-registered G-ACAN within a few weeks. It joined the first customer, Hillman's Airways, at their base at Maylands Aerodrome during December 1932 and was later joined by a further five Dragons.

which were merged into Scottish Airways in 1938. The Dragon 2 was introduced after 62 of the initial version had been built, and this later model was identifiable by the individually framed cabin windows which replaced the continuous glazing of the Dragon 1. Quite a number of Dragons were operated on floats (particularly in Canada), which necessitated an increase in side area and these aircraft were fitted with an extended vertical fin which stayed on even when they reverted to the normal wheeled landing gear.

An early purchaser of the Dragon was the Iraqi air force, which had probably prompted the D.H.84 development in

43 Wing root attachment rib
44 Diagonal engine nacelle bracing struts
45 Passenger entry door
46 Cabin roof escape hatch
47 Ventilating air duct
48 Starboard side baggage compartment, capacity 50 cu ft (1.42 m³)
49 Starboard wing folded (ground handling) position
50 Skin panel external stiffening strip
51 Fuselage upper longeron
52 Horizontal spacers
53 Fin/tailplane root fillet
54 Starboard tailplane
55 Fin construction
56 Sternpost
57 Rudder horn balance
58 Fabric covered rudder construction
59 Tailplane upper bracing wires
60 Rudder operating lever
61 Elevator hinge control
62 Port fabric-covered elevator construction
63 Fabric-covered tailplane construction
64 Diagonal tailplane spar
65 Castoring tailwheel
66 Tailwheel shock absorber mounting
67 Tailplane lower bracing wires
68 Trimming tailplane screw jack
69 Access hatches
70 Fuselage plywood skinning
71 Lower longeron
72 Vertical spacers
73 Tailplane control cables
74 Cabin rear bulkhead
75 Rear passenger seat
76 Wing rear spar
77 Outer wing panel joint rib
78 Rear spar hinge fixing
79 Trailing edge ribs
80 Wing lattice rib construction
81 Port upper aileron construction
82 Aileron interconnecting rod
83 Port lower aileron
84 Wing tip construction
85 Leading edge inter-rib stiffeners
86 Wing internal wire bracing
87 Aileron pulley and operating lever
88 Outboard interplane struts
89 Lower wing panel rib construction
90 Front spar
91 Front spar latched joint
92 Outer wing panel joint rib
93 Folding segment of trailing edge
94 Inboard interplane struts
95 Diagonal wire bracing
96 Nacelle tail fairing
97 Boarding step
98 Fuel filler cap
99 Fuel tank; total capacity 60 Imp gal (273 litres)
100 Engine oil tank
101 Inboard wing panel rib construction
102 Plywood-covered leading edge
103 Oil cooler air scoop
104 Engine bay bulkhead
105 Engine accessory equipment
106 Nacelle-mounted engine instruments
107 de Havilland Gipsy Major I four-cylinder inline engine
108 Engine mounting points
109 Engine bearer struts
110 Cooling air intake
111 Propeller hub fixing
112 Spinner
113 Two-bladed wooden propeller
114 Engine cowling panels
115 Main undercarriage leg strut
116 Diagonal bracing struts
117 Mainwhel spar fairing
118 Port mainwheel

The de Havilland Dragon Rapide served with many domestic operators, including British European Airways, which acquired 45 aircraft in the first half of 1947. Utilized on many of the BEA routes, the aircraft were given individual names in 1950, with subsequent 'Islander' class operations connecting many outlying communities around the north and west coasts of Scotland and other areas of Britain.

de Havilland Dragon and Dragon Rapide variants

D.H.84 Dragon 1: six-passenger cabin biplane powered by two 130-hp (96.9-kW) Gipsy Major 1 piston engines
D.H.84 Dragon 2: Dragon 1 with framed cabin windows, faired-in landing gear legs and 6-mph (9-km/h) maximum speed improvement
D.H.86: scaled-up version of D.H.84 with four Gipsy Six engines and increased passenger capacity
D.H.89 Dragon Six: developed Dragon with new, non-folding wings and construction based on D.H.86 Express; powered by 200-hp (149-kW) Gipsy Six engines
D.H.89A Dragon Rapide: D.H.89 fitted with split trailing-edge flaps; some D.H.89s retrospectively modified
D.H.89B Dominie Mk 1: D.H.89A for RAF as W/T and navigation trainer
D.H.89B Domine Mk 2: communications transport

version of DH.89B for RAF
D.H.89A Rapide Mk 2: post-war civil Rapide with six passenger seats, pilot and radio operator
D.H.89A Rapide Mk 3: post-war Rapide with eight passenger seats and pilot
D.H.89A Rapide Mk 4: D.H.89A converted with 200-hp (149-kW) Gipsy Queen Mk 2 engines fitted with constant-speed propellers
D.H.89A Rapide Mk 5: Rapide converted with Gipsy Queen 3MVP engines and manually operated variable-pitch propellers
D.H.89A Rpaide Mk 6: Rapide fitted with Fairey X5 fixed-pitch metal propellers
D.H.89M: military version of D.H. 89A with extended fin, twin nose-mounted Vickers Mk V guns and open mid-upper turret with one Lewis Mk III gun on ring mounting.

de Havilland D.H.89

Specification

de Havilland D.H.89A
Type: light piston-engine transport biplane
Powerplant: two 200-hp (149-kW) de Havilland Gipsy Queen 3 inline piston engines
Performance: maximum speed 157 mph (253 km/h); cruising speed 132 mph (212 km/h); initial rate of climb 867 ft (264 m) per minute; service ceiling 19,500 ft (5944 m); maximum range with standard fuel tanks 578 miles (930 km); take-off run 870 ft (265 m); landing run 510 ft (155 m)
Weights: empty 3,276 lb (1486 kg); maximum take-off 5,500 lb (2495 kg)
Dimensions: 48 ft 0 in (14.63 m); length 34 ft 6 in (10.52 m); height 10 ft 3 in (3.12 m); wing area 336 sq ft (31.21 m²)

The five-seat D.H.90 Dragonfly was a small, luxury development of the Rapide but was constructed with a pre-formed plywood fuselage. One of the 67 examples is G-AEDU which was originally in Mozambique as CR-AAB. It was restored as G-AEDU in 1979, and in June 1983 it was sold to an owner in Louisville, Kentucky, as N190DH

G-ACTM is a D.H.89A Dragon Rapide (c/n 6746) which was originally delivered during the war as a Dominie for RAF use. When the war was over it was civilianized and, in 1953, sold to Lebanon as OD-ABP. It subsequently flew in Jordan and, in 1964, returned to England and is shown in its Rothman parachuting livery.

the first place. It ordered eight of the D.H.84M version, and these were delivered to Baghdad during 1933 to be used for patrolling the rather turbulent tribally-controlled areas of the country. A gunner's open position was provided on top of the fuselage just aft of the wings and the pilot was able to take aggressive action using two machine-guns fitted one on each side of the nose of the Dragon. The D.H.84M was also fitted with a seaplane-style extended fin. Other air forces which ordered the type were the Danish army air force (two aircraft), the Portuguese air force (three aircraft) and the Turkish and Irish military forces which purchased standard civil Dragons as general duties transports.

Long-distance record attempt

The most famous of all Dragons was G-ACCV (c/n 6014) named *Seafarer* and owned by Jim and Amy Mollison. As Amy Johnson, Mrs Mollison had become famous through her epic flight to Australia in 1930 and subsequent flights from England to South Africa. Together, the Mollisons planned to use *Seafarer* in an attempt on the world long-distance record, which would start with a flight to New York. The Dragon made its first attempt to leave Croydon on 8 June

G-AGSH, a Dragon Rapide Mk 6, is seen here in the markings of the Royal Air Force Sport Parachute Association. The predominantly red colour scheme reflected its use by the 'Red Devils' parachute team as the jumpship at many air displays.

Rejected by the RAF in favour of the Avro Anson for general reconnaissance, the D.H.89B Dragon Rapide was ordered for communications and training duties as the Dominie Mk I and II. This example served with No. 2 Radio School and has the direction finding loop on the upper fuselage to facilitate the training of wireless operators.

1933 but was so heavily loaded that it failed to evade a ditch and the aicraft nosed over. The aircraft was repaired and flown to Wales where it successfully took off from Pendine Sands and, after 39 hours in the air, arrived over Bridgeport, Connecticut. Attempting to land downwind *Seafarer* overshot and was damaged beyond repair, the Mollisons ending up in hospital. The remains of G-ACCV were later cannibalized to be used in the Dragon 2 *Seafarer II* which was used by Ayling and Reid to fly the Atlantic from Canada to England in August of the following year.

In 1934, de Havilland had rushed through development of a new four-engine airliner designated D.H.86. Aimed at the requirement for a fast 10-seater which could operate the Singapore to Australia section of the proposed Croydon to Brisbane passenger service, the D.H.86 (Express Air Liner, as it was known) used much of the design layout of the Dragon but was scaled up, had a completely new wing cellule and was powered by four of the new 200-hp (149-kW) de Havilland Gipsy Six inline engines. There was also a degree of pressure from existing Dragon operators for a more comfortable and faster replacement for the D.H.84, and this led to the company scaling down the D.H.86 and fitting it with two Gipsy Six engines to produce the D.H.89 Dragon Six. Outwardly, the Dragon Six was not a great deal different from the Dragon, but it used the completely new tapered wings without the folding mechanism of the previous model and the maximum speed of 128 mph (206 km/h) which had been achieved by the Dragon 1 rose to 157 mph (253 km/h) because of improved streamlining and the higher engine power. The D.H.89 prototype (E-4, c/n 6250) was first flown from Hatfield on 17 April 1934. It had a fully faired landing gear, which was a major contributor to drag reduction, and the nose cone was tapered upwards to give a new profile to the cockpit area.

Once again, Mr Hillman was a keen purchaser of the new model, which was now named the Dragon Rapide, and the first three production examples were delivered to Hillman's Airways between July and September 1934. A further four Dragon Rapides were delivered to this operator, and these were finally transferred to British Airways when Edward Hillman sold his business in December 1935. Another Rapide operator was Railway Air Services Ltd, which had been formed by the principal railway companies in 1934 and had begun flying on routes from Croydon to the Isle of Wight, Plymouth, Birmingham and Liverpool. The expansion of mail services to Glasgow and Belfast prompted the company to buy the D.H.86 and also a total of eight D.H.89s. Other British operators of the Dragon Rapide included Olley Air Service Ltd, Northern & Scottish Airways Ltd, Jersey Airways Ltd and British Continental Airways Ltd. All of these small air carriers used the Dragon Rapide intensively, and in all weather conditions, right up to the outbreak of World War 2 in 1939.

The D.H.89 built up a good export reputation, 41 of the first 100 aircraft being sold to overseas customers. Several of the Middle East petroleum companies bought Rapides for communications with the desert oil extraction sites, and Canadian companies including Quebec Airways and Canadian Airways Ltd had fleets of them, often fitted with the extended fin and twin floats. Once the Rapide production line had built up to a fair volume, de Havilland introduced the D.H.89A version

which featured split trailing edge flaps fitted just outboard of the engine nacelles on the lower wings, and optional metal propellers. Many of the earlier D.H.89s were retrospectively modified with the flap system, and production of the D.H.89A started at G-AERN (c/n 6345) which was sold to West Coast Air Services and delivered in March 1937. At about this time, also, the Rapide was given an effective cabin heating system, the rear cabin windows were enlarged and optional provision was made for a toilet in the rear of the cabin.

Several Rapides had been sold abroad for military purposes during 1936 and 1937. The Imperial Iranian war ministry bought three, the National Government of China had five (delivered in December 1937) and the Spanish government ordered three for police work in its North African territories. These were, in fact, never used in North Africa and they joined the Republican forces when the Spanish Civil War broke out. Three ex-civil D.H.84s and approximately 10 D.H.89s also reached one side or the other. These were all aircraft which were sold by dealers who had purchased them in England and were able to break the blockade which both the British and French governments established in the summer of 1936. Both the Nationalists and the Republicans were desperate to obtain aircraft, and a number of Airspeed Envoys, Monospars, Fokker transports and Rapides were despatched, although a fair number never reached their destinations. The Rapides were fitted in Spain with open gun turrets and there is no evidence that any of these machines survived the war.

Coastal patrol version

In 1935, the British Air Ministry carried out evaluations to see if the Rapide would be suitable for the coastal patrol role

The D.H.90 Dragonfly first appeared in 1936 as a smaller version of the Dragon Rapide, intended as a luxury airliner. Most of the 66 machines built went to buyers abroad.

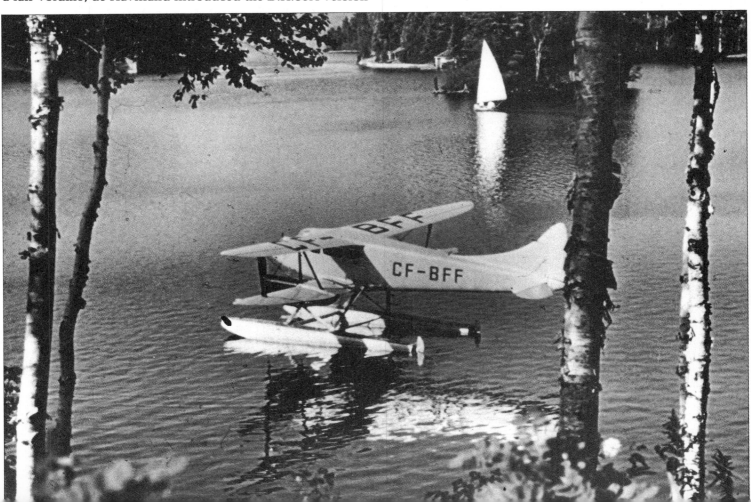

de Havilland Dragon and Rapide

set out in Specification G.18/35. One example (K4772, c/n 6271) was built as a D.H.89M with the extended fin and a dorsal upper turret which housed a Lewis Mk III machine-gun, and it was tested at Martlesham Heath and Gosport but the patrol contract was awarded to the Avro 652 (which became the Anson). Despite this setback two Rapides were ordered as communications aircraft and several were ordered as navigation trainers by Airwork Services Ltd, which had gained substantial contracts from the Air Ministry during the build-up to the outbreak of war. As 1938 gave way to the fateful 1939 the Rapides in use at the School of Navigation at Shoreham received a coat of camouflage paint, and the Rapide went into battle.

Up to the start of the war on 3 September 1939, de Havilland's civil Rapide output had numbered about 180 aircraft and this gave way to military production at Hatfield

The glassed-in, very narrow cockpit of the D.H.84 gave the pilot an excellent all-round view. This type, of which 115 were built, flew successfully with a large number of civil airlines.

as the company started to receive direct Air Ministry orders for D.H.89s equipped as W/T and navigation trainers. These were designated D.H.89B Dominie Mk I and were externally identical to the civil model with the exception of the large loop antenna on the roof just behind the cockpit and, of course, the camouflage paint scheme. Dominies entered service with the air navigation schools, particularly No. 6 Air Observers' Navigation School (AONS) at RAF Staverton and No. 7 AONS at RAF Perth (Scone). They were also delivered as the D.H.89B Dominie Mk II for general communications duties and employed as the mainstays of station flights both with the RAF and the Royal Navy. The Air Transport Auxiliary (ATA) took over responsibility for the ferrying of military aircraft from airfield to airfield in May 1940 and used Dominies for positioning crews all over the United Kingdom and Europe. It also set up a Medical Section which used Dominies with up to two stretchers fitted into the modified D.H.89 cabin to ferry medical cases from isolated locations to its central hospital at White Waltham.

The arrival of the war had brought complete suspension of all civil air services. Once the military priorities had been sorted out some of the aircraft used by the airlines were put back in service with civil markings to run priority routes under the control of the Associated Airways Joint Committee (AAJC). Typical of the Rapides so employed were G-ACPP and G-ACPR of Great Western and Southern Air Lines, which were put to work flying three return flights each day between Land's End (St Just) and the Scilly Isles. Most of the Dragons and Rapides on the civil register, however, were impressed into military service with standard service markings and serials. Many of them suffered accidents during their war service with the result that few were still airworthy when peace came in 1945.

The overall total of Dragon Rapides built by de Havilland was 728 and the production line was closed in 1945 to make way for new types. The last 346 aircraft were built by the Brush Coachworks at Loughborough and, in common with many other aircraft, the D.H.89 was subject to some cancellation of Air Ministry contracts when peace arrived. In fact, the last batch of approximately 100 Rapides was built for post-war civil sale. These were known as the Rapide Mk 2, which was fitted with six passenger seats, and the Rapide Mk 3 which had eight passenger seats in addition to the pilot. The Rapide Mk 4 was a conversion of the standard Dominie with the Gipsy Queen 3 engines replaced by Gipsy Queen 2s with constant-speed propellers, and the single example of the Rapide Mk 5 had manually-operated variable-pitch propellers and a special version of the Gipsy Queen 3 engines. The final post-war variant was the Rapide Mk 6 which, again, was a modification of earlier aircraft with fixed-pitch Fairey X5 propellers which provided performance equivalent to that of the Rapide Mk 4 but with less mechanical sophistication.

The majority of post-war Rapides were Dominies, which had survived to be declared surplus and sold at bargain prices to various overhaul companies such as W.A. Rollason, Field Aircraft Services and Lancashire Aircraft Corporation. These Dominies initially supplemented the fleets of the AAJC operators to Shetland, Guernsey and Scilly Isles.

The Rapides found their way to small air taxi companies like Air Kruise. They were used by Skegness Air Taxi and Airwork Services, both of which did circular trips for only £1 a person.

Boeing P-26

One of the first successful breaks with the established biplane tradition, Boeing's classic little P-26 was America's first all-metal fighter to achieve production status, and the last to feature open cockpit and fixed landing gear.

The Boeing Airplane Company in Seattle, Washington, became a leading manufacturer of fighters for the US Army Air Corps between 1921 and 1935. This was after it had built the Thomas-Morse MB-3 followed in the mid-1920s by the Boeing PW-9. The classic P-12, the parallel to the US Navy's F4B, was still being built by the company well into the 1930s. but in 1931 Boeing proposed a small monoplane to the US Army, the Boeing Model 248. This fighter would use the successful air-cooled Pratt & Whitney R-1340 nine-cylinder radial engine.

While the US Army showed enthusiasm for these proposals, evidence of caution was provided by the stipulation in the Bailment Contract of 5 December 1931 that while the US Army would supply engines and instruments, Boeing would bear the cost of building three prototypes (XP-936) and their initial testing. The airframes remained with the company.

Construction of the first prototype started in January 1932, and in no more than nine weeks the aircraft was complete, its first flight being made on 20 March before being delivered for service trials at Wright Field; the second aircraft underwent static tests at Wright and the third went to Selfridge Field, Michigan, prior to evaluation by active USAAC squadrons. All three prototypes were successful in their various trials and were then purchased outright by the USAAC and accorded the successive designations XP-26, Y1P-26 and finally P-26.

Despite Boeing's experience in cantilever wing design and previous work on retractable landing gear, the P-26 embodied an externally-braced monoplane wing and fixed, spatted landing gear. Despite use of an engine of only 525 hp (392 kW), the prototype XP-936 returned a maximum speed of 227 mph (365 km/h) at 10,000 ft (3050 m) compared, for example, with the biplane P-12E's 189 mph (304 km/h) with

a 500-hp (373-kW) engine. All-metal semi-monocoque construction was employed, comprising aluminium bulkheads, top-hat section longerons, stiffeners and skins. The thin-section, low aspect ratio, low-set wing was supported by landing wires attached to the fuselage and by flying wires attached to the landing gear, and the pilot's cockpit was located above the wing's mid-chord. An armament of twin 0.3-in (7.62-mm) forward firing machine-guns was provided, as well as provision to carry up to 112 lb (51 kg) of bombs externally. Compared with the P-12's wing span of 30 ft 0 in (9.14 m), the XP-936 spanned only 27 ft 5 in (8.36 m).

Signed up for the Army

Trials with the XP-936 at Wright Field occupied most of 1932, and on 7 November a new specification was drawn up incorporating the experience of these trials. Thus on 11 January 1933 the US Army Air Corps and Boeing signed a contract for 111 examples of this improved design (the Model 266) to be designated the P-26A. In due course this order was increased to 136 in the largest single production order for a US military aeroplane since that for the 200 MB-3As in 1921.

Production versions of the P-26A differed externally from the prototypes only in that the streamlined wheel spats did not extend aft of the landing gear strut fairings, and span was increased. However, another alteration was included after an early aircraft overturned during landing on soft ground; the pilot was killed although the aircraft itself was scarcely damaged. Accordingly the streamlined headrest fairing was strengthened and deepened to provide better protection, and production was delayed while this modification was incorporated.

The third prototype Boeing XP-936. Trials with the Pratt & Whitney R-1340-21 engined prototypes occupied many months before a production standard was agreed, the principal differences lying in the increased depth of the pilot's headrest and the shortening of the streamlined mainwheel fairings.

Resplendent in olive drab fuselage and orange-yellow wings, wheel spats, engine cowling, tail surfaces and fuselage bands, this Boeing P-26C belonged to the 19th Pursuit Squadron, 18th Pursuit Group, based at Wheeler Field, Hawaii, in 1939. Not many were built, some ending their days in Guatemala.

Looking more like a 1930s sport roadster than a fighting machine, this P-26A is resplendent in the blue-and-yellow standard paint scheme of the mid-1930s US Army Air Corps, modified suitably by the addition of a fuselage flash and leading edge decor on the tail surfaces. The kicking mule insignia identifies the 95th Pursuit Squadron, 17th Pursuit Group, based at March Field, California. That unit operated its 'Peashooters' during 1934 and 1935. The plane was truly a design in transition, mixing features of earlier aircraft with pioneering trends that would characterize the next fighter generation. First of the Air Corps' monoplane fighters, its landing speed was deemed fast enough to warrant reduction to a less-dangerous level by the use of wing flaps.

Boeing P-26

Specification

Boeing P-26A
Type: single-seat fighter
Powerplant: one 500-hp (373-kW) Pratt & Whitney R-1340-27 nine-cylinder air-cooled radial piston engine
Performance: maximum speed 234 mph (377 km/h) at 6,000 ft (1830 m); initial climb rate 2,360 ft (719 m) per minute; service ceiling 27,400 ft (8350 m); normal range 360 miles (579 km)
Weights: empty 2,271 lb (1031 kg); maximum take-off 3,012 lb (1366 kg)
Dimensions: span 27 ft 11½ in (8.52 m); length 23 ft 10 in (7.26 m); height 10 ft 5 in (3.17 m); wing area 149.5 sq ft (13.89 m²)
Armament: two synchronized forward-firing 0.3-in (7.62-mm) machine guns on sides of nose, plus provision to carry up to two 100-lb (45-kg) or five 30-lb (13.6-kg) bombs under fuselage and wings

The P-26s had a short service life; by the time World War 2 broke out they had been relegated to second-line duties. But daring Chinese and Filipino pilots actually flew them into combat against the best that Japanese invaders could put into the air and, in some rare cases scored victories.

142

Partially concealed behind the wing is the Snowy Owl insignia on this P-26A belonging to the 17th Pursuit Squadron, 1st Pursuit Group; colour scheme was olive drab fuselage and orange-yellow wings and tail, and white diagonal fuselage band outlined in black.

Boeing P-26A of the 95th Pursuit ('Kicking Mule') Squadron, 17th Pursuit Group; the olive drab finish preceded the adoption of an all-over blue scheme, and for a short time the aircraft carried the squadron number in large characters under the fuselage. The kicking mule emblem originated during World War 1 when the unit was the 95th Aero Squadron.

Boeing P-26 variants

Model 248: three prototypes (XP-936, subsequently XP-26, Y1P-26 and P-26), with Pratt & Whitney R-1340-21 engines; serial nos 32-412, -413 and -414
Model 266 (P-26A): 111 aircraft built, with R-1340-27 engines; 33-028 to -138; some subsequently to Guatemala
Model 266A (P-26B): two aircraft built, with R-1340-33 engines with fuel injection; 33-179 and 33-185
Model 266 (P-26C): 23 aircraft built, initially with R-1340-33 engines without fuel injection, but later modified to P-26B standard; 33-186 to -203; some subsequently to Guatemala
Model 281: 12 aircraft built, with R-1340-33 engines; one to Spain and 11 to China

Internally, however, the P-26A had undergone much improvement with the inclusion of US Army radio and the addition of flotation gear in the wing roots. Tare weight remained much the same although the 525-hp (392-kW) Pratt & Whitney R-1340-21 engine was replaced by a 500-hp (373-kW) R-1340-27 engine, though top speed was increased to 234 mph (377 km/h). The armament installation was altered to allow one of the 0.3-in (7.62-mm) guns to be replaced by a 0.5-in (12.7-mm) weapon, and the bomb rack attachment points changed to permit carriage of either two 100-lb (45-kg) or five 30-lb (13.6-kg) bombs under the wings and fuselage.

Deliveries of the first production P-26As started on 16 December 1933 and the last of the original order for 111 aircraft was completed on 30 June 1934. Unit cost per aircraft, less government-furnished equipment (GFE), came out at $9,999.00 (marginally less than the cost of a Boeing P-12E biplane).

When the P-26A entered service early in 1934 it gained the nick-name 'Peashooter' and quickly became a firm favourite among US Army pursuit pilots, being light and sensitive on the controls, and remaining the fastest US Army Air Corps fighter until joined four years later by the Seversky P-35 and Curtiss P-36A in 1938. Many of the pilots who were to achieve fame in World War 2 served their flying apprenticeships on the aircraft, and a remarkable proportion of the pre-war P-26 group and squadron commanders rose to high rank in the USAAF and USAF in later years.

Squadron service

First deliveries were made to the 1st Pursuit Group, commanded by Lieutenant Colonel Ralph Royce (who later, as a major general, commanded the III Fighter Command in 1942 and the US 1st Air Force in 1943), based at Selfridge Field, Michigan. The group included the 17th, 27th and 94th Pursuit Squadrons – the last famous as the 'Hat in the Ring' squadron. The 27th and 94th gave up their Peashooters in 1938, but the 17th continued flying them until 1941 when they were finally replaced by Curtiss P-40s.

Also equipped with P-26As in 1934 was the 17th Pursuit Group (commanded by Major Frank O'D. Hunter, who succeeded Major General Royce at the head of the 1st Air Force from 1943 until 1945). Based at March Field, California, the 34th and 95th Squadrons retained their P-26As for only one year before the group was assigned to the attack role.

Third and last of the initial P-26A pursuit groups in 1934 was the 20th at Barksdale, Louisiana, commanded by Lieutenant Colonel Armin F. Herold: the group's 55th and 77th Squadrons took delivery in 1934 and the 79th Squadron

Boeing P-26A cutaway drawing key

1 Starter dog
2 Propeller hub sleeve
3 Sleeve attachment
4 Two-blade propeller
5 Engine face plate
6 Cooling inlets
7 Engine cowling ring
8 Pratt & Whitney R-1340-27 Wasp engine
9 Cylinder heads
10 Gun barrel blast tube
11 Exhaust pipes
12 Engine bearer ring
13 Louvred exhaust stacks
14 Carburettor cold air intake
15 Engine bearer upper support struts
16 Starter primer access
17 Cowling panel fasteners
18 Hot air intake
19 Cockpit heater
20 Exhaust stub
21 Gun blast tube
22 Oil cooler
23 Lower panel access
24 Wingroot stub
25 Port gun barrel
26 Bulk head/lower longeron attachment
27 Fuselage forward frame
28 Air intake/starter controls
29 Support strut attachment
30 Cooling louvres
31 Oil tank, capacity 8 US gal (30 litres)
32 Upper louvres
33 Oil filter access
34 Gunsight tube supports
35 Tubular gunsight
36 Starboard wing fuel tank
37 Starboard landing wires support strut and brace
38 Fuel filter cap
39 Landing wires outboard attachment
40 Front spar
41 Pitot tube
42 Wing panelling
43 Aerial spring brace attachment
44 Starboard navigation lights (upper and lower surfaces)
45 Aerial lead-in
46 Electrical leads
47 Wing main rib stations

Displaying an experimental camouflage scheme evaluated in 1935, this P-26A served with the 34th Pursuit Squadron, 17th Pursuit Group, based at March Field, California. Basic finish was 'desert sand' with olive drab and neutral grey superimposed. This squadron was unusual in retaining its P-12 biplanes longer (until 1936) than its P-26s, which were relinquished in 1935.

48 Starboard aileron
49 Aileron hinge points
50 Transmitter aerial mast
51 Aerials
52 Aileron tab
53 Aileron control linkage
54 Control rods
55 Rear landing wire
56 Windscreen panel
57 Main instrument panel
58 Landing wires/fuselage attachment points

59 Fuselage upper longeron
60 Lower instrument panel (fuel cocks and light switches)
61 Rudder pedal assembly
62 Ammunition loading access (magazines in cockpit floor)
63 Transmitter
64 Landing wires spacer
65 Ammunition feed
66 Port 0.30-in (7.62-mm) machine-gun
67 Underseat control linkage
68 Seat support frame

80 Bulkhead hatch (rear fuselage access)
81 Fuselage main frame
82 Access panel
83 Liquid oxygen vapouriser
84 Holding tray
85 Tail surface control cables
86 Receiver lead-in insulator
87 Abbreviated upper longeron
88 Fuselage frames
89 Rudder control cables
90 Elevator control cables
91 Elevator tab controls

97 Elevator control runners
98 Fuselage aft main frame/ tailplane support
99 Fin root fillet
100 Starboard elevator linkage
101 Starboard tailplane
102 Tailplane spar
103 Elevator outer hinge

104 Starboard elevator
105 Fin front spar
106 Tail identification light
107 Fin structure
108 Rudder upper hinge
109 Receiver aerial mast
110 Rudder inner frame
111 Rudder hinge
112 Elevator torque tube
113 Rudder post
114 Rudder control horns
115 Elevator tab
116 Port elevator

117 Elevator hinge
118 Tailplane structure
119 Elevator tab control linkage
120 Tailplane front spar/ fuselage attachment

121 Tailwheel leg fairing
122 Tailwheel
123 Tailwheel leg
124 Tailwheel control runs
125 Fuselage skinning
126 Wingroot fillet
127 Aileron control rod assembly
128 Rear spar/stub wing attachment
129 Fuselage angled main frame attachment
130 Fuselage main fuel tank
131 Fuel filler access
132 Front spar/stub wing attachment
133 Mainwheel leg attachment
134 Front spar
135 Landing wires support strut and brace
136 Undercarriage 'V'-strut rear member
137 Stub wing structure
138 'V'-strut/rear spar attachment
139 Fuel filler cap
140 Port wing fuel tank
141 Rear spar
142 Transmitter aerial
143 Trailing edge ribs
144 Port aileron
145 Aileron tab
146 Aileron hinges
147 Aileron control linkages
148 Rear landing wire anchor point
149 Aileron control rods
150 Wing main rib stations
151 Outboard rib stations
152 Transmitter aerial lead-in
153 Port wingtip
154 Port navigation lights (upper and lower surfaces)
155 Wing structure
156 Front spar section
157 Landing wires anchor points
158 Flying wires brace

159 Outboard flying wires
160 Undercarriage trouser fairing
161 Brake cable assembly
162 Cross-brace member
163 'V'-strut front member
164 Flying wires attachment fairing
165 Wheel spat
166 Treadle
167 Brake arm
168 Port mainwheel
169 Axle
170 Spat inner frame
171 Spat/leg join
172 Mainwheel oleo leg
173 Inboard flying wires
174 Centre-line spacer
175 Starboard wheel fairing attachment
176 Spat panel
177 Starboard mainwheel
178 Under-fuselage bomb-rack installation (inc items 179– 183)
179 Arming handle
180 Bomb release wire (to cockpit)
181 Bomb-rack main member
182 Support frame
183 Forward sway braces
184 Possible loads inc (items 184–186)
185 30-lb (13.6 kg) practice bombs (five) or
186 100-lb (45-kg) bombs (two)

69 Pilot's seat
70 Throttle quadrant
71 Maps and document holder
72 Hinged entry flap
73 Equipment pouch
74 Cockpit coaming
75 Pilot's headrest
76 Headrest fairing
77 Receiver aerial brace
78 Turnover structure
79 Wireless receiver

92 Abbreviated lower longeron
93 Tailwheel control cables
94 Turnbuckles
95 Rear fuselage structure
96 Tailwheel control linkage

Representative of the colourful schemes carried by the P-26A in service with the US Army Air Corps was this example of an aircraft of the 94th Pursuit Squadron, 1st Pursuit Group, based at Selfridge Field, Michigan. Aircraft of this group carried the squadron colour in a diagonal band around the fuselage.

One of the ex-USAAC Boeing P-26As that served with the Guatemalan Cuerpo de Aeronautica Militar in the immediate post-war era. This aircraft (FAG 0816, previously 33-135) flew with the Escuadron de Caza at Campo de la Aurora, Guatemala City, in 1947.

in 1935. All were re-equipped with P-36s in 1938.

As the P-35s and P-36s entered service with home-based front-line squadrons in 1938 the P-26 was moved farther afield, initially to the Panama Canal Zone, and soon after to Wheeler Field. The 16th Pursuit Group, commanded by Lieutenant Colonel Willis H. Hale (later commander of the 6th Air Force in 1947–9, and of the 1st Air Force, 1950–1), included the 24th and the 29th Squadrons based at Albrook Field, Canal Zone, in 1938–9, and the 78th Squadron at Wheeler Field, Territory of Hawaii, in 1940. The 37th Pursuit Group received P-26s in 1940, its 28th and 30th Squadrons retaining them for only one year, but the 31st Squadron was still flying them in 1942 (after the US entered World War 2) and was the last first-line squadron to fly the Peashooter. This group and the 32nd Group were both based at Albrook Field: the latter, commanded by Captain Roger J. Browne (yet another commander of the 1st Air Force, in 1954–5) was equipped with P-26s for one year in 1941.

One other group, the 18th (with the 6th and 19th Pursuit Squadrons) flew P-26s from Wheeler Field between 1938 and 1941, but they had been discarded in favour of P-40s by the time of the Japanese attack on Pearl Harbor.

Returning to the development of the P-26 itself, the addition of 25 aircraft to the original order brought changes to the powerplant; the first two aircraft, designated P-26Bs and first flown on 10 January 1935, were powered by R-1340-33 engines with fuel injection, and were followed by 23 P-26Cs, also with R-1340-33 engines but initially without fuel injection. Delivery of the P-26C started in February 1936, and all were eventually modified to the P-26B standard. Both versions had a top speed of 235 mph (378 km/h) at 6,000 ft (1830 m).

Perhaps somewhat surprisingly, the P-26 was not widely exported in the late 1930s to the world's smaller air forces, for its cost and performance compared favourably with many other aircraft being offered on the international market.

Nevertheless Boeing underwrote the development of an export version, the Model 281, subsequently producing a total of 12 examples. Originally these were little different from the standard USAAC P-26A, but it soon became clear that the Peashooter's lively landing performance was not suited to the rough field surfaces of foreign air force bases, and split landing flaps were introduced to reduce approach speeds. Such flaps were also fitted to all Peashooters of the USAAC, either on the production line or as a retrofit.

One of the Boeing 281s was sold to Spain and the remainder were purchased by the Chinese for operation against the Japanese. The first arrived in China on 15 September 1934 but was destroyed in a crash during a demonstration by an American pilot; the other 10 reached Canton during the next 15 months, equipping one fighter squadron and being flown in constant action against the vastly superior numbers of Japanese aircraft. They succeeded in gaining occasional air victories, however, before the survivors were eventually forced out of service by lack of spares.

After the P-26 was declared obsolete in 1941 and given up by the USAAC, a few of the remaining machines which had been used in the Panama Canal Zone were transferred to the Cuerpo de Aeronautica Militar in Guatemala, to form that country's first fighter unit stationed in La Aurora near Guatemala City. Six of these aircraft were still in use immediately after the end of World War 2.

Led by Major (later Lieutenant Colonel) Armin F. Herold (whose aircraft featured blue, yellow and red bands round the engine cowling), this formation of 20th Pursuit Group Boeing P-26As included aircraft of the 55th, 77th and 79th Pursuit Squadrons flying from Barksdale Field, Louisiana just after 1934.

Junkers Ju 52

For all its seemingly archaic appearance, with fixed landing gear, angular lines and corrugated skin, the classic Junkers Ju 52/3m represented the common denominator of every land operation by Germany's Wehrmacht, whether in advance or retreat. 'Tante Ju' was indeed the German counterpart of America's Douglas C-46 Skytrain.

Towards the end of the 1920s, the German Lufthansa was widely regarded as the most efficient airline in the world, while other aviation companies were having problems keeping their heads above water in the major economic crisis that was occurring at the time. The company offered convenient flights throughout Europe with its large fleet of aircraft, mostly consisting of developments of the all-metal monoplane built by Professor Hugo Junkers in 1915, the J 1.

The great majority of these early aircraft (the J 10, F 13, A 20, F 24, W 33, W 34, Ju 46 and Ju 52) were single-engined low-wing monoplanes, but in 1924 there appeared a three-engine airliner, the G 23, powered by a 195-hp (145-kW) Junkers L 2 and two 100-hp (75-kW) Mercedes engines. It is thought that, as a result of Versailles Treaty restrictions imposed on German aircraft manufacture, this prototype was produced at Junkers' Fili factory near Moscow; production of about nine aircraft (as well as that of the much more numerous G 24) was subsequently undertaken in Sweden. The G 24, usually powered by three 280/310-hp (209/231-kW) Junkers L 5 inline engines, served in numerous con-

This Ju52, designated C-352-L, was built by CASA in Spain with BMW 132 radial engines produced under licence.

figurations and with a number of airlines, including Lufthansa which retained them in service until 1933–4.

The year 1926 was busy for the Junkers concern, two new designs (the G 31 tri-motor transport and the W 33/34) being the most important to fly. The former was a beefier version of the successful G 24, and the latter an excellent single-engine transport which was built in large numbers. Almost at once the Junkers designers embarked on a new, but considerably enlarged single-engine transport, the Ju 52, which embodied the cumulative experience of earlier designs and was primarily intended for freight carrying. Like its predecessors it was of standard Junkers all-metal construction with corrugated, load-sustaining duralumin skinning, and featured the patented Junkers full-span double wing. Five aircraft were built, of which four underwent development with various powerplants in Germany and one (CF-ARM) went to Canada. The first aircraft flew on 13 October 1930.

Despite its single engine (usually of around 780-825 hp/582–615 kW) the Ju 52 was able to carry 15–17 passengers when required. However the following year the Junkers design team, under Dipl. Ing. Ernst Zindel, undertook work to adapt the Ju 52 to feature three 525-hp (392-kW) Pratt & Whitney Hornet nine-cylinder radials, and the prototype of

The 18-seat Ju 52/3mg7e, shown here, was a major production variant and featured automatic pilot and wide cabin doors. Subsequent versions had the wheel fairings removed, as sand and mud tended to clog the wheels.

Three Junkers Ju 52/3mg6e mine clearance aircraft of the Minensuchgruppe, probably over the Mediterranean; the rudder markings are said to have denoted the number of minesweeping sorties flown – a somewhat hazardous task.

this version, the Ju 52/3m (*Dreimotoren*, or three-motor), made its maiden flight in April 1932. Subsequent deliveries were made to Finland, Sweden and Brazil, as well as to Deutsche Lufthansa. Ultimately Ju 52/3ms flew with airlines in Argentina, Austria, Australia, Belgium, Bolivia, China, Colombia, Czechoslovakia, Denmark, Ecuador, Estonia, France, Great Britain, Greece, Hungary, Italy, Lebanon, Mozambique, Norway, Peru, Poland, Portugal, Romania, South Africa, Spain, Switzerland, Turkey and Uruguay. Powerplants included Hispano-Suiza, BMW, Junkers Jumo, Bristol Pegasus, Pratt & Whitney Hornet and Wasp engines. Commercial Ju 52/3ms delivered to Bolivia were employed as military transports towards the end of the Gran Chaco war of 1932–5.

Starting late in 1932, Ju 52/3ms were delivered to Lufthansa, with D-2201 *Boelcke* and D-2202 *Richthofen* inaugurating the airline's Berlin–London and Berlin–Rome services before the end of that year. In due course no fewer than 230 Ju 52/3ms were registered with Deutsche Lufthansa, continuing to fly commercial services to Spain, Portugal, Sweden, Switzerland and Turkey almost to the end of World War 2.

Despite the stringencies of treaty restrictions imposed on Germany since 1919, clandestine adventures had continued by which potential military personnel had undergone training in foreign lands, particularly the USSR. Thus when, following her walk-out from the disarmament talks in 1932, Germany set about the covert establishment of a military air force, it fell to such aircraft as the Ju 52/3m to provide the basis of its flying equipment, and in 1934 the first military version, the Ju 52/3mg3e, appeared.

The Ju 52/3mg3e was an attempt to produce a bomber version quickly and without unduly interrupting the highly profitable commercial production line. Powered by three 525-hp (392-kW) BMW 132A-3 radials, this version normally carried a bomb load of 600 kg (1,321 lb), comprising six 100-kg (220-lb) bombs, and featured a dorsal gun position and a ventral 'dustbin', each mounting a single 7.92-mm (0.31-in) MG 15 machine-gun. Deliveries of the Ju 52/3mg3e to the new Luftwaffe totalled 450 in 1934–5, the first unit thus equipped being Kampfgeschwader 152 'Hindenburg'. In 1937 this Geschwader's IV Gruppe was re-designated KGrzbV1; this designation (*Kampfgruppe zur besonderen Verwendung*, or bomber group for special operations) was roughly comparable to the RAF's 'bomber transport' category, and was intended to reflect a dual role, bombing and military transport duties. It thereby perpetuated the originally intended function of the Ju 52/3m. In the event Ju 52/3m-equipped KGrzbV seldom if ever during World War 2 engaged in bombing operations.

When, on 18 July 1936, the Spanish Civil War broke out and Germany quickly aligned herself with the right-wing Nationalists, 20 Ju 52/3ms and six Heinkel He 51s were sent

to Spain, being assembled into the Legion Cóndor under General Hugo Sperrle during the following November. And it was as transports that the Junkers were initially employed, bringing 10,000 Moorish troops to Spain from Morocco. Thereafter they were developed in three bomber *Staffeln* of Kampfgruppe 88, and were flown in raids on the Republican-held Mediterranean ports and in support of the land battle for Madrid. By mid-1937 they were deemed to be poor bombers and were largely replaced by such aircraft as the Dornier Do 17 and Heinkel He 111. Nevertheless the Ju 52/3m3ge continued to serve both as a bomber and a tran-

Junkers Ju 52/3mge cutaway drawing key

1 Starboard navigation light
2 Drooping aileron section of Junkers 'double wing'
3 Aileron hinge fairings
4 Control linkage
5 Underwing inspection panels
6 Corrugated wing skin
7 Aerial mast
8 Wing strut diagonal bracing
9 Starboard oil filler cap
10 House-flag mast
11 Starboard engine cowling (NACA cowling)
12 Junkers metal two-blade propeller
13 Centre BMW 132A radial engine (in Townend ring)
14 Exhaust
15 Filter intakes
16 Engine bearers
17 Bulkhead
18 Centre oil tank
19 Oil filler cap
20 Flat windscreen panels
21 Co-pilot's seat
22 Radio-operator's jump-seat
23 Pilot's seat
24 Control column
25 Rudder pedals
26 Raised cockpit floor level

Equipped with large dural hoops below the fuselage, Ju 52/3mg6e aircraft of the Minensuchgruppe were flown over coastal waters round Europe in attempts to render Allied minelaying harmless. The aircraft shown, 3K+IB, belonged to the Gruppenstab and operated from Malmi over the Gulf of Finland during the winter of 1943–4.

A Ju 52/3mg7e (1Z+NA) of Stab IV/TG 1 (previously KGzbV 1) on the Courland Front during the last winter of the war; by then the Luftwaffe's transports were mainly engaged in parachuting supplies to beleaguered Wehrmacht units.

27 Control linkage
28 Control lines
29 Port BMW 132A radial engine (in NACA cowling)
30 Bulkhead
31 Engine bearers
32 Engine oil tank
33 Oil filler cap
34 Fuel filler cap
35 Mainwheel support strut
36 Mainwheel spat
37 Exhaust
38 Port mainwheel
39 Corrugated wing skin
40 Multi-spar wing structure
41 Diagonal cross-brace members
42 Pitot head

43 Port navigation light
44 Drooping aileron section of Junkers 'double wing'
45 Aileron hinge fairings
46 Trim tab
47 Tab control
48 Control runs
49 Inner section trailing-edge flap
50 Control linkage
51 Port wing fuel tanks
52 Fuselage/wing ball-and-socket attachment points
53 Centre aisle
54 Single-seat cabin arrangement (17 maximum)
55 Upper fuselage longeron
56 Luggage rack
57 Ceiling lights
58 Aerial
59 Two-seat rear bench
60 Passenger entry door
61 Underfloor control lines
62 Entry vestibule
63 Entry steps attachment
64 Toilet compartment

65 Rear cabin bulkhead
66 Cabin ventilation
67 Cargo compartment
68 Luggage loading hatch
69 Baggage shelves
70 Aft fuselage frames
71 Inspection walkway
72 Lower fuselage longeron
73 Fuselage construction
74 Control lines
75 Rear fuselage frame
76 Fin/fuselage attachment
77 Tailskid spring
78 Tailskid
79 Port tailplane structure
80 Port elevator
81 Lower rudder hinge
82 Control linkage
83 Multi-spar tailplane construction
84 Elevator corrugated skin
85 Fin construction
86 Rudder control linkage
87 Rudder post
88 Rudder structure
89 Corrugated skin
90 Rear navigation light

Junkers Ju 52

Specification

Junkers Ju 52/3mg7e
Type: 18-seat military transport
Powerplant: three 830-hp (619-kW) BMW 132T-2 nine-cylinder air-cooled radial engines
Performance: 183 mph (295 km/h) at sea level; initial climb rate 680 ft (208 m) per minute; service ceiling 18,045 ft (5500 m); range 802 miles (1290 km)
Weights: empty 14,462 lb (6560 kg); maximum take-off 23,180 lb (10515 kg)
Dimensions: span 95 ft 11½ in (29.25 m); length 62 ft 0 in (18.90 m); height 14 ft 9 in (4.50 m); wing area 1,189.45 sq ft (110.50 m²)
Armament: (typical) one 7.92-mm (0.31-in) MG 15 machine-gun in dorsal position and two 7.92-mm (0.31-in) machine-guns mounted to fire abeam through side windows

A Junkers Ju 52/3mg7e of 2.Staffel, KGzbV 1, based at Milos, Greece, in May 1941 prior to the invasion of Crete. Under the command of Generalmajor Gerhard a fleet of 493 Ju 52/3ms was assembled for the landings, known as Operation 'Mercury', but owing to confusion over the island during the initial assault subsequent waves of transports were delayed and the element of concentration was lost; of every four paratroopers dropped, one was killed or wounded. By the end of the operation more than 170 Ju 52/3ms had been lost or seriously damaged.

One of the first tasks of the German air force contingent in Spain was to lift 10,000 Moroccan troops from North Africa to the war zone. The aircraft shown, a Ju 52/3mg3e, is depicted in the markings of the Legion Cóndor's Kampfgruppe 88 late in 1936.

sport with German and Spanish Nationalist forces until the end of the Civil War.

To war in earnest

Operations from Germany's poorly surfaced military airfields had resulted in 1935 in the introduction of the Ju 52/3mg4e with tailwheel in place of tailskid, and by 1938 this version was being standardized among the KGrzbV. In March that year, at the time of the Austrian *Anschluss*, German troops were carried forward by KGrzbV 1 and 2 in a massive show of strength, the former based at Fürstenwalde with 54 aircraft, and the latter at Brandenburg-Briest.

By the time Germany was ready to crush Poland the Luftwaffe's *Transportverband* possessed an inventory of 552 aircraft, of which 547 were Ju 52/3mg3e and Ju 52/3mg4e aircraft (the balance being two obsolete He 111 transports, a Junkers G 38, a Ju 90 and a Focke-Wolf Fw 200). Losses in the month-long campaign of September amounted to 59 Junkers Ju 52/3ms, all but two to ground fire or flying accidents. In the course of 2,460 flights the aircraft carried 19,700 troops and 1,600 tons of supplies.

In the relatively swift and clinically organized invasion of Norway in the following year, the number of Ju 52/3ms available had risen to 573, equipping all four *Gruppen* of KGzbV 1, and KGrzbV 101, 102, 103, 104, 105, 106 and 107, an average of 52 aircraft in each *Gruppe*. A small number of twin float-equipped Ju 52/3m Wasser aircraft was also employed in the Norwegian campaign, alighting in the fjords to disembark troops, engineers and supplies. A new version, the Ju 52mg5e, with provision for alternative wheel, float or ski landing gear had been introduced, powered by three 830-hp (619-kW) BMW 132T-2 engines.

Among the important operations undertaken by the Junkers in Norway were the capture by airborne forces of Stavanger-Sola airport and of the Vordingborg bridge. A total of 29,000

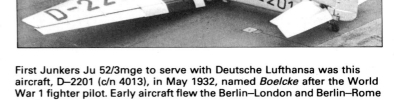

First Junkers Ju 52/3mge to serve with Deutsche Lufthansa was this aircraft, D–2201 (c/n 4013), in May 1932, named *Boelcke* after the World War 1 fighter pilot. Early aircraft flew the Berlin–London and Berlin–Rome services.

men, 259,300 Imp gal (1,180,000 litres) of aviation fuel and 2,376 tons of supplies were airlifted during the campaign, for the significant loss of 150 aircraft.

However, before the conclusion of the Norwegian campaign, the majority of Ju 52/3ms were being withdrawn back to Germany in preparation for Operation 'Yellow', the great assault in the West. As a result of losses in Norway the number of Junkers available was only 475, to which was now added 45 DFS 230 assault gliders, the whole transport force being commanded by General Putzier. Because of the need to conserve the Ju 52/3ms for a likely air assault on the UK, the Luftwaffe's transports were largely confined to airborne attacks in the initial stage, and it was against the Netherlands and Belgium that most of these were launched, in particular on the Moerdijk bridges and on Rotterdam's Waalhaven airport. Large numbers of Ju 52/3ms were employed in each attack and losses, mainly from anti-aircraft gunfire, were extremely heavy; in the five days that it took the Wehrmacht to crush the Netherlands, no fewer than 167 Junkers were totally destroyed, and a similar number badly damaged.

By the end of 1940 a total of 1,275 Ju 52/3ms had been delivered to the Luftwaffe, of which some 700 aircraft had already been struck off charge for one reason or another. After the collapse of France no further major operations involving the use of Ju 52/3ms were launched until the advance by German forces through the Balkans in April 1941. By then a number of new versions had appeared, namely the Ju 52/3mg6e, which was similar to the Ju 52/3mg5e but equipped with improved radio and the Ju 52/3mg7e with automatic pilot, accommodation for up to 18 troops and wider cabin doors; it also featured provision for two 7.92-mm (0.31-in) machine-guns to fire through the cabin windows. Operations in the Balkans and Aegean also saw the first operations by the *Minensuchgruppe* (minesweeping group), equipped with the Ju 52/3mg6e fitted with large dural hoops energized by an auxiliary motor to explode Allied mines sown in abandoned harbours.

Despite its ultimate capture, Crete proved a disaster for the *Transportverband*. Assigned to the task of an airborne invasion of the island, the 493 Ju 52/3ms and about 80 DFS 230 gliders were intended to attack in three waves. However, as a result of confusion on the ground caused by dense clouds of

South African Airways flew a total of 15 Ju 52/3ms, of which the first, ZS-AFA *Jan Van Riebeeck* is seen here. Nine aircraft were handed on to the South African Air Force, these being employed on a transport shuttle between South Africa, Egypt and Italy.

Since April 1986, this Junkers Ju-52 has been flying for Lufthansa again, exactly 50 years after it was first brought into service by the same airline with the registration D-AQUI. Later it was used in Norway and the USA before returning to Germany to be restored. (*Photo: Lufthansa, with the consent of Senat. Bremen, No. MBB 86-0402/32*)

Junkers Ju 52

As well as serving with the German Legion Cóndor, Ju 52/3ms were supplied to the Spanish Nationalist forces, this 3mg4e bearing the markings of the Grupo de Bombardeo Nocturno 1-G-22 early in 1938. In Spanish service the Ju 52/3m was nicknamed *Pava* (turkey), its last bombing sortie being against Belmez on 26 March 1939.

dust, there were numerous collisions and delays, so that what had been planned as an attack concentrated in time and area degenerated into widespread confusion and dissipated effort. German causualties were more than 7,000 men (of whom about 2,000 were paratroops) and 174 Ju 52/3ms, representing more than a third of the Luftwaffe's available transport force.

It has often been averred that the Balkan campaign was a lost cause for the Allies, yet the heavy losses inflicted on this vital enemy assault arm proved of immense importance when Germany launched Operation 'Barbarossa' less than two months later, and henceforth (apart from isolated instances of commando-type operations) the use of air transport was confined within the Luftwaffe to logistic supply and evacuation. Indeed, on the opening day of 'Barbarossa' the Luftwaffe could field no more than 238 serviceable Ju 52/3ms, a far cry from the numbers available in 1939 and 1940.

The nature of warfare on the Eastern Front quickly determined the role to be played by the Ju 52/3m, with scorched earth tactics employed by the retreating Russians demanding considerable dependence by the Wehrmacht on air supplies. Production of the Ju 52/3m increased to 502 in 1941, 503 in 1942 and 887 in 1943. New versions continued to appear; the Ju 52/3mg8e dispensed with the wheel spats (found to be a hindrance in the quagmire conditions on the Eastern Front), but included a 0.51-in (13-mm) MG 131 gun in the dorsal position, while some aircraft had 850-hp (634-kW) BMW 132Z engines; the Ju 52/3mg9e, which appeared in 1942, featured strengthened landing gear to permit a take-off weight of 25,353 lb (11500 kg) and was equipped to tow the Gotha Go 242 glider; the Ju 52/3mg10e was a naval version with provision for floats, and the Ju 52/3mg12e had 800-hp (597-kW) BMW 132L engines. Only one other version reached the Luftwaffe (late in 1943), namely the Ju 52/3mg14e with an MG 15 machine-gun mounted in a streamlined position over the pilot's cabin.

It may be said of the Ju 52/3m that its star shone brightest in adversity from 1942 onwards. When in February that year six German divisions were trapped at Demyansk, the Luftwaffe performed the prodigious task of sustaining 100,000 troops, and in three months delivered 24,300 tons of material, airlifted 15,446 men into the pocket and evacuated 20,093 casualties: the cost of this effort was a loss of 385 flying personnel (including Major Walter Hammer, commanding KGrzbV 172) and 262 aircraft. Far greater disasters befell the German armies at Stalingrad and in North Africa, and in a single raid on Sverevo in the dreadful winter of 1942–3 52 Junkers were destroyed by Russian bombers. In the final attempts to succour (and eventually to evacuate) the Axis armies in Tunisia in April 1943 the Luftwaffe lost 432 transport aircraft, almost all of them JU 52/3ms, in less than three weeks.

The story of 'Tante Ju' did not end on VE-Day, when fewer than 50 such aircraft remained airworthy of the 4,835 said to have been built in Germany. The principal post-war operator of the aircraft was France where Ateliers Aéronautiques de Colombes produced more than 400 examples of a version known as the AAC1 Toucan; apart from 85 which flew post-war services for Air France, others were operated by Aéro-

A ground view of a Ju 52/3mg4e showing the ventral gun position retracted; this version differed from the Ju 52/3mg3e in having a tailwheel in place of a skid. The photo emphasizes the characteristic corrugated skinning, a feature that, although ridiculed, bestowed considerable strength with lightness on the airframe.

Cargo, Air Atlas, Aigle Azur, Air Nolis, Air Ocean, TAI and many other airlines. The Toucan served with the Armée de l'Air and Aéronavale, and was used in fairly large numbers in the Algerian and Indo-China wars. In Spain CASA produced 170 aircraft, known as the C-352-L, with licence-built BMW 132 radials. Ten aircraft were reconditioned by Short Bros and Harland at Belfast, and entered service with British European Airways as G-AHOC to G-AHOL on 18 November 1946 on the Croydon–Liverpool–Belfast service. In Switzerland three Ju 52/3mg4e transports which were originally delivered to the Swiss Fliegertruppe on 4 October 1939 were still flying in the early 1980s.

In common with most of Germany's successful wartime aircraft, the Ju 52/3m underwent extensive development, resulting in the appearance of the Ju 252 and Ju 352. The former, whose prototype first flew in October 1941, was a larger aircraft than the Ju 52/3m, powered by three 1,340-hp (1000-kW) Junkers Jumo 211F liquid-cooled engines in annular cowlings, and had accommodation for 21 passengers in a pressurized cabin; the corrugated skinning was dispensed with. Originally it was intended to produce 25 aircraft for Lufthansa, but in view of the deteriorating war situation the order was reduced to 15, and all were delivered to the Luftwaffe. Some Ju 252As served with Lufttransportstaffel 290 (later redesignated Transportstaffel 5).

A quartet of early Ju 52/3mg3es bearing pre-war Luftwaffe markings; note the extended and awesomely situated ventral 'dustbin' gun positions and tailskids. The ventral gunner was protected from the slipstream by a fairing in which very exposed steps were incorporated to allow entry to the fuselage while the aircraft was airborne.

Grumman Single-seat Biplane Fighters

Grumman has been associated with US Navy fighters for so long that the names Tomcat, Cougar, Panther, Bearcat, Tigercat, Hellcat and Wildcat awake vivid memories of the last 45 years of carrier-based flying. To the older generation who remember the days before American naval aircraft had official names, the Grumman image evoked is that of the brightly coloured single-seaters with the F2F/F3F designations.

These sturdy-looking aircraft were almost the last biplanes when most other aircraft manufacturers had gone over to monoplanes. The Boeing P-12F acquired by the US Army in May 1932 was their last-ever single-seater biplane, more than a year before the first Grumman single-seater was produced for the Navy. Leroy Grumman's first aircraft was the two-seater FF-1, flown for the first time on 21st December 1931; this was also the first fighter in the US Navy to have a retractable undercarriage and closed cockpit. The plane was much faster than others of the same format, and this led to the conviction that a smaller, single-seat version would give much better performance than the Boeing F4B-4 and Curtiss F11C-2 fighters which the US Navy had ordered.

On 2 November 1932 the US Navy ordered an XF2F-1

The predecessor of the Grumman F2F and F3F fighters, the two-seater FF-1, was fitted with the 4½ ft (1.37 m) Wright R-1820 nine-cylinder radial engine.

155

Though the majority of the Grumman single-seat fighters were to serve with US Navy squadrons, the US Marine Corps did buy examples of the types. Their most significant acquisition was a fleet of F3F-2s ordered to equip VMF-1 at Quantico and VMF-2 at San Diego. An aircraft of the former squadron illustrates the typically colourful markings worn in the 1930s, and the 'M' prefix added to the squadron letter on the fuselage from July 1937 to identify Marine aircraft.

Grumman F3F

Specification

Grumman F3F-3
Type: single-seat shipboard fighter
Powerplant: one 950-hp (708-kW) Wright
R-1820-22 9-cylinder radial piston engine
Performance: maximum speed 264 mph
(425 km/h); cruising speed 150 mph (241
km/h); service ceiling 33,200 ft (10120 m);
range 980 miles (1577 km)
Weights: empty 3,285 lb (1490 kg);
maximum take-off 4,795 lb (2175 kg)
Dimensions: span 32 ft 0 in (9.75 m); length
23 ft 2 in (7.06 m); height 9 ft 4 in (2.84 m);
wing area 260.0 sq ft (24.15 m²)
Armament: two 0.3-in (7.62-mm) Browning
machine-guns

Grumman Biplanes

The first and last active US Navy squadron to operate the Grumman F2F-1 was VF-2B, operating from USS *Lexington*. 'Fighting Two' received its first aircraft in February 1935, and saw continuous service with the yellow-tailed fighters until September 1940. The aircraft were then passed to NAS Pensacola for training duties.

single-seat prototype, and on 19 December the small Grumman company also received its first production contract for 27 FF-1 two-seaters. A factory was rented in Farmingdale, Long Island, and construction began. The US Navy had decided on air-cooled radial engines for all of its fighters back in 1927. Instead of the 54 in (1.37 m) wide Wright R-1820 Cyclone of the FF-1, with its nine cylinders circled in a single row, a new 44 in (1.12 m) diameter twin-row 14-cylinder Pratt & Whitney XR-1535-44 Twin Wasp Junior was selected better to fit into the shape of the XF2F-1's short, deep all-metal fuselage.

The main wheels retracted into the fuselage behind the engine, wound up by about 32 turns of a hand crank, and the tail wheel also disappeared, along with the arresting hook in the tail. The small size (span of 28 ft 6 in/8.69 m and length of 23 ft 1 in/8.56 m) promised to occupy less space on aircraft-carrier decks. Another advantage was that the water-tight compartments in the fuselage below the cockpit floor provided flotation in an emergency water landing, eliminating the complicated rubber bags in the wings of older types. Like previous US Navy fighters, the XF2F-1 was armed with two synchronized 0.3-in (7.62-mm) machine-guns, under the cowl ahead of the enclosed cockpit.

On 18 October 1933 the XF2F-1 (serial number 9342) was first flown from Farmingdale and soon displayed its superior performance. With the XR-1534-44 giving 625 hp (466.1 kW) at 8,400 ft (2560 m), top speed was 229 mph (369 km/h) at that critical altitude compared with 207 mph (333 km/h) for

the production FF-1s delivered in the same year. Weighing only 3,536 lb (1604 kg) compared with 4,677 lb (2121 kg) for the two-seater, the XF2F-1 showed so much better manoeuvrability than its predecessor that the US Navy gave up the two-seat fighter configuration until after World War 2.

Grumman still faced competition from five other single-seat fighter designs built for the US Navy within a year of the XF2F-1's appearance. Curtiss was able to get its XF11C-3 into the air first, on 11 March 1933, because the airframe was essentially that of the 1925 Curtiss Hawk with fabric-covered fuselage and open cockpit. Like the Grumman aircraft, it had the wheels retracting into the fuselage, just behind a 700-hp (522.0-kW) R-1820 Cyclone.

Boeing offered the most modern-looking design, a low-wing monoplane flown on 14 September 1933 that made 239 mph (385 km/h) on only 550 hp (410.1 kW). Unfortunately it was judged unsuitable for carrier work because it required too long a take-off run and landed too fast. Northrop's low-wing XFT-1 and the high-wing Curtiss XF13C-1 monoplane appeared in January 1934 with most of the Boeing's speed and much of the same problems, while the Berliner-Joyce XF3J-1 biplane delivered in March 1934 had a conservative

Success with the two-seat Grumman FF-1 fighter provided the fledgling design team with a sound basis for a single-seat development with better performance. As the Grumman F2F-1, it began replacing the Boeing F4B-2s of VF-2B in 1935. This example carries the red tailplane and fuselage codes of VF-5B 'Red Rippers'.

Looking rather sombre in its black trim when compared with the bright colours of other US Navy squadrons, this F3F-1 served with VF-7 (later designated VF-72), the last squadron to operate the F3F-1, with final withdrawal taking place on 10 February 1941. This model continued to serve in the pilot training role at NAS Norfolk and Miami.

In this view of the Grumman XF2F-1 fighter prototype, the barrel-like lines of the fuselage are well illustrated. Various modifications were introduced, including a smaller-diameter engine cowl with rocker arm blisters, a Mk III Mod 2 telescopic gunsight, and various radio aerials.

design that was much too slow and too late to be competitive.

The US Navy ordered 27 Curtiss biplanes on 26 February 1934 and 54 Grumman F2F-1s on 17 May. When the first Curtiss was delivered on 8 October 1934, it carried a BF2C-1 (for Bomber Fighter) designation, as it could carry a 474-lb (215-kg) bomb or a drop tank; neither was provided on the Grummans. A severe vibration problem caused the retirement of the BF2C-1 by March 1936, and Curtiss won no more US Navy fighter production contracts.

Far more success was enjoyed by the F2F-1, first delivered on 19 January 1935, which remained in squadron service more than five years. Powered by a production Twin Wasp Jr, the R-1535-72 of 700 hp (522.0 kW) at take-off and 650 hp (484.7 kW) at 7,500 ft (2286 m), the F2F-1's top speed went from 203 mph (327 km/h) at sea level to 231 mph (372 km/h) at 7,500 ft (2286m). Landing at a reasonable 66 mph (106 km/ h), the fighter climbed to 5,000 ft (1524 m) in 2.1 minutes and reached a 27,100-ft (8260-m) service ceiling. The 110-US gal (416-litre) fuel capacity allowed an 985-mile (1585-km) maximum range. It might be mentioned that the Royal Navy's standard carrier fighter at that time, the Hawker Nimrod, had a maximum speed of 195 mph (314 km/h).

As was the custom of the time, the first production F2F-1 (9623) went to the US Navy's test station at Anacostia, in Washington DC, during January 1935. The next 22 were painted in the markings of VF-2B, the fighter squadron of the USS Lexington, and flown across the country from Farmingdale to San Diego, California, by US Navy pilots.

During this movement, the US Navy lost a Grumman when the aircraft painted 2-F-10 ran into a blinding dust storm over Mississippi on 16 March 1935. Lieutenant-Commander Arthur W. Radford bailed out at 3,000 ft (914 m), landed safely, and went on to become the top admiral in the US establishment in 1953, as the chairman of the Joint Chiefs of

Staff. A replacement aircraft (9997) was ordered on 29 June 1935, at a price of $12,000.

Twenty F2F-1s went to the USS Ranger for VF-3B from April to June 1935 while production continued until the last two of 55 aircraft were delivered on 2 August 1935, the last group going to the Battle Force Storage Pool in San Diego. Nine of these were issued to replace the FF-1s of VF-5B on the Ranger in October 1935.

Improved design

Even before F2F-1 deliveries began, Grumman prepared a new design intended to improve that design's directional stability and manoeuvrability, spin tendencies, and to add a bombing capability. On 15 October 1934 the US Navy ordered the design and construction of one XF3F-1 for $75,850, but Grumman would have to build three aircraft, all with the serial 9727, to complete the contract.

The XF3F-1 had the same R-1535-72 engine, but the fuselage was lengthened, and the wing area increased from 230 to 260.6 sq ft (21.37 to 24.21 m²). Reduction of the wheel diameter from 32 to 26 in (0.81 to 0.66 m) eliminated the bulge behind the engine and allowed a more streamlined fuselage. Jimmy Collins, company test pilot and a well-known aviation writer, made the first three XF3F-1 test flights on 20 March 1935.

Two days later tests resumed with two flights by US Navy pilots in the morning and then Collins began a series of six flights to demonstrate recovery from high-speed dives. The tenth dive was begun from 18,000 ft (5486 m) with a pull-out planned at 5,000 ft (1524 m) at 9g, nine times the stress of gravity on the airframe. But this time the biplane pulled out at 8,000 ft (2438 m) so sharply that the accelerometer

Despite the loss of the first and second prototypes (the first machine crashed during a test flight) the US Navy was convinced of the XF3F-1's performance improvements over the F2F-1. The second prototype was re-built and successfully completed the test phase. Operating squadrons included VF-6B, one of whose aircraft is shown here.

indicated some 14 g, the overstressed airframe broke up in mid-air and crashed in a cemetery, and Collins was killed.

A second strengthened prototype was quickly built and flown on 9 May at Farmingdale and delivered to the Anacostia test station. During a 10-turn spin demonstration, the XF3F-1 failed to recover, company pilot Lee Gehlbach bailed out, and the prototype struck the ground after 42 flat turns. The wreck was shipped back to Grumman and rebuilt in three weeks and redelivered to Anacostia on 20 June 1935 by William McAvoy.

On 24 August 1935 the US Navy ordered 54 F3F-1 fighters for $1,102,885; the batch was enough for two 18-plane squadrons with 50 per cent spares. The R-1535-84 engine had the same 650-hp (484.7-kW) rating as the R-1535-72, with the addition of a dynamic damper and fittings for the hydraulic pitch control of the Hamilton Standard 96-in (2.44-m) two-bladed propeller. While gross weight increased from 3,847 lb (1745 kg) on the F2F-1 to 4,170 lb (1892 kg) on the F3F-1, top speed remained 231 mph (372 km/h) at 7,500 ft (2286 m), and landing speed remained 66 mph (106 km/h), while range could be stretched to 998 miles (1606 km). Service ceiling was elevated to 28,500 ft (8687 m) by the slightly lower wing loading.

Armament included the usual 0.3-in (7.62-mm) M2 gun under the port side of the cowl with 500 rounds, but the starboard weapon was a 0.5-in (12.7-mm) M2 with 200 rounds. A 116-lb (52.6-kg) MkIV bomb could be attached below each wing and was aimed in a dive by the same three-power telescopic sight used for the guns. Other equipment included a radio, life raft, and oxygen, as on the F2F-1.

Wing span was now 32 ft (9.75 m) and length 23 ft 3 in (7.09 m). The typical Grumman biplane wing structure with metal ribs, twin spars, and leading edges, had fabric surfaces and was joined by metal N struts. Between the wings was a 5-ft (1.52-m) gap, and the lower wing had 2° dihedral.

The first F3F-1 (0211) was delivered 29 January 1936 and went to Anacostia as was usual. Squadrons VF-5B on the *Ranger* and VF-6B on the USS *Saratoga* got new F3F-1s between March and July, while the last delivery was made on 21 September 1936. A new US Marine squadron, then VF-4M at San Diego, got six in January 1937.

Grumman proposed a version to take advantage of the power offered by the new Wright Cyclone G series with a two-stage super-charger. Work on a prototype began before the contract, which was not approved until the aircraft was completed. On 27 July 1936 the XF3F-2 (0452) was flown to Anacostia by James Taylor. Powered by a single-row XR-1820-22 of 950 hp (708.4 kW) at take-off and driving a 9-ft (2.74-m) three-bladed propeller, the SF3F-2 achieved 255

mph (410 km/h) at 12,000 ft (3658 m) and could take off from a carrier in a 25-kt wind in only 131 ft (40 m). The increased engine diameter of 54 in (1.37 m) again altered the barrel-shaped appearance.

A civilian version, the G-22, was built for the Gulf Oil company's Major Alford Williams and delivered 6 December 1936 in bright orange paint and blue trim. Costing $12,225, the *Gulfhawk II* was flown on promotional tours. Powered by a 1,000-hp (745.7-kW) Wright R-1820-G1 and looking like an F3F-2, it actually had F2F wings of 28 ft 6 in (8.69 m) span

Sentiment for the biplane and a lack of belief in the attributes of monoplane fighters for the US Navy helped to buy time for the F3F. Fitted with a large-diameter Wright Cylcone powerplant, which necessitated a major revision of the nose contours, the F3F-1 became the F3F-2, and 81 were ordered for the US Navy, deliveries of which were all completed during 1936.

Grumman F3F-3 cutaway drawing key

1 Three-bladed constant-speed controllable-pitch 9-ft (2.74-m) diameter Hamilton Standard propeller
2 Propeller pitch change mechanism
3 Carburettor air intake
4 Supercharger air intake
5 NACA-type cowling
6 Wright R-1820-22 Cyclone nine-cylinder single-row radial air-cooled engine
7 Exhaust pipe
8 Oil cooler intake
9 Oil cooler (9 in/22.9 cm diameter)
10 Upper engine mounting struts
11 Lower engine mounting struts
12 Starboard gun blast tube
13 Port gun blast tube
14 Oil tank (9 US gal/34 litre capacity)
15 Oil filler cap
16 Engine bulkhead
17 Main fuel tank (83 US gal/314 litre capacity)
18 Fuel tank filler cap
19 Tank fixing
20 Fuselage main longeron
21 Centre section forward strut
22 Centre section aft strut
23 Strut attachment lug
24 Light alloy interplane N-struts
25 Flying wires
26 Upper wing centreline joint
27 Aircraft sling attachments
28 Mk VII gun camera
29 Front spar
30 Rear spar
31 Spar bracing rib
32 Diagonal wire bracing
33 Wing ribs (of truss construction)
34 Starboard aileron
35 Aileron actuating arm
36 Aileron control rod
37 Aerial cable
38 Starboard navigation light
39 Mk III Mod 4 telescope sight
40 Windscreen frame
41 Port 0.3-in (7.62-mm) Browning machine-gun
42 Starboard 0.5-in (12.7-mm) Browning machine-gun
43 Ammunition tanks (500 rounds 0.3-in/7.62-mm and 200 rounds 0.5-in/12.7-mm)
44 Ammunition feed chute
45 Cartridge case ejector chute
46 Pressure fire extinguisher
47 Auxiliary fuel tank (47 US gal/178 litre capacity)
48 Auxiliary tank filler
49 Very pistol cartridge holder
50 Rudder pedal
51 Instrument panel
53 Pilot's seat
54 Throttle and propeller controls
55 Bomb release levers
56 Tailplane trim control
57 Access step
58 Cockpit floor structure
59 Adjustable seat support structure
60 Headrest
61 Aft-sliding canopy
62 Life raft stowage
63 D/F loop
64 Junction box
65 Equipment bay access door
66 Dynamotor unit
67 Radio transmitter
68 Radio receiver
69 First aid kit
70 Emergency rations and water supply
71 Dorsal light
72 Fuselage frames (Z section)
73 Tailplane incidence control rod
74 Lift/hoist tube
75 Controls access cover
76 Rudder and elevator control cables
77 Fin structure (solid section ribs)
78 Fin/fuselage attachment
79 Rudder post
80 Rudder structure (fabric covered)
81 Rudder hinge
82 Trim tab
83 Trim actuator
84 Tailcone
85 Arrester hook fairing
86 Tail light
87 Variable-incidence tailplane
88 Tailplane structure
89 Elevator (fabric covered)
90 Arrester hook (extended)
91 Retractable tailwheel (solid rubber tyre)
92 Tailwheel shock absorber strut
93 Port upper wing structure
94 Port navigation light
95 Interplane 'N' struts
96 Lower wing front spar
97 Lower wing rear spar
98 Spar bracing rib
99 Wing ribs
100 Leading edge construction
101 Wire bracing
102 Retractable landing light
103 Mk XLI bomb rack
104 Mk IV 116-lb (52.6-kg) demolition bomb
105 Fuse unit
106 Wing spar root fitting
107 Flying wire attachment
108 Wing root fillet
109 Port mainwheel (26 in × 6 in/66 cm × 15 cm)
110 Oleo strut
111 Radius arms
112 Fairing door
113 Retraction strut
114 Lock actuator
115 Wheel well
116 Retraction strut axle mounting
117 Retraction chain drive
118 Starboard mainwheel

AVIAGRAPHICA

Grumman single-seat biplane fighter variants

XF2F-1: first prototype (BuNo. 9342) with metal semi-monocoque fuselage, fabric-covered metal wings and XR-1535-44 Twin Wasp Junior powerplant; minor changes introduced during test programme
F2F-1: production model; 54 ordered by US Navy (BuNo. 9623–9676 and 9997) and delivered during 1935; front-line service until September 1940; armament of two 0.3-in (7.62-mm) Browning machine-guns
XF3F-1: prototype development of F2F-1 offering improved handling and increased overall performance; extra fuselage length and wing span and minor aerodynamic improvements; first aircraft crashed during testing; second aircraft crashed but rebuilt to complete the test phase
F3F-1: production model built to a US Navy order for 54 aircraft (BuNo. 0211-0264); R-1535-84 Twin Wasp Junior powerplant; 0.3-in (7.62-mm) and 0.5-in (12.7-mm)

Browning machine-guns; all aircraft delivered 1936
XF3F-2: last production F3F-1 converted to XF3F-2 with 850-hp (634-kW) Wright XR-1820-22 Cyclone radial; increased fuel capacity
F3F-2: production model built to US Navy order for 81 aircraft (BuNo. 0967-1047) for Navy and Marine service; entered service in December 1937 with deliveries completed in May 1938; major revision to nose contours to accommodate new powerplant
XF3F-3: F3F-2 (BuNo. 1031) converted with minor drag-reducing modifications to airframe, revised cowling and forward fuselage decking
F3F-3: incorporating modifications of XF3F-3 and built to an order for 27 aircraft (BuNo. 1444-1470) which equipped VF-5, VMF-1 and VMF-2; relegated to second-line duties after little more than a year on carrierborne operations, mainly as advanced pilot trainers

The urgent need to replace the obsolescent F2F-1s in service with VF-2 and VF-5, while development of the first generation of monoplane fighters continued, led to a contract for 27 'improved' F3F-2s in 1938, which were designated F3F-3. Various modifications helped to reduce drag in addition to new features such as the curved Plexiglas windscreen and revision of the engine cowling.

and was credited with 290 mph (467 km/h). In October 1948 it was donated to the Smithsonian Institution (which now operates the National Air and Space Museum) and is the only Grumman single-seat biplane surviving today. Gulf also purchased a two-seat version, the G-32 delivered on 12 May 1938.

New Model welcomed

Eighty-one production F3F-2s, ordered on a contract approved on 23 March 1937, were built in the new Grumman factory at Bethpage, New York, except for the wings and tail, which were subcontracted to Brewster. The first F3F-2 (0967) was flown to Anacostia by Lee Gehlbach on 17 July 1937. Although not officially accepted until November the new model was hailed in the test report as 'the most satisfactory single-seat fighter developed for the Navy to date, taking into account all the factors . . .'.

Powered by a Wright R-1820-22 with 950 hp (708.4 kW) for take-off and 750 hp (559.3 kW) at 15,200 ft (4633 m), the F3F-2 had a wing span of 32 ft (9.75 m) and was 23 ft 2 in (7.06 m) long. According to US Navy characteristics charts it weighed 3,254 lb (1476 kg) empty and 4,498 lb (2040 kg) with normal load, the top speed went from 234 mph (377 km/h) at sea level to 260 mph (418 km/h) at 15,250 ft (4648 m). Landing speed was 69 mph (111 km/h). Rate of climb began at 2,800 ft (853 m) per minute and the service ceiling was 32,300 ft (9845 m), while 130 US gal (492 litres) of fuel allowed a range between 975 to 1,130 miles (1569 and 1819 km). Armament remained the same as on the F3F-1.

The second F3F-2 was delivered 1 December 1937 for VF-6 on the USS *Enterprise*, and by April 1938 26 had been allocated to replace that squadron's F2F-1s. US Marine Squadron VMF-1 at Quantico got some to replace, at long last, its 188-mph (303-km/h) Boeing F4B-4s in March

The Grumman J2F 'Duck' was a special version of the F2F with a large main float. A small rudder at the end of the float made manoeuvring on water easier.

1938, while VMF-2 (formerly VF-4M) at San Diego also re-equipped with the F3F-2.

When the last F3F-2 was accepted in May 1938, all seven US Navy and US Marine fighter squadrons had Grumman single-seaters. These units had been renumbered in 1937, the US Navy squadrons now corresponding to their carriers: VF-2 with CV-2, etc. All of their fighters were painted chrome yellow on the upper wing surface to facilitate their location in emergencies, and a tail colour went with each carrier. Thus the F2F-1s of VF-2 on the *Lexington* wore yellow tails, the F3F-1s of VF-3 the *Saratoga*'s white and the F3F-1s of VF-4 the *Ranger*'s green, the F2F-1s of VF-5 the *Yorktown*'s red, and the F3F-2s of VF-6 the *Enterprise*'s blue. Colourful stripes on the cowls and fuselages denoted each machine's place within the squadron, and US Marine F3F-2s had vertical red, white, and blue rudder stripes.

By this time the biplane fighter seemed ready for replacement, for the US Navy ordered 54 Brewster F2A-1 monoplanes in June 1938 and Grumman's own XF4F-2 monoplane was showing great promise. Nevertheless, the US Navy decided to order 27 F3F-3 fighters on 21 June 1938 as these could be delivered before the Brewsters. These aircraft incorporated drag-reducing refinements made to F3F-2 number 1031, which became the XF3F-3. That plane had been returned to Grumman for modification of the cowling and windshield, a new 105-in (2.67-m) Hamilton propeller, and other details. At one point, it also tried an upper wing with landing flaps that had been made for a company aircraft, the G-32A two-seater version of the F3F-2, but tests in August indicated this change was unnecessary, and the standard wing was restored.

The XF3F-3 arrived at Anacostia in October, and after successful tests some of its improvements were incorporated on the production F3F-3. On 16 December 1938 the first F3F-3 (1444) came to Anacostia for Production Acceptance Trials. The first 18 were painted with the red tails of VF-5 on the *Yorktown*, whose F2F-1s they were replacing, while the others remained ashore as spares.

Using the same engine and armament as its predecessor, the F3F-3 weighed 4,543 lb (2061 kg), had a top speed of 239 mph (385 km/h) at sea level and 264 mph (425 km/h) at 15,200 ft (4633 m), and landed at 68 mph (109 km/h). Service ceiling was 33,200 ft (10119 m), and range varied from 980 to 1,150 miles (1577 to 1851 km).

When the last F3F-3 was delivered on 10 May 1939, American production of biplane fighters ended, although abroad the Gloster Sea Gladiator, Polikarpov I-153, and Fiat CR.42 would continue into World War 2. Grumman's plump single-seaters would retire from US Navy service without firing a shot in combat.

In December 1939, VF-3 received ten Brewster F2A-1 monoplanes and was able to exchange half of its F3F-1s for VF-7s. This was the squadron with black tailplanes set up for the new USS *Wasp*. From September 1940 deliveries of F2A-2s replaced VF-2's F2F-1s and the remaining machines still in use by VF-3.

Dornier's Flying Pencils

From 1937 the Dornier 'Flying Pencil' was one of the most notorious and active fast bomber and reconnaissance aircraft in the world. Subsequently, it was tripled in weight and quadrupled in power, but without real success, and the overall production total of all models only just exceeded 3,000.

It is generally accepted that in the mid-1930s the Luftwaffe was clandestinely developing its new fast bombers in the guise of civil transport aircraft. Anyone looking closely at the Do 17 V1, the first prototype of a completely new high-speed land plane built in mid-1934 by Dornier's factory in Friedrichshafen, could be in no doubt about its purpose. This aircraft type, whose slim fuselage soon earned it the nickname of 'Flying Pencil', with its sleek lines, small, simple tail and undercarriage which retracted into the nacelles of the BMW engines, looked distinctly like a fast bomber. As a transport plane this aircraft, which squeezed two passenger seats in behind the cockpit, and a further four in a 'cabin'

Fitted with BMW-Bramo 323P Fafnir engines rated at 1,000 hp (745.7 kW) for take-off, the Dornier Do 17Z-2 appeared in 1939 capable of carrying a 2,205-lb (1000-kg) bombload. This example was one of the last in front-line service, fighting on the Eastern front in 1942 with 15.(Kroat)/KG 53.

behind the wings with a clear height of only 4 ft (1.22 m), would have been wholly unsuitable. It was obvious that the high-wing configuration allowed room for a large bomb compartment underneath the wing.

From first flight on 23 November 1934 the Do 17 handled well, but though two further prototypes were speedily completed and tested by the airline Deutsche Lufthansa, it was reluctantly agreed that the type was not suited to carrying passengers. For despite all appearances, the Do 17 really had been designed as a fast six-passenger mailplane! The prototypes languished in a hangar at the Löwenthal factory, where by chance they were spotted by Flugkapitän Robert Untucht, famed Lufthansa test pilot and RLM (air ministry) liaison officer. He instantly drew the obvious conclusion, which apparently had not occurred to anyone else, and tested one of the aircraft. His enthusiasm led to the Do 17 V4, a bomber prototype with twin fins. Further prototypes followed, the

Dornier Do 217

Specification

Dornier Do 217E-2
Type: four-seat bomber
Powerplant: two 1,580-hp (1178-kW) BMW 801ML 14-cylinder radial piston engines
Performance: maximum speed 320 mph (515 km/h) at 17,060 ft (5200 m); service ceiling (with bombload) 24,600 ft (7500 m); range with normal fuel 1,430 miles (2300 km)
Weights: empty 18,522 lb (8855 kg); maximum loaded 26,299 lb (16465 kg)
Dimensions: span 62 ft 4 in (19.0 m); length 59 ft 8.5 in (18.2 m); height 16 ft 6 in (5.03 m); wing area 613.5 sq ft (57.0 m²)
Armament: (as depicted) one fixed 20-mm MG 151/20 in nose fired by the pilot, one hand-aimed 20-mm MG FF, one 13-mm MG 131 in turret and one hand-aimed MG 131 to lower rear; two Hs 293A anti-ship missiles

One of the ultimate sub-types of the basic Do 217E-series was the E-5, built from the start with wing pylons for the Hs 293A stand-off radio-guided anti-ship missile, together with the associated Kehl/Strassburg guidance system. This model entered service with II/KG 100 in April 1943 and quickly made its mark against Allied ships in the Bay of Biscay and Atlantic, the first attack being against British destroyers on 25 August 1943. This Do 217E-5, from 6/KG 100, is very unusual in retaining its fixed MG 151 cannon under the nose; normally this was removed when the 20-mm MG FF hand-aimed cannon was added in the glazed part of the nose.

Dornier Do 17

Many of the Do-17s surviving into 1941 served with KG 2, and this Do 17Z-2 flew with that unit's I Gruppe based at Tatoi, Greece, in May 1941. Do 17Zs could undertake shallow diving attacks at speeds up to 370 mph (595 km/h) on account of their sturdy structure. KG 2 was soon to take its Do 17s to the USSR.

Early in 1942, Hermann Goering presented 15 ex-Luftwaffe Do 17Z-2s to the Finnish air force where they supplanted Bristol Blenheims with PLeLv 46 and enjoyed considerable success against the Russians. This example survived the war and was flown for several years after by PLeLv 43 on reconnaissance duties.

Hispano-engined Do 17 V5 reaching 243 mph (391 km/h). As this was well above the speed of any fighter in service it was hoped defensive guns would not be needed, but eventually the Do 17E-1 went into production at the company's new factories at Löwenthal, Manzell and Allmansweiler in 1936 with hand-aimed MG 15s firing above and below at the rear, and with a bomb load of up to 1,653 lb (750 kg). With a shortened, glazed nose the Do 17E-1 and corresponding Do 17F-1 reconnaissance aircraft were not quite so elongated, but when a *Staffel* of 15 F-1s went to Spain in spring 1937 its Do 17s easily outpaced Republican fighters, and aircraft of this type quickly replaced the Heinkel He 70 in reconnaissance wings. Do 17E-1s also served in Spain, with 1 and 2/K 88, along with a more powerful version, the Do 17P with 865-hp (645-kW) BMW 132N radials. Both remained standard types, serving with Grupo 27 of the Spanish EdA (air force) until 1949.

Foreign service and operations

In July 1937 the Do 17 V8 (also known as the Do 17M V1) appeared at the prestigious International Military Aircraft Competition at Zurich. It impressed everyone with its clean lines, and when it easily won the Circuit of the Alps, pulling far ahead of every fighter at the meeting, the media had a field-day. What was not reported was that its 1,000-hp (746-kW) DB 600A engines had been earmarked for fighters, so the production Do 17M bomber had Bramo 323A-1 Fafnir radial engines of the same power. They also had the short rounded nose of the Do 17E and Do 17F, but Yugoslavia was so impressed at Zurich that its delegation bought 20 Do 17Ks plus a manufacturing licence, this model retaining the original long nose but being powered by Gnome-Rhône 14N

The original 'flying pencil': Dornier's Do 17V1 fast mailplane caused much anxiety in Britain and France when it appeared in late 1934, as its military potential was both obvious and frightening. A year later all fears were realized when the twin-fin Do 17V4 bomber prototype was rolled out.

The initial production bomber version was the Do 17E-1, which began equipping the *Kampfgeschwader* in 1937. It was soon to receive its baptism of fire in Spanish skies, alongside the similar Do 17F-1 reconnaissance version. This E-model of 7./KG 255 is seen with national insignia painted over the 1938 war games.

radials of 980 hp (731 kW). The Do 17K had a 20-mm cannon and three machine-guns, but still reached 259 mph (417 km/h). When Germany invaded Yugoslavia on 6 April 1941 70 Do 17Ks of various sub-types were on strength, 26 being destroyed on the ground but others seeing prolonged and hectic action. A few were eventually put into service by the Croatian puppet air force against Soviet partisans, while on 19 April 1941 two escaped to Heliopolis, Egypt, with cargoes of gold, afterwards serving with the RAF as AX 706/707.

Fighting over Spain against the Polikarpov I-16 had suddenly showed the Dornier's vulnerability, and in late 1937 a completely new forward fuselage was designed to provide much more room for an enlarged crew and better arcs of fire for the guns. First flown in early 1938 on the DB-engined Do 17s and Do 17U versions, the new front end went into major production with the Do 17Z series of bombers, reconnaissance aircraft and night-fighters, all powered by the Fafnir. With a maximum load of 2,205 lb (1000 kg) the Do 17Z-2 was virtually the standard 'Dornier' during the great battles of 1940. Over 500 had been built when production was stopped in mid-year, and these aircraft saw much service with KG 2, KG 3, KG 53 (Croatian) and the Finnish air force.

The Do 17Z-7 Kauz (screech-owl) was a night-fighter fitted with the nose of a Ju 88C-2 complete with one cannon and three MG 17s. This was followed by the properly planned Do 17Z-10 Kauz 11, with the world's first FLIR (forward-looking infra-red) detector, two cannon and four machine-guns. The first of several Do 17Z-10 kills was gained by Oberleutnant Becker on 18 October 1940; it was a Vickers Wellington over the Zuyder Zee. By late 1940 the Do 17Z-10 was being

Laid down to a Swedish air force order, this Do 215B-1 was converted on the production line for Luftwaffe use following the arms embargo in 1939. It was configured for long-range reconnaissance and served with 3.Aufkl. St./Ob.d.L. attached to the Luftwaffe High Command at Stavanger in April 1940.

replaced by the Do 215B. The 215 designation was chosen by the RLM for export versions of Do 17Z, the only sale being to Sweden in late 1939, which selected the 1,100-hp (820-kW) DB 601A engine. The 18 Do 215B-1 aircraft involved were never exported, but were taken over by the Luftwaffe as fast reconnaissance machines. At least 20 of the last batch of Do 215B-4s were completed as Do 215B-5 night-fighters with not only the IR sensor but also the first Lichtenstein radar. Again Becker scored the first kill, on 9 August 1941, with four more by 2 October to become the first night ace.

In 1937 the RLM had called for an enlarged Do 17Z with much heavier bombload and considerably greater fuel capacity, able to accept any of a range of engines, and equally capable at level or dive bombing. First flown in August 1938, the Do 217 V1 was powered by 1,075-hp (802-kW) DB 601A engines, but despite its similar appearance to the Do 17/215 it was a totally new design. It soon showed that it was less pleasant to fly, and in fact crashed, but development continued. Prototypes flew with Junkers Jumo 211A and BMW 139 engines before the big BMW 801 was used in the Do 217 V9 prototype of January 1940. By this time handling was acceptable, the leading edges of the fins being slotted, but the unique dive brake, which opened like a giant cross at the extreme tail, caused endless difficulty. In mid-1941, after wing brakes had been tried and several aircraft lost, the RLM abandoned its stance that the heavy Do 217 had to be a dive bomber.

The heavyweight arrives

First to enter service, in late 1940, the Do 217E-1 was the first bomber model, with the massive bombload of 8,818 lb

(4000 kg), of which 5,550 lb (2517 kg) was inside the bomb bay. A handful to fly, but still a most effective bomber, the Do 217E-1 had a hand-held 20-mm MG FF in the nose, used by KG 40 against ships in the Atlantic, and seven MG 15s. The Do 217E-2 introduced the EDL 131 electric dorsal turret with the excellent MG 131 gun, a hand-aimed MG 131 being in the ventral position, a fixed MG 151/15 firing ahead and three hand-aimed MG 15s completing the defence, though R19 (the 19th in the *Rüstsatz* series of field kits) added twin or quadruple MG 81 machine-guns firing aft from the tailcone. Other *Rüstsätze* added barrage cable cutters and various weapon kits, by far the biggest of which hung two Hs 293 anti-ship missiles under the wings, with Kehl/Strassburg radio command guidance link. The first operational missile carrier was the Do 217E-5 flown by II/KG 100, which went into action with increasingly devastating effect against British ships from 25 August 1943.

With the Do 217E subtypes Dornier got the much heavier Do 217 family into service, and all subsequent models proved adequate but generally (and in the case of the Do 217K-2, severely) underpowered. Despite this, and the absence of the 2,000-hp (1491-kW) engines that were needed, Dornier proposed in early 1941 to develop a night intruder fighter version. The result was the Do 217J, with plenty of fuel and weapons for missions over the UK, but Hitler personally stopped further such flights from 12 October 1941 so the Do 217J served only over Germany and, from September 1942, over Italy with the Regia Aeronautica. Equipped with early radar, usually FuG 202 Lichtenstein BC, the Do 217J-2 retained the turret and lower rear gun of the Do 217E-2 but had a new nose with four MG FFs and four MG 17s. Eight 100-lb (50-kg) SC50 bombs could be carried in the rear bomb bay, though this provision was removed from the Do 217J-2 version.

On 31 July 1942 Dornier flew the first Do 217N, with 1,850-hp (1380-kW) DB 603A engines. A much better, but

Featuring a redesigned nose packed with guns, the Do 217J was the night fighter/intruder version of the Do 217E. This example, the Do 217J-2, differed from the J-1 by having no rear bomb bay. Do 217Js often operated in concert with Messerschmitt Bf 110s, whose manoeuvrability and speed were greater than the Do 217.

KG 2 became the only *Geschwader* to be completely equipped with the Do 217. Originally beginning replacement of the Do 17Z in 1941, KG 2 pulled back from the Russian front and relocated to the Netherlands for bombing and anti-shipping strikes over the North Sea. This is a Do 217E-2/R19 of 9./KG 2 with two MG 81 machine-guns in the tailcone.

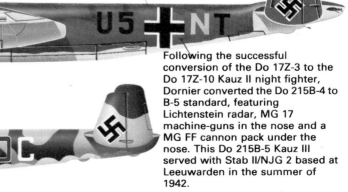

Following the successful conversion of the Do 17Z-3 to the Do 17Z-10 Kauz II night fighter, Dornier converted the Do 215B-4 to B-5 standard, featuring Lichtenstein radar, MG 17 machine-guns in the nose and a MG FF cannon pack under the nose. This Do 215B-5 Kauz III served with Stab II/NJG 2 based at Leeuwarden in the summer of 1942.

The Do 317 was an advanced extension of the Do 17/217 line, featuring a pressurized cabin. No real increase in performance over the Do 217P was found, and apart from the Do 317V1 (illustrated), the other five prototypes were completed without pressurization and used by KG 100 as missile carriers.

of this family reached heights up to 53,000 ft (16155 m) and speeds of over 400 mph (644 km/h). (Dornier's literature states 785 km/h, or 488 mph, but this is an error.)

Total production of Do 217s amounted to 1,541 bombers and 364 night fighters, not including the five Do 217Rs. These were five of the six prototypes of the Do 317 with which Dornier wanted to ensure the order for highly developed 'B-bombers' — fast, long-range bombers with pressurised cabins which were intended to raze Britain to the ground, and remote-controlled machine guns. In 1943 test flying of the Do 317-V1 began; this aircraft resembled a Do 217M with triangular tail fins, and the Do 317B with DB 610A/B twin engines of 2,870 hp (2,140 kW) never actually flew.

still not brilliant, night-fighter, the Do 217N carried a heavier load of avionics and, for use on the Eastern Front, restored the rear bomb bay. The Do 217N-2 had wooden fairings in place of the turret and lower rear gun, but most had the new SN-2 radar and an increasing number were fitted with *schräge Musik* oblique upward-firing cannon, the usual fit being four 20-mm MG 151 of the type which by the start of Do 217N-2 production had also replaced the forward-firing MG FFs. Only 364 Do 217Js and Do 217Ns were delivered, and they had faded from the NJG (night fighter wings) front line by mid-1944. The blind spot in most bombers was directly below the centre section and the upward-firing 20-mm cannon took full advantage of this.

In come the guided bombs

In 1941 Dornier had again enlarged the crew compartment, this time eliminating the windscreen and glazing the whole nose as in many other German types of the period. The Do 217K-1 bomber entered service with KG 2, replacing the last of the Do 17Z-2s, in October 1942. Crews initially felt vulnerable surrounded by Plexiglas, but the Do 217K-1 was better arranged and also introduced a braking parachute made of Perlon, a Nylon-like material. In December 1942 the Do 217K-2 followed it into service, this having the span greatly increased to lift two of the formidable FX, or FX 1400 or Fritz X, guided bombs. Each of these weighed 3,461 lb (1570 kg) and the Kehl/Strassburg command link steered it in azimuth and pitch.

Major Bernhard Jope's III/KG 100 based at Istres had a field-day on 9 September 1943 when the Italian fleet sailed from La Spezia to join the Allies. One of the world's biggest battleships, the brand-new *Roma*, took two direct hits, blew up and sank in minutes; and her sister *Italia* just reached Malta with 800 tons of water on board. Later FX sent many other ships to the bottom. Most Do 217K-2 aircraft had a paired R19 *Rüstsatz* in the tail with four aft-firing MG81 guns.

Last production Do 217 was the Do 217M, essentially a Do 217K-1 with DB 603As, or alternatively a bomber version of the Do 217N. Only a few were built, the priority being on the Do 217N night-fighter, but one hit by AA fire near London on 23 February 1944 was abandoned by its crew and then flew on to make an excellent belly landing near Cambridge! Even at light weights height could not be maintained on one engine, and as with all the Do 217s the feeling was that there was too much aeroplane for the available wing area and power.

The last of the Do 217s, and by far the fastest, the Do 217P family was for high-altitude use and had the same complex *HZ-Anlage* system as the Henschel Hs 130: a DB 605T in the rear fuselage drove a giant two-stage blower which supercharged the two DB 603B propulsion engines, the underside of the fuselage and inboard wings being filled by giant radiators and intercoolers. The three engines provided 2,880 hp (2148 kW) at 45,000 ft (13715 m), and aircraft

Do 217Es served with KG 40 in France on anti-shipping strikes under the command of Fliegerführer Atlantik from March 1941 onwards. The type was successful in this role and was later adapted to carry the Henschel Hs 293A and Fritz-X anti-ship missiles.

Seen wearing hastily applied RAF roundels and Air Ministry registration, this Do 217M-1 shows the Daimler-Benz DB 603A engines which distinguished it from the BMW 801D-powered Do 217K-1. Later Do 217M versions featured carriage for Fritz-X and Hs 293A missiles, but these did not attain series production.

Dornier Do 217K-1 cutaway drawing key

1. Starboard rudder tab
2. Rudder controls
3. Rudder mass balance (lead insert)
4. Starboard tailfin
5. Leading-edge slot
6. Tailplane/tailfin attachment
7. Elevator
8. Elevator mass balance
9. Fixed tab
10. Trim tab
11. Tailplane construction
12. Elevator controls
13. Rear navigation light
14. Four aft-firing 7.9-mm MG 81 machine-guns (Rüstsatz [field conversion set] 19)
15. Ammunition boxes
16. Tailplane trim control
17. Fuel emergency jettison
18. Mudguard
19. Tailwheel
20. Tailwheel doors
21. Tailwheel retraction mechanism
22. Tailplane carry-through
23. Fuselage skinning
24. Master compass
25. Dipole antenna
26. Anti-collision beacon
27. Elevator mass balance
28. Port tailfin
29. Leading-edge slot
30. Bomb bay division
31. Bomb bay hinge line
32. Bomb bay rear bulkhead entry/inspection hatch
33. Spherical oxygen cylinders
34. Starboard mainwheel
35. Mudguard
36. Mainwheel doors
37. Mainwheel retraction mechanism
38. Mainwheel well
39. FuG 25 (A-A recognition)
40. EuG 101 radio altimeter
41. Outer section split flaps
42. Starboard aileron
43. Aileron tab
44. Control lines
45. Rear spar
46. Braced wing ribs
47. Intermediate ribs
48. EGS 101 antenna
49. Starboard navigation light
50. Front spar
51. Leading-edge hot-air de-icing
52. Hot-air duct
53. Balloon-cable cutter in leading-edge
54. Starboard outer fuel tank (35 Imp gal/160 litre capacity)
55. Starboard oil tank (51.7 Imp gal/235 litre capacity)
56. Flame-damping exhaust pipes
57. Sliding-ring cooling air exit
58. BMW 801D 14-cylinder two-row radial engine
59. Annular oil cooler
60. VDM Three-blade metal propeller of 12.79 ft (3.90 m) diameter
61. Cooling fan
62. Cowling sliding nose-ring
63. Propeller boss
64. Starboard inner fuel tank (175 Imp gal/795 litre capacity)
65. Fuselage main fuel tank (231 Imp gal/1050 litre capacity)
66. Wing spar carry-through
67. Bomb bay top hinge line
68. Load-bearing beam
69. Bomb shackle
70. Bomb bay centre hinge line
71. Typical bomb load: two 2,250-lb (1000-kg) SC 1000 bombs
72. Forward bomb doors
73. 13-mm MG 131 machine-gun in ventral position (1,000 rounds)
74. Ammunition ejection chute
75. Ventral gunner's station
76. Armoured bulkhead
77. Cartridge collector box
78. Batteries (two 24-Volt)
79. Radio equipment
80. Dorsal gunner's seat support
81. Cabin hot-air
82. Dorsal gunner's station
83. Armoured turret ring
84. Aerial mast
85. Gun safety guard
86. Starboard beam-mounted 7.9-mm MG 81 machine-gun (750 rounds)
87. 13-mm MG 131 machine-gun (500 rounds)
88. Electrically-operated dorsal turret
89. Revi gunsight
90. Angled side windows
91. Jettisonable decking
92. Bomb-aimer's folding seat
93. Navigator's position
94. Pilot's contoured table seat
95. Rear-view gunsight
96. Upper instrument panel
97. Nose glazing
98. Control horns
99. Engine controls
100. One 13-mm MG 131 in strengthened nose glazing (alternatively twin 7.9-mm MG 81Z)
101. Balloon-cable cutter in nose horizontal frame
102. Cartridge ejection chute
103. Ammunition feed
104. Lotfe 7D bombsight
105. Bomb aimer's flat panel
106. Control column counterweight
107. Nose armour
108. Ventral gunner's quilt
109. Ammunition box (nose MG 131)
110. Cartridge collector box
111. Entry hatch
112. Entry hatch (open)
113. Entry ladder
114. Port mainwheel doors
115. Mudguard
116. Port mainwheel
117. Mainwheel leg cross struts
118. Port engine cowling
119. Landing light (swivelling)
120. Control linkage
121. Pitot head
122. Port navigation light
123. Port aileron
124. Aileron trim tab

Dornier Do 17, 215 and 217 variants (simplified, omitting many prototypes)

Do 17 V1: original civil mailplane prototype, two 750-hp (559-kW) BMW VI engines, wing area 592 sq ft (55 m²), speed 270 mph (435 km/h)
Do 17 V4: first bomber prototype, twin fins, BMW VI
Do 17 V8: first Do 17 M-series, DB 600 engines, long glazed nose
Do 17E: initial production bomber, 750-hp (559-kW) BMW VI, short rounded nose, speed 221 mph (355 km/h)
Do 17F: initial production reconnaissance version, similar to Do 17E
Do 17M: bomber, 900-hp (671-kW) Bramo 323A engines, broadly as E
Do 17P: day/night reconnaissance, 865-hp (645-kW) BMW 132N engines
Do 17R: test-beds with 1,100-hp (820-kW) DB 601A or other engines
Do-17S: new forward fuselage with roomy crew compartment, 1,000-hp (746-kW) DB 600C engines
Do 17U: five-seat pathfinder (two radio/radar operators) with new nose and DB 600A engines (according to Dornier, Bramo 323A)
Do 17Z: four-seat bomber with new nose, basically Do 17M with modified crew compartment; later **Do 17Z-2** with 1,000-hp (746-kW) Bramo 323P engines, **Do 17Z-3** reconnaissance bomber, **Do 17Z-4** crew trainer and **Do 17Z-5** maritime reconnaissance aircraft
Do 17ZKauz: Do 17Z-6 Kauz 1 night-fighter with nose of Ju 88C-2, followed by **Do 17Z-10 Kauz II** designed from start for role, both with Bramo 323P engines
Do 215B: most four-seat reconnaissance/bomber with 1,100-hp (820-kW) DB 601Aa; **Do 215B-5** night-fighter with first Lichtenstein radar
Do 217 V1: new enlarged bomber/dive bomber with 614-sq ft (57-m²) wing and 1,075 (802-

kW) DB 601 As
Do 217 V2/3/4: prototypes with 1,200-hp (895-kW) Jumo 211As
Do 217 V7/8: prototypes with 1,550-hp (1156-kW) BMW 139
Do 217A: long-range reconnaissance/bomber, long-span 700-sq ft (65-m²) wing, 1,350-hp (1007-kW) DB 601R/C3
Do 217C: similar to Do 217A but regular 614-sq ft (57-m²) wing, revised ventral contour, no cameras, more defensive guns
Do 217E: major family of four-seat bombers, 1,580-hp (1178-kW) BMW 801 MA or ML engines: **Do 217E-2** introduced turret, **Do-217E-4** BMW 801 C engines, **Do 217E-5** either Hs 293 or FX 1400 missiles
Do 217J: interim three-seat night-fighter, 1,580-hp (1178-kW) BMW 801L, FuG 202 Lichtenstein BC radar
Do 217K-1: four-seat night bomber, 1,700-hp (1268-kW) BMW 801D engines, new glazed nose
Do 217K-2: carrier for FX 1400 missiles, long-span 721-sq ft (67-m²) wing. R19 tail guns
Do 217L: high-altitude reconnaissance aircraft, 2,000-hp (1491-kW) DB 603HC-3 engines, 753-sq ft (70-m²) wing, 360 mph (580 km/h), ceiling 42,650 ft (13000 m)
Do 217M: bomber, 1,850-hp (1380-kW) DB 603A engines
Do 217N: four-seat night-fighter and intruder, 1,850-hp (1380-kW) DB 603A engines
Do 217P: ultra-high altitude pressurized bomber with third supercharging engine to boost DB 603B main engines, Do 217K-2 wing
Do 217R: Hs 293 missile carrier modified from Do 317A prototypes
Do 317A: four-seat high-altitude bomber, 1,750-hp (1305-kW) DB 603A engines

The Lockheed Twins

The introduction of the small Lockheed airliner in the mid-1930s pulled the company back from penury, and set the Burbank-based organization on the road to recovery. When war came the shortage of patrol bombers and fast transports immediately became evident, and Lockheed grasped the opportunity with both hands.

In 1932, Lockheed was on the verge of financial ruin. Its trustees valued the assets of the company at $129,961 and ordered it to sell them. While the founder of the firm, Allan Loughead, tried to raise the money to buy his old company, the stockbroker and banker Robert Ellsworth Gross snapped up the almost totally run-down aircraft company for the legendary amount of $40,000. Like many other businessmen who speculated with their money, Gross had little idea of the complex world of the flying industry, but had plenty of sound business sense and gradually came under the spell of the new generation of commercial transport planes. After he had made a careful assessment of the company, Gross declared that the company's future lay not in the production of mail planes or military aircraft, but in the development of fast and relatively small commuter and supply planes, which could eventually represent a challenge to the new machines from Boeing and Douglas which dominated the market at the time. With Gross came Hall Hibbard, a young aircraft engineer from the Massachusetts Institute of Technology, who worked with Lloyd Stearman on a number of different projects which looked promising. But it was Gross who gradually developed the idea of a small, twin-engine all-metal plane. The construction team was joined by George Prudden and James Gerschler, and later on by C. L. 'Kelly'

Johnson, who early on demonstrated his brilliant ability by solving the problems of the new Lockheed in the wind tunnel which later became known as the Lockheed Model L-10.

Roll-out for the Lockheed Model L-10 Electra took place on 23 February 1934. It was a beautiful little twin-engine aircraft resplendent in glistening polished natural aluminium. Power came from two 450-hp (336-kW) Pratt & Whitney R-985-SB radials, cabin and crew seats numbered 12, empty weight was 6,454 lb (2928 kg), and the gross weight was 10,300 lb (4672 kg). Tests gave a maximum speed of 202 mph (325 km/h), and a spanking maximum continuous cruising speed of 190 mph (306 km/h). After exhaustive tests the prototype L-10 Electra was flown by Marshall Headle to Mines Field, Los Angeles, for FAA certification which was granted a few weeks later. On the return to Burbank a heart-

Lockheed A-29 in US Army Air Force colours of early 1942 vintage. Initially all 800 A-29 and A-29A aircraft were allocated to the RAF under Lend-Lease, but with the crisis taking place in the Pacific and the Far East a large number were repossessed and pressed into service with the USAAF: some were used as crew trainers, and others as bombers and maritime patrol aircraft, one being the first USAAF aircraft to sink a U-boat in World War 2.

This Howard 500 is a conversion of a Lockheed Super Ventura. It has a newly-built fuselage and two Pratt & Whitney R-2800 engines. It now belongs to the British company, Baker Petroleum.

Lockheed PV2 Harpoon

Specification

Type: four/five-seat patrol bomber
Powerplant: two 2,000-hp (1491-kW) Pratt & Whitney R-2800-31 Double Wasp 18-cylinder radials
Performance: maximum speed (clean) 282 mph (454 km/h) at medium altitudes; service ceiling 23,900 ft (7285 m); range (with outer-wing tanks available, after curing major sealing problem) 1,790 miles (2880 km)
Weights: empty 21,028 lb (9538 kg); maximum 36,000 lb (16330 kg)
Dimensions: span 74 ft 11 in (22.84 m); length 52 ft 0½ in (15.86 m); height 11 ft 10 in (3.63 m); wing area 686 sq ft (63.77 m²)
Armament: internal bay for bombload of 4,000 lb (1814 kg), plus underwing racks for two 1,000-lb (454-kg) bombs, depth charges or other stores, or (as illustrated) eight HVAR (high-velocity aircraft rockets) in addition to drop tanks

This Lockheed PV-2 Harpoon served at the end of World War 2 with US Navy squadron VPB-142 in the Marianas Islands. It was one of the original and most common variant with a forward-firing armament of five guns, two high in the nose and three below; later the number was increased to eight. In fact hardly any of the PV-2 was identical with the corresponding parts of any PV-1, the unchanged portions being confined to small portions of the fuselage, inboard wing ribs and the cowlings (but not the nacelles). Another item common to some PV-1s was the type of Martin dorsal turret, but the lower rear guns were changed to the same 0.5-in (12.7-mm) calibre as used elsewhere.

The Lockheed Twins

Lockheed PV-1 of the US Navy's VB-135 operational over the Pacific area in 1944. Powered by twin 2000-hp (1491-kW) Pratt & Whitney R-2800-31 radials, the first PV-1s entered service with Navy Squadron VP-82 to replace the PBO-1 (Hudsons) in December 1942. Approximately 1,600 PV-1s were procured by the US Navy. The much cleaner Martin turret helped boost the PV-1 maximum speed to 312 mph (502 km/h) at 13,800 ft (4200 m).

The Lockheed XC-35 was built to a US Army Air Corps contract of 1936, to investigate high-altitude flight. Modified from a Model 12, its circular-section fuselage was stressed up to 10 lb/sq in (0.69 bars) pressure differential. It was the first aircraft to feature a pressure cabin and engine-driven turbo-superchargers, and flew for the first time on 7 May 1937.

stopping incident took place. Up to the time of the L-10's first flight Lockheed had gone into debt for $139,404 for its development, and as its priceless prototype, newly certificated, made its approach all attempts by the crew to lower one of the main wheels ended in stubborn failure: only a skilfully handled one-wheel landing at nearby Union Air Terminal by pilot Headle, with minimal damage to the Electra, prevented a major lay-off of the work force and the renewal of financial straits. There the matter rested: sales of the Model L-10 Electra rocketted skywards with examples going to Mid-Continent Airlines, Northwest Airlines, Northeast Airlines, Cia Nacional Cubana, Pan American Airways, Panair do Brasil, Braniff Airways, National Airlines, British Airways, Delta Air Lines, Eastern Air Lines, Chicago and Southern, LAV (Venezuela), LOT (Poland), LARES (Romania), AEROPUT (Yugoslavia), LAN-Chile, and to a host of private buyers including Amelia Earhart.

An L-10 Electra was the seventh Lockheed successfully to fly the Atlantic Ocean when Dick Merill and John Lambie flew NR16055 on a round-trip to London to collect photos of King George VI's coronation in 1937. Also that year, somewhere in the Pacific Ocean wastes between Lae, New Guinea, and Howland Island, aviatrix Amelia Earhart and her navigator disappeared for ever during a record attempt in their L-10 Electra. A total of 149 L-10s was built and delivered between 29 June 1934 and 18 July 1941, and many saw military service in the RCAF and Argentine navy, and with the US Army, US Navy and US Coast Guard as redesignated C-36, C-37, R20 and R30 sub-types.

Bigger and better

The interim Model L-12 Electra Junior was taken into the air for the first time by Marshall Headle at 12.12 on 27 June 1936, exactly on the scheduled time. By now business was booming, with Lockheed getting $2 million worth of orders in the previous year. Price-tagged at $40,000 the Model L-12, with six-seat capacity, was aimed squarely at the business and commuter markets, and in fact was a scaled-down version of its predecessor with two Pratt & Whitney R-985-SB radials. Grossing 8,650 lb (3924 kg), the Electra Junior's top speed was 225 mph (362 km/h) and service ceiling 22,300 ft (6800 m). Its performance and handling qualities exceed those of the majority of contemporary fighters, and it became another good seller. Several records fell to the Model L-12, including a new route average of 210 mph (338 km/h) by test pilot E. C. McLead, despite four fuel stops, from Amsterdam to India on a delivery flight of a L-12 for the Maharaja of Jodhpur. A total of 130 Model L-12s was built before work stopped in mid-1942.

Incorporating many of the latest aviation developments, the larger and more powerful Lockheed Model L-14 Super Electra took to the air for the first time on 29 June 1937. New features on this 14-seat aircraft included use of 24SRT

The Lockheed Model 14 Super Electra of South African Airways is very similar in design to the models succeeding the Hudson which was destined to have a memorable career in World War 2 in a number of very useful roles. The Model 14 was all-metal, with Fowler flaps, two 820 hp (611 kW) Wright Cyclones GR-1820-G3B radial engines and flew for the first time on 29 July 1937.

One of the 625 Lockheed Model L-18 Lodestars, with its higher-mounted tail designed to avoid pitch and Pratt & Whitney engines. The Model 18 was flown for the first time on 2 February 1940 by Marshall Headle and was used by several airlines. Only a few were sold in Europe. There were also US Army and RAF versions.

After World War 2 many Venturas remained in service around the world. This former GR.Mk V of the Royal Canadian Air Force was replaced by a Lancaster MR.Mk 10, but went on into the 1950s as a target tug at Sea Island, Vancouver. The orange/black livery was called 'Oxydol special' after a popular brand of soap powder.

By far the most important of the post-war users of the Ventura was the South African Air Force, which gathered its own survivors (including this GR.Mk V) and many former B-34s and PV-1s to serve as ocean patrol and medium bomber aircraft until Shackletons arrived in 1958. No 6472 served with No. 17 Sqn.

duralumin, high-speed aerofoil (NACA 23018 and 23009 at root and tip respectively), single main spar, and high wing loading, massive Lockheed-Fowler flaps, and two of the latest Wright Cyclone engines, the GR-1820-G3B. With an empty weight of 10,700 lb (4854 kg) and a gross of 17,500 lb (7938 kg), the new L-14 had a top speed of 257 mph (414 km/h): its cruising speed was some 30 mph (48 km/h) faster than that of any other commercial transport in the United States and, at a cruise speed of 237 mph (381 km/h) the Super Electra cut the West Coast—New York flight time of the Douglas DC-3 by four hours. Such was the reputation of the company that even before roll-out over 30 L-14s were on the order book, and the aircraft itself was soon to justify all expectations. Millionaire Howard Hughes purchased a Model L-14, and increased tankage from the normal 644 to 1,844 US gal (3438 to 6980 litres) for a round-the-world record attempt. Departing from New York on 10 July 1938, Hughes and his crew flew via Paris, Moscow, Yakutsk, Fairbanks and Minneapolis to land at Floyd Bennett Field after a 14,709-mile (23670-km) flight achieved within the time of three days 17 hours 14 minutes and 10 seconds. But the 112 Model L-14s are remembered today as the progenitors of what was to be one of Lockheed's most successful warplanes. Licence production of the L-14 in Japan amounted to 64 by Tachikawa and 55 by Kawasaki.

Enter the Hudson

To the United States in April 1938 came the British Purchasing Commission in search of good-quality American aircraft to bolster the strength of the Royal Air Force in its preparations for an inevitable war: the mission had $25 million with which to acquire its finds. At that time Lockheed engaged only 2,000 workers, and had eschewed the design of military types in favour of the commercial market. But in 10 days of frantic labour the concern had cobbled together something that might whet the appetites of the commission: this was nothing other than a mockup of a Model L-14 provided with bomb-bay, bomb-aimer's panel and nose-glazing, and provision for various armaments. The British, with a need for a medium-range maritime patrol bomber for North Sea operations with RAF Coastal Command, were impressed. At the invitation of Sir Henry Self, the contracts director at the Air Ministry in London, Courtlandt Gross (brother of Robert Gross) travelled to the UK with Carl Squier, C. L. Johnson, Robert Proctor and R. A. van Hake for consultations. The

initial order for 175 Model B14s, now known as the Hudson, was signed on 23 June 1938, with provision of up to a maximum of 250 by December 1939: it was the largest military order gained by a US company to date. The first Hudson Mk I bomber took to the air on 10 December 1938, with the company, now numbering a work force of 7,000, hard at work to fill the orders which rose in value with additional orders for P-38s and B-34s to an impressive $65 million.

Arriving by sea, the first Hudson Mk Is reached the UK on 15 February 1939. The type was powered by two 1,100-hp (820-kW) Wright GR-1820-G102A Cyclones with two-speed Hamilton propellers. For reconnaissance duties the Hudson Mk I carried an F.24 camera, assorted flares and a bombload of up to 1,100 lb (499 kg) comprising either four 250-lb (114-kg) GP, SAP or AS, or 10 110-lb (50-kg) anti-submarine bombs; an overload of 12 112-lb (51-kg) Mk VIIc AS bombs could be carried, but in this event the bomb doors could not be fully closed. Modified with extra items at the Lockheed-Vega subsidiary at Speke (Liverpool), the first Hudson Mk Is and Mk IIs (the latter differing in the installation of Hamilton Standard Type 611A-12/3E50-253 constant-speed propellers) were delivered to Wing Commander E. A. Hodgson's No. 224 Squadron at Leuchars, Scotland, in

Venturas of the Royal New Zealand Air Force featured prominently in the campaigns in the south-west Pacific, in the Solomons and against the Japanese bastions at Rabaul and Kavieng. These PV-1s, three of 388 procured under Lend-Lease, flew as the Ventura GR.Mk V with the RNZAF in the Solomons during 1943-4. The nearest aircraft is NZ4534, coded ZX-D. They are demonstrating single-engine flight.

The Lockheed Twins

August 1939. Although less manoeuvrable than the lighter Avro Anson, the Hudson was considered by the squadron to be eminently suitable for its patrols over the North Sea as far as Norway, the Skaggerak and the German Bight. Cruising at 2,000 ft (610 m) at 190 mph (306 km/h), a fuel consumption of 71 Imp gal (323 litres) per hour gave the Hudson an endurance of over six hours with 20 per cent reserves and a 570-mile (917-km) radius of action. Armament was light initially, and the twin 0.303-in (7.7-mm) nose guns, beam guns and the Boulton Paul Type 'C' Mk II turret were retrofitted during the autumn of 1939 and the spring of 1940.

With the outbreak of war the Hudsons of RAF Coastal Command were among the first RAF aircraft to go into action, and the first combat with a German aircraft was recorded on 4 September 1939, when No. 224 Squadron's T-Tommy (N7214), captained by Flying Officer H. D. Green, engaged a Dornier Do 18 over the Dogger Bank. In addition to No. 224 Squadron, Nos 206, 269, 233, 320 and 220 Squadrons were equipped with Hudsons during 1939–40, and much action was seen off Norway during the *Altmark* incident and the subsequent German invasion of Scandinavia, and over the Channel during the Dunkirk evacuations in addition to patrol work over the Western Approaches and the North Sea. During 1941 RAF and RCAF Hudsons, operating from the UK, Iceland, and Newfoundland, conducted a difficult war against the U-Boat menace: on 27 August 1941 a Hudson of No. 269 Squadron from Kaldadarnes forced the crew of the *U-570* to surrender after repeated attacks. Use of the Hudson was not limited to the RAF and RCAF, and in early 1942 US Army A-28s and A-29s, and US Navy PBO-1s did much work along the eastern seaboard of the United States, while in the Far East those of Nos 1 and 8 Squadrons RAAF fought well against great odds during the Japanese invasions of Malaya, Java and Burma. Six primary marks of Hudson, in maritime and transport work, came from Lockheed's 2,941 made up to June 1943 when production ceased, seeing service on all Anglo-American war fronts.

Ventura Mk II of No. 21 Sqn, RAF, operating from Methwold airfield, Norfolk, under No. 2 (Bomber) Group. RAF Venturas entered service in November 1942, and one of their first large missions was that against the Philips concern at Eindhoven on 6 December 1942. The spring and summer of 1943 saw Nos 21, 464 and 487 Sqns operating the Ventura over enemy-held France, Belgium and Holland, often at considerable loss.

The Lockheed PV-2 was the last version of the twin-engined Lockheed craft, with a wingspan almost 10 ft (3 m) longer than that of the PV-1.

Lockheed Hudson Mk 1 cutaway drawing key

1 Starboard navigation/ identification lights
2 Starboard wingtip
3 De-icing slots
4 Internal vanes
5 Aileron internal mass balance
6 Starboard aileron
7 Aileron tab
8 Tab mechanism
9 Control cables
10 Wing main spar structure
11 De-icing tubes
12 Leading-edge de-icing boot
13 Main wing rib stations
14 Wing skinning
15 Flap control cables
16 Flap tracks
17 Flap cables/pulleys
18 Track fairings
19 Port flap (extended)
20 Aerial mast

35 Central instrument console
36 Starboard nose compartment entry tunnel
37 Bulkhead
38 Starboard engine oil tank
39 Fixed forward-firing 0.303-in (7.7-mm) Browning machine-guns (two)
40 Carburettor intake
41 Wright R-1820-G102A radial engine
42 Starboard nacelle
43 Cowling nose ring
44 Three-blade propeller
45 Spinner

69 Pilot's radio control boxes
70 Forward (canted) fuselage frame
71 Frame wing pick-up
72 Hydraulics reservoir
73 Wireless-operator's table
74 Wireless-operator's seat
75 Transmitter
76 Receiver
77 Main spar centre-section carry-through

21 D F loop fairing
22 Supported structure
23 Aerial lead-in
24 Cockpit cold air
25 Flight deck sun-blind frames
26 Windscreen wiper motor
27 Jettisonable canopy hatch
28 Console light
29 Windscreen wipers
30 Second-pilot's jump seat
31 Adjustable quarterlight
32 Windscreen frame support member
33 External gunsight
34 Second-pilot's (back-up) control column (cantilevered)

46 Nose compartment cold air
47 Machine-gun muzzles
48 Nose structure
49 Roof glazing
50 Window frames
51 Nose cone
52 Navigator's side windows
53 Compass
54 Navigator's table
55 Navigator's (sliding) seat
56 Bomb-aimer's flat panels
57 Bomb-aimer's prone position
58 Bomb selector switch panel
59 Navigator's instrument panel
60 Forward flare chute
61 Bombsight support
62 Nose frames
63 Nose compartment warm air
64 Windscreen de-icing tank
65 Machine gun ammunition magazine
66 Rudder pedal assembly
67 Pilot's control column
68 Pilot's seat

78 Spar/frame attachment
79 Wireless bay racks
80 Cabin cold air
81 Astrograph table/supply locker
82 Wing flaps actuating cylinder
83 Smoke-float stowage rack
84 Port cabin windows
85 Beam machine-gun positions (field modification)
86 Gun support frame
87 Tailfin de-icing boot
88 Astrodome (Mk III and retrofit)
89 Fuselage frames
90 Stringers
91 Flare stowage racks
92 Parachute stowage
93 Aft fuselage bulkhead
94 Aerials
95 Boulton Paul dorsal turret
96 Turret support canted frame

97 Turret ring
98 Dorsal cut-out former
99 Bulkhead
100 Rear bulkhead/tailplane support
101 Tail surface control linkage
102 Starboard tailplane
103 Twin 0.303-in (7.7-mm) machine-guns
104 Rudder control quadrant
105 Cable linkage
106 De-icing tube
107 Starboard end plane
108 Tailfin de-icing boot
109 Tailfin skinning
110 Rudder tab actuator
111 Aerial attachment
112 Rudder upper balance
113 Rudder tab
114 Starboard rudder
115 Starboard elevator
116 Starboard elevator
117 Tab actuating linkage
118 Elevator control mechanism

119 Fixed centre-section
120 Tail navigation light
121 Port elevator
122 Elevator tab
123 Port tailfin de-icing boot
124 Tailfin structure
125 Rudder upper balance
126 Rudder upper hinge
127 Rudder tab
128 Port rudder structure
129 Port end plane
130 Rudder lower balance
131 Fixed tailwheel
132 Port tailplane structure
133 Tailwheel shock-absorber leg
134 Tailplane support bulkhead
135 Warm air conduit
136 Bulkhead cover plate
137 Control pulley quadrant
138 Turret mechanism support
139 Aft flare tube
140 Toilet location
141 Step
142 Entry door (jettisonable dinghy housing)
143 Ammunition feed magazine
144 Dinghy release cylinder/ hand lever
145 Tunnel (ventral) gun station (optional)
146 Cabin entry walkway (port)
147 Ventral camera port
148 Ventral gun well
149 Bomb-doors operating quadrant
150 Bomb-bay rear well
151 Port flap section
152 Flap track fairings
153 Aileron tab
154 Port aileron
155 Aileron internal mass balance
156 Port wing tip structure
157 Port navigation identification lights
158 Internal vanes
159 Wing slots
160 Wing structure

161 Main spar
162 Nose ribs
163 Port wing leading-edge de-icing boot
164 Rib assembly
165 Mainwheel recess
166 Port nacelle fairing
167 Rear spar wing join
168 Main spar wing join
169 Port wing aft fuel tank
170 Fuselage bomb-bay actuating cylinder
171 Port wing foward fuel tank
172 Control servos
173 Undercarriage retractor cylinder
174 Undercarriage support attachment strut
175 Port engine oil tank bay
176 Engine support frame
177 Carburettor anti-icing tank
178 Engine bearer assembly
179 Bomb-bay forward wall
180 Carburettor intake
181 Battery
182 Smoke floats
183 Propeller anti-icing tank (fuselage)
184 Engine bearer ring
185 Cowling nose ring
186 Spinner
187 Three-blade propeller
188 Starboard mainwheel
189 Pitot head
190 Oil cooler intake
191 Exhaust louvres
192 Landing gear fulcrum
193 Drag strut
194 Exhaust stub
195 Side strut
196 Mainwheel oleo leg
197 Torque links
198 Port mainwheel
199 Axle hub
200 Towing lug
201 Undercarriage door
202 Float marker
203 250-lb (113.5-kg) A S bomb

The Model 18 Progeny

A direct development of the L-14 series, the Lockheed L-18 Lodestar first flew on 21 September 1939: the fuselage had been stretched by 5 ft 6 in (1.68 m), and to minimize tail flutter the elevator was raised slightly. By the end of 1940 some 54 of the 17-seat Model 18s had been sold to such varied customers as Mid Continent (first to buy the $90,000 aircraft), Regie Air Afrique and the Netherlands East Indies, BOAC and South African Airways. During World War 2 the Model 18 series was adopted by the US Army and the US Navy as a transport: US Army versions included the C-56 (in models up to C-56E), C-57 and C-57B, C-59, C-60 and C-60A, C-66 and C-111, all of which featured differences either in engines, seating or ancillary equipment. Naval versions included the R50 (in models up to R50-6), while the RAF used Lodestar Mks I, IA and II models.

In response to a request from the British, Vega Aircraft Corporation developed a military version of the Model L-18 series which was employed by the RAF as the Ventura, by the US Army Air Force as the B-34 and B-37, and by the US Navy as the PV-1 patrol bomber. All were powered by two 2,000-hp (1492-kW) Pratt & Whitney R-2800-31 radials, with the exception of the RAF's Ventura Mk I which had Pratt & Whitney R-2800-S1A4G engines, and the few B-37s which featured Wright R-2600-13s. The first Ventura Mk I flew on 31 July 1941 and, together with the up-rated Mk II and Mk IIA versions, entered service with No. 2 (Bomber) Group in November 1942. On daylight missions over France and the Low Countries the Ventura fared badly against the dangerous Focke-Wulf Fw 190As of the Luftwaffe, and losses to flak and enemy fighters were consistently high. During the summer of 1943 the type was withdrawn from No. 2 Group, its place being taken by North American Mitchells and Douglas Boston Mk IIIA bombers. The B-34s of the USAAF saw little action, while the B-37 (Ventura Mk III) saw none at all. However, in the Solomons and South Pacific

A Lockheed Hudson Mk IVA in the colours of the Royal Australian Air Force. In the 1970s this machine belonged to the Stathallan Collection in Scotland, and has since been moved to the RAF Museum, Hendon.

area Ventura Mk IVs and GR.MK Vs of the RNZAF saw considerable action against the Japanese bastions at Kavieng and Rabaul, and proved their worth. The last-mentioned marks were known in the US Navy as PV-1s, of which 1,800 were built. Carrying a crew of four or five, the PV-1 weighed in at 20,197 lb (9161 kg) empty and 31,077 lb (14097 kg) gross, and was capable of a maximum speed of 312 mph (502 km/h) at 13,800 ft (4205 m). Armament consisted of two forward-firing 0.5-in (12.7-mm) guns, two more guns of the same calibre in a Martin CE250 dorsal turret, and two 0.3-in (7.62-mm) guns in the ventral position: up to four 1,000-lb (454-kg) bombs could be stowed internally, with another two under the wings, while an alternative was a single Model 13 Mk II torpedo. US Navy PV-1s operated from Aleutian bases during 1943–5 in all weathers on anti-shipping strikes and attacks on the Japanese bases at Paramushiro and Shimushu, and fought off frequent aggressive attacks by the Mitsubishi A6M3 Reisens of the 13th Koku Kantai (Air Fleet) which defended the area. The PV-1 more than compensated for the relatively poor showing by the Ventura in Europe, and performed useful service against the Japanese in all sectors of the Pacific.

The last version of this long and successful series of twin-engine Lockheed aircraft, begun in 1934 with the little Model L-10, was the maritime patrol bomber, the PV-2 Harpoon. In this model, the fuselage and tailplane were rebuilt and the wingspan increased from 65 ft 6 in (19.96 m) to 75 ft (22.86 m). The PV-2's maiden flight was on 3 December 1943, and the first planes were delivered to the US Navy for use on its supply bases in the Aleutians. Wing flexing caused additional problems during production, but PV-2s flew until the end of the war and remained in service for years afterwards with reserve squadrons of the US Navy.

Wartime-vintage Lockheed Venturas were converted in many instances to luxury executive-type aircraft in the years of peace. This smart twin, N5390N, is a Howard Aero Super Ventura.

Featuring a luxury custom-fitted interior, new fuselage contours and a totally new nose section, this beautifully finished ex-US Navy PV-1 illustrates one of several executive conversions of the type.

Swordfish: Taranto Tinfisher

Archaic in appearance even when it first flew, the venerable Swordfish survived as an anachronism throughout World War 2, outlived its replacement and destroyed a greater tonnage of enemy shipping than any other Allied torpedo bomber.

The beginnings of the Swordfish came with the privately-financed tender for Specification S.9/30 from the Air Ministry made by the Fairey Aviation Company. The tender went out at the beginning of the 1930s and was for a torpedo bomber. The TSR I prototype, with an air-cooled 635 hp (474 kW) Bristol Pegasus IIM nine-cylinder radial engine, flew on 21 March 1933. But it soon became apparent that its engine was underpowered and the plane's directional stability left something to be desired. Six months later it crashed after failing to recover from a spin.

A revised specification, S.15/33, was drafted and Fairey produced the TSR II with lengthened fuselage, revised tail unit and an uprated Pegasus IIIM3 developing 775 hp (578 kW). Its structure was largely of fabric-covered metal with split-axle wheel landing gear capable of replacement by twin single-step Fairey floats. With a maximum sea level speed of 146 mph (235 km/h) and first flown on 17 April 1934, this aircraft exceeded the specified performance demands and three prototype development aircraft, named Swordfish, were ordered to meet Specification S.38/34; the third aircraft was completed as a floatplane, making its first flight on 10 November 1934.

The first production order for 86 aircraft was placed in 1935 and initial deliveries were made the following February to No. 823 Squadron, which embarked in HMS *Glorious* later that year, replacing Shark Mk IIs. The standard three-seat production aircraft had a maximum speed of 138 mph (222 km/h) and was easily capable of lifting a standard 18-in (457-mm) 1,610-lb (731-kg) torpedo from the decks of all British carriers with full load, its range in this configuration being 546 miles (879 km).

Further orders continued with Fairey until by the outbreak of war in 1939 a total of 689 Swordfish aircraft had been completed or were on order. Mk I floatplanes were serving with Nos 701, 702 and 705 Catapult Flights of the Fleet Air Arm, being embarked in most of the Royal Navy's battleships, battle-cruisers and cruisers in commission, as well as serving with wheel landing gear in 13 squadrons, of which eight were at sea in the carriers HMS *Ark Royal*, *Argus*, *Courageous*, *Eagle*, *Furious*, *Glorious* and *Hermes*.

Swordfish were in action from the earliest days of the war and it was a floatplane flown by Lieutenant Commander W. M. L. Brown from HMS *Warspite* during the Battle of Narvik on 13 April 1940 that was used to direct the fire of

A Swordfish Mk II of the main Blackburn-built production batch. Carrying a smoke float under the starboard wing, this aircraft would probably have been from a carrier-based squadron.

Fairey Swordfish

Specification

Fairey Swordfish Mk II
Type: two/three-seat deck-landing or float-equipped torpedo-carrying naval aircraft
Powerplant: one 750-hp (560-kW) Bristol Pegasus 30 radial piston engine
Performance: maximum speed 138 mph (222 km/h); climb to 5,000 ft (1525 m) in 10 minutes 0 seconds; service ceiling 10,700 ft (3260 m); range without weapons 1,030 miles (1658 km); with torpedo 550 miles (885 km)
Weights: empty 5,200 lb (2359 kg); maximum take-off 9,250 lb (4196 kg)
Dimensions: span 45 ft 6 in (13.92 m); length 36 ft 4 in (11.12 m); height 12 ft 10 in (3.93 m); wing area 607.0 sq ft (56.39 m²)
Armament: one fixed forward-firing 0.303-in (7.7-mm) Vickers machine-gun and one flexible 0.303-in (7.7-mm) Vickers 'K' or Browning machine-gun in rear cockpit, plus provision for one 18-in (457-mm) 1,610-lb (731-kg) torpedo, or 1,500-lb (681-kg) mine or bombs under the fuselage, or up to eight 3-in (76.2-mm) 60-lb (27-kg) rockets or four 250-lb (113-kg) bombs under wings

Although fairly anonymous in being bare of serial number, Royal Navy ship and squadron markings, this Swordfish is shown in a colour scheme typical of around 1940–1 (the period of the Battle of Taranto) and is carrying a standard naval 18-in (457-mm) torpedo. The horizontal bar suspended from the top wing centresection, visible in the front view, is the aim-off sight, used for attacks on ships, and the emergency dinghy stowage was located in the top wing immediately outboard of the wing-fold; the rear Lewis gun is shown in the stowed position.

Super wartime photo of a Swordfish Mk 1 (P4084) with float undercarriage being launched from a slipway. These aircraft were widely used aboard Royal Navy ships during World War 2 for reconnaissance and gunnery spotting duties.

Fairey Swordfish II cutaway drawing key

1	Rudder structure
2	Rudder upper hinge
3	Diagonal brace
4	External bracing wires
5	Rudder hinge
6	Elevator control horn
7	Tail navigation light
8	Elevator structure
9	Fixed tab
10	Elevator balance
11	Elevator hinge
12	Starboard tailplane
13	Tailplane struts
14	Lashing down shackle
15	Trestling foot
16	Rear wedge
17	Rudder lower hinge
18	Tailplane adjustment screw
19	Elevator control cable
20	External bracing wires
21	Elevator fixed tab
22	Tailfin structure
23	Bracing wire attachment
24	Aerial stub
25	Bracing wires
26	Port elevator
27	Port tailplane
28	Tailplane support struts
29	Dinghy external release cord
30	Tailwheel oleo shock absorber
31	Non-retractable Dunlop tailwheel
32	Fuselage framework
33	Arrester hook housing
34	Control cable fairleads
35	Dorsal decking
36	Rod aerial
37	Lewis gun stowage trough
38	Aerial
39	Flexible 0.303-in (7.7-mm) Lewis machine gun
40	Fairey high-speed flexible gun mounting
41	Type O-3 compass mounting points
42	Aft cockpit coaming
43	Aft cockpit
44	Lewis drum magazine stowage
45	Radio installation
46	Ballast weights
47	Arrester hook pivot
48	Fuselage lower longeron
49	Arrester hook (part extended)
50	Aileron hinge
51	Fixed tab
52	Starboard upper aileron
53	Rear spar
54	Wing ribs
55	Starboard formation light
56	Starboard navigation light
57	Aileron connect strut
58	Interplane struts
59	Bracing wires
60	Starboard lower aileron
61	Aileron hinge
62	Aileron balance
63	Rear spar
64	Wing ribs
65	Aileron outer hinge
66	Deck-handling/lashing grips
67	Front spar
68	Interplane strut attachments
69	Wing internal diagonal bracing wires
70	Flying wires
71	Wing skinning
72	Additional support wire (fitted when underwing stores carried)
73	Wing fold hinge
74	Inboard interplane struts
75	Stub plane end rib
76	Wing locking handle
77	Stub plane structure
78	Intake slot
79	Side window
80	Catapult spool
81	Drag struts
82	Cockpit sloping floor
83	Fixed 0.0303-in (7.7-mm) Vickers gun (deleted from some aircraft)
84	Case ejection chute
85	Access panel
86	Camera mounting bracket
87	Sliding bomb-aiming hatch
88	Zip inspection flap
89	Fuselage upper longeron
90	Centre cockpit
91	Inter-cockpit fairing
92	Upper wing aerial mast
93	Pilot's headrest
94	Pilot's seat and harness
95	Bulkhead
96	Vickers gun fairing
97	Fuel gravity tank (12.5 Imp gal/57 litre capacity)
98	Windscreen
99	Handholds
100	Flap control handwheel and rocking head assembly
101	Wing centre section
102	Dinghy release cord handle
103	Identification light
104	Centre section pyramid strut attachment
105	Diagonal strengtheners
106	Dinghy inflation cylinder
107	Type C dinghy stowage well
108	Aileron control linkage
109	Trailing edge rib sections
110	Rear spar
111	Wing rib stations
112	Aileron connect strut
113	Port upper aileron
114	Fixed tab
115	Aileron hinge
116	Port formation light
117	Wing skinning
118	Port navigation light
119	Leading-edge slot
120	Front spar
121	Nose ribs
122	Interplane struts
123	Pitot head
124	Bracing wires
125	Flying wires
126	Port lower mainplane
127	Landing lamp
128	Underwing bomb shackles
129	Underwing strengthening plate
130	Rocket-launching rails
131	Four 60-lb (27-kg) anti-shipping rocket projectiles
132	Three-blade fixed-pitch Fairey-Reed metal propeller
133	Spinner
134	Townend ring
135	Bristol Pegasus IIIM3 (or Mk 30) radial engine
136	Cowling clips
137	Engine mounting ring
138	Engine support bearers
139	Firewall bulkhead
140	Engine controls
141	Oil tank immersion heater socket
142	Filler cap
143	Oil tank (13.75 Imp gal/62.5 litre capacity)
144	Centre section pyramid struts
145	External torpedo sight bars
146	Fuel filler cap
147	Main fuel tank (155 Imp gal/705 litre capacity)

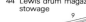

the battleship's guns, resulting in the destruction of seven German destroyers, one of which was finished off by a bomb from Brown's aircraft; he also sank with bombs the German submarine *U-64* in Herjangsfjord.

In 1940, as production of the Fairey Fulmar fleet fighter increased at Fairey's Hayes factory, responsibility for the Swordfish was taken over entirely by Blackburn Aircraft Limited at Sherburn-in-Elmet, Yorkshire, the first aircraft being completed on 29 December. After 300 Mk Is had been delivered in nine months, Blackburn production switched to the Mk II with strengthened lower wing with metal skin to permit the carriage of eight rocket projectiles. The provision for interchangeability of wheel and float landing gear was discarded after termination of the Mk I production.

Mk Is continued in service throughout 1940, and once again it was Lieutenant Commander Brown who provided excellent spotting services for HMS *Warspite*'s main armament in the action off Calabria against the Italian fleet on 9 July.

Later that year, however, the brilliantly executed attack on the Italian fleet in Taranto harbour on 11 November constituted the pinnacle on which the Swordfish's fame was forever to stand. Following a remarkable feat of low-level reconnaissance by a Maryland crew which disclosed a concentration of Italian naval vessels in the port, it was decided to launch a night strike by the Swordfish of Nos 813, 815, 819 and 824 Squadrons from HMS *Illustrious* (Rear Admiral Lumley Lyster, himself an experienced naval pilot who had served at Taranto during World War 1). Led by Lieutenant Commander Kenneth Williamson, the first wave of 12 aircraft (six with torpedoes, four with bombs and two with bombs and flares) was launched 10 minutes before a second wave of nine aircraft (five with torpedoes, two with bombs and two with bombs and flares) led by Lieutenant

Fairey Swordfish variants

Fairey TSR 1: one prototype to Specification S.9/30; Pegasus IIM of 635 hp (474 kW); crashed from spin and destroyed
Fairey TSR II: one prototype (K4190) to Specification S.15/33; Pegasus IIIM3 of 775 hp (578 kW); first flight 17 April 1934
Fairey Swordfish Mk I: to Specification S.38/34, and powered by Pegasus IIIM3 of 690 hp (515 kW) (three prototypes, K5660-K5662 being completed as floatplane)
Fairey Swordfish Mk I: Fairey production 1935–40, with Pegasus IIIM3; all convertible to floatplanes; K,L and P serials (689 built)
Fairey Swordfish Mk I: Blackburn production 1940–

1, aircraft as Fairey-built Mk Is; V serials (300 built)
Fairey Swordfish Mk II: Blackburn production 1941–4, with Pegasus 30 of 750 hp (560 kW); wheel landing gear only and metal-covered lower wings; W, DK, HS, LS, NE and NF serials (1,080 built, some later converted to Swordfish Mk IV with enclosed cockpit)
Fairey Swordfish Mk III: Blackburn production 1944, with Pegasus 30; wheel landing gear only; ASV radar (most aircraft with provision for rocket projectiles); FF, NF, NR and NS serials (327 built, many converted to Swordfish Mk IV with enclosed cockpit)
Fairey Swordfish Mk IV: conversions from Mks II and III with enclosed cockpit

An enclosed-cockpit, Blackburn-built Swordfish Mk II of No. 1 Naval Air Gunnery School, Canada, in 1944. Although a feature more usually associated with later Swordfish versions, the cockpit canopy on this aircraft would have been added as part of the winterizing modifications available in 1944.

The only two RAF squadrons to fly Swordfish on a regular basis were Nos 119 and 202. Painted black overall and carrying ASV radar and 250-lb (113-kg) bombs, the Swordfish Mk IIIs of No. 119 Sqn (NF410, shown here, was based at Knocke/Le Zoute, Belgium, early in 1945) were used against enemy E- and R-boats operating off the Dutch coast.

148 Vickers gun trough
149 Fuselage forward frame
150 Oil cooler
151 Fuel filter
152 Stub plane/fuselage attachment
153 Fuel feed lines
154 Dinghy immersion switch
155 Exhaust
156 Port Dunlop mainwheel
157 Jacking foot
158 1,610-lb (730-kg) 18-in (45.7-cm) torpedo
159 Access/servicing footholds
160 Torpedo forward crutch
161 Radius rod fairing
162 Undercarriage axle tube fairing
163 Undercarriage oleo leg fairing
164 Starboard mainwheel
165 Hub cover
166 Underwing bombs
167 Underwing outboard shackles
168 Depth-charge
169 250-lb (113-kg) bomb
170 Anti-shipping flares

183

Blackburn-built Swordfish Mk II, HS275, of No. 1 Naval Air Gunnery School, Yarmouth, Nova Scotia, 1943. By this stage in the war most Swordfish had acquired a wide variety of camouflage schemes, that shown here being fairly commonplace.

Commander John Hale. Achieving almost total tactical surprise, the Swordfish crews attacked at low level, sinking the new 35,000-ton battleship *Littorio* at her moorings, and crippling the two older battleships *Conte di Cavour* and *Caio Duilio*, as well as a heavy cruiser and a destroyer. At a single stroke Italy's naval power in the Mediterranean was reduced by a half, at a cost of two Swordfish (Williamson himself being shot down and taken prisoner). A postscript to this attack lay in the fact that the Japanese naval attaché in Rome was recalled to Tokyo and became the architect of the Japanese attack on Pearl Harbour one year later.

Thereafter, and for many months to come, Fleet Air Arm Swordfish, based on Malta, became the scourge of Axis shipping in the Mediterranean, between them sinking more than a million and a half tons of German and Italian ships during 1941–3. Among their other widely varying tasks in that theatre were minelaying, fleet reconnaissance, gunnery spotting, coastal bombing attacks and even agent-dropping. One Swordfish is recorded as having flown 12 minelaying sorties in a single 24-hour period.

The attack on *Bismarck*

The most famous of all Swordfish pilots now joins the story. Lieutenant Commander Eugene Esmonde, a peacetime Imperial Airways pilot from Ireland, and who now commanded a Swordfish squadron aboard HMS *Victorious*, led a torpedo attack by nine aircraft on the German battleship *Bismarck* at large in the Atlantic on 26 May 1941 as it made its way towards Brest. The attack resulted in at least one vital hit, which crippled the vessel's steering mechanism, thereby allowing the British fleet to catch and sink her. Esmonde was awarded the DSO for his part in the operation, and now joined HMS *Ark Royal* in the Mediterranean; however, when the carrier was torpedoed he managed to fly off all his Swordfish and make for Gibraltar before the ship sank.

By the end of the year Esmonde was stationed in Kent, commanding No. 825 Squadron, deployed to counter any attempt by the German warships *Scharnhorst* and *Gneisenau* to break out of Brest and escape up the English Channel to Germany. On 12 February 1942 the worst British fears were realized when the German ships evaded all patrols and reached the eastern end of the Channel before being spotted. Esmonde's six Swordfish were thus the only aircraft readily available for an initial strike. Flying from Manston, the Swordfish crews missed their fighter rendezvous but pressed home their attack in the face of overwhelming enemy fighter and flak defences. Esmonde, in a Swordfish Mk II (W5984), was himself one of the first to be shot down by a Focke-Wulf Fw 190, followed by all five of his fellow pilots; none of their torpedoes found their mark. Of the 18 crew members only five survived to be rescued from the sea and all received the DSO or CGM. Esmonde was awarded a posthumous Victoria Cross.

Meanwhile efforts had been made to speed a replacement

A formation of early Swordfish Mk Is in November 1938 from the second and third production batches; these aircraft had provision for interchangeable wheel and float undercarriage. The aircraft shown here were clearly squadron aircraft, although probably not embarked in a carrier (note absence of fuselage chevron).

Originally referred to as the Fairey TSR 2, the prototype Swordfish, K4190, was designed and built to Specification S.15/33 and carried the Fairey works no. F2038 in small characters aft of the service serial number on the rear fuselage.

One of the last working examples of the Fairey Swordfish is now owned by the Fleet Air Arm Museum in Yeovilton, and regularly appears at air displays in the UK. (*Photo: Air Portraits*).

A Swordfish Mk 1, K5972, of the initial Fairey-built production batch in the markings of No. 823 Sqn, embarked in HMS *Glorious* in 1936. The fin stripes identify the Flight aircraft.

for the now-famous old 'Stringbag' biplane. The Fairey Albacore had been in production for some months but never lived up to its modest expectations (800 were produced, but manufacture stopped in 1943, while that of the Swordfish continued for a further year). The Fairey Barracuda (a Merlin-powered monoplane) for all its grotesque appearance might have had a distinguished career had it not been severely delayed after the abandoning of its original Rolls-Royce Exe engine.

Later Blackfish

As it was, Blackburn continued to produce Swordfish Mk IIs (known locally as 'Blackfish') until 1944, completing the last of 1,080 examples on 22 February that year. Production then switched to the Mk III, which was fitted with a large ASV scanner between the landing gear legs, thereby preventing carriage of the torpedo; when employed on anti-shipping torpedo strikes it was normal practice for one Mk III to assume the search role, while Mk IIs in the strike unit carried bombs and torpedoes. Swordfish were widely used aboard

the relatively small escort carriers which were hurriedly introduced for convoy duties, particularly in the North Atlantic in the mid-war years, their normal complement of six Swordfish and six Grumman Martlet fighters being permanently ranged on their steeply pitching decks at the mercy of the elements.

The final version was the Mk IV, retrospectively modified Mk IIs and Mk IIIs with a rudimentary cockpit enclosure, and this version continued in service until the end of the war in Europe. A small number of Swordfish were sent to Canada for operational and training purposes, some serving with No. 1 Naval Air Gunnery School at Yarmouth, Nova Scotia.

The last Mk III (N204) was completed on 18 August 1944 in Sherburn, and on 28 June 1945 a Swordfish was the last biplane to fly a solo mission for the Fleet Air Arm. By 1967 there were only six complete Swordfish left out of the 2,396 production aircraft built. One of these (LS326, previously registered as G-AJVH), is still in working order and often makes appearances at air displays in England.

This Swordfish, the same aircraft as that pictured on the previous page, is taxying during a display by the Fleet Air Arm Memorial Flight. The aft navigators' compartment must have seemed frighteningly exposed during World War 2 actions.

PBY Catalina: Ocean Patroller

Designed in 1935, the PBY transformed the oceanic patrolling capability of the US Navy. It was evaluated and purchased for the RAF before the war and was also built under licence in the Soviet Union; as a result, there were more Catalinas than any other flying-boat in history. And nearly 50 years after its inception, it still flies many oceans.

The Consolidated Catalina was one of the slowest fighters of World War 2. It was jokingly said of this plane that there was no point in its crew using a stop watch to rendezvous with a convoy because it took a whole month to get to its destination. It was already flying in 1935 and therefore, even when war broke out, it was not a young aircraft. What was more, the US Navy had ordered the next generation of flying boat, the Martin PBM, to replace the Catalina, even before the war. But the much-loved 'Cat' did not accept defeat that easily. In 1938 the Soviet Union had declared that it was better than anything built by their own factories, and throughout the war it was built under licence in Russia. Furthermore, the original American craft lived on in many new versions and more of these were sold during the war than the newer machines that replaced them.

The genesis of the PBY, as the aircraft was known to US forces, lay in a 1933 requirement by the US Navy for a new long-range patrol flying-boat. At that time the principal aircraft in this category was the Consolidated P2Y, designed at Buffalo by Isaac M. 'Mac' Laddon, a gifted seaplane engineer and a director of Consolidated Aircraft. To meet the new demand he cleaned up the P2Y by giving it an almost cantilever wing mounted above the shallow but broad hull on a central pylon housing the flight engineer. The wing differed from that of the P2Y in having a rectangular centre section and tapered outer panels, all of stressed-skin all-metal construction (ailerons were fabric-skinned). A unique feature was that the wing-tip floats were mounted on pivoted frames which could be retracted electrically so that in flight the floats formed the wingtips. The hull, likewise all-metal, was quite different from that of most large boats in being all on one deck, with a broad semicircular top. In the bows was a mooring compartment and transparent sighting window with a venetian blind giving seawater protection. The bow cockpit was a turret with large all-round windows in pro-

A US Navy PBY-5A pictured in 1944 over the Aleutians. In areas such as this, with consistent bad weather, the range and endurance of these reliable amphibious boats brought many crews to a safe landing either on land or water.

One of the more unusual aircraft handed over from the inventory of the US Army Air Force to the newly formed USAF in October 1947 was this OA-10A amphibian of the Air Rescue Service. Built during the war by Canadian Vickers, it was one of a batch of 230 which served from early 1944 on several fronts and remained in the active inventory until at least 1954. After the war they were unarmed, but were otherwise broadly similar to the PBY-5A to which the specification applies. In the European theatre the RAF handled air/sea rescue, but from the start of 1945 the USAAF used the OA-10A in the 5th Emergency Rescue Squadron, together with the P-47 and lifeboat-dropping B-17G.

Consolidated PBY Catalina

Specification

Consolidated PBY-5A (OA-10A)
Type: long-range patrol and rescue amphibian (PBY, anti-submarine)
Powerplant: two 1,200-hp (895-kW) Pratt & Whitney R-1830-92 Twin Wasp radial piston engines
Performance: maximum speed 175 mph (282 km/h); patrol speed 113 mph (182 km/h); initial climb rate 620 ft (189 m) per minute; service ceiling 13,000 ft (3960 m); range with full military load 2,350 miles (3782 km)
Weights: empty (typical) 20,910 lb (9485 kg); maximum take-off 35,420 lb (16067 kg)
Dimensions: span 104 ft 0 in (31.7 m); length 63 ft 10 in (19.47 m); height 20 ft 2 in (6.15 m); wing area 1,400 sq ft (130 m²)
Armament: one 0.5-in (12.7-mm) machine-gun in each waist blister, one or two 0.3-in (7.62-mm) machine-guns in bow turret and one 0.3-in (7.62 mm) machine-gun in rear ventral hatch, plus up to four stores of 1,000 lb (454 kg) each on wing racks

Consolidated PBY Catalina

This Catalina IVA from Royal Air Force No. 210 Squadron shows the standard colour scheme for maritime patrol aircraft of Coastal Command from 1942 onwards. This particular machine has ASV Mk II radar without the dipole aerial array on the hull. One 'Cat' skipper from No. 210 won a VC and another sank the Command's last U-boat.

duction aircraft, with a machine-gun above. Two pilots sat side-by-side in the wide cockpit with large windows all round. Aft of the wing were left and right gunner's stations each with a sliding hatch. Unlike the P2Y the tail was clean and simple, with the horizontal tail mounted well up the single fin. The powerplant switched from Cyclones to the new two-row Pratt & Whitney Twin Wasp, neatly cowled on the centre section with cooling gills and driving Hamilton variable-pitch propellers.

Designated Consolidated Model 28, the new boat received the US Navy designation XP3Y-1, the prototype (BuAer number 9459) flying from Lake Erie on 28 March 1935. It proved to be an excellent aircraft, though tests at Coco Solo (Panama Canal Zone) showed the need for a larger rudder. The new Douglas XP3D-1 was also good, but the Consolidated boat was cheaper, at $90,000, and an order for 60 was placed on 29 June 1935. The designation was changed to PBY-1 because of the increase in underwing weapon load to 2,000 lb (907 kg). Defensive armament comprised four 0.5-in (7.62-mm) Browning machine-guns, one in the manual nose turret, one in each waist position and the fourth in a tunnel hatch which was located on the underside of the rear fuselage.

With the massive order for 60, Consolidated had plenty of work to support its 2,000-mile (3220-km) move to San Diego, in southern California, where weather was fine all through the year. In October 1935 the XP3Y made a non-stop flight of almost 3,500 miles (5633 km) from Coco Solo to San

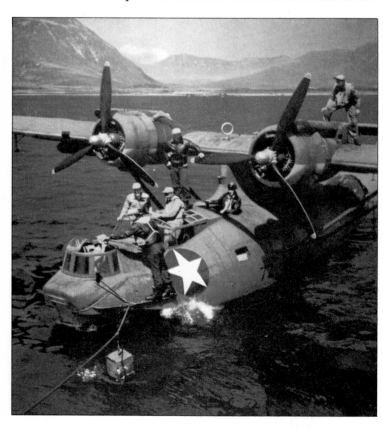

An original colour photograph taken at about the time of the start of the long Aleutians campaign in early 1942 shows a PBY-5 of the US Navy before slipping its moorings for a patrol. A pair of bombs can be seen under the wing (maximum load was four at 1,000-lb [454-kg]). Defensive guns would be two 0.3-in (7.62-mm) and two 0.5-in (12.7-mm). The photographer picked an unusually sunny, clear day.

NZ4017 was one of a batch of Boeing-built PB2B-1 Catalinas, approximately equivalent to the PBY-5, which were supplied under the Lend-Lease Act to the Royal New Zealand Air Force in 1943–4. Equipped with ASV radar transmitters on the wings, it served in the South West Pacific theatre until after VJ-Day.

Consolidated PBY-5A Catalina cutaway drawing key

1 Starboard tailplane
2 Tailplane leading edge de-icing
3 Tail navigation light
4 Starboard fabric-covered elevator
5 Elevator tab
6 Rudder trim tab
7 Fabric-covered rudder construction
8 Tailcone
9 Elevator push-pull control rod
10 Rudder control horn
11 Tail mooring point
12 Lower fin structure integral with tail fuselage
13 Tailplane centre section attachment
14 Upper fin construction

15 Aerial cables
16 Fin leading edge de-icing
17 Port tailplane
18 Cooling air intake
19 Rear fuselage frame and stringer construction
20 Ventral tunnel gun hatch
21 0.3-in (7.62-mm) machine gun
22 Fuselage skin plating
23 Target-towing reel
24 Flare launch tube
25 Rear fuselage bulkhead
26 Bulkhead door
27 0.5-in (12.7-mm) beam machine gun
28 Starboard beam gun cupola
29 Cupola opening side window
30 Flexible gun mounting
31 Port beam gun cupola
32 Gunner's folding seat
33 Semi-circular gun platform
34 Walkway
35 Hull bottom V-frames
36 Wardroom bulkhead
37 Crew rest bunks
38 Wardroom
39 Starboard mainwheel
40 Hull planing bottom step

41 Planing bottom construction
42 Fuselage skin plating
43 Mainwheel housing
44 Hydraulic retraction jack
45 Telescopic leg strut
46 Fore and aft wing support struts
47 Wing mounting centre pylon construction
48 Pylon tail fairing
49 Starboard wing integral fuel tank, capacity 875 US gal (3312 litres)
50 Fuel jettison pipe
51 1000-lb (454-kg) bomb
52 Smoke generator tank
53 Trailing edge ribs
54 Fabric covered trailing edge
55 Rear spar
56 Aileron trim tab
57 Starboard retractable wing-tip float
58 Float support struts
59 Retraction linkage
60 Fabric-covered starboard aileron
61 Static discharge wicks
62 Wing-tip aerial mast
63 Float up-lock
64 Float leg housing
65 Starboard navigation light

66 Leading edge de-icing boot
67 Float retracting gear
68 Front spar
69 Wing rib-stringer construction
70 ASV radar aerial
71 Outer wing panel attachment joint
72 Wing lattice ribs
73 Bomb carrier and release unit
74 Two 500-lb (227-kg) bombs
75 Leading-edge nose ribs
76 Position of pitot tube on port wing
77 Landing lamp
78 Landing lamp glare shield
79 Starboard engine nacelle fairing
80 Hydraulic accumulator
81 Engine oil tank
82 Fireproof bulkhead
83 Exhaust stub
84 Engine bearer struts
85 Detachable engine cowlings
86 Curtiss Electric three-bladed constant-speed propeller, 12-ft (3.66-m) diameter
87 Propeller hub pitch-change mechanism

88 Pratt & Whitney R-1830-92 Twin Wasp two-row radial engine
89 Aerial cable lead-in
90 D/F loop aerial
91 Oil cooler
92 Control runs through pylon front fairing
93 Pylon step
94 Engineer's control panel
95 Flight engineer's seat
96 Wing mounting fuselage main frame
97 Radio and radar control units
98 Cabin heater
99 Front cabin walkway
100 Port main undercarriage leg strut
101 Torque scissor links
102 Port mainwheel
103 Mk 13-2 torpedo
104 450-lb (204-kg) depth charge
105 Forward fuselage frame construction
106 Navigator's seat
107 Radio/radar operator's seat
108 Radio rack
109 Cabin side window
110 Autopilot servo controller
111 Navigator's chart table
112 Fuselage chine member
113 Cockpit bulkhead
114 Co-pilot's seat
115 Pilot's seat
116 Pilot's electrical control panel

117 Sliding side window
118 Engine cowling cooling air gills
119 Port engine nacelle
120 Cockpit roof escape hatch
121 Overhead throttle and propeller controls
122 Windscreen wipers
123 Curved windscreens
124 Instrument panel
125 Control column yoke and handwheels
126 Rudder pedals
127 Cockpit flooring
128 Nose undercarriage hatch doors
129 Nosewheel bay
130 Port aileron
131 Nosewheel
132 Port retractable wing-tip float
133 Float support struts
134 Port navigation light
135 Leading edge de-icing boot
136 Nosewheel forks
137 Nose undercarriage retraction jack
138 Front gunner/bomb aimer's station
139 Curtained bulkhead
140 Gunner's footboards
141 Spare ammunition containers
142 Front rotating gun turret
143 0.3-in (7.62-mm) machine gun
144 Bomb aimer's instrument panel
145 Drift sight
146 Bomb aiming window with protective blind
147 Anchor cable

This Catalina was the third of a batch of 36 GR.IIAs produced by Canadian Vickers, ex-RCAF and the only ones of this species. They were assigned mainly to No. 209 Squadron, the original Catalina operator, after having been fitted with ASV.II radar complete with the hull-mounted dipole aerials ahead of the struts.

Shown in 1942 markings, this PBY-5 was supplied to the Royal Australian Air Force and assigned to No. 11 Squadron. It was one of a batch of 18 ordered as a commercial sale before the Lend-Lease Act became law. British ASV radar was fitted in 1942 (on this aircraft without the wing-mounted transmitter aerials).

Francisco. It then went on to participate in the dedication of the giant new San Diego plant on 20 October before returning to Buffalo to be modified to PBY standard with a broad rounded rudder, de-icer boots on all leading edges (with pull-out steps up the leading edge of the fin), full armament and combat equipment. It flew again in March 1936 and reached US Navy squadron VP-11F at the same time as the first production machines in October 1936. Unquestionably this was the best patrol flying-boat in the world at that time.

In July 1936 Consolidated received a contract for 50 PBY-2s with all four wing racks stressed to 1,000-lb (454-kg) loads and with 0.5-in (12.7-mm) guns in the waist positions. In November 1936 an order followed for 66 PBY-3s with R-1830-66 Twin Wasps uprated from 900 to 1,000 hp (671 to 746 kW), and in December 1937 a contract followed for 33 PBY-4s, all but one with large bulged transparent blisters instead of lateral sliding hatches for the beam gunners and with 1,050-hp (783-k/W) engines. Two more PBYs were sold in 1937 to explorer Dr Richard Archbold, who named them *Guba I* and *Guba II* (Motu word for a sudden storm). *Guba II* spent an arduous year in New Guinea, finally making the first flight across the Indian Ocean to survey the route known in World War 2 as the 'horseshoe route' on which hundreds of military and BOAC Catalinas were to fly. It then crossed Africa and the Atlantic, the first aircraft to circle the globe near the Equator. *Guba I* was sold to a Soviet expedition led

by Sir Hubert Wilkins which flew 19,000 miles (30600 km) through the worst weather in the world fruitlessly searching for S. A. Levanevskii, who vanished near the North Pole on 13 August 1937. So outstanding was the Model 28 in this work that the Model 28-2 was put into production at Taganrog on the Azov Sea as the GST (civil transport version, MP-7), over 1,000 being used in World War 2 with 950-hp (709-kW) M-62 engines in Polikarpov I-16 type shuttered cowlings and with Soviet equipment and armament.

Another Model 28-5 (PBY-4) was bought by the British Air Ministry and tested at Felixtowe as RAF P9630, proving so outstanding that it was adopted as a standard boat for Coastal Command. Named Catalina I – a name later adopted by the US Navy – the first RAF variant was similar to the latest US Navy type, the PBY-5 with 1,200-hp (895-kW) R-1830-92 engines, an order for 200 of which had been placed on 20 December 1939. No flying-boat – in fact no large US Navy aircraft – had ever been ordered in such quantities, and the vast open-ended British orders called for massive extra capacity. British officials helped arrange for licence production by Canadian Vickers at Cartierville (Montreal) and Boeing of Canada at Vancouver. The San Diego plant also much more than doubled in size and was joined by an even larger plant a mile down the road building B-24s.

Amphibian conversion

On 22 November 1939 Consolidated flew a PBY-4 rebuilt as the XPBY-5A with retractable tricycle landing gear. This excellent amphibian conversion was a great success and had only a minor effect on performance. The final 33 PBY-5s were completed as PBY-5As, and another 134 were ordered in November 1940. At the time of Pearl Harbor (7 December 1941) the US Navy had three squadrons of PBY-3s, two of PBY-4s and no fewer than 16 flying the new PBY-5. Before sunrise on that day a PBY crew spotted the periscope of a Japanese submarine at Pearl Harbor, marked it with smoke and guided the destroyer USS *Ward*, which sank it – the first US shots of World War 2, over an hour before the air attack began.

By this time a further 586 PBY-5s had been ordered, and the export list had risen to: Australia 18, Canada 50, France 30 and the Netherlands East Indies 36. In 1942 another 627 PBY-5As were added, of which 56 were to be OA-10s for the USAAF, used for search and rescue. The first Lend-Lease batch for the RAF comprised 225 non-amphibious PBY-5Bs (Catalina IAs) followed by 97 Catalina IVAs fitted in Britain with ASV Mk II radar. RAF Catalinas usually had a Vickers K (VGO) machine-gun in the bow and twin 0.303-in (7.7-mm) Brownings in the waist blisters.

This PBY-1 of VP-12, the second squadron of the US Navy to receive these boats in 1937, shows the appearance of the pre-war version with sliding rear hatches instead of blisters. Pre-war aircraft were finished in silver or natural metal.

An unusual stern view of a US Navy PBY-5 shows the waist gunners (who appear to have non-standard installations of 0.5-in/12.7-mm guns, with saddle-type ammunition boxes). This close-up shows how the rudder, almost divided into upper and lower halves, swings across a fixed portion of tailplane.

Based on a PBY-6A, this Catalina is one of a substantial number modified in the immediate post-war era for use as civilian water-bombers to fight forest fires, mainly on the US West Coast and in Canada. They were the ancestors of today's purpose-designed Canadair CL-215, which has a similar layout but engines of twice the power.

Operational with the RAF

RAF Catalina operations began in spring 1941 with Nos 209 and 210 Squadrons, and one of the first to become operational was a machine of No. 209 from Castle Archdale which on 26 May 1941 was far out over the Atlantic, with the crew under Pilot Officer Briggs being checked out by a 'neutral' lieutenant in the US Navy. Suddenly they spotted a giant warship; it was the *Bismarck*, which had eluded all pursuers for 31½ hours. Despite heavy flak the Catalina radioed the battleship's position and kept her in view until another Catalina from No. 240 Squadron took over and guided the British fleet to the spot. Apart from this epic, almost all Coastal Command missions by over 650 Catalinas were against U-boats, many of the 15- to 20-hour trips ending at Grasnaya (Murmansk) and Arkhangelsk protecting convoys supplying the Soviet Union. The only shortcoming of the Catalina was that its slow speed often gave a U-boat time to dive after being spotted. By 1943 they stayed on the surface, bristling with guns, and two Catalina skippers won the VC, one posthumously, for pressing home their attacks on heavily armed U-boats under almost unbelievable conditions.

Black Cats

Life was equally tough in the Pacific where the Catalina was from 7 December 1941 by far the most important US patrol aircraft. In the northern campaign along the Aleutians many Catalinas had to make overloaded downwind take-offs in blizzards at night, with ice over the windscreen. The PBY was the first US aircraft (other than the obsolete Douglas B-18) to carry radar. They fulfilled diverse missions including those of torpedo-bomber, transport and glider-tug. Perhaps the most famous of all Catalinas were the Black Cat PBY-5A amphibians which, painted matt black, roamed the western

Pacific from December 1942 finding Japanese ships of all kinds by radar at night and picking up Allied survivors from ships and aircraft in boats and dinghies. In addition to radar, bombs, depth charges and fragmentation grenades, the Black Cats often carried crates of empty beer bottles whose eerie whistling descent deterred Japanese gunners and caused wasted time looking for unexploded bombs.

By late 1941 the Cartierville plant was in full production. Canadian Vickers delivered 230 amphibians ordered as PBV-1As but actually passed to the USAAF as OA-10As, as well as 149 Canso I amphibians for the RCAF. Boeing, which came on stream later, built 240 PB2B-1 flying-boats, mainly as Catalina IVBs for the RAF, RAAF and RNZAF, and 17 Catalinas and 55 Cansos for the RCAF. Yet a further plant was brought into the programme in 1941 to produce its own improved models. The NAF (Naval Aircraft Factory) at Philadelphia had been the source of all US Navy flying-boat designs, and its experience enabled it to improve on 'Mac' Laddon's design in a way that could have been done by the parent company had it not been for the frantic demand for production. The NAF Catalina, the PBN-1, had a restressed wing for 38,000-lb (17237-kg) gross weight, with increased tankage, redesigned wing-tip floats and struts, and a new hull with a longer and sharper bow, 20° step amidships, and rear step extended about 5 ft (1.52 m) aft; most obvious of the changes was the tall vertical tail, with a horn-balanced rudder, and armament was generally increased to three or more 0.5-in (12.7-mm) machine-guns (only the ventral tunnel retained the rifle-calibre gun) with a rounded bow turret and improved continuous-feed magazines. Another change was a redesigned electrical system of increased capacity, with the batteries moved from the leading edge down to the hull.

The NAF itself delivered 138 PBN-1 Nomads, and Consolidated (by this time Convair) opened yet another plant at New Orleans to build the best Catalina of all, the amphibious version of the PBN. Called PBY-6A, this usually carried a

This PBY-6A, US Navy number 46648, was one of the last Catalinas built, and one of the few delivered from the Consolidated-Vultee plant at New Orleans. Among their many modifications were the improved hull, tail and floats of the PBN-1, plus pylon-mounted radar and a new nose turret with twin 0.5-in (12.7-mm) guns.

Typical of the ultimate form of Catalina, remaining in use after World War 2, this PBY-6A served until the late 1950s with the Royal Danish air force (Flyvevåbnet) No. 721 Squadron at Vaerlose, mainly in the maritime rescue role. After the war a different radar was fitted and the bow was remodelled without the turret.

centimetric radar in a neat pod above the cockpit, and the bow turret usually had twin 0.5-in (12.7-mm) guns. An order was placed for 900, but the end of the war cut this to 48 for the Soviet Union (which also received all but one of the PBNs), 75 as OA-10Bs for the USAAF and 112 for the US Navy. Fifty more were delivered by Boeing from Vancouver as PB2B-2s, designated Catalina VI by the RAF.

Total production of all versions of the Consolidated Model 28 considerably exceeded 4,000. Of these 2,398 were delivered by Consolidated Aircraft and Convair (the March 1943 name for the merged Consolidated and Vultee-Stinson companies). Some 892 were built in Canada and by the two Canadian plants, and about 1,500 built in Russia.

After the war most users of the Catalina continued to operate the type. In the Soviet Union the GST remained the chief patrol boat until replaced by the Beriev Be-6 in 1950–3, but continued in fishery protection and other offshore roles until 1959. Likewise the lower-powered (870-hp/649-kW M-62IR) MP-7 transport remained in civil use until at least 1958. The RAF withdrew Lend-Lease aircraft after VJ-Day, but the USN continued to use flying-boat and amphibious versions until after 1950. In the 1950s the Naval Reserve and Coast Guard used the PBY-6A and the JSAAF and USAF used the OA-10B in most cases in the air-sea rescue role with an airborne lifeboat under each wing. France and Israel made important use of the Catalina in the 1950s, together with Argentina, Brazil, Ecuador, Dominica, Indonesia, Nationalist China, Mexico and Peru. The last active PBY-6A was retired from NARTU (Naval Air Reserve Training Unit), Atlanta, Georgia, on 3 January 1957. Canada, Australia and New Zealand retained Catalinas of various marks after 1960, and the last in service was Latin American air forces were retired in 1965–6.

Post-war Catalinas found wide employment as civil transports and water bombers for firefighting. The amphibious variants were in special demand, at one time more than 80 being in use by Latin American civil operators (headed by Panair do Brasil which used them on a major network with 22 passenger seats). Some dozen served mainly as freighters in North America, and the water bomber was the first aircraft able to scoop up a load and dump it on a forest fire.

One disadvantage of the later, heavier versions of the Catalina, which was criticised, perhaps justly, was its inadequate engine performance, particularly when one engine stopped working. Various American companies, including Timmins and Steward-Davis, offered conversions or conversion packages to improve the performance and reliability

of the aircraft with a heavier payload. In 1966 the Bird Innovator led to a bigger change. The Bird Corporation, the largest manufacturer of respirators for medical purposes, was using a PBY-5A as a company aircraft. To improve its performance, the company mounted two 340-hp (254 kW) Lycoming piston engines on the outer wing sections, strengthened the tailplane, increased the fuel capacity, rebuilt the tail fin and with other alterations the four-engined Catalina could cruise at 200 mph (322 kmph).

Catalina variants

Consolidated 28 XP3Y-1: original prototype; two 825-hp (615-kW) Pratt & Whitney R-1830-58 Twin Wasp engines.; redesignated XPBY-1 after modification
Consolidated PNY-1: first production model, 900-hp (671-kW) R-1830-64 engines
Consolidated PBY-2: various modifications
Consolidated PBY-3: two 1,000-hp (746-kW) R-1830-66 and other changes
Consolidated PBY-4: two 1,050-hp (783-kW) R-1830-72 and other changes, e.g. waist blisters
Consolidated PBY-5: two 1,200-hp (895-kW) R-1830-92 and numerous other changes, e.g. further modified vertical tail (RAF Catalina I and II)
Consolidated PBY-5A: retractable tricycle landing gear (RCAF: Canso; RAF: Catalina III; USAAF: OA-10 and OA-10A
NAF PBN-1: revised design by Naval Aircraft Factory (USAAF: OA-10B)
Consolidated PBY-6A: amphibian version of PBN
Consolidated PB2B-1: Boeing-built PBY-5 (RAF/RAAF/RNZAF: Catalina IVB)
Consolidated PB2B-2: Boeing-built PBY-6A (RAF/RAAF: Catalina VI)
GST: Licence-built version in Soviet Union, two 950-hp (709-kW) M-62
MP-7: civil transport version of GST; two 850-hp (634-kW) M-621R

Even today a considerable number (probably more than 100) of Catalina flying-boats and amphibians are still in operation. One of these survivors is OB-T-051 of Lorasa (Loretana de Aviaçion SA) of Peru. It is a PBY-5A, used for charters and for passenger and cargo services. Note the spats of a Cessna Skyhawk parked just beyond.

194

Douglas DC-3/C-47/Dakota: world workhorses

The Douglas C-47 and its numerous derivatives has for nearly half a century remained the most versatile workhorse aviation has known. Born in the brassy years of the American mid-1930s as the Douglas DC-3, it became the standard pre-war airliner, went to war in uniform the world over, and returned to civilian clothes afterwards.

In the middle of 1935 C. R. Smith, then President of American Airlines, ordered a larger and more luxurious version of the DC-2 from Douglas, so as to gain the upper hand over competing companies with their Boeing 247s and DC-2s.

The project leader at Douglas, Fred Stineman, had his team design a new type of aircraft known as the Douglas Sleeper Transport, with 14 sleeping berths. Soon, however, it was realised that if 21 seats were installed instead, and a pair of

The Finnish Air Force was still using four Douglas C-47s in its Transport Flight at Utti in 1983.

Douglas C-47 Skytrain

Specification

Douglas C-47 Skytrain

Type: cargo, supply or 21/28-seat troop transport, 14-litter ambulance, or glider tug

Powerplant: two 1,200-hp (895-kW) Pratt & Whitney R-1830-92 radial piston engines

Performance: maximum speed 227 mph (365 km/h) at 7,500 ft (2285 m); initial climb rate 940 ft (287 m) per minute; service ceiling 24,000 ft (7315 m); range 1,600 miles (2575 km)

Weights: empty 18,200 lb (8256 kg); maximum take-off 26,000 lb (11794 kg)

Dimensions: span 95 ft 6 in (29.11 m); length 63 ft 9 in (19.43 m); height 17 ft 0 in (5.18 m); wing area 987 sq ft (91.69 m²)

Payload: 8,000 lb (3629 kg) to 10,000 lb (4536 kg) of military cargo (depending on aircraft variant)

General Eisenhower is on record as having stated that the C-47 was one of the four principal instruments of Allied victory in World War 2 (the others being the bazooka, Jeep and atom bomb). Typical example of the Skytrain was this C-47A-65-DL of the 81st Troop Carrier Squadron, 436th Troop Carrier Group, based at Membury in England between 3 March 1944 and February 1945 (it also took part in the airborne assault on Southern France, based at Voltone, Italy, during July and August 1944). The mission tally on 'Buzz Buggy', together with invasion stripes, suggest participation in the Normandy, South France, Nijmegen and Bastogne operations, both as a paratrooper and glider tug.

One of the 98 US Navy R4D-8s, modified to 'Super DC-3' standard with swept wings, lengthened fuselage, enlarged tail and fully enclosed undercarriage. Redesignated the C-117D, this version had a top speed of 270 mph (435 km/h).

The RCAF contributed three Article VI transport squadrons with Dakotas (Nos 435, 436 and 437) to the RAF during World War 2, the first two in the Far East and No. 437 in Europe. Shown here is an RCAF Dakota used for training pilots in airborne forces duties.

Wright Cyclone 900 hp (671 kW) engines installed, the increased payload could increase their income by 50% more than the DC-2, with fuel costs rising by only 3%. At 3 p.m. on 17 December 1935, the 32nd anniversary of the Wright Brothers' first flight, the prototype, X14988, set off on its maiden flight from Clover Field (now Santa Monica). It was piloted by Carl A. Cover and still designated DST (Douglas Sleeper Transport).

The prototype entered service as American Airlines' flagship on 11 July 1936 as orders poured in to Douglas. By the end of 1939 the DC-3 (third Douglas Commercial) had joined Braniff, Eastern, Northwest, Pennsylvania-Central, Transcontinental & Western, and United, as well as American in the United States, while overseas KLM was the first to take deliveries, followed by Panagra, Panair do Brasil, LAV, CMA, Australian National, Sweden's ABA, Czechoslovakia's CLS, Swissair, Air France, Sabena, LOT, LARES, and MALERT. Licences to build were negotiated with Nakajima in Japan (the first aircraft being completed on 30 September 1938), and with the Soviet Union, which purchased 18 DC-3s before World War 2 and went on to produce huge numbers which served with Aeroflot and the military, first as the PS-84 and later as the Lisunov Li-2.

When war broke out in Europe most of the commercial airlines reduced their operations and in due course many of the DC-3s of subjugated nations found themselves serving with Lufthansa, while others were seized by the Italians.

Douglas C-47 Dakota IV cutaway drawing key

1 Hinged nose cone access to instruments and controls
2 Rudder pedals
3 Instrument panel
4 Windscreen de-icing fluid spray nozzle
5 Starboard propeller
6 Windscreen panels
7 Co-pilot's seat
8 Engine throttles
9 Control column
10 Cockpit floor level
11 Access panels to control cable runs
12 Pitot static tubes
13 Aerial cables
14 Propeller de-icing fluid tank
15 Pilot's seat
16 Cockpit bulkhead
17 Cockpit roof escape hatch
18 Whip aerial
19 Starboard landing/taxying lamp
20 Windscreen de-icing fluid tank
21 Starboard baggage compartment
22 Electrical fuse panel
23 Crew entry door
24 ADF loop aerial housing
25 Life raft stowage
26 Port baggage compartment
27 Main cabin bulkhead
28 Radio operator's seat
29 Air scoop
30 Heating and ventilating system heat exchanges
31 Astrodome observation hatch

The single Douglas XC-47C (42-5671) of 1943 had Edo amphibious floats, each incorporating two retractable landing wheels and a 300-US gal (1136-litre) fuel tank.

The Argentine air force and navy operate helicopters and fixed wing aircraft in support of that nation's bases in Antarctica, and ski-equipped C-47 of the 1st Escuadron Antartico, Fuerza Aerea Argentina, based at Marambio.

Pending the arrival in service of the two-seat TF-104G Starfighter trainers, the Force Aérienne Belge flew the C-47 with a specially modified nose to accommodate the NASRR radar of the F-104G single-seater to provide an air experience vehicle.

32 Starboard outer wing panel
33 Pneumatic leading-edge de-icing boot
34 Starboard navigation light
35 Starboard aileron
36 Aileron cable controls
37 Trim tab
38 Trim tab control gear
39 Flap control shaft
40 Starboard outer flap
41 Fuselage frame and stringer construction
42 Centre fuselage main frames
43 Centre wing section corrugated inner skin
44 Port main fuel tank, capacity 201 US gal (794 litres)
45 Port auxiliary fuel tank, capacity 210 US gal (760 litres)

46 Wing spar attachments
47 Flap hydraulic jack
48 Centre section flap
49 Floor beam construction
50 Cabin window panels
51 Window panel grommets for small arms attachments
52 Paratroop seating, 28-paratroops
53 Starboard emergency exit window
54 Port emergency exit window
55 Cabin lining panels

56 Overhead heating and ventilating duct
57 Rear cabin frames
58 Fuselage skin plating
59 Rear cabin bulkhead
60 First aid kit
61 Access door to tail controls
62 Fin root fillet
63 Starboard tailplane

64 Starboard elevator
65 Fin leading-edge pneumatic de-icing boot
66 Fin construction
67 Aerial cables
68 Rudder aerodynamic balance
69 Hinge post
70 Rudder construction
71 Fabric covering
72 Rudder trim tab

73 Trim tab control gear
74 Rudder and elevator control horns
75 Fuselage tail fairing
76 Elevator trim tab
77 Port elevator construction
78 Fabric covered elevator
79 Leading-edge pneumatic de-icing boot
80 Tailplane construction
81 Tailplane attachment joint
82 Rudder stop cables
83 Tailplane centre section
84 Tailwheel
85 Shock absorber leg strut
86 Tailwheel mounting plate
87 Tailwheel strut
88 Rudder and elevator control cables
89 Tail fuselage joint frame
90 Toilet

91 Rear freight door
92 Forward freight door
93 Paratroop/passenger door
94 Fuselage stringer construction
95 Freight floor
96 Wing root trailing-edge fillet
97 Inboard split trailing-edge flap
98 Flap shroud construction
99 Fuel filler caps
100 Outer wing panel bolted joint
101 Wing panel joint capping strip
102 Outer split trailing-edge flap
103 Port aileron
104 Aileron fabric covering
105 Detachable wing tip joint rib
106 Port navigation light
107 Leading-edge pneumatic de-icing boot
108 Wing stringer construction
109 Rear spar
110 Centre spar
111 Wing rib construction
112 Front spar
113 Leading-edge nose ribs

114 Leading-edge stringers
115 Port landing/taxiing lamp
116 Port mainwheel
117 Main undercarriage rear strut
118 Shock absorber leg strugs
119 Undercarriage knee joints
120 Exhaust pipe
121 Undercarriage bungee cables
122 Engine nacelle fairing
123 Oil tank capacity 29¼ US gal (109 litres)
124 Undercarriage retraction jack
125 Mainwheel well
126 Engine fireproof bulkhead
127 Engine bearer struts
128 Oil cooler
129 Cooling air exit flaps
130 Exhaust collector pipe
131 Engine air intake
132 Engine cowlings
133 Pratt & Whitney R-1830-90C air-cooled 14-cylinder two-row radial engine
134 Propeller hub pitch change mechanism
135 Hamilton Standard constant speed three-bladed propeller

Douglas DC-3, C-47

A Douglas Dakota III of No. 24 Squadron, RAF. The squadron was strictly speaking a communications unit, based at Hendon during World War 2, and flew Dakotas on mail and VIP services to Malta from 1943 onwards.

Douglas C-47 of the small Arkia Israel Inland Airlines Ltd, shown carrying military recognition markings at the time of the Israeli-Egyptian conflict of 1956 (the Suez Crisis).

In the USA, however, Air Transport Command had, between the wars, grown into a sizeable military carrier, albeit to a great extent employing aircraft leased from commercial operators. Indeed it was not until September 1940 that transport aircraft featured significantly in the procurement programme. At this time an order was placed for 545 DC-3s, to be designated C-47 Skytrain. None of these had been delivered at the time of Pearl Harbor when the total transport inventory consisted of about 50 Douglas C-32s, Douglas C-33s and Douglas C-39s – all military versions of the DC-2. By the end of 1941 military orders had been increased by 70 C-47s and nearly 100 C-53s – the US Army's passenger version. In the meantime the USAAC had established the 50th Transport Wing (on 8 January 1941) to administer all transport duties, this being followed by the 51st, 52nd and 53rd in 1942, the 54th, 60th and 61st in 1943, and the 322nd in 1944. Together these Wings comprised a peak total of 32 Groups, in turn comprising over 190 transport squadrons during the war.

The military C-47 differed from the DC-3 principally in its stronger cabin floor and rear fuselage, large loading doors and 1,200-hp (895-kW) Pratt & Whitney R-1830-92 engines. Utility bucket seats along the cabin walls replaced the airline type, window grommets were inserted to permit the use of small-arms in combat, and the all-up weight increased from 25,000 lb (11340 kg) to 29,300 lb (13290 kg).

Production of the C-47 was undertaken at a new plant at Long Beach, California, a total of 953 being completed before production switched to the C-47A, which differed principally in having a 24-volt electrical system in place of the previous 12-volt system. Long Beach could not cope with the quickly increasing military orders, however, and in 1942 a Douglas-operated plant at Tulsa, Oklahoma, joined the programme, producing 2,099 C-47s while Long Beach completed 2,832. The third major production version was the C-47B, characterized by R-1830-90 or Dash-90B engines with superchargers and extra fuel (originally intended specifically for flight over the 'Hump' in the China-Burma-India theatre); of this variant Long Beach built 300 and Tulsa, 2,808, plus 133 TC-47B trainers with Dash-90C engines. Almost all the 600-odd US Navy R4D Skytrain and Skytrooper transports procured during the war were diverted from US Army contracts, and acquired sub-designations under the overall designation R4D.

In service the C-47 went wherever Allied troops served, being among the first to cross to the UK after the USA's entry to the war. In 1942 Troop Carrier Command was formed to provide mobility for airborne forces, and as a result the C-47 assumed the roles of paratroop transport and glider tug. In the first major Allied airborne assault, the invasion of Sicily in July 1943, C-47s (with a handful of other aircraft types) dropped 4,381 paratroops; in the massive assault on Normandy in June the following year C-47s carried more than 50,000 airborne troops in the first 50 hours.

In the RAF the C-47 and its derivatives were named Dakota (the choice of name being alliterative rather than geographically significant), the Dakota I corresponding to the C-47, the Dakota II to the C-53, the Dakota III to the C-47A and the Dakota IV to the C-47B. Some 1,895 aircraft served with 25 RAF squadrons, first joining No. 31 Squadron on the Burma front in June 1942. It remained with that service until 1950, when it was replaced by the Vickers Valetta.

As transport demands increased, so variations of the basic C-47 proliferated. A float-equipped amphibian, the XC-47C (42-5671) was produced with twin Edo floats each accommodating two retractable wheels and a 300-US gal (1136-litre) fuel tank. The impressed DC-3s were all accorded distinct US Army designations to distinguish between those equipped as 21-seat or 14-berth aircraft, variations in sub-type of Twin Wasp or Cyclone engines, entry and loading door configuration (some had doors on the starboard side of the fuselage), and all-up weight limitations. Most of these ex-airliners were retained for staff transport purposes so as to avoid maintenance and operating complications on the operational squadrons. The ex-DC-3s were designated C-48 to C-52 (with many sub-variants), while the C-53 Skytrooper included not only 193 impressed DC-3s but also many new-built aircraft to airliner standard. The two C-68s were late model DC-3s impressed in 1942, but the four C-84s were early 28-seat DC-3Bs with Wright R-1820-71 engines. The C-117 was a Tulsa-built VIP transport version with 28 seats in an airliner-style cabin; only 17 were completed of a contract for 131 (the remainder being cancelled after VJ-day), some of them having their superchargers removed and being given the designation C-117B. Eleven VC-47 staff transports were restyled C-117Cs, and as late as 1962 were serving as VC-117As and VC-117Bs. Finally there was a strange experiment involving the conversion of a C-47 (41-18496) to a glider, the XCG-17, in an attempt to produce a suitable vehicle for towing behind a C-54 Skymaster.

After the war many Skytrains and Skytroopers were declared surplus and sold to civil operators at home and abroad. The superchargers were removed from the C-47Bs, these aircraft becoming C-47Ds, service staff transports being designated VC-47As and VC-47Ds. When the Military Air Transport Service (MATS) was formed on 1 June 1948, 248

This Douglas C-47 Dakota is still in use, over 50 years after the first flight by this sturdy aircraft type, flying between Antigua and neighbouring islands for Seagreen Air Transport.

Douglas DC-3 of SMB Stage Lines, USA. The DC-3 played an important part in developing a network of national air routes in America during the pre-war period from 1936–41 when air transport increased by 600 per cent, much of it carried in the ubiquitous DC-3s that then dominated airline fleets.

One of the most recent developments in the DC-3 story is the re-engineering of existing airframes with three Pratt & Whitney PT6A-45 turboprops giving improved performance in high altitude/high temperature conditions. But despite these enhancements few significant sales have been made. It is known as the Conroy Tri-Turbo 3.

C-47s were taken on charge, including a batch of SC-47Bs and SC-47Ds equipped to carry a lifeboat for sea rescue. A total of 105 C-47s operated with MATS during the Berlin Airlift of 1948.

During the Korean War Combat Cargo Command of the USAF employed C-47s to drop and supply parachute forces, while RC-47Ds, were used for flare dropping during night bombing raids. In 1953 26 aircraft were modified as AC-47Ds for use by MATS to check air-ways navigation aids.

Service with the US Navy ...

As mentioned above, the C-47 and its derivatives served with the US Navy as the R4D. The R4D-1 with R-1830-82 engines corresponded to the early C-47; two R4D-2s (equivalent to the C-49) were staff transports, later styled R4D-2F and R4D-2Z, and were the only R4Ds with Wright R-1820 engines. The R4D-3 and R4D-4 matched the US Army's C-53 and C-53C Skytrooper, while the US Navy's principal cargo variant was the R4D-5 with Dash-92 engines and 24-volt system, corresponding to the C-47A. The R4D-6 was equivalent to the C-47B with Dash-90B engines, and the R4D-7 to the TC-47B trainer.

Immediately after Pearl Harbor the Naval Air Transport Service came into being, almost exclusively equipped with R4Ds, and Squadrons VR-1, VR-2 and VR-3 were soon flying naval and marine personnel on quasi-airline schedules throughout the Pacific theatre. US Marine Corps paratroops were flown on combat missions in R4D-3s and R4D-5s.

All manner of technical duties demanded special US Navy variations, radio and radar countermeasures being undertaken by the R4D-4Q, R4D-5Q and R4D-6Q, electronic warfare by the R4D-5E and R4D-6E, Antarctic operation by the ski-equipped R4D-5L and R4D-6L, and navigation training by the R4D-5T and R4D-6T. Other versions of this remarkable aircraft included the R4D-5S and R4D-6S air-sea warfare trainers and the R4D-5Z and R4D-6Z (and R3D-2Z already mentioned) staff transports.

The other major US Navy variant was the R4D-8 which materialized from Douglas' venture to modernize the DC-3 as the Super DC-3 after the war, with swept-back, angular wings, lengthened and strengthened fuselage, enlarged tail, uprated R-1820-80 engines and deepened engine nacelles. Some 98 conversions from earlier R4Ds were authorized, and these appeared in R4D-8L (winterized), R4D-8T (trainer) and R4D-8Z (staff transport) versions, while in Korea the US Marine Corps night fighter squadron VMF(N)-513 flew R4D-8s as flare droppers on close support missions.

... and other forces

Dakotas (to use their RAF name) served with the British Commonwealth air forces during World War 2, being flown by Nos 33, 34, 36 and 38 Squadrons of the Royal Australian Air Force in the Far East; Nos 435, 436 and 437 Squadrons of the Royal Canadian Air Force; and Nos 40 and 41 Squadrons of the Royal New Zealand Air Force. Many of their aircraft continued to serve in the post-war services, No. 38 Squadron of the RAAF flying operational sorties in Malaya, and No. 91 Wing, RAAF, in Korea. Ex-USAAF C-47s and derivatives were supplied to the air forces of Argentina, Belgium, Bolivia, Brazil, Burma, Cambodia, Chile, Nationalist China, Colombia, Cuba, Denmark, Ecuador, Egypt, Ethiopia, France, West Germany, Greece, Guatemala, Haiti, Honduras,

The cockpit of one of the oldest DC-3s still in use, built in 1937. It has 85,000 hours on the clock and belongs to Air BVI (British Virgin Islands) and still looks in good condition.

Brainchild of Captain Ronald Terry at the USAF Aeronautical Systems Division, the AC-47 gunships of the 1st Special Operations Wing carried a number of laterally-firing multi-barrel guns with which to saturate jungle targets in Vietnam as the aircraft circled slowly overhead.

India, Indonesia, Iran, Israel, Italy, South Korea, Laos, Mexico, Netherlands, Norway, Nicaragua, Paraguay, Peru, Philippines, Portugal, Rhodesia, Salvador, Saudi Arabia, South Africa, Spain, Sweden, Syria, Thailand, Turkey, Uruguay, Venezuela, Vietnam, Yemen and Yugoslavia. Russian-built Li-2s were also provided for the air forces of Bulgaria, Communist China, Czechoslovakia, Hungary, North Korea, Mongolia, Poland and Romania. To these should be added aircraft supplied during the past 30 years, either by the USA or from surplus stocks held by the above

nations, to the air forces of Chad, Congo, Benin, Finland, Gabon, Ivory Coast, Kampuchea, Libya, Malagasy, Malawi, Mali, Mauretania, Morocco, Niger, Nigeria, Oman, Pakistan, Panama, Papua/New Guinea, Rwanda, Senegal, Somalia, Sri Lanka, Togo, Uganda, Zaire and Zambia. At the last count it was estimated that more than 2,200 C-47s (etc) were still performing quasi-military duties outside the United States, not to mention the many commercial DC-3s still giving useful service among the smaller airlines of the world.

Vietnam

It is perhaps also worth mentioning that a handful of ageing C-47s are still being used by the US Air Force, particularly for shuttle flights. The aircraft made a notable comeback in 1972 after the delivery of the military AC-47, nicknamed 'Puff the Magic Dragon', for use at the air support base at Ton Son Nut. This version had three rapid-firing 7.62-mm 'miniguns' on swivel mounts on the port side of the cabin and was used by a special activity group of the US Air Force for overflying jungle targets: the on-board gunners would spray the area concerned with a veritable hail of bullets from their miniguns. This method was also used later on by newer, more heavily-armed aircraft. The EC-47 was used by tactical electronic warfare squadrons for radio monitoring purposes, and the EC-47Q was so laden down with electronic defence equipment that it could only get off the ground using more powerful Pratt & Whitney R-2000 engines. Of the total of nearly 13,000 machines built, there are now, half a century after the DC-3's first flight, nearly 700 still in use for both civil and military purposes. In short-distance transport and as a supply plane, it is still very much holding its own. It has become a legend in its own time.

An example of the vast spectrum of duties undertaken by the ubiquitous DC-3 is afforded by this aircraft operated by the Finnish company Kar-Air for geophysical survey duties featuring sensors in nose, wings and tail.

Douglas DC-3/C-47 variants

DST: prototype plus six aircraft in initial production batch, plus 18 built subsequently; majority for American Airlines; Wright Cyclone engines
DST/DC-3: mix of 14-berth, and 18- or 21-seat aircraft built 1936–7; 13 aircraft for TWA; Cyclone or twin Wasp engines
DC-3: commercial airliner to individual furnishing requirements; 417 aircraft, many subsequently commandeered for military use
C-41(DC-3-253): only one, modified from DC-2(38-502)
C-41A(DC-3-253A): only one, equivalent to luxury DC-3 for 23 passengers (40–70)
C-47: 953 aircraft for War Department built at Long Beach; 12-volt system. Twin Wasp engines (41-7722/7866;-18337/18699;-38564/38763; 42-5635/5704; -32768/32923; 43-30628/36639; 49-2612/2641 for Greece post-war; among these were 106 US Navy **R4D-1s** 3131-3143; 4692-4706; 01648-01649; 01977-01990; 05051-68687/89,-1074222, 44-83228/29)
C-49J: 34R-1820-71 powered ex-DC-3s fitted as troopers with side seating (43-1961/94)
C-49K: 23 R-1820-71 powered ex-DC-3s fitted as troopers with side seating (43-1995/-2017)
C-50: designation applied to ex-DC-3s with minor variations to interiors and engine powers; four R-1820-85-powered aircraft (41-7697/7700)
C-50A: two aircraft similar to above but fitted as troopers (41-7710/11)
C-50B: three R-1820-81 powered ex-DC-3s with starboard door (41-7703/05)
C-50C: one R-1820-79 powered ex-DC-3 (41-7695)
C-50D: four R-1820-79 powered ex-DC-3s fitted as troopers (41-7696, -7709,-7712/13)
C-51: one R-1820-83 powered ex-DC-3 (41-7702)
C-52: one Pratt & Whitney R-1830-51 powered ex-DC-3 with 27,700-lb (12565-kg) all-up weight (41-7708)
C-52A: one R-1830-51 powered ex-DC-3 (41-7714)

C-52B: two R-1830-51 powered ex-DC-3s fitted as troopers (41-7706/07)
C-52C: one R-1830-51 powered ex-DC-3 (41-7701)
C-53: named Skytrooper, 193 impressed aircraft and 16 new-build aircraft, all powered by Pratt & Whitney R-1830-92 engines (41-20045/46,-20051,-20053,-20060, -20136, 42-6455/79,-6481-6504,-15530/69,-15870/94, -47371/82, 43-14404/05; included 20 **R4D-3** for US Navy 05073-05084, 06992-06999)
SX-53A: one prototype with full span slotted flaps (42-6480) and 15 production **C-53A** examples (42-6455/79)
C-53B: five ex-airline long-range DC-3s (41-20047, -20052,-20057/59)
C-53C: 17 ex-DC-3s fitted as troopers with side seats (43-2001/34; included 10 **R4D-4** for US Navy, 07000-07003, 33815-33820)
C-53D: similar to C-53C; 159 aircraft (42-68693/851)
C-68: two 21-seat ex-DC3s impressed in 1942 with Wright R-1820-92 engines (42-14297/98)
C-84: four 1937-type DC-3b 28 seat airliners with R-1820-71 engines (42-57157, 42-57511/13)
C-117A: 17 Tulsa-built military airliner-style aircraft completed in 1945 with R-1830-90C supercharged engines; some converted to **C-117B** (45-2545/61); **C-117C** designation covered 11 VC-47C staff transport conversions which later became VC-117As and VC-117Bs
05072; 12393-12404; 30147; 37660-37685; 91104)
C-47A: 4,931 aircraft built at Long Beach and Tulsa; 24-volt system (42-23300/24419; -32924/32935; -92024/93158;-93160/93823;-100436/101035; -108794/108993; 43-15033/16132; -30640/30761; -47963/48262; among these were 248 US Navy **R4D-5s** 12405-12446; 17092-17248; 39057-39095)
C-47B: 3,241 aircraft built at Long Beach and Tulsa with supercharged R-1830-90 or -90B engines; included 133 TC-47B trainers (42-93159; 43-16133/16432; -48263/

49962; 44-76195/77294; 45-876/1139; among these were 147 **R4D-6s** for US Navy 17249-17291; 39096-39098; 39100; 50740-50752; 50753-50839, and 43 **R4D-7s** 39099, 39101-39108; 99824-99857)
YC-47F: prototype Super DC-3 (51-381/) originally termed **YC-129**; transferred to US Navy as prototype **R4D-8**
C-48: designation applied to 36 DC-3s impressed from US airlines in 1941; all with R-1830 engines and maximum all-up weight of 26,850-lb (12179 kg); one C-48 21-seater (41,7681); three **C-48A** 18-seaters (41-7682/4); 16 **C-48B** 14-berth DSTs (42-38324/26, 42-56089/91, 42-56098/102, 42-56609/12, 42-56629); 16 **C-48C** 21 seat DC-3s with R-1830-51 engines (42-38327, 42-38332/38, 42-38358/60, 42-78026/28)
C-49: designation applied to six impressed Wright R-1820-powered DC-3s (41-7685/89, 41-7694; two of these became US Navy **R4D-2F** and **R4D-2Z** VIP transports)
C-49A: one R-1820-powered ex-DC3 (41-7690)
C-49B: three R-1820-powered ex-DC-3s with seating variation and starboard entry door (41-7691/93)
C-49C: two R-1820-powered ex-DC-3s fitted as troopers with side seats (41-7715 and 41-7721)
C-49D: 12 R-1820-71-powered ex-DC-3s fitted as troopers with side seats (41-7716/20, 42-38256,-43624, -65583/84,-68860, 44-52999)
C-49E: 23 R-1820-79-powered ex-DC-3s (42-43619/23, -56092/97,-56103/07,-56617/18,-56625/27,-56634)
C-49F: nine R-1820-71-powered 14-berth ex-DSTs (42-56613,-56616,-56620/21,-56623,-56628,-56633, -56636/37)
C-49G: eight R-1820-97-powered ex-DC-3s (42-38252, -38255,-56614/15,-56630/32,-56635)
C-49H: 19 R-1820-97-powered ex-DC-3/DSTs (42-38250/51,-38253/54,-38257,-38328/31,-57506,-65580/82)

Quetzalcoatl, the feathered snake-god of the Toltecs, creates a very unusual green and brown livery on the fuselage of this DC-3 belonging to a club in Fort Lauderdale, Florida.

Hawker Hurricane

Never displaying the glamour of Mitchell's immortal Spitfire, Sydney Camm's Hurricane nevertheless represented the vital instrument on which the RAF's newly formed Fighter Command cut its teeth during the 18 months before World War 2. It was the RAF's first eight-gun monoplane fighter and the first to exceed 300 mph.

The Hawker Hurricane came into being in 1933, as a result of specification no. F.7/30, which did not represent the most up-to-date technology. It was an attempt to bring out a new monoplane version of the Hawker Fury biplane. But the aircraft builder, Sydney Camm, was limping along a whole generation behind the monocoque construction method which Mitchell consistently used for the Spitfire. In fact it was due to precisely the simple construction of the Hurricane that it made such a good showing in the hectic months of 1939 and 1940, when RAF fighters had to fly and fight in extremely primitive conditions, for it sustained considerable damage but was easy to repair.

The first Hurricane (K5083) was flown from Brooklands on 6 November 1935 by the late Group Captain P. W. S. Bulman. Powered by a 1,025-hp (764-kW) Rolls-Royce Merlin 'C' 12-cylinder liquid-cooled inline engine, developed from the private-venture PV-12, the prototype weighed 5,420 lb (2460 kg) all-up and featured a two-blade wooden Watts propeller; its top speed was 315 mph (507 km/h) at 15,000 ft (4575 m).

As production of the first 600 Hurricanes, ordered in June 1936, built up during 1937 (albeit somewhat delayed by abandonment of the Merlin I in favour of the Merlin II, necessitating alterations to the nose contours), the wing-mounted eight-Browning gun battery was confirmed and minor alterations were made to the airframe, including an improved radiator bath, a strengthened hood canopy and the discarding of tailplane struts.

Initial service deliveries were made to No. 111 (Fighter) Squadron at Northolt before the end of 1937, and the next year Nos 3 and 56 Squadrons followed suit. Early spinning trials disclosed a need to increase keel area, provided by a ventral fairing added forward of the fixed tailwheel, and by a 3-in (7.62-cm) downward extension of the rudder.

Within the limitations imposed by the basic airframe structure and by the desperate need to accelerate production in the threatening international climate, little could be done initially to improve the Hurricane I before the outbreak of war. However, the fixed-pitch wooden propeller was replaced by a two-position, three-blade de Havilland metal propeller, and later by a Rotol constant-speed propeller – the latter bestowing much improved climb and performance at altitude. These alterations were made possible by the arrival of the 1,030-hp (768-kW) Merlin III with universal propeller shaft. Metal-covered wings also appeared in production by 1939.

By the outbreak of war a total of 497 Hurricane Is had been completed for the RAF, and 18 home-based fighter squadrons had taken deliveries. Some export orders had been authorized to friendly nations, these including Yugoslavia (12, plus licence production), South Africa (7), Romania (12), Canada (20), Persia (2), Poland (1), Belgium (20, plus licence production) and Turkey (15). Plans were

Amid the dust and sand of the Western Desert, which not only reduced visibility but caused severe wear to aircraft engines, these Hurricane IID anti-tank fighters of No. 6 Squadron taxi out for take-off at Sidi Bu Amud in January 1943 during the rout of the Afrika Korps which followed the 2nd Battle of Alamein.

This Hawker Hurricane belongs to the Battle of Britain Flight, a group of enthusiasts who re-enact scenes from the Battle of Britain at air displays. *(Photo: Air Portraits)*

Hawker Hurricane

Specification

Hawker Hurricane Mk I
Type: single-seat interceptor fighter
Powerplant: one 1,030-hp (768-kW) Rolls-Royce
Merlin III inline iston engine
Performance: maximum speed 318 mph (511 km/h)
at 18,000 feet (5500 m); initial climb rate 2,520 ft
(770 m) per minute; service ceiling 36,000 ft (10970 m);
maximum range 460 miles (740 km)
Weights: empty 4,670 lb (2118 kg); maximum take-off
6,600 lb (2994 kg)
Dimensions: span 40 ft 0 in (12.20 m); length
31 ft 4 in (9.59 m); height 12 ft 11½ in (3.96 m); wing
area 257.6 sq ft (23.93 m²)
Armament: eight 0.303-in (7.7-mm) Browning
machine-guns with 2,660 rounds of ammunition

Representative of the classic RAF Battle of Britain Hurricane I, P3059
served with No. 501 (County of Gloucester) Squadron during August
1940. Aircraft of this Gloster Aircraft-produced batch, equipped from the
outset with Rotol constant-speed propellers, started delivery to RAF
fighter squadrons in May and continued throughout the Battle of Britain;
it has been said that the Rotol propeller transformed the Hurricane's
performance from 'disappointing' to one of 'acceptable mediocrity', and
modified aircraft were certainly much sought after among squadrons
equipped with aircraft having the older de Havilland two-position
propeller.

P3059

The Hurricane prototype (K5083) in a relatively late photograph of the aircraft being flown by P. G. Lucas in 1937 after removal of tailplane struts, installation of gunsight, modification to the radiator bath and with additional strengthening members on the cockpit canopy.

well advanced to create another production line at the Gloster Aircraft Company, and tooling up to produce Hurricanes at the Canadian Car and Foundry Company at Montreal was under way (a total of 1,451 Hurricanes was built in Canada during the war). In 1941 the Austin Motor Company, Longbridge, also produced 300 Hurricanes.

Into successful action

Four Hurricane I squadrons (Nos 1, 73, 85 and 87) accompanied the RAF to France in September 1939, and it was to Pilot Officer P. W. O. Mould of No. 1 Squadron that the first German aircraft, a Dornier Do 17, fell on 30 October. The Hurricane proved able to cope with the primitive airfield conditions in France, principally on account of its sturdy, wide-track landing gear – while the Spitfire was held at home to meet any threat to the British Isles.

By 1940 Hurricane Is were beginning to roll off the Gloster production line, as well as from the new Hawker factory at Langley, Bucks. A Hurricane squadron, No. 46, served at Narvik during the last days of the Norwegian campaign but all its aircraft were lost when the carrier HMS *Glorious* was sunk while bringing them home. Over Dunkirk, and in the closing stages of the Battle of France, Hurricanes were in constant action against the Luftwaffe, and those of the

Hawker Sea Hurricane II cutaway drawing key

1 Fabric-covered rudder construction
2 Tail navigation light
3 Rudder tab
4 Elevator tab
5 Fabric-covered elevator construction
6 Elevator horn balance
7 Tailplane construction
8 Rudder control horn
9 Elevator hinge control
10 Sternpost
11 Tailfin construction
12 Fabric covering
13 Rear aerial mast
14 Rudder balance weight
15 Aerial cable
16 Tailfin aluminium leading edge
17 Port tailplane
18 Control cable pulleys
19 Port access panel to tailplane controls
20 Ventral fin
21 Tailwheel
22 Dowty shock absorber tailwheel strut
23 Fin framework
24 Fin/tailplane root fillet
25 Fuselage fabric covering

26 Lifting bar socket
27 Arresting hook latches
28 Dorsal stringers
29 Fuselage diagonal wire bracing
30 Upper longeron
31 Aluminium alloy fuselage frames
32 Bolted joint fuselage tubular construction
33 Deck arrest hook
34 Arresting hook pivot point
35 Bottom longeron
36 Arresting hook damper
37 Wooden dorsal fairing formers
38 Aerial mast
39 Upper identification light
40 Upward firing recognition flare launcher
41 Tailplane control cables
42 Fuselage access panel
43 Ventral stringers
44 Trailing edge wing root fillet
45 Downward identification light

46 Radio racks
47 Radio equipment (R3002 and R3108)
48 Parachute flare launch tube
49 Sliding canopy track
50 Canopy rear fairing construction
51 Turn-over crash pylon struts
52 Radio equipment (TR1196 and R1304)
53 Radio equipment (TR1143 and TR1133)
54 Battery
55 Oxygen bottle
56 Hydraulic system equipment
57 Dinghy stowage
58 Seat back armour plate
59 Head armour
60 Rearward sliding canopy cover
61 Canopy framework
62 Safety harness
63 Pilot's seat
64 Seat adjusting lever
65 Fuselage/wing spar attachment joint
66 Ventral oil and coolant radiator
67 Position of flap hydraulic jack (fitted on port side only)
68 Gun heater air duct
69 Inboard flap housing
70 Trailing edge ribs
71 Outer wing anel rear spar joint
72 Breech-block access covers

The Sea Hurricane IB was a conversion of the RAF's Mk I, and this Fleet Air Arm version featured catapult spools, arrester hook and naval radio. The Gloster-built aircraft shown here features exhaust glare shields forward of the windscreen. Sea Hurricanes were in constant action in the Mediterranean, particularly in 1942.

This Hurricane I (V7476) was the
only such aircraft to carry RAAF
colours and was flown by Nos 2
and 3 Communications Flights.

73 Cannon breech-blocks
74 Outboard flap housing
75 Rear spar
76 Aluminium aileron
   construction
77 Fabric covered starboard
   aileron
78 Aileron control gear
79 Wing tip construction
80 Starboard navigation light
81 Intermediate wing spars
82 Aluminium wing ribs

83 Front spar
84 Leading edge nose ribs
85 Starboard landing lamp
86 Wing stringer construction
87 Ammunition feed drums
88 Ammunition boxes (total
   364 rounds)
89 Main undercarriage
   swivelling joint
90 Hispano 20-mm cannon
91 Starboard wing-cannon
   bays
92 Cannon barrel front
   mounting

93 Main undercarriage door
   fairing
94 Oleo-pneumatic shock
   absorber leg strut
95 Starboard mainwheel
96 Cannon barrel fairings
97 Recoil springs
98 Cannon muzzles
99 Landing gear pivot point
100 Camera aperture
101 Cine camera
102 Front spar outer panel joint
103 Position of 9 Imp gal
   (41 litres) leading-edge oil
   tank (port side only)
104 Landing gear hydraulic
   retraction jack

105 Retraction linkage
106 Fuel filler cap
107 Port wing main fuel tank
   (34.5 Imp gal/157 litre
   capacity)
108 Main undercarriage wheel
   well
109 Centre section strut
   framework
110 Cockpit floor level
111 Pilot's foot boards
112 De-icing fluid tank
113 Rudder pedals
114 Instrument anel
115 Control column

116 Elevator trim tab control
   wheel
117 Engine throttle control
118 Reflector gunsight
119 Bullet proof windscreen
120 Canopy handgrip
121 Rear view mirror
122 Port outer split trailing edge
   flap
123 Fabric covered port aileron
124 Pitot tube
125 Aileron control gear
126 Port wing tip
127 Port navigation light
128 Aluminium alloy wing skin
   panels
129 Port landing lamp
130 Port cannon barrels
131 Hispano 20-mm cannon
132 Port wing cannon bays
133 Outboard ammunition box
134 Ammunition feed drums
135 Fuel filler cap
136 Fuselage (reserve) fuel tank
   (28 Imp gal/127 litre
   capacity)
137 Exhaust anti-glare shield
138 Oil filter
139 Engine compartment
   fireproof bulkhead
140 Pneumatic system air
   bottle
141 Front wing spar centre
   section
142 Engine bearer support strut
143 Port mainwheel
144 Carburettor air intake
145 Supercharger

146 Engine control rods
147 Coolant filler cap
148 Coolant system header
   tank
149 Magneto
150 Engine bearer struts
151 Rear engine mounting
152 Hand turning crank fitting
153 Lower engine cowlings
154 'Fishtail' exhaust pipes
155 Rolls-Royce Merlin XX-
   engine
156 Coolant pipes
157 Upper engine cowlings
158 Cowling fairings
159 Propeller reduction
   gearbox
160 Engine front mounting
161 Propeller oil spill shield
162 Spinner back plate
163 Propeller hub pitch-change
   mechanism
164 Rotol R.S.5/2 three-bladed
   propeller
165 Spinner

209

Ninth production Hurricane I
(L1555) of No. 111 (Fighter)
Squadron, Northolt, December
1937. Carrying the Co's pennant,
this aircraft was flown by
Squadron Leader John
('Downwind') Gillan. Note the
absence of ventral fin fairing that
was added in 1938 and was a
characteristic of the Hurricane in
later years.

Dramatic dusk launch of a Sea Hurricane IA from the bow-mounted
catapult of a merchant ship. Introduced to provide Allied convoys with on-
the-spot fighter defence against enemy aircraft, the catapult Sea
Hurricanes enjoyed limited success in 1941; with nowhere to go, the pilot
was forced to bale out or ditch in the hope he would be fished out of the
sea by a passing ship.

small Belgian air force suffered almost total destruction.

The Hurricane I provided Fighter Command's mainstay in
the Battle of Britain, equipping a maximum of 32 squadrons
(compared with 18½ of Spitfires) between July and October
1940, no fewer than 2,309 having been delivered by 7
August. Top speed of the Rotol-equipped Hurricane I was
328 mph (528 km/h) at 16,500 ft (5030 m), a performance
which fell far short of that of the superlative Messerschmitt
Bf 109E, and it was this shortfall that caused it to be
committed – whenever possible – against enemy bombers
rather than the German single-seaters. The Hurricane proved
to be exceptionally popular among its pilots as a highly
manoeuvrable dogfighter with rock-steady gun-aiming pro-
perties and the tightest of turning radii, which helped
to make the type particularly effective against the heavy
Messerschmitt Bf 110 fighter. It was, however, the extraordinary teamwork between the various elements of the air
defences that won the great battle.

In September 1940, when the battle was still at its height,
the first Hurricane Mk IIs were beginning to appear with the
1,185-hp (883-kW) two-stage supercharged Merlin XX with
Rotol propeller and slightly lengthened nose. Still armed
with eight Browning guns in the Mk IIA Series 1 version, this
Hurricane possessed a top speed of 342 mph (550 km/h). The
Mk IIA Series 2 introduced pick-up points for a 'universal'
wing capable of mounting 44-Imp gal (200-litre) underwing
fuel tanks; this variant was originally developed to enable
Hurricanes to be supplied by air to the Middle East, but the
fall of France ended this venture after fewer than a dozen
aircraft had attempted the flight. Hurricane IIAs were also

capable of carrying a pair of 250-lb (113-kg) bombs under
the wings and were flown on offensive sweeps across the
English Channel early in 1941.

The Hurricane IIB introduced a new 12-Browning gun
wing (as well as retaining the bomb shackles) and came to be
known as the Hurribomber, while the Mk IIC featured an
armament of four 20-mm Oerlikon/Hispano cannon – at that
time (mid-1941) still regarded as an extraordinary armament
for a single-seater (although one such Hurricane had been
fought experimentally in the Battle of Britain with limited
success). These two sub-variants equipped no fewer than 96
RAF squadrons during 1941–4 and saw continuous action in
northern Europe, North Africa and the Far East, being
employed principally in the ground attack role. They also
played a significant part in the Greek, Iraqi, Syrian
and Malayan campaigns. Last of the Merlin XX-powered
Hurricanes was the Mk IID, introduced in 1942, with a 40-
mm Vickers or Rolls-Royce anti-tank gun under each wing.
Although a small number of this variant remained home-
based, the majority was shipped to the Western Desert
(where the type played a major part in the Battle of Bir
Hakeim) and later to Burma. Following early experience in
the Western Desert, whose abrasive dust and sand wrought
havoc with aero engines, all Hurricanes supplied to the
Middle and Far Eastern theatres were fitted with Vokes air
filters over their carburettor intakes, an ungainly but
necessary modification which reduced performance by some
8 per cent.

The Hurricane II remained the principal variant in service
during the war, eventually providing the major ground-
attack element of the RAF in the Far East. A total of 2,952

Hurricane IIC night-fighter of No. 87 (Fighter) Squadron being flown by
Sqdn Ldr D. G. Smallwood, DSO, DFC; note the CO's pennant aft of the
exhaust glare shield. No. 87 Squadron, which flew Hurricane IICs from
June 1941 until March 1944, was one of the longest-serving Hurricane
night-fighter squadrons in the RAF.

Hurricanes was supplied to the Soviet Union, of which all but about 30 were Mk IIs or their Canadian-built equivalents. The majority was shipped as deck cargo on the North Cape convoys (and suffered heavy losses accordingly), though many were also supplied from Middle East stocks. Another important duty undertaken by the Mk II was night fighting, at one time participating in the almost fruitless Turbinlite venture over the UK but also serving as night intruders over France and Belgium during 1941 and 1942 until this task was taken over almost exclusively by the Bristol Beaufighter and de Havilland Mosquito.

Final variant for the RAF was the Hurricane IV (the Mk III was an unbuilt project intended to introduce the Packard-built Merlin 28 into the Hawker production line). This version, originally termed the Mark IIE, featured the 1,280-hp (954-kW) Merlin 24 or 27 and a new universal wing capable of mounting anti-tank guns, rocket projectiles or other external stores. Owing to the need for only limited airframe modifications, many Mk IIs were converted to accommodate the new wing and, with new engine, remained in service with the RAF until after the war. The final Hurricane built for the RAF, a Mark IIC (LF363), was delivered to No. 309 (Polish) Squadron in February 1944, while the last of all to be built (also a Mark IIC, PZ865), was purchased by the manufacturers and survives to this day.

When the Hawker Hurricane Mk IIC was fitted with four Oerlikon/Hispano 20 mm cannons it was somewhat unprecedented and gave the fighter an awesome punch against enemy aircraft and ground armour. Approximately 3,400 of this model were built.

Hurricane IIB (Z3768) of No. 134 Squadron of No. 151 Wing, Vaenga, North Russia, September 1941. This wing (comprising Nos 81 and 134 Squadrons) was hurriedly assembled in the UK and shipped to the Soviet Union with aircraft previously destined for the Western Desert, hence the inclusion of tropical filter under the nose.

Possibly captured at Merville, France, in May 1940, this Rotol propeller-equipped Hurricane I was evaluated by the Germans at Magdeburg. The Luftwaffe was disdainful of the Hurricane, yet lost more aircraft to its guns than to those of the Spitfire in the first 30 months of the war.

Total production of the Hurricane amounted to 14,231, including those produced in Canada. In addition the extensive repair organization, created in 1939, returned 4,537 repaired Hurricanes to the RAF.

Sea Hurricanes

Loss of the French Atlantic seaboard in 1940 exposed the vital British convoys to increasing action by long-range German bombers such as the Heinkel He 111 and Focke-Wulf Fw 200, and it was decided to adapt the Hurricane I for

catapulting from merchant ships (CAM-ships) to provide some measure of protection against this menace. The first such variant, the Sea Hurricane IA, was a simple adaptation of ex-RAF Hurricane Is to feature catapult spools. Limited success attended these operations in 1941, for it was intended that, once launched, the 'Hurricat' pilot had no alternative after action but to ditch his aircraft or make a forlorn search for land.

The next venture was to convert a number of merchantmen (MACs) to provide a small flight deck from which Sea Hurricane Mk IBs might operate, and these aircraft featured

Unofficially adorned with peacetime squadron flash, this tropicalized Hurricane IIB (BD930) was flown by No. 73 Squadron in the Western Desert in 1942. Veteran of the French campaign and Battle of Britain, No. 73 Squadron was rushed to the Middle East to meet the crisis of 1940, becoming separated from its ground crews and losing many aircraft en route.

A No. 6 Squadron Hurricane IID with 40-mm anti-tank guns, based at LG89 and LG91 in the Western Desert, July 1942. First to receive this Hurricane version, No. 6 Squadron played a major part in destroying enemy vehicles in the desert during the months immediately prior to the decisive 2nd Battle of Alamein.

an arrester hook. A third version, the Sea Hurricane Mk IC, carried the four-cannon armament but was still powered by the Merlin III. It was followed by a full conversion of the Hurricane IIC, the Sea Hurricane IIC with Merlin XX, four-cannon wing, catapult spools, arrester hook, underwing store provision and naval radio. It possessed a top speed of 318 mph (512 km/h) at 17,500 ft (5340 m), a service ceiling of 30,500 ft (9300 m) and a maximum range of 1,062 miles (1710 km). It was withdrawn from service at sea in October 1943.

At one time, late in 1942, the Fleet Air Arm held on charge a total of more than 600 Sea Hurricanes, and almost every fleet and escort carrier of the Royal Navy at one time or another mustered at least a partial complement of these aircraft. One of their most memorable actions was fought over the Malta convoy of August 1942 when Sea Hurricanes from HMS *Indomitable*, *Eagle* and *Victorious* beat off attacks by 600 Axis aircraft, destroying 39 for the loss of seven of their own number.

Although RAF Hurricanes were relegated to second-line duties at home from mid-1944 onwards, particularly in the training role and on meterological and radar calibration work, Hurricane IIs and IVs remained in first line service in the Mediterranean and Far East theatres until 1945, providing outstanding support for the 14th Army's advance through Burma in the latter theatre.

Many experiments were carried out on Hurricanes between 1939 and 1945, mostly aimed at increasing the theatre-reinforcement capabilities (i.e. ferry range); these experiments included the carriage of a jettisonable auxiliary upper wing (the Hillson Bi-Mono project), pickaback trials aboard a Consolidated B-24 Liberator, and towing trials behind an Avro Lancaster. Other trials included the carriage of outsize rocket projectiles and the fitting of a semi-laminar flow wing. A floatplane version was proposed at the time of the 1940 Norwegian campaign, and skis were fitted to at least one Canadian Hurricane. Alternative engines were proposed from time to time although the only such project believed to

have reached construction was a Yugoslav Hurricane fitted with a Daimler-Benz DB 601A in 1941.

After the war, many Hurricanes were declared surplus to requirements in Britain and many of them were refitted for export. During the war, the Irish Air Corps had acquired a few Mk Is, and from 1945 to 1947 a further 13 aircraft were delivered. In the mid-1940s, Hurricanes were also flying in the Turkish, Egyptian and South African air forces. Around 50 Hurricane IIBs and IICs were sent to Portugal (although some of these were used only as sources of spare parts), and 16 were delivered to Persia to fulfil an order received before the war. A further Hurricane, a unique two-seater trainer converted from a Mk IIC, was also sold to Persia (now Iran) in 1947.

Hawker Hurricane variants

F.36/34 prototype: one aircraft (K5083) with 1,025-hp (764-kw) Merlin C; eight-gun armament fitted later; first flown 6 November 1935
Hurricane I: original production model with 1,030-hp (768-kW) Merlin II or III, eight Browning 0.303-in (7.7-mm) guns; early aircraft with fabric-covered wings, later metal-clad (total 2,719 excluding Canadian-built; about 90 exported)
Canadian Hurricane I: built by Canadian Car and Foundry Co. in Montreal, 1940; Merlin III and DH propellers; batch included Hillson Bi-Mono slip-wing Hurricane (total 40)
Hurricane IIA Series 1: introduced 1,185-hp (883-kW) Merlin XX two-stage supercharged engine in September 1940; eight-gun wing; some converted from Marks Is
Hurricane IIA Series 2: introduced provision for wing stores on Universal wing; some converted from Mark I; included some PR Mk I Conversions and PRMkIIA
Hurricane IIB: introduced 12-Browning gun wing and bomb-tank shackles for 500-lb (227-kg) bombs (total approximately 3,100 built by Hawker, Gloster and Austin, plus many converted from other versions; included the PR Mark IIB)
Hurricane IIC: introduced four 20-mm gun armament in 1941; bomb and drop tank provision; worldwide service; also tropicalized (total approximately 3,400 built by Hawker, Gloster and Austin, plus many conversions)
Hurricane IID: introduced pair of 40-mm Vickers or Rolls-Royce anti-tank guns plus two Brownings in 1942; many tropicalized (total approximately 800 built, plus many conversions)

Hurricane IV: introduced 1,280-hp (954-kW) Merlin 24 or 27 and Universal wing to carry alternative rockets, drop tanks, bombs or anti-tank guns in 1942, many tropicalized (total approximately 2,000 built plus numerous coversions)
Hurricane V: two prototypes (KZ193 and NL255, converted Mark IVs) with ground-boosted Merlin 32 and four-blade Rotol propeller
Canadian Hurricane X: Packard Merlin 28, about 100 with eight-gun wing, remainder with IIB wing; many converted to IIC wing (total 489 built in 1940–1)
Canadian Hurricane XI: 150 aircraft with 12-gun or four-cannon armament; majority shipped to Russia
Canadian Hurricane XII: 248 aircraft with Hurricane IIC modifications; one ski-equipped example
Canadian Hurricane XIIA and Sea Hurricane XIIA: Packard Merlin 29; 150 aircraft shipped principally to Soviet Union and Burma in 1943
Sea Hurricane IA: catapult fighter for CAM-ship operations (50 aircraft converted from Hurricane I, 1941)
Sea Hurricane IB: catapult spools and arrester hook for operations from CAM-ships or MACs (total approximately 340 converted from Hurricane IIA Series 2 in 1941–2)
Sea Hurricane IC: as Sea Hurricane IB but four-cannon armament included (total approximately 400 converted from Hurricane IIB and IIC in 1942–3)
Sea Hurricane IIC: full-standard conversion of Hurricane IIC with hook, spools and naval radio (total approximately 400 converted from Hurricane IIC)
Although it is possible to state the total number of Hurricanes built, no exact records exist – or were ever kept – of the number of each variant owing to ad hoc conversions both by the manufacturers and in the field

Junkers Ju 87 Stuka

No aircraft in history was ever quite so deadly effective (when unopposed) as the infamous Stuka, nor so vulnerable (when it ran into opposition). Its terrifying effect in Poland, Norway, France and the Low Countries was equalled only by its complete failure to survive against RAF Fighter Command a few weeks later.

Virtually no other aircraft struck such terror into the hearts of battle-hardened infantry as the Junkers Ju 87, known as the Stuka (for *Sturzkampfbomber*, or dive bomber). It holds the world record for sinking ships and still today comes second only to the Soviet Ilyushin Il-2 for the number of tanks it destroyed. Its most important feature in battle was its ability to place heavy bomb-loads accurately onto pinpoint targets, and only enemy fighters could put a halt to its progress. So during the first year of World War 2 it acquired legendary status, which it lost suddenly and irretrievably in the Battle of Britain. For the rest of the war it operated only at night and at low level, and only one group on the Eastern Front flew it during the daytime. The commander of this group himself flew 2,530 missions.

The technique of dive-bombing was familiar in World War 1, but no aircraft designed for the job existed until the 1920s. One of the first was the Junkers K 47, of which two were flown in 1928 with Jupiter engines and 12 with Pratt & Whitney Hornet engines sold to China. These did extensive research, and demonstrated that a 90° dive is the most accurate. In turn this demands a strong aircraft and resolute pilot, as well as an indicator of dive angle (60° feels like almost 90°). Many who later were to head Hitler's Luftwaffe became convinced that the dive-bomber had to be a central weapon in an air force dedicated to close support of ground forces. When plans could be made for new combat aircraft for the Luftwaffe, in 1933, the immediate need was ultimately met by a trim biplane, the Henschel Hs 123, while Junkers worked on the definitive Stuka.

The design staff under Hermann Pohlmann adopted the same configuration as that of the K 47; a single-engined low-wing monoplane with prominent fixed landing gear and twin fins and rudders. The Ju 87 differed in having an all-metal stressed-skin structure, without the corrugated skin previously used on Junkers all-metal aircraft, and a cranked wing of so-called inverted-gull form. Like that of the K 47, the entire trailing edge was occupied by patented double-wing flaps and ailerons, and the crew of two sat back-to-back under a large glazed canopy. The prototype flew in the spring of 1935 with a 640-hp (477-kW) Rolls-Royce Kestrel engine. Divebrakes were then added under the outer wings,

One of the surviving colour photographs from World War 2, this was taken by the 'backseater' of a Ju 87B-2 flying with StG 77 on a mission over the Balkans — believed to be after dive-bombing British ships during the invasion of Crete. Identical markings can be seen in the colour profile of Ju 87R coded S2 + MR.

Like another famed, or infamous, Nazi warplane, the Bf 109 fighter, the Ju 87 first took to the air on the power of a Rolls-Royce Kestrel engine. This photo shows the original appearance of the V1 (first prototype) at Dessau in mid-1935. The dive-brakes were not ready at this time and the radiator required changes.

All the Luftwaffe's early Stukageschwäder (dive-bomber wings) using the Ju 87 were formed on the Ju 87A, with 600-hp (448-kW) engine and trousered landing gear. This Ju 87A-2 was assigned to III/StG 165 (later renumbered StG 51) in early 1938. The camouflage and Balkankreuz insignia were revised in October 1939.

but on one of the first pull-outs the tail collapsed and the aircraft crashed.

Full-scale production

After much further development, in the course of which the engine was changed to the intended German unit, the 640-hp (477-kW) Junkers Jumo 210Ca, driving a three-blade variable-pitch propeller, a new single-fin tail was adopted, and the JU 87A-1 entered full-scale production in early 1937.

About 200 of the A-0, A-1 and A-2 series were built, all with large trouser fairings over the landing gears and the A-2 with the 680-hp (507-kW) Jumo 210Da and an improved VDM propeller. They equipped four Gruppen, of which StG 163 sent three aircraft to see action with the *Legion Cóndor* in Spain, where the type proved outstandingly effective. But in 1939 all A-series aircraft were transferred to training units, and the swelling ranks of Stukageschwäder (dive-bomber wings) were equipped with the much more capable Ju 87B. Visually this differed in having neater spats over the main wheels, but the chief difference was that it had double the power, in the form of the new Jumo 211A, driving a broad-blade constant-speed propeller. The full production sub-type, the B-1, had the 1,200-hp (895-kW) Jumo 211Da with a direct-injection fuel system giving immunity from icing, or engine-cuts in inverted flight, or negative-g manoeuvres (the Ju 87 could perform all normal aerobatics). Another important feature was an automatic dive-control, set by the pilot to a chosen pull-out height on a contact altimeter. Having gone through a list of 10 vital actions the pilot opened the underwing dive-brakes, which automatically set up the dive, the pilot adjusting the angle manually by lining up the visual horizon with red lines painted at various angles on the canopy. The pilot then aimed at the target manually as in a fighter, using aileron alone to achieve the correct bomb line. Often the angle was 90°, the dive being entered in a wing-over from directly above the target. Curiously, the Ju 87 was the one aircraft in which 90° did not feel like an over-the-vertical bunt; indeed, it seemed more at home in its rock-steady dive than in normal cruising flight, when its vulnerability (accentuated by the transparent canopy down to elbow-level) was all too evident. When a signal light on the contact altimeter came on, the pilot pressed a knob on top of the control column for the pull-out at 6 g to happen by itself, with usual terrain clearance of 450 m (1,476 ft). If it did not, the pilot had to haul back with all his strength, assisted by very careful use of elevator trimmer.

There was a pair of MG 81s, light but fast-firing weapons with belt feed instead of 75-round magazines. Additionally, the entire aircraft was refined to reduce drag, the most noticeable improvement being to the cowling and canopy. The landing gear was cleaned up, but from 1942 the spats and leg fairings were increasingly discarded.

The most numerous variant was the Ju 87D-3, which embodied better protection for the crew and vital parts of the aircraft, reflecting the Ju 87's increasing use as a *Schlachtflugzeug* (close-support aircraft). From 1942 all versions were often called upon to fly missions other than dive-bombing, such as glider-towing, anti-partisan attacks and general utility transport with a great diversity of loads. A few Ju 87D-4s were equipped as torpedo-bombers, but the next main variant was the Ju 87D-5 with extended wingtips to help counter the considerably increased weight of Ju-87D versions. Reflecting the increasing peril of day operations, the Ju 87D-7 was a night variant with the more powerful Jumo 211P engine and long exhaust pipes extending back across the wing. Together with the day-flying Ju 87D-8 it replaced the wing guns by the far more powerful 20-mm MG 151, and dive-brakes were at last omitted. The Ju 87D-8 was the last version in production, the total number built by late September 1944 – when almost all aircraft other than fighters were terminated – being generally accepted as 5,709.

Anti-armour

There were several schemes for successors, including the Ju 87F and Ju 187, but the only other Stuka variants were built by conversions of the ubiquitous D models. The most important sub-type was the Ju 87G series, of which only the Ju 87G-1 became operational. The Ju 87G was a specialized anti-armour version, fitted with two BK 3.7 (Flak 18) guns hung under the wings just outboard of the landing gears. This 37-mm gun was a formidable weapon weighing over 800 lb (363 kg) and in wide service as ground-based flak (anti-aircraft artillery) equipment. In 1942 a trial installation was tested in a converted Ju 87D-5 and found more effective than the many other Luftwaffe anti-tank aircraft such as the Henschel Hs 129 and Junkers Ju 88P. Fed by clips of six rounds, the BK 3.7 had a muzzle velocity with armour-piercing ammunition exceeding 2,790 ft (850 m) per second, and the greatest exponent of the Ju 87G-1, Hans-Ulrich Rudel, was ultimately credited with the personal destruction of 519 Russian armoured vehicles. It was he who flew 2,530 combat missions mentioned above and continued to lead Stuka formations in daylight long after the other Stukagruppen had replaced their vulnerable aircraft with the Focke-Wulf Fw 190.

Another variant produced by converting aircraft of the Ju 87D series was the Ju 87H dual-control trainer. No trainer had been considered necessary in the early days of Ju 87 service, but by 1943 the art of surviving in the type had become so specialized and important on the Eastern Front that even experienced bomber and fighter pilots had to go out with a Ju 87 instructor before taking up their places in the decimated ranks of the Stukagruppen. Almost all versions of Ju 87D were converted into H models, retaining the same suffix numbers. Outwardly the differences included removal of armament and the addition of bulged side panels in the rear cockpit to give the instructor a measure of forward vision.

Possibly the first Ju 87B to drop bombs in anger, this early B-1 served in Spain with the *Staffel Jolanthe*, a very active *Legion Cóndor* unit which grew out of the *Kette Jolanthe* to which personnel from the newly formed StG 163 were posted in 1937. The name came from a pig in a Berlin comedy, painted on Ju 87A trousers.

This Ju 87B-2 crash-landed near Selsey, Sussex, on 'the hardest day' (16 August 1940) of the Battle of Britain after bombing Tangmere. It was assigned to 3/StG 2 'Immelmann', and carried the Gruppe emblem, the coat of arms of the city of Breslau. The adjacent red triangle denoted 87-octane fuel.

The Ju 87R was a long-range version with two 66-Imp gal (300-litre) external fuel tanks under the wings outboard of the dive brakes and a 33-Imp gal (150-litre) tank in each outer wing. This example operated in the Balkan campaign with 7./StG 77 from early 1941. The yellow areas were theatre markings for mainland Europe.

Use of the Ju 87 by the Italian Regia Aeronautica gave rise to the incorrect belief it was made in Italy as the Breda 201. This Ju 87B-2 was based at Gars el Arid in September 1941 with the 209ª Squadriglia, 101° Gruppo Autonomo (independent group). This unit painted its emblem on the wheel spats.

Seen in temporary white finish for the winter of 1941–2, this Ju 87B-2 also wears the yellow theatre band which by that time was becoming standard on the Eastern Front. It flew with Stab II/StG 1 (originally III/StG 51) whose unit emblem was painted on the cowling. The projection from the main leg is the siren.

Sand and snow

All versions could fly with tropical equipment and sand-dust filters, and many aircraft on the Eastern Front operated on skis in winter. There were several experimental variants, mainly concerned with tests of weapons intended for later aircraft. One of the most striking test programmes concerned one Ju 87D-3 fitted with large streamlined overwing passenger cabins. The idea was that the Ju 87, an aircraft well used to front-line operations, should become a vehicle for putting down agents behind enemy front lines. The trials programme got under way in early 1944 at the Graf Zeppelin Research Institute at Ruit, and the final design of cabin seated two men in tandem, both facing foward, with ample side windows which gave the pilot some lateral vision. In a shallow dive the two pods were to be pulled off the wing by streaming large parachutes, but there is no record of this actually being done, though the pods were flown with passengers.

The Ju 87 was widely used by all the Axis air forces, including those of Italy, Hungary, Slovakia, Romania and Bulgaria. When Ju 87s were discovered in Italian markings the totally fictitious belief arose among the British that the type was being made in Italy, even the invented type-

Junkers Ju 87 Stuka

Specification

Junkers Ju 87G-1
Type: anti-tank aircraft
Powerplant: one 1,400-hp (1044-kW) Junkers Jumo 211J-1 inline piston engine
Performance: maximum speed about 195 mph (314 km/h); cruising speed normally about 118 mph (190 km/h); rate of climb and service ceiling not known, but extremely poor; combat radius about 199 miles (320 km)
Weights: empty about 9,700 lb (4400 kg); maximum take-off about 14,550 lb (6600 kg)
Dimensions: span 49 ft 2½ in (15.00 m); length 37 ft 8¾ in (11.50 m); height 12 ft 9¼ in (3.90 m); wing area 362.6 sq ft (33.69 m²)
Armament: two 37-mm BK 3.7 cannon and one flexible 0.331-in (7.92-mm) MG 81 machine-gun, plus a useful bombload when the underwing cannon were not been carried

The last variant of the Ju 87 to become operational apart from the Ju 87H trainer was the Ju 87G-1 anti-tank model. This was not built as such, but rather converted from Ju 87D-5 airframes. The concept was the brainchild of the extraordinary Hans-Ulrich Rudel, who despite being shot down 30 times flew no fewer than 2,530 combat missions and destroyed 519 Russian tanks: the basic Ju 87D-5 was adapted to carry a pair of massive Flak 18 (BK 3.7) 37-mm cannon pods under its outer wing panels. The aircraft illustrated was on the strength of II/Schlachtgeschwader 3, more specifically the unit's 5. Staffel, serving on the Eastern Front in late 1944. The Ju 87G-1 could carry bombs instead of guns, but had no dive-brakes.

designation of Breda 201 Picchiatelli being widely published! In fact, from 1939 every Ju 87 was made by Weser in the same Tempelhof building.

The usual load on the Ju 87B series was an SC 500 (1,102-lb) bomb on crutches which swung out from the belly to let go of the bomb well away from the propeller. Speed built up to about 324 mph (550 km/h), and it became common practice to fit sirens to the landing gears – they were called 'Trombones of Jericho' – to strike extra terror into those near the target. Over short ranges, four SC50 (110-lb) bombs could also be hung under the wings. The pilot could fire two 0.31-in (7.92-mm) MG 17 guns mounted in the wings outboard of the kink, while the radio operator had an MG 15 of the same calibre to give protection above and behind. Production was transferred from Dessau to Weser Flugzeugbau in the great oval building at Berlin-Tempelhof airport, where it built up to 60 a month by mid-1939. Three B-1s made the first combat mission of World War 2 when they took off from Elbing at 04.26 on 1 September 1939 and devastated the approaches to the Dirschau bridge over the Vistula at 04.34, some 11 minutes before the Nazis declared war on Poland. Subsequently the Ju 87B-1 played a trememdous part in the Polish campaign, destroying all but two of the Polish surface warships, heavily bombing Polish troops on many occasions within 330 ft (100 m) of advancing German forces, and on one ghastly occasion virtually wiping out an entire Polish infantry division at Piotrkow railway station.

Carrier-borne variant

Alongside the improved Ju 87B-2 variants, which as single-seaters could carry an SC100 (2,205-lb) bomb, Weser built a batch of Ju 87C-0s with folding wings, hooks and many other changes to suit them to use abroad the carrier *Graf Zeppelin*, which was never completed. Another derived model was the extended-range Ju 87R series, with extra tanks in the outer wings and provision for underwing drop tanks. They entered service in time for the Norwegian campaign – where one put a radio station off the air by ramming the aerials – and then proved useful in the Balkans, Greece and Mediterranean theatres. One Ju 87R tested a large container, hung on the main bomb crutch, intended to carry spares and other cargo.

The Ju 87B and derivatives wrought havoc throughout Europe in the first two years of World War 2, meeting only one serious setback. Over England its losses were unacceptably heavy, 41 being shot down in the period 13–18 August 1940, so that from 19 August Stukas were withdrawn from attacks against UK targets. The type had already shown that, with German air supremacy, it could knock out the vital British coastal radars; but it was the same radars that enabled the defending fighters unfailingly to intercept, and the

vulnerability of the Ju 87 was suddenly apparent. The aircraft had been designed on the basis of good fighter protection, and in such conditions it had demonstrated such devastating effectiveness that many in the UK – foot-soldiers, journalists and politicians alike – cried 'Where are our dive-bombers?' In fact, the country had dive-bombers, such as the Blackburn Skua and Hawker Henley, but they played little part in the war, and the whole concept of the dive-bomber became a subject of violent argument. The success of the Stuka in ideal conditions also warped German procurement and the large Dornier Do 217 and Heinkel He 177 were wrongly designed as dive-bombers.

Even at the outbreak of war the Ju 87 was recognized as a somewhat dated design, but this was masked by its fantastic successes. As with so many other old Luftwaffe types, lack of a replacement resulted in planned termination of production being countermanded, and like that of the Messerschmitt Bf 110 and He 111, Ju87 output increased from 1941 to 1944. The standard basic type throughout this period was the Ju 87D, designed in 1940, first flown in early 1941 and in action

Junkers Ju 87D-3 cutaway drawing key

1. Spinner
2. Pitch-change mechanism housing
3. Blade hub
4. Junkers VS 11 constant-speed airscrew
5. Anti-vibration engine mounting attachments
6. Oil filler point and marker
7. Auxiliary oil tank (5.9 Imp gal/26.8 litre capacity)
8. Junkers Jumo 211J-1 12-cylinder inverted-vee liquid cooled engine
9. Magnesium alloy forged engine mount
10. Coolant (Glysantin-water) header tank
11. Ejector exhaust stubs
12. Fuel injection unit housing
13. Induction air cooler
14. Armoured radiator
15. Inertia starter cranking point
16. Ball joint bulkhead fixing (lower)
17. Tubular steel mount support strut
18. Ventral armour (8 mm)
19. Main oil tank (9.9 Imp gal/45 litre capacity)
20. Oil filling point
21. Transverse support frame
22. Rudder pedals
23. Control column
24. Heating point
25. Auxiliary air intake
26. Ball joint bulkhead fixing (upper)
27. Bulkhead
28. Oil tank (6.8 Imp gal/31 litre capacity)
29. Oil filler point and marker (Intava 100)
30. Fuel filler cap
31. Self-sealing starboard outer fuel tank (33 Imp gal/150 litre capacity)
32. Underwing bombs with *Dienartstab* percussion rods
33. Pitot head
34. Spherical oxygen bottles
35. Wing skinning
36. Starboard navigation light
37. Aileron mass balance
38. 'Double wing' aileron and flat (starboard outer)
39. Aileron hinge
40. Corrugated wing rib station
41. Reinforced armoured windscreen
42. Reflector sight

No picture could better illustrate the cranked wings of the Stuka than this shot taken through the windscreen by the pilot of an accompanying aircraft. This 1940 Ju 87B is still wearing four-letter factory codes and may be on flight test from Tempelhof. From this angle the dive-brakes are visible, but not the 'double wing'.

This Ju 87B-2 is fully painted in the Luftwaffe's approved style of camouflage for the Mediterranean theatre: colours 78 light blue, 79 sand yellow and 80 olive green, plus white theatre band. This particular Stuka served with 1./Stukageschwader 3 (1./StG 3) from various front-line fields in Cyrenaica in 1942.

Illustrated carying an SC1000 (2,205-lb) bomb, this Ju 87D-1/Trop shows the much imporved aerodynamic shape of the D in comparision with the B which preceded it. S7 + KS was the aircraft of Oberstleutnant Walter Siegel, Geschwaderkommodore of Stukageschwader 3 at Derna, Libra, in June 1942. Its markings indicate 8./StG 3.

43 Padded crash bar
44 Signal flare tube
45 Braced fuselage mainframe
46 Front spar/fuselage attachment point
47 Pilot's seat (reinforced with 4-mm side and 8-mm rear armour)
48 Inter-cockpit bulkhead
49 Sliding canopy handgrip
50 External side armour
51 Pilot's back armour (8 mm)
52 Headrest
53 Aft-sliding cockpit canopy (shown part open)
54 Radio mast cut-out
55 Anti-crash hoop (magnesium casting)
56 Radio mast
57 Radio equipment (FuGe 16) compartment
58 Additional (internal) side armour
59 Canopy track

60 Handhold/footrests
61 Braced fuselage mainframe
62 Rear spar/fuselage attachment point
63 Radio-operator/gunner's seat (folding)
64 Floor armour (5 mm)
65 Armoured bulkhead (8 mm)
66 Ammunition magazine racks
67 Additional (external) side armour with cut-out for hand grip
68 Internal side and head armour

69 Sliding canopy section (shown part open)
70 Ring-and-bead gunsights
71 Twin 7.9-mm Mauser MG 81Z machine gun on GSL-K 81 mount
72 Canopy track fairing
73 Peil G IV D/F equipment
74 Circular plexiglass access panel
75 Back-to-back L-section stringers (fuselage horizontal break)
76 First-aid stowage
77 Z-section fuselage frames
78 Radio aerial
79 Faired elevator mass balance
80 Starboard elevator
81 Tailplane structure
82 Tailplane brace/spar attachment point
83 Tailplane bracing strut
84 Fuselage skinning
85 Control runs
86 Tailfin attachment fairing
87 Tailfin structure
88 Rudder horn balance
89 Rudder
90 Rudder trim tab controls
91 Rudder trim tab
92 Rudder control linkage
93 Rudder post
94 Rear navigation light
95 Elevator tab

96 Port elevator
97 Faired elevator mass balance
98 Tailplane front spar
99 Control pulley circular access panels
100 Rudder lower hinge fairing
101 Tailplane bracing strut
102 Emergency tailskid
103 Tailwheel
104 Tailwheel leg
105 Jacking point
106 Fuselage stringers
107 Master compass
108 Crew entry step (port and starboard)
109 Entry step support (with control run cut-outs)
110 Wing root fairing
111 Non-slip walkway (aft section external metal strakes)
112 Fuel filler point
113 Non-slip walkway (forward section composite surface)
114 Leading-edge structure
115 Self-sealing port inner wing fuel tank (52.8 Imp gal/240 litre capacity)
116 Wing-joint external cover strip
117 Ball-and-socket wing attachment points
118 Armoured coolant radiator (port and starboard)
119 Inboard flap structure
120 Flap hinge

121 Rheinmetall-Borsig MG 17 machine gun of 7.92-mm calibre (port and starboard)
122 Ammunition tank (1000 rounds capacity) inboard of rib
123 Port outer self-sealing fuel tank (33 Imp gal/150 litre capacity)
124 Corrugated wing rib
125 ETC bomb rack support bar
126 ETC bomb rack underwing fairing
127 Port outboard flap
128 Port aileron
129 Aileron mass balance
130 Rear spar
131 Wing rib
132 Wing navigation light
133 Front spar
134 Wing leading edge
135 Underwing bomb load (two 110-lb/50-kg bombs) on multi-purpose carrier
136 Bomb shackles
137 Dienartstab percussion rod attachments
138 ETC 50/VIII fairing
139 Air brake (extended)
140 Air brake activating mechanism
141 Air brake (retracted)
142 Landing lamp
143 Wheel spat
144 Fork/spat attachment
145 Port mainwheel
146 Brake reservoir filler point
147 Cantilever fork
148 Leather shroud
149 Oleo-pneumatic shock absorber
150 Mainwheel leg
151 Siren fairing
152 Barrel of MG-17 machine gun
153 Wind-driven siren
154 Starboard wheel spat
155 PVC ventral bomb rack
156 Bomb cradle
157 Starboard wheel fork
158 Starboard mainwheel
159 Bomb release trapese
160 551-lb (250-kg) bomb with Dienartstab attachment

Another major operator of the Stuka was the Magyar Királyi Légierö (Hungarian air force). This Ju 87D-3 is depicted as it looked in 1943 when it was serving with 102/1 Zuhanöbombazö Szazad (dive-bomber squadron). Most Stukas assigned to 102/1 ZS were of the long-span D-5 variety, and by summer of 1943 had no spats.

Yet another of the minor Axis air forces, and one of the smallest, the Royal Bulgarian used a black/white cross insignia reminiscent of Nationalist Spain. This Ju 87D-5 operated on the Eastern Front and in mid-1944 against anti-Royalist partisans in Bulgaria itself. Note the long-span pointed wingtips.

Even more cumbersome and vulnerable than previous variants, the anti-tank Ju 87G-1 nevertheless proved extremely effective in the hands of an expert. This early example is seen in the markings of the Versuchskommando für Panzerbekampfung (test commando for anti-armour warfare) in April 1943; note the Kommando tank emblem.

on the Eastern and North African fronts by the end of 1941. This was powered by the 1,400-hp (1044-kW) Jumo 211J-1 driving a VS 11 propeller with very broad blades, making a major difference to flight performance, which was put to use in carrying much heavier loads. Maximum bomb load rose to 1800 kg (3,968 lb), the main crutch being able to take the PC1400 (3,086-lb) armour-piercing bomb and the wing racks the SC500 (1,102-lb) or a wide range of other stores including gun pods each housing either twin 20-mm cannon or six 0.31-in (7.92-mm) MG 81 machine-guns.

Junkers Ju 87 variants

Junkers Ju 87 V1: first prototype, with 640-hp (477-kW) Rolls-Royce Kestrel
Junkers Ju 87 V2: second rototype 610-hp (455-kW) Jumo 210Aa, hurriedly fitted single-fin tail unit
Junkers Ju 87 V3: third prototype properly designed tail, engine lowered to improve pilot view
Junkers Ju 87A: first production series, 640-hp (477-kW) Jumo 210Ca or (A-2) 680-hp (507-kW) Jumo 210Da about 200 built 1937–8)
Junkers Ju 87B: 1,200-hp (895-kW) Jumo 211Da, redesigned canopy and fuselage, larger vertical tail, spatted instead of trousered landing gears, bombloads up to 1000 kg (2,205 lb) (total deliveries in various sub-types about 1,300)
Junkers Ju 87C: navalized version intended for use from aircraft-carrier, folding wings, hook, catapult hooks,

jettisonable landing gear, flotation gear and extra tankage, operated from land bases
Junkers Ju 87D: major production version, 1,400-hp (1044-kW) Jumo 211J-1 or 1,500-hp (1119-kW) Jumo 211P-1, redesigned airframe with lower drag, bombload up to 3,968-lb (1800 kg), D-2 glider tug, D-3 increased armour, D-4 for torpedo-carrying, D-5 with extended wingtips, D-7 twin MG 151 cannon and night equipment, D-8 as D-7 without night equipment
Junkers Ju 87G-1: conversion of D-3 to attack armoured vehicles with two 37-mm BK 3,7 (Flak 18) guns
Junkers Ju 87H: dual-control trainers without armament, kinked rear canopy with side blisters
Junkers Ju 87R: derivative of Ju 87B-2 with augmented tankage and provision for drop tanks to increase range normally with single SC250 (551-lb) bomb

Weatherbeaten Ju 87B-2s of II/StG 1 on the Eastern Front, probably in autumn 1941. Nine more Ju 87s are in the distance at lower level. These aircraft are probably returning from a combat mission, with bomb racks empty. Spats were still in use at this time, and opposition to the Stuka still generally feeble.

The Ju 87D-5 introduced a wing of greater span to allow the heavy weapon loads to be carried with a better margin of safety. This D-5 was photographed on final landing approach, with full flap, on return from a mission with 8./StG 2 in the Kursk area in the summer of 1943. Its code was T6 + AS, T6 being that of StG 2 itself.

Boeing B-17 Flying Fortress

The B-17 Fortress flew through frost, flak, fire and fear to set a combat record which in terms of sheer courage and staying power of its crews has never been surpassed, and seldom equalled. At first the great olive-drab armadas returned smoking and riddled with holes. By late 1944 the shining silver Forts had almost defeated the Luftwaffe.

The huge fleet of the US 8th Air Force consisted mostly of Boeing B-17s. These flew the length and breadth of Germany and from 1942 to 1945, with their bombing of factories and other pinpoint targets, dominated the European theatre of war. Under their onslaught, even Goering's powerful Luftwaffe crumbled in the greatest and bloodiest air war the world had ever known. But in 1934, when American bombers were at best flying to such militarily insignificant destinations as Canada, Mexico or a few far-flung British islands, no one believed there would be conflict on such a scale. As money was short in the economic depression of the time, people thought they could bring in the Martin monoplane bomber to help them.

But when the US Army Air Corps put out a request for a new multi-engine bomber a few far-sighted engineers at the Boeing Airplane Company decided to interpret 'multi-engined' as meaning not two engines (as had generally been done before) but four. Admittedly they did this mainly in order to get more height over the target, but it had the effect of making the Boeing Model 299 significantly larger than its rivals. Design began on 18 June 1934, and the prototype made a very successful first flight in the hands of Les Tower

Prior to January 1944, when camouflage paint was generally discontinued in the USAAF, various olive drab and green paint schemes were in use. This 1942 picture of B-17Fs of the 8th Air Force's 91st Bomb Group (322nd Bomb Squadron) shows the irregular blotching of Medium Green (officially styled Shade 42) on a few B-17s.

Boeing B-17F-25-BO Flying Fortress

Specification

Type: heavy bomber with crew 8 to 10

Powerplant: four 1,200-hp (895-kW) Wright R-1820-97 Cyclone radial piston engines

Performance: maximum speed 295 mph (475 km/h); initial climb rate 900 ft (274 m) per minute; service ceiling 36,000 ft (10975 m); combat radius with 5,000-lb (2270-kg) bombload 800 miles (1287 km)

Weights: empty (typical) 34,000 lb (15422 kg); loaded (normal) 56,000 lb (25400 kg), (war overload from 1943) 72,000 lb (32660 kg)

Dimensions: span 103 ft 9 in (31.60 m); length 74 ft 9 in (22.80 m); height 19 ft 2½ in (5.85 m); wing area 1,420 sq ft (131.92 m²)

Armament: maximum bombload 9,600 lb (4355 kg), later increased to 17,600 lb (7983 kg); defensive firepower normally 11 guns of 0.5-in (12.7-mm) calibre and one of 0.30-in (7.62-mm) calibre

Fast Woman was a B-17F serving with the 359th Bomb Squadron, 303rd Bomb Group, 8th Air Force, based at Molesworth. Its finish was olive drab (weathered a purplish hue) and medium green. Lettering at this time was in yellow, black being used after the switch on 1 January 1944 to natural metal finish. Note the pre-July 1943 national insignia.

Boeing B-17

This famed B-17G, *A Bit o' Lace* of the 711th BS, 447th BG, based at Rattlesden, actually had nose art painted and signed by Milton Caniff (nose art, often featuring the female form, was invariably well executed). The 447th did not use squadron code letters only this colourful yellow livery.

KJ109 was a B-17G-55 assigned to the RAF and completely re-equipped with chin and ball turrets replaced by a vast assortment of powerful electronics. It operated from Oulton with No. 223 Squadron on highly secret – and extremely effective – 'Jostle', 'Piperack' and 'Mandrel' missions, part of No. 100 Group's new art of electronic war.

at Boeing Field on 28 July 1935. The main purpose of the new bomber was to defend the United States by bombing an invasion fleet (the only plausible kind of target) and it was the nature of this mission, rather than heavy defensive armament, that resulted in Boeing eventually registering the name Flying Fortress.

Triumph and disaster

On 20 August 1935 the impressive aircraft, unpainted except for US Army Air Corps rudder stripes and civil registration X13372, flew nonstop to Wright Field at an average faster than the maximum possible speed of its twin-engined rivals. But on the first officially observed flight before the USAAC evaluation officers, on 30 October 1935, the great bomber took off, climbed far too steeply, stalled and dived into the ground, bursting into a ball of fire. The accident was caused entirely by someone having omitted to remove the external locks on the elevators, and though the immediate winner of the official trials had to be the Douglas B-18, the much greater potential of the great Boeing bomber resulted in a service-test order for 13, designated Y1B-17, placed on 17 January 1936.

These had many changes, especially to the landing gear, armament and in having 930-hp (694-kW) Wright Cyclone engines instead of 750-hp (560-kW) Pratt & Whitney Hornets. In 1937 the machines were delivered to the 2nd Bombardment Group at Langley Field, which subsequently flew almost 10,000 hours with no serious trouble and did more than any other unit in history to solve the problems of long-distance bombing, especially at high altitude. A 14th aircraft was built as the Y1B-17A with engines fitted with General Electric turbo-superchargers, which increased the speed from 256 mph (412 km/h) to 311 mph (500 km/h) and raised the operating height to well over 30,000 ft (9145 m).

Results with the B-17 (as the Y1B was called after its test period was complete) were so good the USAAC not only

The short-lived Model 299 prototype had Hornet S1EG engines, and twin-strut main landing gears. On the fin is the Boeing Airplane emblem and model number, and the rudder carries US Army stripes and serial. Gross weight of 16 US tons (32,000 lb) was just half that of a laden B-17G. Making the Model 299 was a gigantic financial risk.

Boeing B-17F Flying Fortress cutaway drawing key

1 Rudder construction	23 Aerial attachment	39 Gun support frame
2 Rudder tab	24 Aerials	40 Ammunition box
3 Rudder tab actuation	25 Fin leading edge de-icing boot	41 Ventral aerial
4 Tail gunner's station	26 Port elevator	42 Waist gunners' positions
5 Gunsight	27 Port tailplane	43 Port waist 0.5-in (12.7-mm) machine gun
6 Twin 0.5-in (12.7-mm) machine guns	28 Tailplane leading-edge de-icing boot	44 Ceiling control cable runs
7 Tail cone	29 Dorsal fin structure	45 Dorsal aerial mast
8 Tail gunner's seat	30 Fuselage frame	46 Ball turret stanchion support
9 Ammunition troughs	31 Tailwheel actuation	47 Ball turret stanchion
10 Elevator trim tab	32 Toilet	48 Ball turret actuation mechanism
11 Starboard elevator	33 Tailwheel (retracted) fairing	49 Support frame
12 Tailplane structure	34 Fully-swivelling retractable tailwheel	50 Ball turret roof
13 Tailplane front spar	35 Crew entry door	
14 Tailplane/fuselage attachment	36 Control cables	
15 Control cables	37 Starboard waist hatch	
16 Elevator control mechanism	38 Starboard waist 0.5-in (12.7-mm) machine gun	
17 Rudder control linkage		
18 Rudder post		
19 Rudder centre hinge		
20 Fin structure		
21 Rudder upper hinge		
22 Fin skinning		

Numerous B-17s and B-24s landed more or less undamaged in Sweden and Switzerland during World War 2. B-17F-115 was *Veni Vidi Vici* of the 388th BG based at Knettishall on 29 February 1944, but on that day landed in Sweden. Eight months later it emerged from AB Aerotransport's shops as a 14-passenger airliner.

SWEDEN
SE-BAK

124585

B-17F No. 41-24585 was delivered to the 303rd BG's 360th BS, became *Wulf Hund* and at the very start of operations, on 12 December 1942, arrived almost undamaged in France. Its subsequent career was extremely active, initially as a special target for developing anti-B-17 tactics and finally on secret tasks with KG 200.

51 Twin 0.5-in (12.7-mm) machine guns
52 Ventral ball turret
53 Wingroot fillet
54 Bulkhead
55 Radio operator's compartment
56 Camera access hatch
57 Radio compartment windows (port and starboard)

70 Horizontal bomb stowage (port side shown)
71 Dinghy stowage
72 Twin 0.5-in (12.7-mm) machine guns
73 Dorsal turret
74 Port wing flaps
75 Cooling air slots
76 Aileron tab (port only)
77 Port aileron
78 Port navigation light
79 Wing skinning
80 Wing leading edge de-icing boot
81 Port landing light
82 Wing corrugated inner skin
83 Port out wing fuel tank (nine inter-rib cells)

98 Windscreen
99 Central control console pedestal
100 Side windows
101 Navigation equipment
102 Navigator's compartment upper window (subsequently replaced by ceiling astrodome)
103 Navigator's table
104 Side gun mounting
105 Enlarged cheek windows (flush)
106 Ammunition box
107 Bombardier's panel
108 Norden bombsight installation
109 Plexiglass frameless nose-cone
110 Single 0.5-in (12.7-mm) nose machine gun
111 Optically-flat bomb aiming panel

117 Wing front spar/fuselage attachment
118 Battery access panels (wingroot leading edge)
119 No 3 engine nacelle spar bulkhead
120 Intercooler pressure duct
121 Mainwheel well
122 Oil tank (nacelle inboard wall)
123 Nacelle structure
124 Exhaust
125 Retracted mainwheel (semi-recessed)
126 Firewall
127 Cooling gills

135 1,000 hp Wright R-1829-65 radial engine
136 Exhaust collector ring
137 Engine upper bearers
138 Firewall
139 Engine lower bearers
140 Intercooler assembly

58 Ammunition boxes
59 Single 0.3-in (7.62-mm) dorsal machine gun
60 Radio compartment roof glazing
61 Radio compartment/bomb-bay bulkhead
62 Fire extinguisher
63 Radio operator's station (port side)
64 Handrail links
65 Bulkhead step
66 Wing rear spar/fuselage attachment
67 Wingroot profile
68 Bomb-bay central catwalk
69 Vertical bomb stowage racks (starboard installation shown)

84 No 1 engine nacelle
85 Cooling gills
86 Three-blade propellers
87 No 2 engine nacelle
88 Wing leading edge de-icing boot
89 Port mid wing (self sealing) fuel tanks
90 Flight deck upper glazing
91 Flight deck/bomb-bay bulkhead
92 Oxygen cylinders
93 Co-pilot's seat
94 Co-pilot's control column
95 Headrest/armour
96 Compass installation
97 Pilot's seat

112 Pitot head fairing (port and starboard)
113 D/F loop bullet fairing
114 Port mainwheel
115 Flight deck underfloor control linkage
116 Wingroot/fuselage fairing

128 Exhaust collector ring assembly
129 Three-blade propellers
130 Undercarriage retraction struts
131 Starboard mainwheel
132 Axle
133 Mainwheel oleo leg
134 Propeller reduction gear casing

141 Oil tank (nacelle outboard wall)
142 Supercharger
143 Intake
144 Supercharger waste-gate
145 Starboard landing light
146 Supercharger intake
147 Intercooler intake
148 Ducting
149 No 4 engine nacelle spar bulkhead
150 Oil radiator intake
151 Main spar web structure
152 Mid-wing fuel tank rib cut-outs

153 Auxiliary mid spar
154 Rear spar
155 Landing flap profile
156 Cooling air slots
157 Starboard outer wing fuel tank (nine inter-rib cells)
158 Flap structure
159 Starboard aileron
160 Outboard wing ribs
161 Spar assembly
162 Wing leading edge de-icing boot
163 Aileron control linkage
164 Wing corrugated inner skin
165 Wingtip structure
166 Starboard navigation light

fought for massive production numbers, in the teeth of opposition from the US Navy, but also with Boeing collaboration even planned a next-generation bomber which became the B-29. US Navy anger was so intense that production numbers had to be scaled down, and the production batch of the first series model, the B-17B, numbered only 39. These had numerous minor changes as well as a redesigned nose and larger rudder. They were the first aircraft in the world to enter service with turbocharged engines. The B-17B entered service in 1939 and was the fastest, as well as the highest-flying, bomber in the world. The US Army Air Corps had by this time embarked on a major programme of perfecting long-range strategic bombing by day, using the massed firepower of a large formation to render interception hazardous. It was expected that, because of the B-17's speed and height, opposing fighters would be hard-pressed to keep up and would present an almost stationary (relative to the bombers) target that could be blasted by the fire from hundreds of machine-guns.

Provision of adequate forward-firing defensive armament was always a problem with the B-17, but culminated in the B-17G series with four 0.5-in (12.7-mm) guns in two turrets (dorsal and chin, each with two guns) supplemented by a pair of manually operated cheek guns, one on each side of the nose.

Further power and speed

Boeing and Wright Field continued to improve the B-17 and in 1939 a further 39 were ordered under the designation B-17C. These were much heavier, weighing 49,650 lb (22520 kg) compared with about 43,000 lb (19505 kg) for a B-17, because of increased armour, self-sealing tanks, heavier defensive armament (with twin 0.5-in/12.7-mm guns above and in a new ventral 'bathtub', twin 0.3-in/7.62-mm guns in the nose and new flush side gun positions) and extra equipment. Despite the greater weight, the fitting of 1,200-hp (895-kW) engines made this the fastest of all versions, with a maximum speed of 320 mph (515 km/h). In spring 1941 a batch of 20 was assigned to the RAF, following 15 months of negotiations which finally resulted in the aircraft being supplied in exchange for complete information on their combat performance (this was prior to the 1940 Lend-Lease Act). As RAF Fortress Is they had a disastrous and mismanaged career which dramatically reduced their numbers to a handful (about nine) which were transferred to Coastal Command and the Middle East.

Further extensive internal improvements, a new electrical system and engine-cowl cooling gills, led to the B-17D, of which 42 were ordered in 1940. This was the latest model in

Some idea of how deadly the German heavy radar-predicted flak could be is afforded by this picture taken during the bomb run of the 486th Bomb Group on the hated Merseburg oil plants on 2 November 1944. One of the 100-plus heavy guns scored a direct hit through solid cloud on a B-17G of the 834th Bomb Squadron.

service at the time of Pearl Harbor (7 December 1941) when 30 were destroyed on the ground at Hickham Field and at Clark Field, Philippines, the following day. But by this time Boeing had developed a visually different model which incorporated all the lessons learned in World War 2 in Europe. Called Boeing 299O, it entered US Army Air Force service in December 1941 as the B-17E. Its most striking change was the much larger tail, with a giant dorsal fin and long-span tailplane giving better control and stability at high altitude. Armament was completely revised, with paired 0.5-in (12.7-mm) guns in a powered turret behind the cockpit, in a ventral turret at the trailing edge, and in a new manual turret in the tail. Another pair of guns could be fired by hand from the roof of the radio compartment, and with a single hand-aimed gun at each waist position this made a total of 10 heavy machine guns, plus two 0.3-in (7.62-mm) guns aimed from the nose. Further improvements in armour and equipment all helped to increase gross weight to 54,000 lb (24494 kg), so cruising speed inevitably fell from 231 to only 210 mph (338 km/h). This was the first B-17 in large-scale production, and deliveries totalled 512 including 45 sent to the RAF as Fortress IIAs.

Massive production

On 30 May 1942 Boeing flew the first B-17F with many further changes which allowed gross weight to soar to 65,000 lb (29484 kg) with a potential bomb load for short ranges of 20,800 lb (9435 kg), though on normal combat missions the load seldom exceeded 5,000 lb (2268 kg). The only obvious external change on the F-model was the more pointed nose moulded in one piece of Plexiglas. This type went into production not only at Boeing but also in a great nationwide pool with assembly lines at Douglas (Long Beach) and Vega (a Lockheed subsidiary at Burbank). Boeing built 2,300 of this model, and Douglas and Vega added 605 and 500.

With the B-17E and B-17F the US 8th Air Force built up its early strength in England. The first combat mission was flown on 17 August 1942 by 12 B-17Es of the 97th Bomb Group against a marshalling yard near Rouen. This was the small beginning to the greatest strategic striking force ever created, which was to lead to a three-year campaign in the course of which 640,036 US tons of bombs were dropped on German targets and, at the cost of grievous losses, supremacy was eventually obtained even over the heart of Germany in daylight.

By far the most numerous model of B-17 was the last. The B-17G was the final result of bitterly won combat experience and among other changes it introduced a chin turret firing

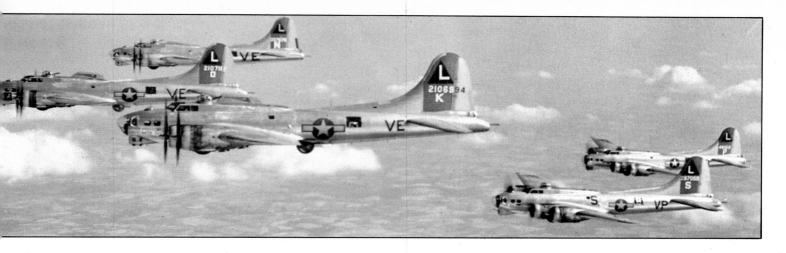

ahead with twin accurately aimed 0.5-in (12.7-mm) guns. Previously German fighters had brought down many B-17s with head-on attacks, but the B-17G, with the chin turret plus two more 0.5-in (12.7-mm) cheek guns (and possibly the dorsal turret) firing ahead was a tougher proposition. The B-17G had enclosed waist positions, much greater ammunition capacity and, like most B-17Fs, paddle-blade propellers to handle the greater weight and prevent too much deterioration in performance. Most B-17Gs had improved turbochargers which actually increased service ceiling to 35,000 ft (10670 m), but these bombers were so heavy the cruising speed fell to 182 mph (293 km/h). This increased the time the gigantic formations were exposed to rocket and cannon attack by the German fighters; conversely, of course, it lengthened the time the B-17 guns had to destroy those fighters.

Electronic versions

Boeing built 4,035 B-17Gs. Douglas 2,395 and Vega 2,250, a total of 8,680. The total of all versions was 12,731, of which 12,677 were formally accepted by the USAAF. The B-17F was used by the RAF as the Fortress II and the B-17G as the Fortress III, the main user being Coastal Command. Some were modified with a radar in place of the chin or ball turret, and for use against surfaced U-boats a 40-mm Vickers S gun was fitted in a nose mount. The B-17G was also the chief heavy carrier of special electronics for the RAF's No. 100 Group, Nos 214 and 223 Sqns being the pioneers of spoofing, decoy, jamming and intelligence missions with 19 distinct types of electronic or related device including the superpower emitters coded 'Jostle' and 'Piperack'. The only electronic device often carried by USAAF B-17s was the early H_2X or Micky Mouse radar used for bombing through cloud. This set's scanner was normally housed in a retractable radome under the nose or in place of the ball turret.

Elimination of paint from the B-17 gave a measurable gain in speed or reduced fuel consumption (because cruising speed was preset at a figure all aircraft could easily maintain at full load). These B-17Gs, built by Douglas, were photographed with the 381st Bomb Group (VE code, 532nd BS; VP, the 533rd). Home base was Ridgewell.

The ball turret, a retractable installation on the B-24 Liberator, was fixed on the B-17. Originally the B-17E had been fitted with a drum-type ventral turret aimed by a gunner in the fuselage, sighting via a periscope. This was soon replaced by the aptly named spherical ball-turret made by the Sperry company. The gunner had to climb into this and squat with his knees fully bent for perhaps five or six hours. A belly landing could flatten the ball-turret and its occupant, and there were many occasions when because of combat damage the turret doors jammed and a belly landing would have killed the ball-turret gunner. Normal procedure for a belly landing was to get the gunner out and then, using special tools, disconnect the whole turret from the aircraft and let it fall free. On one occasion a B-17 returned with severe combat damage and jammed landing gears, and near its home airfield it was found that the special tools were not on board. The executive officer of the station was notified by radio; within minutes he had grabbed a set of tools and taken off. For more than two hours he circled in close formation with the stricken B-17 trying to pass the tools on the end of a cable. He succeeded.

In 1942 various special versions of B-17 were produced by Vega to serve as escort fighters. The first was the second Vega-built B-17F, which was rebuilt as an XB-40 with many armament changes including a second dorsal turret and a bomb bay full of ammunition. It was followed by 20 YB-40s

The subject of this colour profile is a B-17C, which introduced the ventral bathtub also used on the D, but had flush waist gun positions instead of blisters. The B-17D's differences were mainly internal.

Ship 41-9023 was named *Yankee Doodle*, and was one of the most famous of all US bombers. Assigned to the 414th BS, 97th BG, it carried General Ira C. Eaker, commanding general of the VII Bomber Command, on the very first mission in Europe, to Rouen railway workshops on 17 August 1942. The total force: just 12 Fortresses.

Boeing B-17

In a typical story of amazing nerve and skulduggery, the infant Israeli air force, the Heyl Ha'Avir, managed to get hold of three B-17Gs in 1948. Devoid of guns, and with turret holes gaping open or with wood/plaster sealing (for the chin hole), and devoid of navigation gear, they bombed Cairo on their way to Israel!

Boeing B-17 variants

Boeing 299: prototype with four 750 hp (560 kW) Pratt & Whitney Hornet engines often called XB 17 but in fact had no military designation (total 1)
Y1B-17: service test batch four 930 hp (694 kW) Wright R-1820-39 engines operational equipment five 0.3 in (7.62-mm) guns, 4,800 lb (2177 kg) bombload later redesignated B-17 (total 13)
Y1B-17A: single aircraft with R-1820-51 turbocharged Cyclone engines
B-17B: Boeing 299E; later styled 299M first production model (total 39)
B-17C: Boeing 299H four R-1820-65 engines improved armament and equipment (total 38)

B-17D: Boeing 299H further improvements (total 42)
B-17E: Boeing 2990 complete redesign and heavier armament, first major production version (total 512)

B-17F: Boeing 299P, restressed for higher weights R-1820-97 engines, frameless plastic nose (total 3,405)

Boeing B-17C

Boeing B-17E

Boeing B-17F

B-17G: standard bomber from 1943 Dash 97 engines with B 2 (from late 1944 B-22) turbo, chin turret (normal detensive armament 13 .05 in (12.7 mm) guns) basis for numerous conversions and post war variants (total 8,680)

---

with even heavier armament including quadruple gun mounts at nose and tail and a total of as many as 30 guns of up to 37- or 40-mm calibre! So heavy were these 'fighters' that they could not even keep formation with the B-17 bombers, and though they flew nine combat missions in 1943 they were judged unsuccessful.

In 1943 Boeing converted the ninth production B-17E to have liquid-cooled Allison engines of 1,425 hp (1063 kW) each; these naturally resulted in improved performance but it remained a one-off prototype (designated XB-38). Another unique machine was the plush XC-108 VIP transport which began life as a B-17E (41-2593) but was converted for General Douglas MacArthur, supreme commander in the Pacific, with a comfortable interior for 38 passengers. The XC-108A was a similar conversion but for cargo, with a large door on the left side. The YC-108 was a VIP conversion of a B-17F, and the XC-108B was a B-17F tanker which ferried fuel 'over the hump' from India to China.

Oddities and other developments

The F-9s were a batch of 16 B-17Fs rebuilt by United Airlines at Cheyenne as strategic reconnaissance machines with from six to ten cameras in fuselage installations. Another 45 B-17Fs were converted as F-9As or F-9Bs, while 10 B-17Gs were turned into F-9Cs, the post-war designation for survivors being FB-17 up to 1947 and RB-17 thereafter. One B-17F served with the US Navy, and late in the war 40 B-17Gs were transferred to the US Navy to pioneer the technique of AEW (airborne early warning) with the newly developed APS-120 radar in a vast chin blister; this variant was designated PB-1W.

A strange wartime rebuild was the Aphrodite cruise-missile conversion in which war-weary B-17Fs and B-17Gs were stripped of everything that could be removed and packed with 10 tons of Torpex, a British explosive with 50 per cent greater blasting power than Amatol. Under the project names 'Perilous' and 'Castor' many tests were made, the take-off being made by two pilots in an open cockpit who then baled out to leave the Fortress (official designation BQ-17) under radio control from an accompanying aircraft such as a B-17 or PV-1. Though 11 combat launches were made on German targets the idea was judged rather too perilous after one BQ-7 had made a crater over 100 ft (30 m) in diameter in England and another had broken radio link and orbited a British city before heading out to sea.

In 1944 British experience was used in converting B-17Gs into B-17H air/sea rescue aircraft with an airborne lifeboat and search radar; post-war these were designated SB-17G. Other post-war variants included the CB-17 and VB-17 transports, TB-17 trainers, radio-guided QB-17 versions and DB-17 radio director aircraft. These soldiered on with the USAF after its formation in 1947, and also with various minor air forces. Many others became civil airliners.

No history of the B-17 would be complete, however, without reference to its exciting cloak-and-dagger operations with I/KG 200, the clandestine Gruppe of the Luftwaffe whose story has only recently come into the open. The B-17, mainly the G model, was its most important captured type, used for numerous long-range missions under the cover-designation Dornier Do 200. These machines carried out daring operations throughout Europe from Norway to Jordan and the Western Desert. They were not specifically intended to deceive the Allies, and wore German markings; they were used just because they were better for the job than any German aircraft!

It is difficult to praise any Allied aircraft more highly. It is undoubtedly due to the B-17 that the Allies gained air supremacy in Europe towards the end of the war.

From a distance this B-17G, ship number 43-37716, merely looks a trifle dirty or weatherbeaten. On closer inspection it can be seen to be the famous 5 Grand, the 5,000th B-17 built by Boeing, covered with the names of every Seattle worker who found a space.

Messerschmitt Bf 109

Longest-serving of all German interceptors, Willy Messerschmitt's classic Bf 109 was the cornerstone of the Luftwaffe's fighter arm throughout World War 2, being built in greater numbers than any other aircraft and credited with more air victories than any other fighter in the history of aerial warfare.

When aircraft designer Willy Messerschmitt began planning the Bf 109 in his Bavarian aircraft factory, he adapted some of the features of his four-seater passenger aircraft, the Bf 108 Taifun, and created a small, angular low-wing monoplane with a retractable undercarriage and an enclosed cockpit. The new Junkers Jumo 210A was to have been the engine, but this was not yet complete. Instead, the 695-hp (518-kW) Rolls Royce Kestrel VI was imported, and the new machine was completed in September 1935.

When flown in competition with the Ar 80 V1, Fw 159 V1 and He 112 V1, at the Travemünde trials, the Bf 109 V1 performed well despite minor problems and, amid general surprise, was rewarded by a contract for 10 prototype development aircraft (although it was not in fact declared the outright winner, 10 Heinkel aircraft also being ordered).

Three further prototypes (the Bf 109 V2 registered D-IUDE, Bf 109 V3 D-IHNY and Bf 109 V4 D-IOQY) were flown in 1936, powered by Jumo 210A engines and with provision for two synchronized Mg 17 machine-guns in the nose decking. However, rumours abounded that the British Hawker Hurricane and Supermarine Spitfire were to be armed with four guns, so that by the time the Bf 109 V4 prototype flew a third Mg 17 was planned to fire through the propeller hub.

The proposed two-gun Bf 109A production version did not therefore materialize, and the first pre-production Bf 109 B-0 examples were flown early in 1937, at the same time as the Bf 109 V5, Bf 109 V6 and Bf 109 V7 prototypes. Considerable operational experience was gained by three Staffeln of Jagdgruppe 88, which were equipped with production examples of the Bf 109B-1, Bf 109B-2 and Bf 109C-1 versions during the Spanish Civil War, experience that not only assisted in the development of the aircraft itself

but of air combat in general; for it was largely through men such as Werner Mölders and Adolf Galland (the former arguably the finest fighter pilot of all time, and the latter to become Germany's General of Fighters during World War 2), who fought in Spain with the Bf 109, that there came to be evolved the basic air fighting tactics which were to last until the end of the era of gun fighting air-combat.

By the beginning of World War 2 in September 1939, the Luftwaffe had standardized its fighter equipment with the Bf 109. The Bf 109D series, although produced in fairly large numbers and still in service, was giving place to the Bf 109E (widely known as the 'Emil'). Ten pre-production Bf 109E-0s appeared late in 1938 with two nose-mounted MG 17 machine-guns and two in the wings, and powered by the 1,100-hp (812-kW) DB 601A engine. Production Bf 109E-1s started leaving the Augsburg factory at the beginning of 1939 with alternative provision for two 20-mm MG FF cannon in place of the wing machine-guns. Maximum speed was 354 mph (570 km/h) at 12,305 ft (3750 m) and service ceiling 36,090 ft (11000 m), performance figures which helped the Bf 109E to eclipse all of its opponents in the first eight months of the war. A sub-variant, the Bf 109E-1/B, introduced soon after, was a fighter-bomber capable of carrying a 551-lb (250-kg) bomb under the fuselage.

Production of the Emil was shifted from Augsburg to Regensburg in 1939 (to make way for the Bf 110 twin-engine fighter) as a massive subcontract programme was undertaken by Ago, Arado, Erla and WNF, no less than 1,540 aircraft being delivered that year. On the eve of the invasion of Poland the Jagdverband comprised 12 Gruppen flying 850 Bf 109E-1s and Bf 109E-1/Bs and one with Ar 68s. Some 235 Bf 109D-1s were still serving with the Zerstörergeschwader.

One of the earliest known air-to-air photographs of a Bf 109, this November 1936 picture shows the Bf 109V4 (no. 4 prototype), with Jumo 210A engine and armament of three MG 17 machine-guns, each with 500 rounds. The similarity to later production Bf 109 versions is strikingly apparent.

To speed production by an as-yet small industry the Bf 109 was licensed in 1937 to Fieseler and in 1938 to Focke-Wulf and Erla. This photograph was taken at Bremen in August 1938 and shows the first 10 Bf 109C-2s completed by Focke-Wulf. The C-2 was the final Jumo-engined version, with five MG 17s.

Introduced into Luftwaffe service midway
through the Battle of Britain in August 1940, the
Messerschmitt Bf 109E-7 featured a modified
fuel system and attachments for a ventral drop
tank. Being equipped to carry the extra fuel, the
new aircraft were able to provide effective
escort for the big daylight raids over London in
September 1940. 'Red 2' (no. 2058), depicted
here, was being flown by Unteroffizier Klick of
3./LG2 when it was shot down by RAF fighters in
the famous raids on London of 15 September.

Messerschmitt Bf 109

Specification

Messerschmitt Bf 109E-7

Type: single-seat interceptor fighter

Powerplant: one 1,200-hp (895-kW) Daimler Benz DB 601N 12-cylinder inverted-vee liquid-cooled inline engine

Performance: maximum speed 359 mph (578 km/h) at 12,300 ft (3749 m);
Initial climb rate 3,300 ft (1006 m) per minute; service ceiling 36,500 ft (11125 m); range 680 miles (1094 km)

Weights: empty 4,440 lb (2014 kg); maximum take-off 6,100 lb (2767 kg)

Dimensions: span 32 ft 4½ in (9.86 m); length 28 ft 8 in (8.74 m); height 11 ft 2 in (3.40 m); wing area 174 sq ft (16.16 m²)

Armament: one hub-firing 20-mm (MG FF/M cannon and four 7.9-mm (0.31-in) MG 17 machine-guns in nose decking and wings

Messerschmitt Bf 109

The first occasion on which Bf 109s fought the RAF was during the daylight raid by 24 unescorted Vickers Wellingtons on Wilhelmshaven on 18 December 1939, 12 of the bombers being destroyed for the loss of two Bf 109Es of JG 77.

Deadly production

In 1940 production of the Emil increased to 1,868 aircraft, the D-series being almost entirely discarded from front-line use. Principal sub-variants produced that year were the Bf 109E-2, Bf 109E-3 (with two MG 17s in the nose and two in the wings, plus an MG FF/M firing through the propeller shaft) and the Bf 109 E (with two nose MG 17s and two wing MG FF cannon). All these versions saw widespread action during the great daylight battles over southern England in the Battle of Britain. When employed in the 'free chase' tactic they proved deadly, being generally superior to the Hurricane and well matched with the Spitfire. However, as is now well known, the capabilities of the Bf 109E were frequently squandered when the aircraft were too often tied to close escort on bomber formations, a role in which the Bf 109Es were deprived of their greatest assets, speed and manoeuvrability. Later in the Battle of Britain they were also employed as fighter-bombers (the Bf 109E-4/B). Other variants, which appeared soon after the Battle of Britain, included the Bf 109E-5 and Bf 109E-6 reconnaissance fighters, the latter with DB 601N engine, the Bf 109 E-7 with provision for belly drop-tank, and the Bf 109E-7/Z with GM-1 nitrous oxide engine boost.

Early in 1941 the Emil was beginning to appear in the Mediterranean theatre, tropicalized versions of the above sub-variant serving with JG 27 in North Africa. However, by the time Germany opened its great attack on the Soviet Union in June 1941, the Bf 109F series was beginning to go in the front-line fighter squadrons although the Emil continued to serve for a long time yet.

Powered by the 1,200-hp (895-kW) DB 601E, the Bf 109F was generally regarded as the most attractive of the entire Bf 109 family introducing extended and rounded wingtips and enlarged spinner while Frise ailerons and plain flaps replaced the Emil's slotted flaps. A fully retractable tailwheel superseded the earlier fixed type, and a cantilever tailplane was introduced. In the matter of gun armament, however, the Bf 109F was widely criticized, for it reverted to the hub cannon and two nose decking MG 17s. While this tended to satisfy the German *Experten* (aces) as benefitting the aircraft's performance, it was pointed out that the majority of Luftwaffe fighter pilots needed a heavier armament with which to achieve a 'kill'.

Pre-production Bf 109F-0s were evaluated by the Luftwaffe during the second half of 1940, and Bf 109F-1s were delivered early the following year. A number of accidents indicated that removal of the tailplane struts left the entire tail unit vulnerable to sympathetic vibration at certain oscillating frequencies of the engine, and strengthening modifications were quickly put in hand. After the Bf 109F-2 (with 15-mm

J-310 was the first Bf 109 to serve Switzerland's Fliegertruppe, delivered on 17 December 1938. Powered by a 680-hp (507-kW) Jumo 210Da engine (like the German Bf 109B) it had an armament of four MG 17 machine-guns (as fitted to the Bf 109C). The Swiss used Bf 109s until the end of 1949, some being assembled locally.

Messerschmitt Bf 109G-14/U4 cutaway drawing key

1 Starboard navigation light
2 Starboard wingtip
3 Fixed trim tab
4 Starboard Frise-type aileron
5 Flush-riveted stressed wing-skinning
6 Handley Page leading-edge automatic slot
7 Slot control linkage
8 Slot equalizer rod
9 Aileron control linkage
10 Fabric-covered flap section
11 Wheel fairing
12 Port fuselage machine-gun ammunition-feed fairing
13 Port Rheinmetall Borsig 13-mm MG 131 machine-gun
14 Engine accessories
15 Starboard machine-gun trough

24 Blast tube
25 Propeller hub
26 Spinner back plate
27 Auxiliary cooling intakes
28 Cooling header tank
29 Anti-vibration rubber engine-mounting pads
30 Elektron forged engine bearer

31 Engine bearer support strut attachment
32 Plug leads
33 Exhaust manifold fairing strip
34 Ejector exhausts
35 Cowling fasteners
36 Oil cooler
37 Oil cooler intake
38 Starboard mainwheel
39 Oil cooler outlet flap

16 Daimler Benz DB 605AM 12-cylinder inverted-vee liquid-cooled engine
17 Detachable cowling panel
18 Oil filter access
19 Oil tank
20 Propeller pitch-change mechanism
21 VDM electrically-operated constant-speed propeller
22 Spinner
23 Engine-mounted cannon muzzle

40 Wing root fillet
41 Wing/fuselage fairing
42 Firewall/bulkhead
43 Supercharger air intake
44 Supercharger assembly
45 20-mm cannon magazine drum
46 13-mm machine-gun ammunition feed
47 Engine bearer upper attachment

Called 'tripala' by the Spanish (the earlier models had a two-blade propeller) the Bf 109E-1 was by far the best fighter in Spain in early 1939, when this picture was taken at a Légion Kóndor base. Armament was two cannon and two MG 17 machine-guns. The Légion transferred 40 Bf 109s to Spain, which built other models post-war.

Right: The Bf 109 V10 flown by Ernst Udet in July 1937 at the Zurich International Flying Meeting. Despite demonstrating an excellent performance, Udet crashed the aircraft during the Circuit of the Alps race after failure of the DB 600 engine.

6D-ISLU

Left: Wearing the insignia of the Gruppen-Kommandeur, I Gruppe, of a Jagdgeschwader in 1939, the Bf 109D was powered by the DB 600A and was in effect the production version developed from the V10 prototype. It carried an armament of one hub-firing MG FF cannon and two MG 17s and its performance was in most respects better than a Spitfire I.

48 Ammunition feed fairing
49 13-mm Rheinmetall Borsig MG 131 machine-gun breeches
50 Instrument panel
51 20-mm Mauser MG 151/20 cannon breech
52 Heelrests
53 Rudder pedals
54 Undercarriage emergency retraction cables
55 Fuselage frame
56 Wing/fuselage fairing
57 Undercarriage emergency retraction handwheel (outboard)
58 Tail trim handwheel (inboard)
59 Seat harness
60 Throttle lever
61 Control column
62 Cockpit ventilation inlet

63 Revi 16B reflector gunsight (folding)
64 Armoured windshield frame
65 Anti-glare gunsight screen
66 90-mm armourglass windscreen
67 Galland-type clear-vision hinged canopy
68 Framed armourglass head/ back panel

69 Canopy contoured frame
70 Canopy hinges (starboard)
71 Canopy release catch
72 Pilot's bucket-type seat (8-mm back armour)
73 Underfloor contoured fuel tank (88-Imp gal/400 litres of 87 octane B4)
74 Fuselage frame

81 Aerial mast
82 D/F loop
83 Oxygen cylinders (three)
84 Filler pipe

85 Wireless equipment packs (FuG 16ZY communications and FuG 25a IFF)
86 Main fuel filler cap
87 Aerial
88 Fuselage top keel (connector stringer)
89 Aerial lead-in
90 Fuselage skin plating sections
91 U-stringers
92 Fuselage frames (monocoque construction)
93 Tail trimming cables
94 Tailfin foot fairing
95 Starboard fixed tailplane
96 Elevator balance
97 Starboard elevator
98 Geared elevator tab
99 All-wooden tailfin construction
100 Aerial attachment
101 Rudder upper hinge bracket
102 Rudder post
103 Fabric-covered wooden rudder structure

75 Circular access panel
76 Tail trimming cable conduit
77 Wireless leads
78 MW 50 (methanol/water) tank (25 Imp gal/114 litres capacity)
79 Handhold
80 Fuselage decking

104 Geared rudder tab
105 Rear navigation light
106 Port elevator
107 Geared elevator tab
108 Tailplane structure
109 Rudder actuating linkage
110 Elevator control horn
111 Elevator connecting rod
112 Elevator control quadrant
113 Tailwheel leg cuff
114 Castoring non-retractable tailwheel
115 Lengthened tailwheel leg
116 Access panel
117 Tailwheel shock-strut
118 Lifting point
119 Rudder cable
120 Elevator cables
121 First-aid pack
122 Air bottles
123 Fuselage access panel
124 Bottom keel (connector stringer)
125 Ventral IFF aerial
126 Master compass
127 Elevator control linkage
128 Wing root fillet
129 Camber-changing flap
130 Ducted coolant radiator
131 Wing stringers
132 Wing rear pick-up point
133 Spar/fuselage upper pin joint (horizontal)
134 Spar/fuselage lower pin joint (vertical)
135 Flaps equalizer rod
136 Rüstsatz R3 auxiliary fuel tank ventral rack
137 Undercarriage electrical interlock
138 Wing horizontal pin forward pick-up
139 Undercarriage retraction jack mechanism
140 Undercarriage pivot-bevel

141 Auxiliary fuel tank (Rüstsatz R3) of 66 Imp gal. (3000 litre) capacity
142 Mainwheel leg fairing
143 Mainwheel oleo leg
144 Brake liners
145 Mainwheel fairing
146 Port mainwheel
147 Leading-edge skin
148 Port mainwheel well
149 Wing spar
150 Flap actuating linkage
151 Fabric-covered control surfaces
152 Slotted flap structure
153 Leading-edge slot actuating mechanism
154 Slot equalizer rod
155 Handley Page automatic leading-edge slot
156 Wing stringers
157 Spar flange decrease
158 Wing ribs
159 Flush-riveted stressed wing-skinning
160 Metal-framed Frise-type aileron
161 Fixed trim tab
162 Wingtip construction
163 Port navigation light
164 Angled pitot head
165 Rüstsatz R6 optional underwing cannon gondola
166 14-point plug connection
167 Electrical junction box
168 Canon rear mounting bracket
169 20-mm Mauser MG 151/ 20 cannon
170 Cannon front mounting bracket
171 Ammunition feed chute
172 Ammunition magazine drum
173 Underwing panel
174 Gondola fairing
175 Cannon barrel

233

Aircraft VK + AB was Bf 109 V24 (prototype no. 24), works number 5604. It was built in 1940 alongside V23 (CE + BP) as the third and fourth development aircraft for the Bf 109F, with round wingtips, a better-streamlined engine installation and other changes. The Bf 109F was the nicest of all 109s to fly.

JG 54 Grünherz ('Green Heart') moved from northern France to the Soviet Union in 1941, and this photograph was taken on an airfield near the Leningrad front in summer 1942. These Bf 109-G2s bear the badges of III/JG 54 (left) and II/JG 54 (right). The G-2 was the first 'Gustav' to enter service, in late April 1942.

MG 151 replacing the 20-mm MG FF) came the principal version, the BF 109F-3, early in 1942 with a top speed of 390 mph (628 km/h) at 21,980 ft (6700 m).

Bf 109Fs had joined the Geschwaderstab and III Gruppe of Adolf Galland's JG 26 'Schlageter' early in 1941 on the Channel coast, and during the early stages of Operation 'Barbarossa' in the East this version equipped Major Günther Lützow's JG 3 'Udet', Werner Mölders' JG 51, Major Günther von Maltzahn's JG 53 'Pik As' and Major Johannes Trautloft's JG 54. The superiority of the new fighter (even over the Spitfire Mk V in the West) quickly became apparent as the German fighter pilots' victory tallies soared.

The Bf 109F underwent progressive improvement and development: the BF 109F-4 had an MG 151 rebarrelled to 20-mm, the Bf 109F-4/R1 could be fitted with *Rüstsatz* (field conversion kit) comprising two 20-mm MG 151 guns in underwing packs for the bomber-destroyer role, the Bf 109F-4/B fighter-bomber was capable of carrying up to 1,102 lb (500 kg) of bombs, and the Bf 109F-5 and Bf 109F-6 reconnaissance fighters were introduced later in 1942. It was principally in the tropicalized Bf 109F-4 that the 22-year-old Oberleutnant Hans-Joachim Marseille became the highest-scoring Luftwaffe fighter pilot in the West with 158 air victories, although he died baling out from a BF 109G-2 on 30 September 1942 in North Africa.

The Bf 109G (dubbed the 'Gustav' by German pilots) was introduced into service in the late summer of 1942 and came to be built in larger numbers than any other version. It was powered by the 1,475-hp (1100-kW) DB 605A, although pre-production Bf 109G-0s retained the DB 601E. Basic arm-

ament remained two nose-mounted MG 17s and hub-firing 20-mm MG 151/20 cannon. The Bf 109G-1 with pressure cabin, was powered by the DB 605A-1 with GM-1 power boosting, and the tropical version, the Bf 109G-1/Trop, carried 0.51-in (13-mm) MG 131s in place of the MG 17s, necessitating larger breech blocks and giving rise to the nickname *Beule* (bump) on account of the raised fairings foward of the windscreen. The Bf 109G-2 dispensed with the pressure cabin and the Bf 109G-2/R1 was a fighter-bomber; the Bf 109G-3 was similar to the Bf 109G-1 but with FuG 16Z radio, and the Bf 109G-4 was an unpressurized version of the Bf 109G-3. The Bf 109G-5 introduced the DB 605D engine with MW-50 water-methanol power-boosting (making possible a maximum power of 1,800 hp/1343 kW) for combat bursts), while the Bf 109G-5/R2 featured a taller rudder and lengthened tailwheel leg in an effort to counter the aircraft's swing on take-off.

Improvements and add-ons

Most important of all the Gustavs was the Bf 109G-6 which, in various sub-variants, was powered by AM, AS, ASB, ASD or ASM versions of the DB 605 engine; basic armament was the hub-firing 30-mm MK 108 cannon, two nose MG 131s and two underwing 20-mm MG 151/20 guns. Numerous *Rüstsatz* kits were produced including those to produce the Bf 109G-6/R1 fighter-bomber with a bombload of

The illustration shows a Bf 109E-4N of Jagdgeschwader 27, used in North Africa in 1941. It was equipped with four 7.92-mm machine guns.

'Red 4' of Jagdgeschwader 3 'Udet', a Bf 109E-3 of the Battle of Britain period. This version carried an armament of four MG 17 machine-guns and a hub-firing MG FF/M 20-mm cannon.

Pending the introduction of custom designed night fighters, obsolete Bf 109Cs formed the initial equipment of ad hoc night fighter units, in this case 10.(Nacht)/JG 77, based at Aalborg, Denmark, in July 1940.

Equipped with dust filter on the nose intake, this Bf 109E-7/Trop fighter-bomber was among the first German fighters to operate in the Mediterranean, equipping 7./JG 26 'Schlageter' at Gela in March 1941 for attacks on Malta.

Displaying the wasp markings of the famous 'Wespen-Geschwader' (Zerstörergeschwader 1) the Bf 109E-4/B fighter-bomber supplement the Bf 110 in the ground-attack role and provided top cover after dropping its bomb.

up to 1,102 lb (500 kg), and the Bf 109G-6/R2 bomber-destroyer with two 21-cm (8.27-in) WGr 210 'Dodel' rockets replacing the underwing cannon. The Bf 109G-6.U4 (with an *Umrüst-Bausatz* or factory conversion set) was armed with two 30-mm MK 108 underwing cannon, and the Bf 109G-6U4N night-fighter carried radar. Tropicalized versions of most of these were also produced. The Bf 109G-7 was not built, but the Bf 109G-8 reconnaissance fighter formed part of the equipment of Nahaufklärungsgruppe 13 late in 1943 on the Channel coast. Fastest of all Gustavs was the Bf 109G-10 with the DB 605D with MW-50 and bulged cockpit canopy (known as the 'Galand hood'); top speed was 429 mph (690 km/h) at 24,280 ft (7400 m); the Bf 109G-10/R2 and R6 possessed the revised tail and tailwheel assembly of the Bf 109G-5/R2 and were equipped with FuG 25a IFF equipment; the Bf 109G-10/U4 had provision for a belly gun pack containing two MK 108 30-mm guns, but this could be replaced by a non-jettisonable fuel tank known as the *Irmer Behalter*. The Bf 109G-12 was a two-seat trainer, field-modified from the Bf 109G-1 to provide conversion training on the Schulejagdgeschwader, notably JG 101, 102, 104, 106, 107 and 108 in 1944. Last operational version was the 'universal' Bf 109G-14 with lightened fixed armament but with provision for external guns, WGr210 rockets or bombs. The Bf 109G-16 heavily armoured ground-attack fighter-bomber entered production before Germany's surrender but did not see operational service.

Development of the Bf 109H high-altitude fighter started in 1943, being a progression from the F-series with increased wing span and the GM-1 boosted DB 601E. Maximum speed was 466 mph (750 km/h) at 33,135 ft (10100 m). Pre-production aircraft were evaluated operationally in France and a few sorties were flown by production Bf 109H-1s, but wing flutter problems caused the H-series to be abandoned, although projects included the Bf 109H-2 with Jumo 213E, and the Bf 109H-5 with DB 605 engines.

Last main operational version of the Bf 109 was the K-series, developed directly from the Gustav; indeed the Bf 109K-0 pre-production aircraft were converted G-series airframes. The Bf 109K-2 and Bf 109K-4 (pressurized) were powered by MW-50 boosted 2,000-hp (1492-kW) DB 605 ASCM/DCM engines and armed with one 30-mm MK 103 or MK 108 cannon and two 15-mm (0.59-in) MG 151 heavy machine-guns, and the Bf 109K-6 had provision for two underwing 30-mm MK 103s. Only two Bf 109K-14s (DB 605L with MW-50 and a top speed of 450 mph/725 km/h) saw action before the end of the war, being delivered to Major Wilhelm Batz's Gruppenstab, II/JG 52, in April 1945.

Trials and experiments

With the Focke-Wulf Fw 190 reaching full operational status only after two years of war, the Bf 109 provided the backbone of the Luftwaffe's fighter arm throughout World War 2: with more than 30,000 examples produced (because of confusion caused by the bombing of factories, an accurate production total could not be arrived at, but only the Russian Ilyushin Il-2 had a higher figure, with 36,163 models built), it was natural that experiments and projects abounded.

For example, among the more bizarre trials were those conducted on Bf 109Es to carry a parachutist in an over-wing 'paracapsule'. Another (in the Starr-Schlepp programme) involving the mounting of a Bf 109E on a DFS 230 troop-carrying glider as a means of delivering airborne forces; this experiment was followed later in the war by the well-known *Beethoven-Gerät* composite weapon system involving the use of Bf 109s and Fw 109s mounted atop unmanned Junkers Ju 88s loaded with explosives. A number of radical operational tactics were pioneered by Bf 109 units, including the aerial bombing of American bomber formations with 551-lb (250-kg)

Wearing the white 'theatre band' on the rear fuselage (denoting service in the Mediterranean), this Bf 109F-4/Trop belonged to 6./JG 53 based at Comiso in May 1942 during the Luftwaffe's assault on Malta.

The Bf 109G-14 with 'Galland' hood was a fighter-bomber version of the G-6, this 'Gustav' bearing the markings of III./JG 53. The 'Spiralschnauze' has no significance in this instance. Note the bulges over the breech blocks of the nose-mounted 13-mm (0.51-in) MG 131 guns.

bombs dropped from Bf 109Gs (pioneered by JG 1 in 1943), and the use by JG 300 of day fighters for freelance night combat against night bombers, known as *wilde Sau* tactics.

A development of the Emil was the Bf 109T carrierborne fighter, intended for deployment abroad the German carrier *Graf Zeppelin*. Featuring folding wings, arrester hook and catapult spools, 10 pre-production Bf 109T-0s and 60 Bf 109T-1s were produced between 1939 and 1941, but when the carrier's construction was abandoned most of these aircraft were delivered to the Luftwaffe for land-based operation.

Perhaps the most ambitious of all projects was the Bf 109Z *Zwilling*, involving the union of two Bf 109F airframes and outer wing panels by means of new wing and tail sections; the pilot was to have been accommodated in the port fuselage and two versions were proposed, a *Zerstörer* with five 30-mm guns and a fighter-bomber with a 2,205-lb (1000-kg) bombload. A prototype was built but this was never flown.

Bf 109s were supplied to numerous foreign air forces from 1939 onwards, and considerable licence-production of the Gustav was undertaken by Avia at Prague and IAR at Brasov in Romania. The most successful of the foreign air arms with Bf 109s was the Finnish air force, its highest scoring pilot, Lentomestari Eino Juutilainen, achieving 94 victories, of which 59 were scored in Gustavs; he was the highest-scoring non-German/Austrian fighter pilot of all time and his aircraft was never once hit in combat.

Despite the absence of unit markings it is known that this Bf109 was serving in autumn 1943 with II/JG 26, one of the crack fighter units in northern France. It is a G-6/R6, the R6 modification adding the pair of 20-mm MG151 cannon and ammunition in underwing gondolas. The slats are clearly visible here.

Taken in 1944, when many Bf 109s were being used in the anti-bomber role with heavy rocket mortars, this photograph shows a pair of G-6/Rs2 with the most common of these weapons, the Wfr Gr21 which lobbed 21-cm rockets from the tubes under the wings. They were called *Pulk Zerstörer* ('formation destroyer').

Messerschmitt Bf 109 variants

Bf109a (later Bf109V1): D-IABI, first prototype; 695-hp (518-kW) Rolls-Royce Kestrel V engine; first flight in September 1935
Bf109 V2, V3 and V4: three prototypes, (D-IUDE, D-IHNY and D-IOQY); Jumo 210A engines
Bf109B: pre-production **Bf109B-0** with Jumo 210B; **Bf109B-1** with Jumo 210D; **Bf109B-2** with Jumo 210E and later, 210G engines
Bf109 V10 and V13: two prototypes, (D-ISLU and D-IPKY); Daimler-Benz DB 600 engines
Bf109C: developed from **Bf109 V8** prototype; **Bf109C-0** and **Bf109C-1** with four MG17 guns; **Bf109C-2** with five MG17s
Bf109 V13: modified with boosted DB 601 engine; world speed record of 379.38 mph (610.54 km/h) on 11 November 1937
Bf109D: developed from Bf109 V10 and V13 prototypes; **Bf109D-0** with DB 600Aa and armament of one 20-mm and two 7.92-mm (0.31-in) guns; **Bf109D-1** similar; **Bf109D-2** with two wing MG 17s; **Bf109D-3** with two MG FFs in wings
Bf109 V14: prototype (D-IRTT); fuel-injection DB 601A engine; two 20-mm and two 7.92-mm (0.31-in) guns; **Bf109 V15** (D-IPHR) similar but one 20-mm gun
Bf109E: **Bf109E-0** with four 7.92-mm (0.31-in) guns; **Bf109E-1** (and **Bf109E-1/B** bomber) similar; **Bf109E-2** with two 20-mm and two 7.92-mm (0.31-in) guns; **Bf109E-3** with one hub 20-mm and four 7.92-mm (0.31-in) guns; **Bf109E-4** (also **Bf109E-4/B** and **Bf109E-4/Trop**) similar to Bf109E-3 but no hub gun; **Bf109E-4/N** with DB610N engine; **Bf109E-5** and **Bf109E-6** reconnaissance fighters with two 7.92-mm (0.31-in) guns; **Bf109E-7** similar to Bf109E-4/N with provision for belly tank (**Bf109E-7/U2** ground attack sub-variant); **Bf109E-7/Z** with GM-1 boost; **Bf109E-8** with DB601E engine; **Bf109E-9** reconnaissance fighter
Bf109F: **Bf109F-0** from E-airframes with DB 601N engine; **Bf109F-1** wih one 20-mm and two 7.92-mm (0.31-in) guns; **Bf109F-2** with one 15-mm and two 7.92-mm (0.31-in) guns (**Bf109F-2/Z** with GM-1); **Bf109F-3** with DB601E engine; **Bf109F-4** and **Bf109F-4/B** with one 20-mm and two 7.92-mm (0.31-in) guns and DB 601E; **Bf109F-5** and **Bf109F-6** reconnaissance fighters with two 7.92-mm (0.31-in) guns; trials aircraft included one with BMW 801 radial, one with Jumo 213, one with butterfly tail and one with wing fences
Bf109G: **Bf109G-0** with DB601E engine; **Bf109G-1** with DB 605A-1 and GM-1; **Bf109G-1/Trop** with one

20-mm and two 15-mm guns (*Beule*); **Bf109G-2** was unpressurized version of Bf109G-1 (also **Bf109G-2/R1** fighter-bomber); **Bf109G-3** with FuG 16Z radio; **Bf109G-4** unpressurized version of Bf109G-3; **Bf109G-5** with enlarged rudder had DB605D with MW-50; **Bf109G-6** with variations of DB 605 (see text) and two 13-mm (0.51-in), one 30-mm and two underwing 20-mm guns (also R and U sub-variants, see text); **Bf109G-8** reconnaissance fighter; **Bf109G-10** with DB605G and MW-50; **Bf109G-12** was two-seat trainer; **Bf109G-14** with one 20-mm and two 15-mm guns plus provision for underwing guns or rockets; **Bf109G-16** ground-attack fighter
Bf109H: high-altitude fighter developed from F-series; **Bf109H-0** pre-production; **Bf109H-1** with DB601E; **Bf109H-2** and **Bf109H-3** with Jumo 213; **Bf109H-5** with DB 605L
Bf109J: proposed Spanish licence-built version, not proceeded with
Bf109K: development from Bf109G-10; **Bf109K-0** with DB 605D and GM-1; **Bf109K-2** and **Bf109K-4** (pressurized) with DB 605ASCM/DCM and MW-50, and one 30-mm and two 15-mm guns; **Bf109K-6** with three 30-mm and two 15-mm guns; **Bf109K-14** with DB605L and MW-50
Bf109L: proposed version with Jumo 213E engine; maximum estimated speed 474 mph (763 km/h); not built)
Bf109S: proposed version with blown flaps; not built
Bf109T: carrierborne version of Bf109E for carrier *Graf Zeppelin*; 10 **Bf109T-0** converted by Fieseler; 60 **Bf109T-1** with DB601N; **Bf109T-2** was conversion of T-1 with deck gear removed
Bf109TL: project based on near-standard Bf109 with two underwing Jumo 109-004B turbojets; abandoned in 1943
Bf109Z Zwilling: twin Bf109F airframes with single pilot and five 30-mm guns (**Bf109Z-1**); **Bf109Z-2** with two 30-mm guns and 2,205-lb (1000-kg) bombload; **Bf109Z-3** and **Bf109Z-4** conversion of Bf109Z-1 and Bf109Z-2 respectively with Jumo 213 engines; one prototype built but not flown; led to Me 609 project
Me 209 V1, V2, V3 and V4: D-INJR, D-IWAH, D-IVFP and D-IRND; high-speed prototypes developed for speed records
Me 309 V1, V2, V3 and V4: GE-CU, GE-CV, GE-CW and GE-CX; high-speed, high-altitude fighter prototypes intended to replace Bf109F
Me609: projected development of Bf109Z *Zwilling* twin-Bf109); abandoned

Heinkel He 111: big Blitz bomber

Although a 1934 design, the Heinkel He 111 not only provided the muscle of Germany's 'strategic' bombing force at the beginning of World War 2 but, with surprisingly little alteration to its basic design, came to constitute the backbone of the Luftwaffe's bomber force until Hitler's eventual defeat in 1945.

When the Luftwaffe asked for a fast commercial transport plane to be built secretly, one which could be converted quickly and cheaply into a bomber, Siegfried and Walter Günter built the He 111. This was a twin-engined, larger version of the He 70 Blitz, which had been put into service by Lufthansa in 1934. The new machine had the same elliptical wings and the same tail. The first prototype, powered by 600-hp (448-kW) BMW VI 6, OZ engines, was flown from Marienehe by Gerhard Nitschke on 25 February 1935. After less than three weeks it was followed by the second. The third prototype, a forerunner of the bomber version of the He 111A, performed much better than many fighter planes of its time.

As six commercial He 111C-0s entered service as 10-seat airliners with Lufthansa during 1936, the first of 10 military He 111A-0s were being evaluated at Rechlin but, owing to inadequate engine power when carrying warload, were summarily rejected, all 10 aircraft being sold to China.

Anticipating the problem of power shortage, Heinkel produced the He 111B, of which the pre-production He 111B-0 series were powered by 1,000-hp (746-kW) Daimler-Benz DB 600A engines. Despite a considerable weight increase this version returned a top speed of 224 mph (360 km/h). By the end of 1936 the first production He 111B-1s, with 880-hp (656-kW) DB 600C engines appeared and, following successful trials, joined 1./KG 154 (later renamed KG 157), KG 152, KG 155, KG 253, KG 257 and KG 355.

Few examples of the He 111D-0 and D-1, with 950-hp (709-kW) DB 600Ga engines, were built as a result of a

Armourers handling an SC 500 (1,102-lb/500-kg) bomb on an airfield at the Eastern Front during the summer of 1941, with a Heinkel He 111H-6 of Kampfgeschwader 55 in the background. The He 111 provided the Luftwaffe's main heavy bomber strength for much of World War 2.

Heinkel He 111

Specification

Heinkel He 111H-16

Type: five-seat medium night bomber/pathfinder and glider tug

Powerplant: two 1,350-hp (1006-kW) Junkers Jumo 211F-2 inline piston engines

Performance: maximum speed 270 mph (435 km/h) at 19,685 ft (6000 m); service ceiling 27,890 ft (8500 m); normal range 1,212 miles (1950 km)

Weights: empty 19,136 lb (8680 kg); maximum take-off 30,864 lb (14000 kg)

Dimensions: span 74 ft 1¾ in (22.60 m); length 53 ft 9½ in (16.40 m); height 13 ft 1¼ in (4.00 m); wing area 931.1 sq ft (86.50 m²)

Armament: one 20-mm MG FF cannon, one 0.51-in (13-mm) MG 131 and up to seven 0.31-in (7.92-mm) MG 15 and MG 81 machine-guns, plus one 4,409-lb (200-kg) bomb carried externally and one 1,102-lb (500-kg) bomb internally, or eight 551-lb (250-kg) bombs all internally

The aircraft depicted here, Wkr Nr 3340, 'Yellow B' of the 9th Staffel, Kampfgeschwader 53 Legion Cóndor is shown with the escort identity wing bars carried during the big Luftwaffe day-light raids on London during Sunday 15 September 1940 – the climax of the Battle of Britain. The three white panels have always been said to indicate the III Gruppe of a Geschwader, although many anomalies exist as to throw doubt on this assumption. This aircraft was in fact damaged in action on that day and force landed at Armentiers with two wounded crew members; recent computerized research suggests that it was probably attacked by Spitfires of No. 66 (Fighter) Sqn.

the F-4. The He 111G series comprised nine examples, of which five (powered variously by B.M.W.132Dc and B.M.W.132H-1 radials and DB 600G inlines) were delivered to Lufthansa and the remainder went to Turkey as He 111G-5s. Produced simultaneously with the He 111G series, the He 111J series was developed as a torpedo-carrying version, of which about 90 were produced, but in fact served as a normal bomber with the Kriegsmarine-allocated KGr 806 in 1939.

Hitherto all He 111s had featured a conventional 'stepped' windscreen profile but, following the appearance of the eighth prototype in January 1938, the He 111P adopted the smooth nose profile with extensive glazing that so characterized the aircraft thereafter. This design incorporated a nose gun mounted offset to port, and a small hinge-up windscreen to improve the pilot's view during landing. The He 111P series entered production before the end of 1938, the type joining KG 157 in the following April. Intended as an interim version pending arrival of the He 111H, it survived in Luftwaffe service long after the outbreak of war in 1939.

Devastation in Poland

By September that year the He 111H was well-established with operational units, the Luftwaffe deploying 400 such

shortage of this engine, and in 1938 production switched to the He 111E with 1,000-hp (746-kW) Junkers Jumo 211A-1s. Some 200 of these aircraft were produced, and they proved capable of lifting a 4,409-lb (2000-kg) bombload – roughly similar to that of the RAF's much slower Armstrong Whitworth Whitley III heavy bomber.

Meanwhile efforts had been made to simplify the He 111's wing structure for ease of production, and a new planform with straight leading and trailing edges had appeared on the seventh prototype. This wing was introduced into production with the He 111F, which emerged from the shops of Heinkel's new showpiece factory at Oranienburg in 1938; powered by 1,100-hp (821-kW) Jumo 211A-3s, 24 He 111F-1s were sold to Turkey, while the Luftwaffe's version was

He 111 variants

He 111a (He 111 V1): 1st prototype, two 600-hp (448-kW) B.M.W. VI6,0Z with two-blade propellers
He 111 V2: 2nd prototype (D-ALIX)
He 111 V3: 3rd prototype (D-ALES)
He 111 V4: 4th prototype (D-AHAO)
He 111C-0: six aircraft (D-ABYE, -AMES, -AQUY, -AQYF -ATYL, -AXAV); two delivered to Kommando Rowehl for clandestine reconnaissance
He 111A-1: 10 aircraft based on V3; rejected
He 111 V5: DB 600A; all-up weight 18,959 lb (8600 kg)
He 111B-0: pre-production version accepted by Luftwaffe; one aircraft with Jumo 21Ga
He 111B-1: production bombers; early aircraft with DB 600Aa, later DB 600C; all-up weight 20,536 lb (9323 kg); maximum bombload 3,307 lb (1500 kg)
He 111B-2: supercharged DB 600CG engines, all-up weight 22,046 lb (1000 kg)
He 111 V7: prototype with straight tapered wing
He 111 G-01: also termed **He 111 V12** (D-AEQU), B.M.W. VI 6.0Zu, passed to DLH
He 111 G-02: also termed **He 111 V13** (D-AYKI), B.M.W. VI 6.0Zu, passed to DLH
He 111G-3: two aircraft, **V14** (D-ACBS) with B.M.W. 132Dc and **V15** (D-ADCF) with B.M.W. 132H-1; both passed to DLH and re-styled **He 111L**
He 111G-4: also termed **He 111 V16** (D-ASAR); DB 600G; used by Milch as personal transport
He 111G-5: four aircraft with DB 600Ga engines, sold to Turkey
He 111 V9: modified from B-2 airframe wit DB 600Ga; became He 111D prototype with wing radiators
He 111D-0: pre-production batch with DB 600Ga and radiators moved to engine nacelles
He 111D-1: small number of production aircraft, abandoned due to shortage of DB engines
He 111V6: prototype (D-AXOH) from modified B-0 with Jumo 610Ga
He 111V10: prototype He 111E (D-ALEQ) from modified D-0 with Jumo 211A-1
He 111E-0: pre-production aircraft, 3,748-lb (1700-kg) bombload; all-up weight 22,740 lb (10315 kg)
He 111E-1: production bombers, 4,409-lb (2000-kg) bombload all-up weight 23,754 lb (10775 kg)
He 111E-3: minor internal alterations, internal bombload only
He 111E-4: half bombload carried externally
He 111E-5: as E-4 with extra internal fuel tanks
He 111 V11: prototype He 111F with straight-tapered wing; Jumo 211A-3
He 111F-0: pre-production aircraft, all-up weight 24,250 lb (11000 kg)
He 111F-1: 24 aircraft sold to Turkey in 1938
He 111F-4: 40 aircraft for Luftwaffe with E-4 bombload
He 111J-0: pre-production aircraft, DB 600CG; external bombload only
He 111J-1: 90 production aircraft intended as torpedo-bombers but served as bombers only
He 111V8: modified B-0 (D-AQUO) with stepped cockpit profile
He 111P-0: pre-production batch similar to V8, following J-1 in factory
He 111P-1: production DB 601A-1; maximum speed 247 mph (398 km/h)

He 111P-2: as P-1 but with FuG 10 radio
He 111P-3: P-1s and P-2s modified as dual-control trainers
He 111P-4: provision for additional defensive armament; extra internal fuel; external bombload
He 111P-6: introduced DB 601N engines; reverted to internal bombload; P-6R2 was later conversion to glider tug; others transferred to Hungary
He 111V19: prototype (D-AUKY); Jumo 211 engines
He 111H-0: pre-production batch similar to P-2 (FuG10) but with Jumo 211
He 111H-2: as H-1 but with Jumo 211A-3 engines
He 111H-3: introduced anti-shipping role with forward-firing 20-mm gun in gondola Jumo 211D-1 engines
He 111H-4: early aircraft had Jumo 211D-1, but later 211F-1 engines
He 111H-5: provision for 5,511-lb (2500-kg) bombload; all-up weight increased to 30,982 lb (14055 kg)
He 111H-6: included all previous modifications and provision for two 1,686-lb (765-kg) LTF5b torpedoes and increased defensive armament; Jumo 211F-1; He 111H-7 and H-9 were similar but with minor equipment changes
He 111H-8: H-3 and H-5 airframes with balloon cable-fender and cutters, H-8 R2 had fenders removed and was modified as glider tug
He 111H-10: H-6 development with 20-mm gun moved from gondola to nose. Kuto-Nase balloon cable-cutters, Jumo 211F-2
He 111H-11: fully enclosed dorsal gun position with increased armament and armour, H-11 R1 had twin MG 81 guns in beam positions, H-11 R2 was glider tug
He 111H-12: ventral gondola omitted to allow carriage of Hs 293A missiles, FuG 203b radio equipment
He 111H-14: pathfinder development of H-10, 20H-14 R2s were glider tugs
He 111H-16: 'standard' bomber H-16 R1 had electric dorsal turret, H-16 R2 was glider tug with rigid boom; H16 R3 was pathfinder with reduced bombload
He 111H-18: pathfinder similar to He 111H-16 R3 with special flame-damped exhausts
He 111H-20: built as glider tug transport, H-20 R1 was paratrooper with jump hatch, H-20 R2 was freighter tug with 30-mm gun in electric dorsal turret, H-20 R3 modified as bomber, H-20 R4 modified as bomber with external load of 20 110-lb (50-kg) bombs
He 111H-21: introduced Jumo 213, maximum speed 298 mph (480 km/h) bombload 6,614 lb (3000 kg), all-up weight increased to 35,275 lb (16000 kg). Rüstsatz as for He 111H-20
He 111H-23: similar to H-20 R1 with Jumo 213 engines
He 111V32: single H-6 modified with turbocharged DB 601U engines as prototype for proposed He 111R high-altitude bomber, **He 111R-1** and **R-2** were proposed but not built
He 111Z-1: two He 111 composited with fifth engine added, glider tug, all-up weight 62,831 lb (28500 kg)
He 111Z-2: long-range bomber project similar to Z-1 intended to carry four Hs 283A missiles
He 111Z-3: proposed version of Z-1 for long-range reconnaissance

A licence-(CASA-) built He 111H-16 of Ala 94, Spanish Ejército del Aire, in the late 1950s. The splinter camouflage scheme remained much the same as had been current during the Spanish Civil War of 1936–9.

Among the small number of German bombers flown by the Slovakian Air Force was this He 111H-3 (possibly licence-built in Romania by the Fabrica de Avione SET of Bucharest), based at Trenčin early in 1943.

Heinkel He 111H-3 cutaway drawing key

1 Starboard navigation light
2 Starboard aileron
3 Wing ribs
4 Forward spar
5 Rear spar
6 Aileron tab
7 Starboard flap
8 Fuel tank access panel
9 Wing centre section/outer panel break line
10 Inboard fuel tank (145 Imp gal/700 litre capacity) position between nacelle and fuselage
11 Oil tank cooling louvres
12 Oil cooler air intake
13 Supercharger air intake
14 Three-blade VDM airscrew
15 Airscrew pitch-change mechanism
16 Junkers Jumo 211 D-1 12-cylinder inverted-vee liquid-cooled engine
17 Exhaust manifold
18 Nose-mounted 7.9-mm MG 15 machine gun
19 Ikaria ball-and-socket gun mounting (offset to starboard)
20 Bomb sight housing (offset to starboard)
21 Starboard mainwheel
22 Rudder pedals
23 Bomb aimer's horizontal pad

24 Additional 7.9-mm MG-15 machine-gun (fitted by forward maintenance units)
25 Repeater compass
26 Bomb aimer's folding seat
27 Control column
28 Throttles
29 Pilot's seat
30 Retractable auxiliary windscreen (for use when pilot's seat in elevated position)
31 Sliding entry panel
32 Forward fuselage bulkhead
33 Double-frame station
34 Port ESAC bomb bay (vertical stowage)
35 Fuselage windows (blanked)
36 Central gangway between bomb bays
37 Double-frame station
38 Direction finder
39 Dorsal gunner's (forward) sliding canopy

40 Dorsal 7.9-mm MG 15 machine gun
41 Dorsal gunner's cradle seat
42 FuG 10 radio equipment
43 Fuselage window
44 Armoured bulkhead (8-mm)
45 Aerial mast
46 Bomb flares
47 Unarmoured bulkhead
48 Rear fuselage access cut-out
49 Port 7.9-mm beam MG 15 machine gun
50 Dinghy stowage
51 Fuselage frames
52 Stringers
53 Starboard tailplane
54 Aerial

55 Starboard elevator
56 Tailfin forward spar
57 Tailfin structure
58 Rudder balance
59 Tailfin rear spar/rudder post
60 Rudder construction
61 Rudder tab
62 Tab actuator (starboard surface)

63 Remotely-controlled 7.9-mm MG 17 machine gun in tail cone (fitted to some aircraft only)
64 Rear navigation light
65 Elevator tab
66 Elevator structure
67 Elevator hinge line
68 Tailplane front spar
69 Semi-retractable tailwheel

70 Tailwheel shock-absorber
71 Tail surface control linkage
72 Fuselage/tailfin frame
73 Control pulley

74 Push-pull control rods
75 Master compass
76 Observation window fairing
77 Glazed observation window in floor
78 Ventral aft-firing 7.9-mm MG 15 machine gun in tail of 'Sterbebett' ('Death-bed') bath
79 Ventral bath entry hatch
80 Ventral gunner's horizontal pad

81 Forward-firing 20-mm (Oerlikon) MG FF cannon (for anti-shipping operations)
82 Rear spar carry-through
83 Forward spar carry-through
84 Oil cooler
85 Anti-vibration engine mount
86 Oil tank
87 Engine bearer
88 Exhaust flame-damper shroud
89 Radiator air intake
90 Radiator bath
91 Port mainwheel
92 Mainwheel leg
93 Retraction mechanism
94 Mainwheel door (outer)
95 Multi-screw wing attachment
96 Trailing-aerial tube (to starboard of ventral bath)
97 Rear spar attachment

98 Port outboard fuel tank (220 Imp gal/1000 litre capacity)
99 Flap control rod
100 Landing light
101 Pitot head
102 Pitot head heater/wing leading-edge de-icer
103 Flap and aileron coupling
104 Flap structure
105 Aileron tab
106 Tab actuator
107 Rear spar
108 Forward spar
109 Port aileron
110 Port navigation light

Heinkel He 111

Though to some extent superseded by the H-series, the Heinkel He 111P continued in widespread service well into the war. This P-2 of Kampfgeschwader 55 flew from Villacoublay, France, during the autumn of 1940 on night raids over Britain and displays the Geschwaderstab marking on the nose; crudely applied mottled camouflage has obscured Geschwaderziechen and fin swastika.

First prototype of the He 111 was the He 111a (later styled the He 111V1), flown by Gerhard Nitschke at Marienehe on 24 February 1934 while powered by 660-hp (492-kW) BMW VI 6.0Z engines. Although built as a bomber, British Intelligence authorities persisted in believing it to be a high-speed commercial aircraft.

aircraft compared with 349 He 111P series, 38 He 111E series and 21 He 111J series aircraft. Of this total of 808 aircraft, 705 were serviceable on the eve of Germany's attack on Poland. In that fateful campaign the Heinkels of KG 1, KG 4, KG 26, KG 27, KG 53, KG 152 and II/LG1 were in constant action, starting with raids far beyond the front line but, as the Poles fell back towards Warsaw, launching devastating raids on the Polish capital.

Owing to the lack of suitable airfields, only three He 111-equipped units (KG 4, KG 26 and KGr 100) operated in the Norwegian campaign, the other Geschwäder deploying in readiness for the German attack in the West, which opened on 10 May 1940. Four days later the campaign was besmirched by the apparently wanton attack by 100 Heinkels of KG 54 on Rotterdam.

By the beginning of the Battle of Britain the He 111H had almost entirely replaced the He 111P series (although most staff crews still flew the older aircraft, and it was in an He 111P that Oberst Alois Stoeckl, commanding KG 55, was shot down and killed near Middle Wallop on 14 August 1940). From the outset the He 111H, with its 270-mph (435-km/h) top speed, proved a difficult aircraft to shoot down (compared with the Dornier Do 17), and showed itself capable of weathering heavy battle damage. The 17 Gruppen flying the He 111H during the battle operated an average strength of about 500 aircraft (compared with about 100 He 111P series aircraft, of which some 40 served in the reconnaissance role with the *Aufklärungsgruppen*), losing some 246 of their number in air combat in the course of the four-month battle. Among the outstanding attacks by He 111s were those by KG 55 on the Bristol aircraft factory on 25 September, and the same unit's devastating raid on Supermarine's factory at Southampton the following day.

The majority of the He 111Hs employed during the Battle of Britain were He 111H-1s, -2s, -3s, and -4s, the latter two initially powered by 1,100-hp (821-kW) Jumo 211D engines, and perhaps the main significance of their losses lay in their five-man crews, whereas the other bombers, the Junkers Ju 88 and Do 17, were crewed by only four.

The next variant to join the Kampfgeschwäder was the He 111H-5, which incorporated additional fuel tanks in place of the wing bomb cells, and featured two external racks each capable of lifting a 2,205-lb (1000-kg) bomb; its maximum all-up weight was increased to 30,985 lb (14055 kg). He 111H-5s were widely used during the winter Blitz of 1940–1, these aircraft carrying the majority of the heavy bombs and parachute mines to fall on British cities in that campaign. The He 111H-5 could also carry a single 3,968-lb (1800-kg) bomb externally.

The He 111H-6 came to be the most widely used of all He 111s, entering production at the end of 1940. With provision to carry a pair of 1,687-lb (765-kg) LT F5b torpedoes, this version was armed with six 7.92-mm (0.31-in) MG 15 machine-guns and a forward-firing 20-mm cannon, and some aircraft featured a remotely operated grenade-launcher

Serving with the Legion Cóndor's bomber element, Kampfgruppe 88, during the Spanish Civil War in 1937, this He 111B-1 carried a variety of individual markings, including the name *Holzauge* (literally 'Wooden Eye') and a black scottie-dog on fin. German aircrews gained much experience over Spain, albeit against soft targets and little opposition.

A Jumo-powered He 111E-1 whose maximum bomb load (carried internally) had been increased to 4,410 lb (2000 kg); this version eventually equipped all four bomber Staffeln of Kampfgruppe 88 of the Legion Cóndor in Spain during the extremely vicious and bloody civil war that gripped the country in 1938.

One of the last surviving operational He 111s was this He 111H-20 of I Gruppe, Kampfgeschwader 4 'General Wever', based at DresdenKlotzsche in April 1945 for supply-dropping missions to isolated Wehrmacht units.

in the extreme tail. Despite its torpedo-carrying ability, most He 111H-6s were used as ordinary bombers, the first unit to fly torpedo-equipped He 111H-6s being I/KG 26, flying these aircraft from Bardufoss and Banak in northern Norway against the North Cape convoys from June 1942 onwards and participating in the virtual annihilation of the convoy PQ 17.

Following the successful use of He 111Hs as pathfinders by KGr 100, this role featured prominently in subsequent development of the aircraft, the He 111H-14, He 111H-16/R3 and He 111H-18 being specially fitted with FuG Samos, Peil-GV, APZ5 and FuG Korfu radio equipment for the task; He 111H-14s were flown on operations by Sonderkommando Rastedter of KG 40 in 1944.

As the He 111 was joined by such later bombers as the Heinkel He 177 Greif, Dornier Do 217 and others, it underwent parallel development as a transport; the He 111H-20/R1 was fitted out to accommodate 16 paratroops and the He 111H-20/R2 was equipped as a freight-carrying glider tug. Nevertheless bomber versions continued to serve, particularly on the Eastern Front where the He 111H-20.R3 with a 4,410-lb (2000-kg) bombload and the He 111H-20/R4, carrying 20 110-lb (50-kg) fragmentation bombs, operated by night.

Perhaps the most outstanding, albeit forlorn of all operations by the He 111H bombers and transports was that in support of the Wehrmacht's attempt to relieve the German 6th Army at Stalingrad between November 1942 and February 1943. As the entire available force of Junkers Ju 52/3m transports was inadequate for the supply task, He 111 bombers of KG 27, KG 55 and I/KG 100 joined KGrzbV 5 and KGrzbV 20 (flying an assortment of He 111D, F, P and H transports) and embarked on the job of flying in food and ammunition to the beleaguered army. Although the bombers were occasionally able to attack the Russian armour as it tightened its grip on the city, bad weather severely hampered the supply operations, and by the end of the Stalingrad campaign the Luftwaffe had lost 165 He 111s, a sacrifice from which the Kampfgeschwäder never fully recovered.

The Heinkel He 111 also underwent two of what were unquestionably the most bizarre of all the Luftwaffe's war-time operational experiments. The first involved the carriage of a Fieseler Fi 103 flying-bomb (the V-1) under one wing. Following trials at Peenemünde in 1943, about 20 He 111H-6s, He 111H-16s and He 111H-21s (all re-designated He 111H-22s) were modified and delivered to III/KG 3 in July 1944. Within six weeks this unit, based in the Netherlands, had launched 300 flying-bombs against London, 90 against Southampton and 20 against Gloucester, the tactics being to approach the British shoreline at low level to escape radar detection before the aircraft climbed to about 1,475 ft (450 m) to release the weapon and then dived to escape.

Believing this campaign to have achieved worthwhile results, the Luftwaffe equipped all three Gruppen of KG 53 with about 100 He 111H-22s and, based in western Germany, these joined the assault on the UK in December, one raid being launched against far-distant Manchester on Christmas Eve. In seven months the four Gruppen launched 1,200 flying-bombs but lost 77 aircraft; no more than 20 per cent of the bombs reached their target cities.

The other experiment involving the He 111 resulted in the extraordinary five-engine He 111Z (Z denoting Zwilling, or twin), achieved by joining together two He 111s by means of a new wing centre-section carrying a fifth engine. The resulting aircraft, with a span of 115 ft 6 in (35.20 m), was intended to tow the huge Messerschmitt Me 321 Gigant glider or three Gotha Go 242 gliders at 140 mph (225 km/h) at 13,125 ft (4000 m).

One of the last important uses to which the He 111 bomber was put was the attack on the airfield at Poltava in the Soviet Union on the night of 21-22nd June 1944. On the previous day, 114 Boeing B-17s of the United States Army Air Force and the North American P-51s which had been escorting them were flown to the USSR after the bombing of Berlin. The Americans were taken by surprise by Heinkel 111s of the 4th, 27th, 53rd and 55th Kampfgruppen, and by the light of flares the bombers destroyed 43 B-17s and 15 P-51s on the ground. More than 7,300 He 111s were produced.

The Heinkel He 111H-6 was the most widely-used version of the aircraft and is pictured here carrying a pair of practice torpedoes on fuselage PVC racks. Among the operational units to employ torpedo-carrying He 111s was KG 26, based in Norway for attacks on the Allied Murmansk-bound convoys.

The Heinkel He 111H-11 with 13-mm (0.51-in) MG 131 heavy machine gun in the extreme nose and five 550-lb (250-kg) bombs on a special rack-plate under the fuselage; this version also featured considerably increased armour protection, some of which could be jettisoned in the interests of speed in an emergency.

North American Harvard/Texan

There may have been more versions of this aircraft than of any other in history. Certainly it was in its day the world's most widely used trainer, though it was used for many other purposes — as a dive-bomber, fighter, tug, racer, forward air control (FAC) aircraft, crop sprayer, and even as a three-passenger executive transport.

This series of solidly built, all-metal monoplanes is so large and varied that it is difficult to find a name for the whole range. The Swedes called it the Sk 14, the Japanese the K10W or K5Y, the Australians the Wirraway, the Spaniards the C.6 and the Luftwaffe the NAA 57. But most flyers remember it as the AT-6, the T-6, the Texan, Harvard or SNJ. And in fact it is an aircraft that for many people is unforgettable. There are still pilots today who can remember exactly how the trim tab on the rudder should be set for take-off (fully to the right) or the maximum temperature which should not be exceeded on the cylinder heads (240°C or 464°F, reduced after the war to 230°C, or 446°F), or where the

fuel indicators were located (on the upper surface of both wing tanks forming the floor of the cockpit).

Including post-war modifications, but excluding one-offs such as the racers, or the phoney conversion to simulate Zeros for Hollywood, the total number of different sub-types in this family is not fewer than 260. (The chief ones are listed separately.) Their story goes back even before North American

The Harvard Formation Team uses only machines belonging to this successful series of trainers for its flying displays: a Mk IIA, a Mk IIB and two Mk IVs.

The North American Texan/Harvard had the largest production run of any trainer aircraft ever. This Harvard Mk IIB was produced under licence by the Canadian manufacturers, Noorduyn. (*Photo: Austin J. Brown*)

North American Harvard/Texan

AJ955 was one of 450 NA-66s built with what was then (1940) a new designation, Harvard Mk II. No. 955 was the first of 33 in that total that went to the RCAF, and it is depicted as it looked whilst serving in 1943 with No. 2 Wireless School. Oddly, no radio aerial is visible; more than 50 radio fits were used on T-6 variants.

Aviation put its name on its aircraft but served as the parent to General Aviation at Dundalk, Maryland, where types GA-1 to GA-15 were created. In late 1934 the US Army issued a requirement for a new basic trainer, the next type encountered by pupil pilots after they had mastered the lower-powered primary trainer. The General Aviation design team, under vice-president J. Lee Atwood, quickly produced a cantilever low-wing monoplane with all-metal structure (including a wing covered with flush-riveted stressed skin, though the rest of the aircraft was mainly fabric-covered), fixed cantilever main legs, a 400-hp (298-kW) Wright R-975 Whirlwind engine and tandem open cockpits. Instead of becoming the GA-16 it was styled the NA-16, reflecting the company's change of name.

The NA-16 was flown at Dundalk in April 1935, with civil registration X-2080. The US Army pilots at Wright Field thought it the best design submitted, and the nearest approach to a tactical aircraft then achieved in a trainer, but requested several changes. This classic prototype thus became the NA-18 with enclosed cockpits (covered by tandem sliding canopies), a faired landing gear and the 600-hp (448-kW) Pratt & Whitney R-1340 Wasp engine. This aircraft was later sold to Argentina, but in late 1935 the US Army adopted the NAA trainer and placed an order for 42, with the designation BT-9. On the strength of this the company moved to sunny California, paying a $600 annual rental for a site at Inglewood on what is today Los Angeles International Airport and building a completely new factory with 150 employees (nine years later the payroll had reached 91,000).

The BT-9s were delivered in training colours of blue fuselage and chrome-yellow wings and tail, with blue/red/white-striped rudder. Most BT-9s had fixed slats on the outer wings and were used as unarmed pilot trainers, fitted with

First of the many: few photographs exist of the original General Aviation NA-16, but the same machine is pictured here after it had been modified with enclosed cockpits and faired main legs, though retaining the small-diameter Whirlwind engine. Later it was given a Pratt & Whitney 600 hp (448 km) R-1340 Wasp engine and redesignated NA-18 and exported to Argentina.

North American Harvard Mk IIB cutaway drawing key

1 Pitot tube
2 Wing tip fairing
3 Starboard navigation lights
4 Starboard outer wing panel
5 Aileron tab
6 Tab control rod
7 Starboard fabric-covered aileron
8 Aerial mast
9 Starboard split trailing edge flap
10 Flap control rod
11 Aileron hinge control
12 Aileron cables
13 Starboard landing/taxiing lamp
14 Detachable engine cowling panels
15 Hamilton Standard two-bladed variable-pitch propeller
16 Feathering bobweights
17 Propeller hub pitch change mechanism
18 Engine oil tank sump
19 Bottom cowling panels
20 Starboard mainwheel
21 Carburettor air intake duct
22 Exhaust collector
23 Pratt & Whitney R-1340-49 Wasp nine-cylinder radial engine
24 Engine mounting bulkhead
25 Cockpit heater muff
26 Engine oil tank
27 Oil filler cap
28 Battery
29 Engine hand cranking lever attachment
30 Engine bearer struts
31 Filtered air intake
32 Air intake heater duct
33 Lower engine bearers
34 Mainwheel well
35 Fuel pump
36 Intake fairing
37 Engine control rod runs
38 Fireproof bulkhead
39 Forward rudder pedals
40 Fuse box
41 Generator control unit
42 Electrical control panel
43 Front pilot's instrument panel
44 Instrument panel shroud
45 Aerial cable lead-in
46 Windscreen panels
47 Forward sliding canopy section
48 Front pilot's seat
49 Safety harness
50 Throttle mixture and propeller control levers
51 Cockpit light
52 Tailplane trim control wheels
53 Footboards
54 Wing spar/fuselage attachment joint
55 Fuel contents gauge
56 Hydraulic system emergency handpump
57 Fuel cock control
58 Dynamotor
59 Cockpit step
60 Rear rudder pedals
61 Hydraulic reservoir
62 Engine and propeller control rods
63 Radio equipment stowage
64 Sliding canopy rail
65 Rear instrument panel
66 Undercarriage warning horn
67 Roll-over protection frame
68 Canopy fixed centre-section
69 Rear sliding canopy section
70 Rear pilot's seat
71 Canopy emergency exit side panel
72 Emergency exit handle
73 Rear pilot's throttle box
74 Fire extinguisher
75 Trim handwheels
76 Flap lever
77 Rear seat mounting
78 Forward fuselage steel tube primary structure
79 Non-structural side panels
80 Rear cockpit step
81 Baggage compartment
82 Oxygen bottles
83 Oxygen filler valve
84 Rear fuselage frame and stringer construction
85 Control system access panels
86 Upper identification light
87 Fin mounting box
88 Fin root fairing
89 Starboard tailplane
90 Starboard elevator
91 Elevator tab

The Harvard served as standard equipment at RAF Flying Training Schools for more than 16 years, from 1938 to 1955. N7033 was a Harvard Mk I and flew at No. 2 FTS at RAF Brize Norton during the early war years.

N 7033

92 Tailfin construction
93 Tail navigation lights, port and starboard
94 Rudder mass balance
95 H/F aerial cable
96 Fabric-covered rudder construction
97 Rudder tab
98 Tab control rod
99 Elevator hinge control
100 Fabric-covered elevator construction
101 Rudder hinge control cable
102 Elevator tab
103 Elevator mass balance
104 Tailplane construction
105 Tailwheel shock absorber strut
106 Non-retracting tailwheel
107 Tailwheel steering control
108 Rear fuselage/tailplane bulkhead
109 Fuselage skin plating
110 Fuselage lifting bar
111 Tailplane control cable runs
112 Ventral identification lights (red, green and amber)
113 Rear fuselage longeron
114 Forward/rear fuselage joint
115 Wing root fillet
116 Central flap segment
117 Flap hydraulic jack
118 Wing walkway
119 Split trailing edge flap
120 Wing centre-section construction

121 Outer wing panel bolted joint
122 Rear spar
123 Outboard split trailing edge flap segment
124 Aileron hinge control
125 Aileron false spar
126 Fabric-covered aileron construction
127 Aileron tab
128 Starboard navigation lights
129 Wing tip fairing
130 Bottom wing skin/stringer panel
131 Leading-edge nose ribs
132 Outer wing panel main spar
133 Aileron control
134 Wing rib construction
135 Landing/taxiing lamps
136 Port centre-section fuel tank; total aircraft fuel capacity 91.5 Imp gal (416 litres)
137 Fuel filler cap
138 Undercarriage leg locking mechanism
139 Main undercarriage leg pivot fixing
140 Hydraulic retraction jack
141 Mainwheel leg strut
142 Torque scissor links
143 Mainwheel leg door
144 Port mainwheel
145 Air intake to cabin heater

North American Harvard

Specification

Type: two-seat advanced trainer

Powerplant: one 600-hp (447-kW) Pratt & Whitney R-1340-49 Wasp radial piston engine

Performance: maximum speed 210 mph (338 km/h); initial climb rate 1,350 ft (411 m) per minute; range 740 miles (1191 km); endurance 8 hours

Weights: empty typically 4,020 lb (1823 kg); maximum take-off 5,250 lb (2381 kg)

Dimensions: span 42 ft $0\frac{1}{4}$ in (12.81 m); length 28 ft $11\frac{7}{8}$ in (8.836 m); height 11 ft $8\frac{1}{2}$ in (3.57 m); wing area 253.7 sq ft (23.57 m^2)

Armament: none on this aircraft, but see text for many options

This Harvard Mk IIB typified the variants made in great numbers during the middle war years. The penultimate Harvard for the RAF produced under licence by Noorduyn of Canada, it also had the USAAF designation AT-16 (and for a time an assigned US tail number) because most of the 2,485 Mk IIBs were Lend-Lease, paid for by US funds. The pupil (in front) canopy slid back outside the fixed central portion while the instructor's canopy slid forward on the inside. On this Mk IIB the rearmost part of the canopy was fixed, but aircraft fitted for gunnery pupils had a rear section (distinguished by a straight lower edge) which rocked up and over and travelled forward with the main rear hood section.

A fine portrait of a North American BT-9 basic trainer with the R-975 Whirlwind engine and fixed slats and landing gear, of the 46th School Sqn, USAAC, in 1939. This colour scheme was replaced in 1940.

flaps pumped down by a manual hydraulic system. These were probably the first flapped basic trainers, and flaps were provided on all subsequent models. The R-975 Whirlwind fitted to most of the fixed-gear versions, except for the US Navy NJ-1 and a batch for China, was of smaller diameter than the Pratt & Whitney Wasp used on the much more numerous retractable-gear models, and resulted in a slightly better forward view.

The main landing wheels were far forward, making nosing over difficult, and on most of these variants the exhaust was collected at the front of the engine and discharged through the right side of the cowl. Many sub-types including the first two big orders for France, had the original curved wingtips and rudder; but the NA-57 for France had the new wing and tail, first flown on the NA-54, which was structurally better and easier to make. Large numbers of the former type had Et.2 (Entrainement biplace) or P.2 (Perfectionnement biplace) in black on their striped rudders, and they were put to various uses by the Vichy forces and Luftwaffe. Aircraft of the second batch were diverted to become Yales in Canada,

mostly with the exhaust stack extended back over the right wing root.

Export sales came thick and fast, no two batches being exactly alike but all having the R-975 or R-1340 engines, except for wartime licence-built Swedish Sk 14 versions which had to use an Italian Piaggio engine, and the Imperial Japanese Navy models which had a Kotobuki engine driving a wooden propeller. The Japanese variants, designated K10W and K5Y1, had many local modifications, notably to the canopy, rear fuselage and vertical tail.

Competitive attack trainer

The real mainstream began with the US Army Air Corps competition in 1937 for a BC (basic combat) trainer, able to undertake pilot instruction while at the same time simulating the handling and cockpit controls of a combat type, with the option of being able to mount fixed and movable guns and carry bombs if necessary so that one type could almost turn out a fully fledged combat pilot or gunner. The same NA-16 was taken as the starting point, but it was fitted with a big Wasp engine, driving a Hamilton variable-pitch propeller and a hydraulic pump feeding a 1,000-lb/sq in (70.3-kg/cm^2) system which worked the flaps and also the new retractable main landing gears, which folded inwards ahead of the spars with the wheels in compartments causing curved projections ahead of the wing roots. This NA-26 prototype of 1937 won the competition, and the first production model was the US Army's BC-1, some of which were the first specially designed instrument trainers, designated BC-1I.

Further changes, listed in the variants, brought in stressed-skin fuselages, integral wing tanks (soon followed by removable aluminium wing tanks), and the new angular wingtips and rudder. In 1940 the BC category was superseded by AT

SNJs lined up at NAS Pensacola during World War 2. The SNJ was almost identical to the USAAF AT-6 Texan, each major development having variants for both services. A few of the navy trainers were used for carrier training with arrester hooks.

Many well-loved old-stagers were some years ago found in the Royal Netherlands air force light-aircraft units based at Deelen and Soesterberg, and operated on tactical missions mainly for the army. This ex-RAF Harvard Mk 2B (USAAF AT-16 no. 43-13120) was flying until at least 1965 with Deelen's photo flight.

EZ316 was a Harvard Mk IIA (NA-81) supplied under Lend-Lease to the Fleet Air Arm (the large batch involved is often omitted from listings of RN Harvards). It was used from 1942 onwards as an advanced pilot trainer and is shown in post-war (about 1958) markings, still with wartime insignia, serving at Stretton with No. 1832 Sqn, RNVR.

Large numbers of ex-US Navy aircraft were passed on to the French Aeronavale after World War 2. This machine is an SNJ-4, modified with the rear canopy fairing fixed and used in the pilot training role. The unit was 56S, which later became a navigator training unit equipped with C-47s.

Massive production

Almost all the gigantic wartime contracts were for the AT-6A, AT-6C, and AT-6D, plus the corresponding US Navy SNJ-3, SNJ-4 and SNJ-5, which were externally similar with the straight-edged airframe, stressed-skin fuselage and provision for a hand-aimed gun in the rear cockpit, the usual canopy having a rear fairing which rocked up and forward as the main section was slid open. On most earlier versions the rear fairing was fixed. Structurally, the big exception was launched by the NA-88 of 10 April 1941, when production was already on a massive scale even though the United States was still neutral. There was a fear that aluminium would run out, and in this model NAA redesigned the aircraft to have a basic wing structure, flaps, fin and all control surfaces of spot-welded low-alloy steel, and the forward fuselage side panels, whole rear fuselage, cockpit floor and tailplane of plywood. This saved 1,246 lb (565 kg)

(advanced trainer, a category dormant for 13 years), the NAA aircraft becoming the AT-6.

NAA was unable to meet demand, even with an Inglewood plant whose floor areas had expanded from 159,000 sq ft (14770m²) to almost 2,000,000 sq ft (185800 m²)! A new factory was therefore built at Dallas, Texas (others were built elsewhere for other NAA types), and from 1942 the AT-6 was accordingly named Texan, though since 1938 the name Harvard had taken firm hold in the British Commonwealth for the same basic type. British industry had been totally unable to meet the RAF's need for aircraft in 1938, because orders had not been placed in time, and a great outcry went up when foreign aircraft were ordered. The NAA trainer was the first, soon followed by the Lockheed Hudson and Consolidated Catalina. The Harvard Mk I was a BC-1 with British instruments and radio, and bucket seats tailored to the seat-pack parachutes. The first of 400 entered service in December 1938 at No. 3 FTS, Grantham, camouflaged on top and down to the mid-line of the fuselage, and yellow below. Subsequently the RAF received about half of the 4,768 Harvards supplied from NAA or from Noorduyn on US Lend-Lease contract, a further 1,380 Harvards being supplied direct from Noorduyn and (post-war) from Canadian Car and Foundry, as well as 285 post-war T-6Js for European air forces.

One of the post-war T-6G trainers that began life as wartime AT-6s and were then remanufactured in 1949-53. Note the spinner, rear-fuselage D/F loop acorn fairing, larger canopy side windows and flat-tread steerable tailwheel. The total thus updated was 2,068. This one went to the USAF; many went to the Air National Guard.

Most Swedish aircraft of the general NA-16 family were not the locally built Sk 14 series (which were basic trainers with fixed landing gear) but ex-US aircraft supplied as war surplus in 1946-9. This Sk 16A (ex-USAAF AT-6A 41-16098) was still intensively utilized on pilot training at F9 at Sävar as late as 1967.

The Forca Aérea Brasileira (Brazilian air force) was not only one of the last T-6 operators but in fact still had two EMRAs (reconnaissance and attack squadrons) flying armed T-6s as late as 1977! Another operator was the Esquadrilha da Fumaca (Smoke Squadron), shown right, one of the established FAB aerobatic display teams, whose mounts were distinctive. The metal-covered rear canopy is a local modification.

of aluminium or light alloy per aircraft, with a surprisingly modest weight penalty and not much difference in manufacturing cost. Designations were AT-6C, SNJ-4 and Harvard Mk IIA, but after a while it was accepted that there would be no shortage of aluminium and the original structure was restored (still as the NA-88) in the AT-6D, SNJ-5 and Harvard Mk III, though these introduced 24-volt electrics.

One of the electric items much appreciated by ground crew was the starter. Of the inertia type, the flywheel was spun by the pilot depressing his heel on a treadle in the floor between the rudder pedals. A healthy rising whine ensued, and when the pitch was high enough the pilot would instead depress his toe, rocking the treadle and engaging the flywheel.

Trainer variants

NA-16: original prototype, 400-hp (298-kW) R-975 engine; modified as **NA-18** with enclosed cockpit and 600-hp (448-kW) R-1340
Na-19: USAAC BT-9 with R-975, fixed slats, 42 built
Na-19A: USAAC BT-9A with nose and dorsal 0.3-in (7.62-mm) guns and recording camera, 40 for USAAC Reserve
NA-22: ninth BT-9 temporarily evaluated as primary trainer, open cockpits, Townend-ring cowl simpler equipment
NA-23: USAAC BT-9B for 1937 production, 117 built
NA-28: US Navy model, NJ-1, 500-hp (373-kW) R-1340-6, 40 built (last flown temporarily as NJ-2 with 490-hp/366-kW XV-770-4)
NA-29: USAAC Reserve BT-9C with nose and dorsal guns, 67 built, first completed as Y1BT-10 with 600-hp (448-kW) R-1340 and another with RC-1A type wings and tail as BT-9D
NA-30: Y1BT-10 (see above)
NA-58: USAAC BT-14 with stressed-skin fuselage, 450-hp (336-kW) R-985-25 Wasp Junior, BC-1A outer wings and tail, 251 built of which 27 re-engined 1941 with 400-hp (298-kW) R-985-11 as BT-14A
NA-20: (NA-16-2H); R-1340-engined NA-18, sold to Honduras
NA-31 (NA-16-4M); as BT-9 with 450-hp (336-kW) R-975-E3, one sold to Sweden with licence to ASJA, see licence production p. 253
NA-32 (NA-16-1A); two pattern aircraft sold with licence 1937 to Commonwealth Aircraft (Australia); as NA-26 (see below) but fixed landing gear
NA-34(NA-16-4P)I; for Argentine, two nose and one dorsal guns, full radio, bomb racks, 30 built
NA-37 (NA-16-4R); demonstrator for Japan, 450-hp (336-kW) R-985-9CG, three-blade propeller, via Mitsubishi to Imperial Japanese Navy as KXA1
NA-38 (NA-16-4M); one NA-31 supplied in kit form to Sweden
NA-41 (NA-16-4C); as BT-9C with R-975 for China, 35 built
NA-42 (NA-16-2A); as NA-20 plus nose/dorsal guns, two to Honduras
NA-46 (NA-16-4); as BT-9C plus two guns, bomb racks under centre section, R-975, 12 for Brazilian navy
NA-47 (NA-16-4RW); as NA-37 but R-975-E3 with two-

blade prop. supplied as kit to Imperial Japanese Navy.
NA-56: new BC-1A airframe but fixed gear, 600-hp (448-kW) R-1340, 50 for China
NA-57: as NA-23 for French Armée de l'Air (200) and Aéronavale (30); 214 on strength of Luftwaffe, Vichy French air force 1941
NA-64: as NA-57 but new BC-1A wings and tail; for Armée de l'Air (200) and Aéronavale (30), but at 111th delivery France fell and other 119 diverted to RAF and passed on as Yale Mk I to RCAF as wireless (radio) trainer
NA-26: first of retractable-gear family, 600-hp (448-kW) R-1340, combat equipment, one demonstrator evaluated by USAAC as BT-9D
NA-27 (NA-16-2H): European demonstrator as NA-26, sold to Fokker with licence as PH-APG, later air force no. 997, destroyed 11 May 1940
NA-33 (NA-16-2K): second pattern for CAC (Australia), see licence production p. 253
NA-36: USAAC BC-1, armament, 600-hp (448-kW) R-1340-7 or -47, 150 built, plus 30 BC-1 I instrument trainers; last three completed as NA-54
NA-45 (NA-16-1GV): as BC-1, three for Venezuela
NA-48: (NA-16-3C): as BC-1, 15 for China
NA-49 (NA-16-1E): as BC-1 but British equipment, usually unarmed, 400 for RAF as Harvard Mk I (first US aircraft bought for RAF)
NA-52: SNJ-1 for USN, as BC-1 but stressed-skin fuselage and integral tanks, 16 built
NA-54: last three BC-1 completed with redesigned outer wings and rudder to speed production, also R-1340-45 with three-blade propeller, stressed-skin fuselage, integral tanks
NA-55: USAAC BC-1A, as BC-1 but new wings and tail and stressed-skin fuselage, 29 for National Guard and 54 for USAAC Reserve, plus nine more completed as AT-6
NA-59: continuation of BC-1A under new designation AT-6, total 94 including nine ordered as NA-55
NA-61 (NA-16-1E): as NA-49 but for RCAF, 30 built
NA-65: USN, as NA-52 but R-1340-56 and controllable-pitch propeller, 36 built as SNJ-2
NA-66: NA-59 with British equipment as Harvard Mk II with R-1340-49; 600 built, 20 RAF, 67 RNZAF, 511 assigned RCAF but 486 delivered
NA-71 (NA-16-3); as NA-59, three for Venezuela

NA-75: as NA-66, Harvard Mk II, 100 for RCAF
NA-76: as NA-66, order for 450 for Armée de l'Air placed June 1940 two weeks before capitulation, all taken over by RAF as Harvard Mk II of which 259 to RCAF
NA-77: as NA-59 with removable fuel tanks and R-1340-9,517 for US Army as AT-6A plus 120 for US Navy as ANJ-3
NA-78: as NA-77 but built at new Dallas plant, 1,130 AT-6A plus 150 SNJ-3
NA-79: further (1940) contract for 25 SNJ-2
NA-81: Harvard Mk II as NA-66, 24 for RAF, 101 for RCAF
NA-84: as NA-77 but R-1340-AN-1 and one 0.3-in (7.62-mm) dorsal gun (in other AT-6s merely provision for this); AT-6B gunnery trainer, 400 from Dallas
NA-88: as NA-84 but extensive substitutes for aluminium in AT-6C and SNJ-4; during run, decision to revert to original structure but switch to 24-volt electrics, still as NA-88 but with US Army/US Navy designations AT-6D/SNJ-5; totals, all from Dallas, 9,331 comprising 2,970 AT-6Cs (of which 726 to RAF as Harvard Mk IIA), 2,400 SNJ-4s, 2,604 AT-6Ds (351 to RAF as Harvard Mk III), and 1,357 SNJ-5s
NA-119: standard AT-6Ds supplied to Brazil 1944 as 10 assembled airframes, 10 sets of major airframe sections and 61 in kit form for completion by Construcciones Aeronauticas SA
NA-121: final batch of 800 AT-6Ds plus 956 AT-6Fs with redesigned outer wings and rear fuselage for sustained 6g manoeuvres and clear-view rear canopy; 411 (not, as often reported, 931) AT-6Fs transferred to USN as SNJ-6s
NA-168: first major post-war contract for remanufacture of NA-88 to T-6G standard with updated cockpit, new avionics, steerable tailwheel, modified main gears, extended fuel capacity, square-tip propeller (with spinner, often removed in service) and AN-1 series engine; this batch, 691 for USAF (serials 49-2897/3536 and 50-1317/1326), plus 59 LT-6Gs equipped for FAC duties in Korea (49-3537/3596)
NA-182: further batches of remanufactured T-6Gs, total 824 (51-14314/15137)
NA-186: design data for T-6J provided to CCF (see licence production)

NA-188: further remanufactured T-6Gs, total 107 (51-15138/15237 and -16071/16077)
NA-195: more T-6Gs, total 11 (51-17354/17364)
NA-197: June 1952, last T-6G remanufacture contract, total 110 (52-8197/8246, 53-4555/4614) Many T-6G blocks were assigned to friendly air forces under MDAP, and numerous other wartime aircraft were modified without NA type numbers, examples being the AT-6D re-engined with 500-hp (373-kW) Ranger V-770-9 as XAT-6E, the USN SNJ-3Cs, -4Cs and -5Cs with hooks for carrier training, the AT-6Fs rebuilt by the USAF as T-6Fs for front line observation in Korea, and the large numbers of USN aircraft (mainly SNJ-4s) remanufactured at NAS Pensacola in 1951-53 to approximately T-6G standard with designation SNJ-7 and (armed) SNJ-7B. NAA's contract for 240 NA-198 (Navy SNJ-8) new aircraft to similar standard was cancelled

NAA Attack variants

NA-44: prototype attack model with 785-hp (586-kW) Wright R-1820-F52 Cyclone, stressed-skin throughout, two wing guns, two cowl guns, one (optional 0.5-in/12.7-mm) in rear cockpit and 400-lb (181-kg) bombload; prototype became no. 3344 of RCAF, served to 1947

NA-69: batch of 10 for Siam, requisitioned by USAAC and put into combat duty in Philippines as A-27s (41-18890/18899)
NA-72: batch of 30 delivered to Brazil
NA-74: batch of 12 for Chile

Licence production

Sweden: after studying NA-31 and NA-38, ASJA built 35 similar with R-975-E3 with air force designation Sk 14 in 1938–9, while Saab (which took over ASJA) followed in 1940–41 with 18 more; lack of US engines led to Piaggio P.VIIRC 35 (500 hp/373 kW) in next wartime batch of 23 Sk14A, followed by 60 built in 1943–4; these fixed-gear aircraft were unrelated to large Sk16 family of ex-US T-6/SNJ purchases post-war
Australia: CAC began to tool for NA-33 in 1937 with name Wirraway as multi-role aircraft with two 0.303-in (7.7-mm) forward guns and full combat gear including rear gun and up to 500 lb (227 kg) of bombs; total 755 in 10 variants; post-war rebuilds included CA-28 Ceres crop-sprayers
Canada: to meet urgent need, which NAA could not fulfil, Canadian government nominated Noorduyn in 1940 as additional source for Empire Air Training Scheme. Type basically AT-6A, with US instruments and radio (unlike RAF Harvards), but designated Harvard Mk IIB; first batch 100 (1-40), followed by 110 (7-40); then USAAF took over

contracts for remainder under Lease-Lend programme, with US designation AT-16, but delivered with RAF serials as Harvard Mk IIB; total 1,800 (500 + 233 + 67 + 339 + 361 + 300); Noorduyn built a further 900 Harvard Mk IIBs for RAF; in 1946 CCF (Canadian Car & Foundry) took over Noorduyn and in 1951 received order for 270 new aircraft for RCAF designated Harvard Mk IV, basically similar to T-6G; the USAF also bought 285 more for MCAP recipients with designation T-6J
Japan: Imperial Japanese Navy evaluated NA-37 and NA-47 and ordered K10W1 version from Watanabe in 1941 with 600-hp (448-kw) Kotobuki (Bristol Jupiter derived) engine and one/two guns; after 26 delivered, programme transferred to Nippon Hikoki as K5Y1, as which 150 more delivered 1943–4

superseded by T (trainer), and the standard post-war model was defined as the T-6G, with over 250 engineering changes including a redesigned cockpit with better instruments, controls and pilot view, repositioned aerial masts usually with a D/F loop acorn over the rear fuselage), different propeller, increased fuel capacity with extra tanks at the inner end of the outer-panels, and such new avionics as a VHF command set, range receiver and marker-beacon receiver, new interphone, radio compass and ILS, as well as up-to-date instruments training equipment as in the next generation T-28. Most of the remanufactured T-6Gs came from NAA's Downey (Los Angeles) plant, but some were converted at Columbus, where they were at first called T-6H, later reverting to T-6G-NT.

Harvard's vast war experience

Though primarily trainers, the NA-16 family have played a notable part in many wars. Harvard Mk Is carried bombs in July 1940. Much later the USAF 6147th Tactical Air Control Squadron pioneered what were called 'Mosquito' observation tactics over the front line in Korea, and purpose-built T-6F and LT-6G Texans pioneered the FAC (forward air control) mission. In Kenya RAF No. 1340 Flight did similar work, flying round the clock against the Mau Mau. In infant Israel the Heyl Ha'Avir bought all the T-6s it could get, using them from November 1948 as front-line dive-bombers with eight 110-lb (50-kg) bombs and often carrying three guns, at least one being of 0.5-in (12.7-mm) calibre. By 1953 no fewer than 90 were in use, though by this time their main role was that of armed trainer. Even these numbers are small compared with the 450-odd used by the Armée de l'Air and Aéronavale in the bitter Algerian war in 1956–60. As late as 1969 Harvards of all species had been gathered in Biafra to form a mercenary squadron used effectively against Nigeria's jet air force on its home airfields.

For many long years the North American Harvard/Texan wore large numbers of different liveries for many countries and has been the advanced flying training platform for hundreds of pilots, many of whom went on to master the thoroughbreds of the time, the Spitfires and Hurricanes of World War 2. The Harvard bridged the considerable gap between the low powered elementary trainers such as the D.H. Tiger Moth and those fierce, high-powered front line fighters.

Excluding the later aircraft built under licence, 21,342 aircraft of the NA-16 series were built. In addition, NAA built 53 fighters with higher engine performance, and these are shown in the list of variations.

Other familiar items included Ki-Gass manual engine priming, a wobble pump for building up fuel pressure before starting, a manual selector for building up hydraulic pressure, and massive diecast trim wheels and levers for the landing gear and flaps. Every example was pleasant to fly, and of course fully aerobatic, but if harshly handled would flick dangerously through 270°, and landing with excessively vigorous stick pressure would likewise result in violent wing-drop which, at the very least, would break the spars and often caused a write-off. Thus, the NAA trainers fulfilled the requirement in not being so easy that pilots did not have to fly correctly.

New designations and equipment

As far as possible the variants list includes all the models produced by NAA or its licensees, or modified post-war by the USAF or USN. In June 1948 the AT category was

This Harvard Mk 2A was one of several hundred serving with the South African Air Force in 1943–75, many of them passed on from wartime schools in 'The Union' or in Southern Rhodesia to the north. No. 7698 was one of the many used by the ACF (Active Citizen Force) No. 40 Sqn, in both refresher training and COIN roles.

Index

Index